THE TEAHOUSE UNDER SOCIALISM

THE TEAHOUSE UNDER SOCIALISM

The Decline and Renewal of Public Life in Chengdu, 1950–2000

DI WANG

CORNELL UNIVERSITY PRESS
ITHACA AND LONDON

This book has been published with the assistance of a research grant from the University of Macau.

First published 2018 by Cornell University Press

Printed in the United States of America

Library of Congress Cataloging-in-Publication Data

Names: Wang, Di, 1956– author.
Title: The teahouse under socialism : the decline and renewal of public life in Chengdu, 1950–2000 / Di Wang.
Description: Ithaca : Cornell University Press, 2018. | Includes bibliographical references and index.
Identifiers: LCCN 2017040065 (print) | LCCN 2017040970 (ebook) | ISBN 9781501715549 (epub/mobi) | ISBN 9781501715556 (pdf) | ISBN 9781501715488 (cloth : alk. paper) | ISBN 9781501715495 (pbk. : alk. paper)
Subjects: LCSH: Chengdu (China)—Social life and customs—20th century. | Tearooms—China—Chengdu—History—20th century. | Socialism and culture—China—Chengdu—History—20th century. | Chengdu (China)—Politics and government—20th century.
Classification: LCC DS797.77.C48 (ebook) | LCC DS797.77.C48 W355 2018 (print) | DDC 951/.38—dc23
LC record available at https://lccn.loc.gov/2017040065

For my family

CONTENTS

ACKNOWLEDGMENTS

Writing this book has been a long journey. My interest in the teahouses of Chengdu started in the 1980s when I studied the society of the upper Yangzi region, but it was a very hard task at the time because of a lack of sources. In the 1990s, when I conducted research for my dissertation on street culture in Chengdu, I discovered some good material and thought that I might write a hundred-year history of Chengdu teahouses. However, I decided to write two books on teahouses in Chengdu (divided by 1950) after I found the massive records from the Chengdu Municipal Archives in the late 1990s and early 2000s. As soon as the first book on teahouses in the late Qing and Republican periods was completed in 2006, I started to work on the current book. Unbelievably, the time has passed by so quickly, and it has taken more than ten years, the longest time I have ever spent on a book. Now, I feel so relieved to see that the book is going to be published.

My thanks first go to Bill Rowe. The idea of studying teahouses started during my graduate years at Johns Hopkins University under his supervision; he was the first to read the first complete manuscript of this book and gave me constructive comments. I owe special thanks to Karl Gerth, who read the earlier version of the whole manuscript thoroughly and offered the most comprehensive suggestions. I am also very grateful to Howard Goodman, who was my copy editor but did much more than copyediting and helped me shape a better manuscript in many ways. I would like to thank Madeleine Zelin and Richard Smith (as well as Bill) for writing recommendation letters for my grant applications for this project. My gratitude goes to editor Emily Andrew at Cornell University Press for her enthusiastic support of this project; she guided me through the whole procedure, from revisions to final manuscript preparation. I would like to thank the two anonymous reviewers for the press, who offered their expert critiques and constructive suggestions for improving this book.

I thank the National Humanities Center (NHC) and the National Endowment for the Humanities for providing residential fellowship during the 2006–2007 academic year, when I could concentrate my energy and time on this project. The constant discussions with fellows of the 2006–2007 class at the NHC have inspired my thoughts. My thanks also go to the University of Macau for supporting me with its generous Start-up Research Grant at the last stage of this project. I received several grants from Texas A&M University, including an International Research Travel Assistance Grant (2007), a grant through the Program to Enhance Scholarly and Creative Activities (2007), and a Stipendiary Fellowship through the Glasscock Center for Humanities Research and the Confucius Institute (2009). This project also received research grants from the East Asian Institute of the National University of Singapore (2010), L'École des hautes études en sciences sociales (EHESS, 2011), and the Research Center for Urban Culture at Shanghai Normal University (2012). I want to thank the Chengdu Municipal Archives for allowing me to use its collection during 1997 and 2003. Without the access to massive archival material, it would not be possible to complete this project. I also owe thanks to the Sterling C. Evans Library at Texas A&M University for providing me its good services.

During the decade of working on this book, I presented papers based on this project at Association for Asian Studies annual meetings and other conferences and would like to thank the organizers, discussants, panelists, and audiences for their comments on my papers. I also gave talks at several institutions, including the National University of Singapore, the University of Erlangen-Nuremberg (Erlangen, Germany), the Free University (Berlin), L'École des hautes études en sciences sociales, L'Université Paris-Diderot, Nanjing University, Shanghai Normal University, Wuhan University, Central China Normal University (Wuhan), Fudan University, Peking University, and Remin University (Beijing). The questions and comments from audiences inspired my thoughts. Earlier versions of chapter 2 and chapter 6 have been published in the journals *Frontiers of History in China* and *International Journal of Asian Studies* respectively. Some material in chapters 4 and 5 appeared in *Quaderni storici*. I thank the editors and publishers for permission to reuse the materials here.

Many people provided their support in making connections or accompanying me on my fieldwork during 1997 to 2003. Especially, I would like to thank Lai Jun, Wang Jing, Jiang Mengbi, Yang Tianhong, Hou Dechu, and Li Xudong. My deepest gratitude goes to my family for their encouragement and spiritual support, which gave me strength to complete this long journey. I dedicate this book to them.

The Teahouse under Socialism

INTRODUCTION

Urban Political Transitions under Socialism

The last day of 1949 in Chengdu was cold and overcast, and in their usual way residents sought warmth and camaraderie in hundreds of neighborhood teahouses. But December 31 also marked a turning point. News about the war just beyond the city was trickling in, and newspaper headlines announced the destruction of Nationalist troops and a coming political transition for Chengdu.[1] Just a few days earlier, the air was filled with the not-so-distant rumble of cannon and intense gunfire, but on December 27, without firing a shot, the People's Liberation Army (PLA) had marched into Chengdu, preventing the street battles that residents dreaded. During all this, life carried on, and teahouses not only remained open but were packed with customers. Daily life was affected very little.[2] Few patrons would have noticed that on this last day of the year the new government established a Committee for the Takeover of Culture and Education (Wenjiao jieguan weiyuanhui) under the PLA's Military Control Commission in Chengdu (Chengdu shi junshi guanzhi weiyuanhui), an act that would forever change not just teahouses but public life in general (see figure I.1).[3]

Figure I.1 Stove to warm patrons in a teahouse in a Chengdu suburb,
September 2015. Author photo.

People eager to hear the latest about the war went to their neighborhood's information hub. On December 31 the teahouse waiters would have been attending to their usual duties—seating, clearing, and refreshing tea bowls—but today they were too busy to sweep peanut shells and tobacco ash from the floor. Customers did not seem to mind; their sole focus was the PLA's presence in the city and the optimistic speculation that the new Communist government would bring social and economic stability. Large numbers in Chengdu were hopeful that a regime change would end an era filled with civil war, rising prices, and the Nationalist dictatorship. The ordinary people cared little about complex political ideologies but longed for stability and prosperity. In the eyes of many, a regime change might not have been a bad thing.

As night fell, even more people squeezed into the teahouses, as the day's news was put aside in favor of scheduled storytelling. The storytellers quickly lured listeners into strange and fantastical worlds—*Investiture of the Gods* (*Fengshen yanyi*), *Romance of the Three Kingdoms* (*Sanguo yanyi*), and *The Legend of Yue Fei* (*Shuo Yue*).[4] These roiling tales led listeners into well-known historical and political narratives as well as into ghost worlds, and it all overlapped with human society past and present, providing temporary relief from recent difficulties. Many in the audience went home once the storytelling ended at about 10 or 11 p.m., but hard-core teahouse-goers would have stayed much longer, bolstered by naps taken earlier in the bamboo chairs.[5] Also, late nights were when chefs, apprentices, and workers from nearby shops and restaurants gathered in the teahouses to relax with friends and unwind after their long shifts, and to use the hot water to clean their faces and even their feet. The regulars might not have noted the passing of another year before heading home. After all, previous years had blended, one into another, and there was no reason to believe the year ahead would be any different. The common folk of Chengdu followed the generations that went before them, secure in the knowledge that regardless of the world's chaos, they could hold fast to their meager livelihoods and their teahouses (see figure I.2).

But if some of the customers or workers paused to think about teahouses, they might have recalled that like all of Chengdu, the teahouses had already gone through some changes during the first half of the twentieth century. Moreover, even the city's physical landscape had transformed during this time.[6] While the Boxer Rebellion at the turn of the century and the occupation of Beijing by troops of the Eight Powers Alliance had had little effect on Chengdu, which was shielded by high elevation and mountainous borders, this protection was pierced with the regime change brought by the 1911 Revolution. At that time, mutinous soldiers

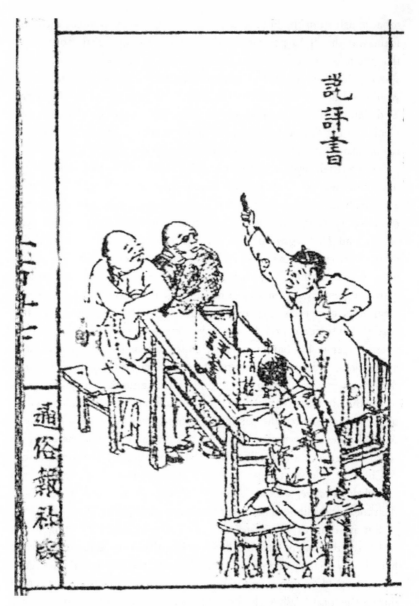

Figure I.2 Storyteller. From Fu Chongju 1910, 117.

burned and looted Chengdu's commercial center, followed by the horrific street battles of 1917 and 1932. Chengdu survived relatively unscathed a few years later, when Japanese invading troops flooded eastern China.

Subsequently, from 1937 to 1949, Chengdu residents could easily frequent teahouses, and they went about their everyday lives without interruption.

Long after midnight on the last day of 1949, waiters finally twisted the knobs to turn off oil lamps or switched off electric lights, leaving their teahouses dark and quiet, a brief respite in the daily cycle of operation.[7] Teahouse workers went home to sleep under thermal quilts after another exhausting day, and quite a few actually lived in the teahouses. This free time was precious, a quick opportunity to rest or stretch sore muscles. After just a few hours, they would make their way back to the commotion of the teahouse, thankful for wages that kept them from starvation and perhaps hoping to someday open their own place. As long as there were teahouses, they would have their livelihoods.

While we cannot construct with any certainty the dreams and aspirations of average teahouse customers and workers, we can be sure that most did not foresee the upheaval soon to come, when teahouses would disappear along with the occupations that they provided. When workers awakened the following morning, January 1, 1950, they would have opened the teahouse doors for business as usual, unaware that Chengdu as well as all other Chinese cities had entered a profoundly different era, one that made the functioning of teahouses and public life more subject to state control.

The City, Modernity, and the Vitality of Teahouses

Chengdu is the capital of Sichuan Province and one of the major cultural, economic, and political centers in West China. It has a long history. During the Three Kingdoms period (220–280 CE), it was the capital of the state of Shu. During the Tang dynasty, Chengdu was one of most prosperous cities in China. Much later, a transition occurred from late Ming governance to that of the early Qing (roughly the 1620s to 1680s), during which Sichuan experienced more than a half century of war that devastated the economy in the region and damaged the cities. Yet in the early Qing, the economy and culture were gradually restored. The Opium Wars (1840–1842 and 1856–1860) had little economic impact on Chengdu, although missionaries increased their activities there, and the city suffered little damage during the Taiping Rebellion (1851–1864). Chengdu had one of the largest populations among the country's inland cities in the late nineteenth and early twentieth centuries. In the 1900s to the 1920s its population was from 340,000 to 350,000. By 1949, it had grown to 650,000. By 2000, its population reached six million.[8]

Like all other provincial capitals, Chengdu experienced almost all the political, economic, social, and cultural transformations from the late-Qing reforms to the Communist victory. During 1900 and 1910, Chengdu, under the influence of the New Policies and self-government movement, became a center and model of industrial, commercial, educational, and social reforms in the upper Yangzi region. Local elites, supported by state power, enthusiastically participated in reforms that expanded their influence over ordinary people and built their social reputation. In 1911 many residents joined the Railroad Protection Movement, but in the post-Republican revolution Chengdu fell into chaos. By 1935, the central government barely controlled Chengdu; instead the city was in the hands of five warlords who shared power under the system of defense districts (*fangqu zhi*). The Nationalist government finally extended its power into Sichuan during 1935 and 1937.[9]

The War of Resistance against Japan (1937–1945) brought Sichuan and Chengdu onto the central stage of national politics. The Nationalist government's move to Chongqing (only 180 miles from Chengdu) had a profound impact on Chengdu and also changed the relationship between Sichuan and the central government. Many offices of the central government and other provincial governments, social and cultural organizations, schools, and factories from East China arrived in Chengdu. A huge number of refugees flooded into the city, bringing new cultural elements with them. Postwar Chengdu became a stage of political struggle between the Guomindang and the Communists. On December 27, 1949, nearly three months after the establishment of the People's Republic of China, the People's Liberation Army captured Chengdu.

During the early socialist period, Chengdu was gradually developed into an industrial city, and its facilities and infrastructure were also gradually improved: streets were widened; there was new residential construction; sewage systems and bridges were built or improved. From 1964, the central government launched a plan called Three Lines of Construction (Sanxian jianshe) in preparation for future wars. This provided a new wave of industrial development. During the Cultural Revolution (1966–1976), the city fell into unrest and even a constant sort of violence in the early stage of the movement, when many factories and schools were shut down, and many young people and government employees were sent to the countryside. The Imperial City, a historic site dating to the Han dynasty, was dismantled entirely.

The post-Mao reforms brought Chengdu rapid expansion and construction. From 1993 to 1998 the dredging of the Funan River that circles the city and the construction of parks with plantings along its banks greatly improved the landscape, environment, and living conditions of the city. In order to balance development between coast and hinterland, the central government launched an ambitious plan called the Great Development of China's West (Xibu dakaifa), which opened even more opportunities for Chengdu to play a broader role in the national economy. Sichuan was usually one of the most populous of China's provinces, but in 1997 its eastern part was separated and became administered by Chongqing at the provincial level; as a result, Chengdu's administrative region shrank. Despite this setback, Chengdu, based on its central position in Sichuan Province, subsequently built up its own momentum by knitting together the economy of western Sichuan, thus providing a great opportunity for its economic development.

With the advent of this kind of modernization, the pace of everyday life has accelerated. As Ágnes Heller pointed out, "Any change in the rhythm of life is bound to affect everyday life, but not everyone's everyday life in equal measure; and not every area of everyday life is affected to the same degree."[10] Chengdu succumbed much less than other major Chinese cities to the fast-paced lifestyle of the twentieth century. Nevertheless, like many Chinese cities, Chengdu has experienced development processes and pressures that are now commonplace in China and around the world. As a result of China's political, economic, and cultural transformation and the impact of globalization, teahouses, teahouse culture, and the public sphere have seen a shift in both the substance and style of the activities and opportunities offered.[11]

By 2000, the city had changed dramatically. It teemed with places of public leisure—coffeehouses, bars, Internet bars, karaoke clubs, ballroom dance halls, cinemas, and other modern entertainment centers—as well as luxury hotels and related facilities. Furthermore, almost every family had one or more color television sets and low-priced VCD and DVD players that brought a huge variety of channels and entertainment genres (especially Hollywood). Entire families, in their own cars, were taking drives out of town to scenic areas or to resorts and the like. Chengdu residents had options for their leisure time, but, almost unbelievably, this tsunami of options failed to drown the teahouse business; instead, in Chengdu today, teahouses enjoy unprecedented popularity and success and are found almost everywhere in the city. No one anticipated such a strong resurgence, given the obstacles teahouses faced during almost every political stage in the twentieth century.

During the War of Resistance, reformist elites and the government all framed their constant attacks on teahouse culture in the larger context of the war. They often compared the plight of soldiers fighting on the bloody battlefields with people whiling away the hours at teahouses, turning leisure pursuits into shameful activities. Lao Xiang, a local writer, defended the habits of Chengdu residents, pointing out, "We do not cry out 'Long live teahouses,' but we also disagree that teahouses should be forbidden. When a better alternative emerges, teahouses may fade away. In the meantime, however, we have to go to teahouses to drink, rest, chat, do business, and meet friends."[12] Lao believed that new types of public facilities might eventually replace the teahouse, which was a token of an "old society" that would be abandoned as society became more "progressive." He of course could not anticipate that more than half a century later, when society came to be considered vastly more "progressive," teahouses would flourish.[13] Today, old, small, and rustic teahouses prosper along with elegant and magnificent ones, and they are shared by elderly retirees who smoke old-fashioned pipes and fashionable youngsters with dyed hair and smart phones.

Chengdu in the past had more teahouses than other cities because of the culture fostered by its geography and economy. Unlike in most regions in China, the rural people of Sichuan, especially on the Chengdu Plain, lived in relative isolation on their farmlands; this prevented the cultivation of village or community life. They relied on rural markets more than did their counterparts elsewhere, who had access to long-distance trade networks. The rural workers of the Chengdu Plain marketed locally and then would stop by a teahouse to socialize or take in entertainment. Some even bought and sold in the teahouses.[14] In addition, the narrow footpaths made the use of transport animals rare; men using equipment such as carrying poles, wheelbarrows, and sedan chairs were much more prevalent. Coolies depended on teahouses as rest places. Poor water quality and limited fuel

Figure I.3 A teahouse in the open air. This photograph was taken by Joseph Needham between 1943 and 1946. Photo reproduced courtesy of the Needham Research Institute, Cambridge University.

made Chengdu further dependent on teahouses. Water carriers brought river water from outside town to sell for drinking. Such transport would have been difficult for many families, so it was common to purchase boiled water directly from teahouses. Firewood, the major fuel in Chengdu, was expensive; many ordinary families lit fires only to cook. They patronized restaurants and teahouses in order to conserve firewood and bought their hot water for washing from neighborhood teahouses (see figure I.3).

By the end of the twentieth century, drinking water, fuel, and transportation were plentiful and affordable, and people could drink tea conveniently at home. So what has made teahouses endure? There are many factors, but the most important is that teahouses always adapted to changes in society and adjusted their business model in parallel with cultural, political, and economic transformations. In particular, they have been able to absorb new technology and new demands for pleasure. In the first ten or fifteen years of the twentieth century, for example, even during the Qing dynasty at its endpoint, teahouses introduced movie shows and record players to the public.[15] In the 1980s, with the rise of videos, many teahouses added video screening equipment. To keep up with economic development and rising living standards, teahouses installed air-conditioning and private box seats. Similarly, teahouses provided space for mahjong. Even the older sort of personal services either survived intact or came back in different forms. For instance, while the hot towel service was gone, foot-soaking has been added. And fortune-telling, earwax picking, and shoe polishing continue today. Sometimes, people in the teahouse feel that they have traveled to a previous era or are on a bridge linking the past to the present.

Coffeehouses and bars have not replaced teahouses or stolen away teahouse customers. Tea drinking is still the best fit for people with limited economic resources, especially the elderly. The main customer base in the teahouse is the middle-aged and older. Young people who are attracted to international trends go to modern Western-style coffeehouses or bars, while others patronize the less-expensive and old-style ones.[16] Coffeehouses and bars in contemporary Chinese cities are entirely Western, with no reflection of Chinese custom, but teahouses are rooted in China's past. In a coffeehouse or a bar, patrons have no access to peddlers, fortune-tellers, earwax pickers, or shoe polishers. The teahouse has always included more of these aspects of the local society and economy than do the modern coffeehouse and bar. Its patrons can linger for hours or even all day, for very little money, adding boiling water to their tea leaves rather than having to buy another cup. In lower-level and street-corner teahouses, people often strike up conversation, adding thus another dimension of vitality to the teahouse environment.

Nearly all of Chengdu has been demolished and rebuilt during the decades spanning the turn of the century. The old streets and neighborhoods in which teahouses were embedded are almost all gone, and the city has been born anew, amid rapid population growth, booming urban development, and the attendant traffic problems. Chengdu's fate is similar to that of almost all other ancient cities in China. Whereas each Chinese city in ancient times had its own charming, distinctive appearance and folk culture, today this uniqueness is all but lost; cities are becoming alike in look and sensation. Therefore, the recovery and restoration of the historical legacies of China's cities form a significant mission for social, cultural, and urban historians. Whether the teahouse will continue to adapt to the challenges of radical social transformation, incorporate today's ubiquitous technological gadgets, manage globalization, and play an important role in modern, urban lifestyles are questions that only time will answer.

Public Life, Public Spaces, and Urban Society under the Socialist State

Why are we looking at teahouses in socialist, that is, post-1949, Chengdu? The teahouse may be considered a "small urban space," following the words of sociologist William H. Whyte in his discussion of such public places as coffeehouses.[17] It is natural, then, that the theory and history of urbanism will be taken up here, since we are dealing with Chengdu as an urban area with many smaller spaces, à la Whyte. I propose that we think beyond simply "small urban spaces" and link the latter to concepts of the public, society, and the state. How does the public (or publics) manifest itself (or themselves) in those small urban spaces? Teahouse life was and is part, but not all, of public life in Chengdu, and was thus susceptible to transformations, along with the rest of the country. We shall see its importance in everyday life and how an ancient cultural institution could remain vital and even thrive despite unprecedented threats during a period of rapid modernization. Post-Mao reforms provided a significant opportunity for the revival of public life, which enhanced the development of the public sphere.

In this book, "the public" means people as they move about outside their private spaces, engaging in livelihoods, commerce, information sharing, and entertainment—all of these giving substance to another aspect of urban society, namely urban culture. The individuals who act in public, in their public spaces, and the resultant life and culture that make up a society, must all deal in numerous ways with the state. In this book I begin to explore examples of the way in which certain policies of Early Socialism created historically game-changing impacts on society. The main evidence of this was the large extent to which urban Chengdu and its culture of public life became pressured and bent by the ruling Communist state entity, which was quite concerned with the public. By looking back at Chengdu and capturing the push and pull of various forces, we can narrate changes in the situation of the urban teahouse (the small spaces) and the publics (smallest human units of society) who frequented them in China's new socialism (the state).

In the first half of the twentieth century, few other institutions in Chengdu were more important in everyday life than teahouses, and no other city in China had as many of them as Chengdu.[18] By examining the economic, social, political, and cultural changes that occurred in the teahouses of Chengdu during the late Qing and Republican periods, we obtain a thorough picture of everyday culture in its most basic unit of public life. We find, as I did in my previous work, that the enduring local culture and customs as represented by the Chengdu teahouse constantly resisted relentless waves of Westernization, which imposed a uniformity of modernist and then postmodern transformation, and which came in parallel with the state's growing role in public life. In other words, two major developments coexisted in the course of urban reform and modernization in this period: the growing role of the state, and the concurrent decline of the uniqueness of local culture and customs. Both of these developments could be seen clearly in a major part of everyday culture—the teahouse.

The book at hand focuses on teahouses in Chengdu after the Communist victory. It deals with different issues and answers different questions from those of the pre-Communist period because of, quite understandably, a new social and political environment. Today, Chengdu still has the largest number of teahouses among all Chinese cities. In the second half of the twentieth century, the role and importance of the teahouse changed, and many more public spaces became available, as compared with the preceding eras and regimes. By the end of the twentieth century the teahouse vied for patrons alongside outdoor places such as streets, squares, sidewalks, open markets, plazas, and parks, as well as such indoor places as theaters, cinemas, galleries, museums, exhibitions, courtyards, arcades, restaurants, and coffeehouses. However, like most popular public spaces, the teahouse remains an enduring symbol of Chinese culture, having already prevailed for centuries through political transformation, modernization, and globalization. Naturally, teahouse life was and is part, but not all, of public life in Chengdu, and was thus susceptible to political and social transformations, along with the rest of the country. We shall see its importance in everyday life and how an ancient cultural institution could remain vital and even thrive despite unprecedented threats to small business per se during a period of rapid modernization. Post-Mao reforms provided a significant opportunity for public life. It is a worthy subject for historical scholarship. A robust understanding of the teahouse's expansive social, cultural, and political roles can take us far in understanding not just Chengdu, but the whole of Chinese urban society, as well as the broader connection between the transformation of Chinese urban society and the politics of the new socialist state.

To study and write about the world brought by the new state, I draw on a general consensus in the field of historians and sociologists working on China by referring here to two major periods: Mao's China (1949–1976), which I frequently call Early Socialism, and the post-Mao Reform Era (1977–2000), or Late Socialism.[19] My study is a type of microhistory of Chengdu, and it concerns the processes, stories, and degrees of change in the public life of that city, from the PLA's takeover and through the stormy political developments of Early Socialism—which were massive and affected both urban and rural people, sometimes violently and tragically—ultimately arriving to the reforms of the post-Mao, or Late Socialism, period.

By examining teahouses in Chengdu through the second half of the twentieth century, this book will hold up for investigation several motivating questions: How did state power intervene in the operation of small businesses? How could such a thing as "socialist entertainment" be established in a local society? What happened to the already established guilds? How did the political movements change the teahouses and public life? How did the teahouse revive and flourish under the post-Mao reforms and the opening up of the economy? Through such questioning, we might enhance our understanding of public life and political culture in Chengdu under the Communist state with its needs.

Four major points run through the book as a type of contextual backdrop, and each point becomes an aspect of political developments that greatly impacted lives in Chengdu, the old-style organizations there, and the city's economy. First of all, during the Mao era, the state achieved tight control over society generally, and it was able to penetrate the very core of society in order to control almost all its resources. The spaces usually available for social give-and-take and for the natural development of social projects were sharply limited. Under the Communist regime, the state attempted to control both the venues of public life and leisure and their forms and content. Immediately after its political installation, the

Communist administration in Chengdu carried out measures to manipulate everyday life and popular entertainment. Resistance after 1949 did exist, as, in historical comparison, popular culture had resisted control by elites and the state during the late Qing and Republican periods. But post-1949 resistance was much subdued by the state's often violent campaigns to root out so-called enemies, quell emergent protests, and impose its own party-determined forms of expression, co-opting expressions and actions by people in public spaces.[20] Public life thus became weakened in the face of the strongest state in Chinese history. We must recall that the blunt harbinger of all this was the arrival in Chengdu in 1949 of a military unit that immediately looked toward a "takeover" of culture. Such a military-ideological clamp on public life and people's minds was a new thing in Chinese history. As a result, many old forms of entertainment and popular culture that did not manage to be recognized as "revolutionary" quickly vanished. Of course, although we perceive distinct conflicts between this expanded state power and the society per se, in fact the reality was much more complex. The two should not be seen as occupying an unvarying binary opposition: gray areas existed everywhere. Furthermore, state policies were not always unalterable. With the intense flux of political movements, the state control of public space and everyday life was also sometimes tight and sometimes loose.

Second, the post-Mao economic reforms, starting around 1977, were a turning point in public life, because the Late Socialist state, caught up in economic forces, had to weaken its control over people and lessen its interventions in daily life. Socialist ideology over time has become less important in the state's planning. On the one hand, the Chinese Communist Party (CCP) and the government closely watch the crucial sectors such as mainstream media, education, and publications. On the other hand, they have withdrawn direct control from many areas, including small business operations, entertainment, and commercial culture. In parallel with economic and social developments, public life gradually became increasingly freer as well. Everyday life was dominated by sweeping "open market" economic reforms that were structured within a unique type of socialist political system, and to a significant degree public life moved away from state control. Public life after the post-Mao recovery differed significantly from before. The emerging new sort of commercialization had a great impact on teahouses and teahouse life, as well as political culture. And ultimately, as components of a long-established, ongoing local culture, teahouses had to find ways to adjust to the massive wave of commercial globalization.

Third, there is no simple distinction between Mao's rule (Early Socialism) and the reform era (Late Socialism). On the surface, we can see certain continuities in the state's policies that span the two eras. In fact, this phenomenon still affects all aspects of Chinese society. In their study of early 1950s China, Jeremy Brown and Paul Pickowicz noted that during the post-Mao Late Socialism, many people praised the 1950s, offering good memories of that time: "It is no coincidence that post-Mao reform-era publications promote positive memories of the early 1950s: the two periods share striking similarities. After the founding of the People's Republic in October 1949—and again in the late 1970s after Mao died—a massive wave of rural migrants entered cities, private factories coexisted alongside large state enterprises, nongovernmental and church groups operated next to Communist Party-led organizations, and capitalists and other nonparty figures supported the regime and played a role in shaping its policies."[21] I agree that there were such similarities, but throughout this book I also emphasize a divergence: that the 1950s and the post-Mao era moved in two different strategic directions. During Early Socialism, we can describe a period of transition from the pre-1949 free market economy, with little state engagement, to a centrally planned economy with a large factor of state control. For example, although rural migrants could move to the city for jobs, by then the powerful state could send out masses of urban residents to rural areas, and eventually a household registration system could also prevent rural people from migrating to the cities (this is discussed in more detail in chapters 1 and 2). With the reforms of Late Socialism, however, the direction of the state, as instituted from the top, was the opposite—going from the planned economy and tight state control to a freer, market economy with less state control.

Fourth, the socialist state is still woven into social and cultural life and still seeks to wield influence. Li Zhang studied migrant workers in the city during the Late Socialism transition and noted that "the retreat of the state" and "the triumph of the market and capitalism" might be incorrect notions.[22] Jing Wang argues similarly that in the years following 1989, the state also actively participated in consumer and commercial culture. She tries to explain "how culture [was] reconstructed in the 1990s as the site where capital—both political and economic capital—can be accumulated." She finds that in what is termed "the postsocialist state," government has taken a different strategy for maintaining influence, namely, by playing an active role in culture. It has "rejuvenated its capacity, via the market, to affect the agenda of popular culture, especially at the discursive level." Therefore, "the state's rediscovery of culture as a site where new ruling technologies can be deployed and converted simultaneously into economic capital constitutes one of its most innovative strategies of statecraft since the founding of the People's Republic."[23]

I would argue slightly differently. The state has merely found a new and more subtle way to influence culture and entertainment in the post-Mao era—top-down homogeneity. Although there is no question that the new consumer culture is more plentiful and laden with choices than ever before, it reflects little that is local, and instead has become homogenized. Thus, a national, even centralized, culture has strengthened. Of course, such a national culture may be driven by modernization and commercialization as well as by the state. For example, the nationally driven policy surrounding urban development encouraged the unifying of culture and further weakened the ability of local architecture and well-established patterns of urban activity and spaces to survive.

In sum, we have considered both the Chengdu teahouse, a long-established institution, and the Chinese state as phenomena that developed distinct shapes over the half century in question. The teahouses per se—their buildings, sites, manner of operation—were not altered at first, so much as culturally supervised and politically controlled, and consequently they withered. The new Communist state too had its distinct shapes over those fifty years, especially going from Early to Late Socialism. At this point, it will aid in the overall argument, and in sustaining my four major points, mentioned just above, if we consider briefly some previous scholarly approaches to the idea of public spaces and their interaction with the political needs and impacts of the state. The two phenomena created an urban confluence of the public and the political in which we can see both the state's hand and the citizenry's means of resisting that hand, while continuing their lives and lifestyles (see figure I.4).

Figure I.4 A teahouse where middle-class people gathered. This photograph was taken by Joseph Needham between 1943 and 1946. Photo reproduced courtesy of the Needham Research Institute, Cambridge University.

The Public and the Political: Urban Culture under Socialism

In premodern China, there always existed a concept of "public" (*gong*); it touched on motives and actions partly official and partly familial and domestic. In this book, "public" is often used in a sense that connects it with "public space." In late-imperial China, people often discussed "the public" (*gongzhong*) in connection with voluntary organizations and "public opinion" (*gongzhong yulun*), something discussed by Mary Rankin and William Rowe.[24] During the period of the 1911 Revolution, the rampant warlordism and emergence of the Nationalist government, the public played an important role in shaping national and local politics and political culture. At this time, "public" could have several meanings, such as media, intellectuals, an amassed body of a local population, various associations, and so on. Often, such "publics" were separated from the government and officials. After 1949, the "public" became a sensitive term, since the state and the party dominated politics, the economy, and culture, and continually changed and grew or shrank in its force, in parallel with Mao's radical ideologies and policies. Until the Cultural Revolution, "the public" did not exist and was replaced by "the masses" (*qunzhong*), sometimes being "revolutionary masses" (*geming qunzhong*)—a term with a negative opposite, namely "counterrevolutionaries" (*fangeming*). In a certain sense, in communist discourse, "the masses" were those people who diligently followed the CCP and its government and actively participated in required political movements. Although "revolutionary masses" had a life in public places, it was hardly voluntary but was sponsored or organized by the state and the party. There were only official and private realms, no actual "public" between those two endpoints. This changed in the post-Mao era. After some relaxation of state controls on many fronts, people acquired relatively more freedom in political and public life. With this opening and "ideological emancipation" (*sixiang jiefang*), people had more opportunities to participate in national and local politics and to form public opinions. "The public" came back from its formerly deflated profile and started to play a role in China's political life and political culture.

There was not a discourse recognized as something like "public life" in the field of Chinese history, even though people did have goings-on in public spaces.[25] In contrast, there has been an important literature about public life and public spaces in the West. Those studies seem to follow one of two approaches—the narrow and the wide. The narrow view, it seems, has focused on people's need to find the spaces that are outside of home, close friends, family, and private service. It sees different groups and types, coming into contact in, and clashing over, public rituals and public venues.[26] The wider approach uses an analytical viewpoint from sociological and communications theory, and in some contexts views both people and the state as occupying the realm of the public together.[27]

In this book, I will remain more or less persuaded by the narrow approach. I favor Richard Sennett's notion of public life as occurring outside of family and close friends, as stated above.[28] Regarding the wider approach and what one might call the mixing of the political into the public space, I hope to show that especially in the case of post-1949 China, the people and the state tended to stake out different directions and were to some extent, but not diametrically or in a binary sense, oppositional. Overall my concept of public life has the following traits: (1) it is human activity in places that people share—in some sense among random people who do not constitute a kin or friendship group; (2) in such a place, people do not have expectations of privacy; (3) their activities can be conducted for social, leisure, or economic reasons; and (4) activities of public life can be affected by specific political situations as well as the overall political culture of the state. In this study, the focus of public life is mainly on everyday habits of association that are relatively voluntary and free. That is, they are not manipulated by the needs of the state and its ruling party, although it will be instructive, further along, to reflect on certain state-sponsored activities or other propaganda-driven events held in public places, using the public as actors.

Yunxiang Yan notes that "a significant change in public life during the post-Mao era has been the disappearance of frequent mass rallies, voluntary work, collective parties, and other forms of 'organized sociality' in which the state (through its agents) played the central role. In its place are new forms of private gatherings in public venues." Under Mao, public life took the form of a highly controlled, "organized sociality" that emphasized the "centrality of the state, the official ideology, and the submission of individuals to an officially endorsed collectivity."[29] Although I do not think there was any "voluntary work" under Mao's rule (any activity under a "voluntary" flag was sponsored or organized by the party or the government), Yan was right in observing the transformation of public life in the post-Mao era from collective to individual. While some have argued that we might do well to look at party-led public events during Early Socialism as a new and transformed sort of public life in public spaces, I would prefer to emphasize the presence or lack of such essential qualities as voluntarism and vocal expression. Under Mao, these latter qualities were suppressed so that controlled propaganda flow and a controlled public ruled out voluntary, vocal public activities.[30] After Mao, "the new sociality celebrates individuality and private desires in unofficial social and spatial contexts." The center of public life and socialization shifted "from large state-controlled public spaces (such as city squares, auditoriums, and workers' clubs) to smaller, commercialized arenas."[31] Recently, we have had studies of dance halls, bowling alleys, and parks, all of which provide such public space. However, in Chengdu, it was the teahouse that provided not just a space, but services to meet the everyday needs of people from all walks of life. Services must be seen as part of the urban culture, and they added relatively more richness to public experiences in these ubiquitous public spaces.

It is clear that public spaces, as typified so well by the Chengdu teahouse, meshed during this period with political forces—at certain times and in circumscribed ways. My overall research on the teahouses of Chengdu has also taken up the way in which they were impacted by the new political culture; this has helped to show how the CCP's agenda transformed public space and public life. Once again, there is a broad and a narrow approach in this literature; and again I will favor, at least in this discussion, the narrower approach.[32] Based on the perspective found in the work of Lynn Hunt, I want to delimit this political culture: for our purposes it means the socialist or Communist Party's political culture. Hunt focused her examination of political culture on specifically that which developed, and evolved and changed, within the long process called the French Revolution.[33] Similarly, we must recognize that the Chinese Communist revolution professed and practiced a culture that changed and revealed new forms over successive political periods. In the following study, without losing site of where we are in this evolution in political culture, we can examine the effect of the wider aspects upon the narrower—through the lens of the teahouse. We can begin to explore how the new Soviet-style state employed political power to manipulate all aspects of Chinese society, how political power determined people's daily lives and cultural lives, and how socialist politics and in some sense its progressivist and modernist culture penetrated the broad public life. As with the French Revolution, we are dealing with a radical, ideologically potent period of time. We will see to what extent the Communist revolution and other political movements affected the relationships among people and between the individual and the state. A great many current studies of political culture in China focus on the wide arenas of national politics, policy making, state ideologies, and elite activities, but here we enter the lowest level of politics and culture in order to see the two interact at the most basic unit of society.

Urban culture might be considered a part of the political culture, and Chengdu gives us much on which to build or correlate, in regard to theoretic and historical studies. I see several approaches as having developed in studies of post-1949 Chinese cities. The first was a macro-political approach, coming mostly from political scientists and sociologists. Its deals mostly with government policies and little with quotidian human activities. There were in fact few studies of post-1949 Chinese cities before the 1980s.[34] Then the field began to explore urban people and their needs, habits, and lifestyles. Martin King Whyte and William L. Parish did much to open this up. Their *Urban Life in Contemporary China* dealt with a vast array—politics, the economy, security, infrastructure, marriage and family structure, the status of women, urban organizations, crime and social control, political control, religions, social values, and personal relationships.[35] A few years later, Whyte wrote the chapter "Urban Life in the People's Republic" for volume 15 of the *Cambridge History of China*; it addressed urban life historically from 1949 to 1980. From Whyte's work we understand how people responded to the Communists' takeover of cities, the party's Soviet model of urban development, the relationship between the urban elite and ordinary people, urban organizations, and the chaotic impact on urban life of political movements such as the Great Leap Forward and the Cultural Revolution.[36] So far his overall work remains the most comprehensive analysis.

In the second approach, studies of modern urban China began to take a historical view, focusing more on personal and individual experiences under the Communist regime through studies (mostly after 2000) based on empirical and archival data. These new and often reliable sources have increasingly enhanced our understanding of the People's Republic of China and its cities. Research topics have focused heavily on the transition from Communist leadership during the warfare leading up to 1950 to urban management later on, as well as how this transition happened and what was its mechanism. Moreover, since so many studies concentrate on Shanghai, historians of urban China face a challenge regarding the picture of Chinese cities taken as an aggregated whole. The recent and perhaps more important of the English-language historical approaches is *Dilemmas of Victory: The Early Years of the People's Republic of China*, edited by Jeremy Brown and Paul G. Pickowicz.[37] The editors recognize that "documents from municipal archives have led to much more detailed accounts of the Communist takeover of city institutions and the reordering of urban society."[38] Like these Western historians of China, Chinese historians in mainland China also started their studies of the CCP's socialist urban agenda generally after 2000. Despite various restrictions of a political nature, in the past decade some important works have emerged that deserve our attention; in particular, there has been notable progress in the discovery and development of new materials and topics, although most of them are on political history, and few of them study cities other than Shanghai.[39]

The newest contribution to this approach of the history of Communist China is *Maoism at the Grassroots: Everyday Life in China's Era of High Socialism*, edited by Jeremy Brown and Matthew D. Johnson, which includes three articles dealing with cities: Beijing, Tianjin, and Shanghai. As the editors point out, the past scholarship has been "mainly top-down and state-focused," but this edited volume focuses on "individual people in villages, factories, neighborhoods, counties, and ethnic minority regions from the bottom up, and in everyday contexts." This book has also found that state and society are "impossible to clearly distinguish" from each other. During the Mao era, politics could be seen everywhere and penetrated everyday life. Therefore, to study public life, we must consider the factors of politics; as Brown and Johnson point out, "Looking at everyday life does not mean ignoring the role of the state."[40] In fact, the relations of state and society have become a main focus in studying the history of socialist China, and also the emphasis of my study of public life. From this book, we will find that almost all major changes in public life during Early Socialism resulted from the government and state policies.

Finally, the most recent studies of cities and urban life in post-Mao China are those by anthropologists, political scientists, and sociologists. Besides demography, they examine the transformation from the planned economy to the market economy and, of more recent interest, from the ideology of socialist idealism to real problems of disparity, urban woes, and lifestyles. These studies pay attention to workers, government employees, intellectuals, and women. Concerning the latter, we now have explorations of women's experiences at work and home, as well as of how women responded to economic and gender inequality, the worker-management relationship, political participation, the public's response to changes, employment opportunities for women, and the status of women in urban and rural migrant families.[41] Another important topic of this approach has been the prominent changes of Late Socialism (the reform period) that have to do with the rise in itinerant people and the demolition and reconstruction of cities.[42]

In studying China's recent urban culture, although we have been discussing concepts, we must nonetheless keep in mind several specifics that impacted society in the cities. First, the Communist regime during Early Socialism established a machine of control sufficient to reach even the lowest level—that is, the street level—of urban society in which random activities occur in the spaces of public life. Second, after the post-Mao reforms, a large "floating population" greatly escaped the state's control of urban society. Third, since the late twentieth century, China has undergone both an urban and commercial revolution that has changed urban public life. Fourth, academic writing about post-1949 China went through changes. Work conducted in the 1970s and 1980s generally offered a national perspective on political systems, policies, control, and management. With the turn of this century, however, the focus shifted to urban life and problems in specific cities, with an emphasis on human experiences.

All these trends point to the form and plan of my book. Because my study is one of microhistory, it tends to combine the historical (including all the new archival material) and the socio-anthropological approaches just mentioned. I rely on both archival material and fieldwork in an effort to build up my interpretation of the changes in an inland city that in some sense are relatively typical of any Chinese city. Built on a foundation of those earlier studies, my method shifts away just a bit, to go in new directions. The first of these shifts has to do with China's enormous social and cultural transformation after 1949. In the past, studies of modern Chinese history regarded the Republic and the People's Republic as two separate eras. Of course they were right, because the two regimes have obvious differences in political systems, governance, economic and cultural policies, and so forth. However, some recent works on PRC history have found a continuity in the CCP regime's emergence from the Nationalist government; they have also pointed out that CCP and Guomindang policies were not so essentially different as we thought before.

For example, in her 1995 article on everyday life of bank employees in Shanghai and the emergence of the *danwei* system, Wen-hsin Yeh pointed out that by the time the Communists took over Shanghai in 1949, "a significant portion of Shanghai's middle-class urbanites had already been socialized by decades of comparable communal experience." Therefore, the Communist victory in 1949 was "not experienced as a raw confrontation between bourgeois individualism and peasant socialism." Instead, Yeh believes that "the very corporate capitalism that the Communists proceeded not so much to dismantle as to reconstitute had prepared middle-class urbanites' transition to socialism."[43] In 2013, the Harvard-Yenching Institute held a workshop, "Rethinking the 1949 Divide: Dialogue between Political Science and History"; the participants were historians from the

United States and China.[44] The topics of the papers included economic policies, the railroad, the rise of socialist entertainment (my own paper), attacking Yiguandao (a popular religious organization), drafting the 1954 constitution, comparisons of the 1911 revolution and the 1949 revolution, American universities in Shanghai, social welfare, mass movements, and so on. Almost all the participants of the workshop agreed, although to different extents, that the Guomindang and the CCP had many connections in the form of ideology, governance, and economic policy.

The present book seeks to strengthen the terms of the debate about continuity and discontinuity after 1949 chiefly by going more deeply into the 1950s through the 1970s and beyond and by using bottom-up data that knit together individual lives and the state—all of this related to one major inland city and its basic units of public space. I fully recognize the changes and continuities in public life, and the important interplay of the two. Yet my relatively concrete evidence helps to determine more precisely what changed and what remained unchanged in public spaces, public life, and urban culture in Chengdu. By examining public life well past 1949, my study reveals how the Communist revolution and subsequently its enormous, top-down political campaigns affected relationships among ordinary people, the CCP, and the state. I describe public life and political culture during periods of unprecedented historical upheaval, covering the upheavals of Early Socialism, through the radical Great Leap Forward and Cultural Revolution, to the post-Mao reforms of Late Socialism. Finally, my shift of focus has to do with the everyday importance of the teahouse: it has always been the hub of neighborhood communication and social interaction, thus the perfect venue that the politically powerful sought to influence.

The teahouse, as a microcosm of society, provides an ideal window for observing social, cultural, and political transformations. To fully understand a city like Chengdu requires that we enter it from the "bottom" in order to examine the basic units of urban social life. My interest is in how Communist political culture was enforced in these public spaces, and how the resulting changes affected public life generally. In short, I will argue that everyday life in China did undergo a truly fundamental change after 1949, perhaps this being the "rupture" that the one side of the debate refers to, and may be thought of as the roiling surface of a swift river. Although we understand its overall magnitude, we know little about the specific, aggregated details, especially concerning life on the bottom rungs of urban society. The latter aspect represents the continuity of sand, pebbles, and quieter undercurrents that adhere and change only very slowly as individual units, over the river's long course.

Evaluation and Use of Sources

New sources available for the study of post-1949 China present new challenges. In 1969, Michel Oksenberg listed five major primary sources for studying PRC history and culture: mainland publications, such as books, journals, and newspapers; interviews of former residents of the PRC; accounts by people who visited China; fictional works; and Chinese documents and other materials. He did not mention mainland archives because at the time scholars did not have access to them. He acknowledged that assessing these works presented challenges, for example, "what perspectives are commandeered by each source." Today, we are in a much better position than scholars in the 1950s and 1960s. We have access to archival materials despite some limitations. However, the sources are uneven. For example, archives related to the 1950s and 1960s are available, but those for the 1970s and after become rare. Therefore, as Oksenberg pointed out, "the study of China must be undertaken in the face of strong discontinuities in the sources."[45]

Although for the events of the 1950s and early 1960s I depend primarily on archival materials, still we find few records on our subject—the teahouse in general—because during the 1960s and 1970s the number of teahouses decreased dramatically, and they became less important. Yet some Chengdu teahouses survived, and these give us broad clues about teahouse life and even details from a variety of writings that are not usually found in archives—personal records, diaries, and memoirs. However, generally the data about teahouses in 1950s Chengdu usefully reveal aspects of the transition from Nationalist to Communist governance that impacted teahouse life and business operations. They touch on the means of state control, employment, and wages, and the reasons for and results of the teahouses' decline. The Cultural Revolution, a time when teahouses reached their nadir, has left little documentation for us, and the situation was made even worse by the fact that the "national press for this period was less informative, more propagandistic."[46]

I have generally relied on post-1949 materials held by the Chengdu Municipal Archives; these are listed at the beginning of the endnotes, along with the abbreviations used to identify them. In the late 1990s, I found these archival materials scattered in the files deposited by the Chengdu Police Force, the Guilds in All Professions, the Bureau of Industry and Commerce, the Registry of Commercial Administrations, the Association of Industry and Commerce, the Chamber of Commerce, the Second Bureau of Commerce, the United Front Section of the Municipal Party Committee, and the Bureau of Culture. They had not been used previously by researchers. During the 1990s, archives in China were much more open than later, so I was able to access not only those related to the 1950s, but also the early 1960s, although the quantity and quality were not as good as in the earlier years.

In addition, I use newspapers, miscellaneous written sources, and my own field investigations. Examples of the newspaper sources are the *Chengdu ribao* (Chengdu daily) and the *Renmin ribao* (People's daily). Both were official newspapers of the Communist Party and the government, but the former was at the city level, while the latter was at the national level. There are rare mentions of teahouses, usually for propaganda purposes, but which are nonetheless useful. It should be mentioned that from the 1950s to the 1970s, local newspapers reported little on teahouses, in sharp contrast to the plentiful and colorful coverage previously, during the Republican period. Beginning in 1949 the newspapers fell under the control of the government and thus became a political propaganda tool of the party. Although teahouses were still permitted, they were regarded as "backward" and were rarely included in "positive publicity," an attitude that we notice in the comments and urgings set forth in the newspapers. Moreover, the Communist government strongly promoted the notion of building a modern, industrial city that eschewed leisure lifestyles and consumption. Therefore people reduced significantly their patronage of teahouses.

My book's sources on Late Socialism present both advantages and disadvantages. The disadvantage is the lack of archival files; for example, even simple facts such as the precise number of teahouses in this period cannot be answered. In China's current political environment, recent issues are more difficult to research using archival sources, because the pertinent archives are either classified or unavailable to the public. As to advantages, because the teahouses underwent revival during the reforms of Late Socialism, and because of the relatively freer media, local newspapers increased their attention to issues and activities concerning teahouses.

One further note: Under socialism, our relevant sources (whether archival or print media) became structured to benefit the prevailing political movements and ideologies. The preservation and distribution of information via newspapers, especially in Mao's China, was the domain of political propaganda, making the authenticity of their reportage questionable in some instances and to varying degrees. The CCP and the government tightly controlled the dissemination of information from the 1950s to the 1970s, making the use of any materials from this era fraught with difficulties. Therefore, we must analyze the background of the news and place it into its larger political context. Sometimes I treat this information not so much as facts but as indicators of how and why the report was presented in a particular way, merely in order to sift out the truth from between the lines.

Journalism changed after the beginning of the reforms. The CCP and its government still controlled the media, but the emergence of non-party newspapers brought a bit more freedom, as long as media did not report on sensitive political topics. This meant that they could generally report accurately on issues in everyday life, including leisure activities. As a result, newspapers reported with increasing frequency on teahouses and public life, providing valuable details. Of course, these reports shared some similarities with writing in the Republican era; they often presented an elite perspective that was critical of teahouses and public life and biased against popular entertainment. Therefore, we should be skeptical about using them: they are simply a source to understand a more or less official view of popular culture.

In addition to archives and journalistic media, the second part of the book relies on fieldwork. I have been able to perform fieldwork in teahouses for several years and have witnessed dramatic changes to the city's landscape, culture, and everyday life. I have observed all types of teahouses, from multilevel balconied places to small street-corner establishments, and I have talked with a variety of people, from patrons and owners to staff and associated workers—waiters, fortune-tellers, shoe polishers, and earwax pickers. When I investigated a teahouse, I did not pass around a questionnaire, take notes, or record conversations, preferring instead unstructured chats; the topic or questions were not prepared but followed the momentary flow. After fieldwork each day, I wrote in my journal what I heard and saw.

What I heard and saw was not selective according to some imposed format: I was able to collect stories of (at some basic level) actual events and information more easily from a casual conversation than from a formal survey. It helped that in an old-style street-corner teahouse, patrons do not have much sense, or right, of privacy. On the other hand, I could not gain sources systematically on certain subjects, and the information I received was sometimes random. Also, I have tried to retain the original flavor of my notes in their first state. I hope that this helped to preserve whatever was spontaneous in them. Although I performed field investigation like an anthropologist, I nonetheless treated what I encountered from a historical point of view—that is, not attempting to establish, or interpret, a person's habits or patterns in particular ways, but to answer historical questions relative to how economic and political changes transformed public life. I have seen that within a mere decade, the old city has virtually vanished before our eyes, subsumed (physically, at least) by the new. The distinctive charm and folk culture of each city in ancient China have been all but obliterated as cities have become increasingly uniform. Therefore, to recover and restructure the history of China's cities is a significant mission for social, cultural, and urban historians.

Apart from the introduction and conclusion, this book has six chapters and is divided into two parts, of three chapters each. The first part, "The Decline of Public Life, 1950–1976," focuses mainly on state control of the teahouse business and popular entertainment and the subsequent transformations they experienced. Chapter 1 explores the fate of local trade organizations in the early 1950s. By examining the transformation and demise of the existing, older Teahouse Guild in Chengdu, we see how the state could manipulate such organizations to achieve control of small businesses. Once the socialist agenda was put into motion and the state used the organizations to gain total control over all aspects of business, it greatly diminished, and nearly destroyed, their functioning as open public spaces. This process by the new Communist state was just one part of a comprehensive elimination of social activities and groups that were seen as threatening because they existed outside the scope of state power. Thus we see how the state's gradual expansion corresponded with the broader society's decline. The fate of the Teahouse Guild after 1949 was a reflection of the attempted elimination of an urbane and culture-filled "society" overall and the attendant public sphere. In the city, all organizations at all levels, from streets to *danwei*, became parts of the state administration and under the control of a new type of officialdom. From the 1950s to the 1970s, no freely formed or evolved social organizations existed in China; any that did were in name only. During the early and middle 1950s, the CCP launched a collectivization movement through which most privately owned teahouses in Chengdu were forcibly brought under collective ownership.

Chapter 2 describes state control over cultural life, which occurred as soon as the People's Liberation Army entered Chengdu. This would over time transform the major teahouse theaters and the performance troupes associated with them. The goal was to usurp old-fashioned performances with "socialist entertainment." The chapter examines a survey of folk performers that the local government undertook in the mid-1950s so as to control and reduce the number of performers and thus weaken all forms of popular entertainment. Through this old-style public arena, the new government disseminated political propaganda, and the teahouse became a political stage for a newly created political culture. Initially, long-established and revolutionary forms of entertainment coexisted, but as time went on the former was increasingly attacked, controlled, and reformed, until socialist entertainment dominated.

The core of chapter 3 deals with the microcosm of the teahouse; it describes people's daily lives in the period from the 1950s to the 1970s under the Communist government, including to what extent people conducted what I refer to as public lives, and to what extent politics and political movements interfered with that. It was the lowest point for teahouses and public life in Chengdu. The relevant places became politically sensitive, and patrons, workers, and those associated therewith might fear grave repercussions from even the most innocent conversation. However, teahouse life in some ways carried on outside the scope of government control. People continued to gossip and spread "rumors," just as they had for centuries. The teahouse seems to have provided a relief from everyday problems, and could remind people of former ways of life.

The second part of the book, "The Return of Public Life, 1977–2000," discusses the process by which teahouses in Chengdu moved from near obliteration to unprecedented development in the reform period and the opening up of a market economy. The development of private business fostered a revival of teahouses, which in turn deepened public life. Chapter 4 shows that at the end of the Cultural Revolution teahouses did not suffer total destruction, as had the city's walls and many popular spaces, as well as forms of folk entertainment. Teahouses were indeed dormant, but not dead; they recovered immediately once conditions were politically favorable, as seen in the renewed popularity of street-corner teahouses and the emergence of the high-end tea balconies. Beginning in the late 1970s and early 1980s, teahouses reemerged on virtually every corner in the city and today thrive as never before.

Chapter 5 focuses on the various types of teahouse patrons and those who made a living in and were associated with the teahouse, especially migrant workers. With the post-Mao reforms and weakening of state control, teahouses could exist in a relatively more open social environment, serving all levels and all kinds of customers across the social spectrum, regardless of outward status, class, gender, and age; in particular they became the domain of the retired and elderly. Furthermore, as local markets strengthened and management practices improved, people once again began to earn a living in teahouses.

By examining mahjong—a mere game but the most popular activity in the teahouse—chapter 6 brings out conflicts among neighbors, examines the role of the residential committee in the neighborhood, and observes the responses of the municipal government and official media concerning the city's image. Mahjong brings us face to face with changes in daily life and popular culture at the turn of the current century, as daily life moves away from Communist control and "socialist morality." It also serves my argument that these changes reflect a much broader political, economic, social, and cultural transformation in which conflicts between individual rights and the collective interests have become prominent.

The conclusion weaves together the broader themes of cultural continuity and discontinuity, of conflicts between national and local cultures, and public life and public sphere. Teahouses, a thoroughly old-fashioned Chinese phenomenon, had never before experienced vicissitudes like those in the second half of the twentieth century. But the fact that they survived and then flourished, aiding urban public life in the process, underscores the vitality of local culture and the rise of the public sphere.

Part I

THE DECLINE OF PUBLIC
LIFE, 1950–1976

From 1949 to 1976, nearly three decades under Mao's rule, the Chinese people experienced intense unrest: small businesses and people's everyday lives were negatively affected by political storms. For some, the military victory of the Communist insurgency in 1949 augured prosperity and a happier life; but the reality was very different. Although during the "New Democracy" of the early 1950s the government carried out relatively moderate policies in the cities, the CCP constantly launched radical political movements, one after another, as reflected in the names of the subperiods of Early Socialism, as often seen in modern historical studies. These were labeled New Democracy, 1949–1952; the Three Antis and the Five Antis, 1951–1952; Collectivization, 1954; Socialist Transformation, 1956; Anti-rightist, 1957; the Great Leap Forward, 1958; the Great Famine, 1959–1961; Socialist Education, 1964; and the Cultural Revolution, 1966–1976.

During the Three Antis and Five Antis Campaigns, owners of small businesses became targets of party harassment. Then, from 1952 to 1954, during collectivization, the government forced many private businesses into collective or state ownership. Furthermore, the Great Leap Forward and commune movements in 1958 pressed heavily on rural and urban populations. For example, in places or moments not concerned with harvests, government staff, factory workers, and peasants all had to participate in mass iron-making, which ultimately contributed very little to the economy. Moreover, the Great Leap Forward must be associated with a long train of ill effects resulting from the cult worship of Mao, bureaucratic fecklessness, and overall political chaos that resulted in the Great Famine of 1959 to 1961. Further summary of these vast disruptions is not needed at this point, only to say that once China entered into, or created, this unfortunate political situation, public life became discouraged and public spaces shrank: "revolutionary culture" dominated cultural life. The stories given in the next three chapters show the immediate causes of the decline in Chengdu's teahouse businesses, popular entertainments, and public life. The discussion examines the great diminution of the Teahouse Guild and teahouse operations. These chapters show clearly that as state control reached its highest point, public life concomitantly fell to its lowest. None of this should imply a permanent disappearance. Teahouses and public life barely held on after the Cultural Revolution, to await a different future in the era of post-Mao reforms.

1

THE DEMISE OF THE CHENGDU TEAHOUSE GUILD AND THE FALL OF SMALL BUSINESS

During its first thirty years, the CCP monopolized not only political power but economic resources, a phenomenon that began as soon as it took over governance of the nation. In Chengdu, one of the new government's first targets for manipulation was the guilds. The long-established Teahouse Guild dominated the city's teahouse business in the first half of the twentieth century, but it quickly disappeared after 1950. In exploring the fate of old economic organizations in one city under Communist rule, we can understand in a fundamental way how the broad political changes altered economic life in all of China. There have been some excellent studies of Chinese guilds, but most have concentrated on the late-imperial period. A few studies of guilds focus on the Republican era, but those concerning post-1949, especially publications in English, are almost absent.[1] Scholarship on the economic history of the early People's Republic of China has assumed a national perspective, and less attention has been paid to small business and social and economic organizations at the local level.[2] Joseph C. H. Chai has collected and reprinted important works published in various journals regarding economic changes and development in China in *The Economic Development of Modern China.* The second volume, *Socialist Modernization, 1949–78,* includes thirty-nine articles whose topics range from the land revolution, collectivization, industry, finance, and communization to agriculture, international trade, and economic policies. But none focuses on the transformation of old-style mercantile and trade organizations.[3]

This chapter deals with the Teahouse Guild in Chengdu; but it also considers the reorganization, transformation, and decline of Chinese guilds generally and describes state control of professional organizations from a microhistorical perspective. I discuss four major issues: First, how the long-established guild was transformed and how it was replaced by the Preparations Committee for the (New) Teahouse Guild in Chengdu (Chengdu shi chashe ye tongye gonghui choubei weiyuanhui, hereafter referred to as "New Teahouse Guild"). Second, the chapter analyzes the nature and organizational structure of the New Teahouse Guild. Third, it explores the roles of the New Teahouse Guild in social and economic life and how it was transformed into an organization that solely carried out government policies. Finally, there is discussion of the impact of the Three Antis and Five Antis Campaigns (1951–1952), in which the former targeted corruption, waste, and bureaucratism, and the latter bribery, tax evasion, cheating on workmanship and materials, theft of state properties, and stealing of state economic information. By following these developments, we can better understand the attitude and policies of the CCP and its new government toward old-style economic organizations during Early Socialism. At first the government used these organizations to control various professions, but it soon forced them off the historical stage. The chapter argues that the decline and final death of the guilds resulted directly from the state's rising strength and restriction of social freedoms.

The Chengdu Teahouse Guild in the Republican Era

In late-imperial and Republican China, guilds played a significant role in urban economic life and society, but a Chengdu guild for teahouses was established only later, in the 1930s, and all Chengdu teahouse proprietors were required to join. This guild went back to 1929, when the Nationalist government issued laws regarding chambers of commerce and guilds (*tongye gonghui*) and ordered their reorganization. Consequently, the Chengdu municipal government required merchants of all professions to set up guilds. By April 1931, eighty-two Chengdu guilds had been established, including the Teahouse Guild, all having completed the transformation from *bang* (i.e., a group that conducts the same trade) to guild (*gonghui*). A new Chamber of Commerce was established, and in 1936 the Teahouse Guild (Chashe ye tongye gonghui) was restructured and registered with the government. This pre-1949 Teahouse Guild was much less autonomous than its predecessors: the government was increasingly manipulating such organizations.[4]

In the Republican era, especially the late period of the Guomindang (GMD, or Nationalist Party) government, guilds steadily increased their dependence on state power. During the War of Resistance (1937–1945), the Teahouse Guild was gradually transformed from an autonomous organization into a state-controlled one. However, to a certain extent it still represented the interests of the teahouse profession and resisted the increasing controls; it performed conventional guild functions such as making professional regulations, unifying prices, registering businesses, restricting new teahouses, and mediating conflicts among the members. At the same time it played a role in the communications between teahouse proprietors and local government. Thus, as observed through its organizational structure, leadership, membership, functions, and activities, the Teahouse Guild before 1949, under the GMD government, could still protect its members' interests and help resist government control.[5]

During the GMD regime, Chengdu's Teahouse Guild often cooperated with the Nationalist government concerning certain local affairs, but it never stopped resisting when the interests of the profession were threatened or damaged. Although in most of the cases the government was always the winner, the guild was sometimes able to force the government to withdraw its policies. For instance, in August 1940, when the government imposed a new tax, the guild resisted by organizing members not to recognize the tax and to plan a market strike if any member was arrested. Facing a threat of a market strike, the government had to postpone the new tax.[6] This example tells us that the guild could become either a bridge between the teahouse profession and the government or an agency that could challenge state power. Teahouses could create a loud voice and force the government to consider the needs of a whole profession. The guild often had conflicts with the government regarding prices and taxes, but it had to retain a good relationship because it often depended on local authorities to regulate the overall teahouse trade.[7] Although guilds under the Nationalist government were increasingly controlled by state power in comparison with the guilds of the late-imperial period, they were still able to fight back if the interests of the profession were jeopardized.

Transformation of the Guild under Party Administration

On January 8, 1950, twelve days after the People's Liberation Army entered Chengdu, the Military Control Commission (Junguan hui) called the heads of the Chamber of Commerce and all guilds for a meeting at which military authorities explained the CCP's "economic principles of the New Democracy" and its "policy to protect national industries and commerce."[8] The following day, the commission, the municipal government, and the Workers' Union of Chengdu had what they termed an informal discussion (*zuotanhui*), calling for increasing production in order to spur the economy. Then, the commission took over all properties of the Nationalist government, their "bureaucratic capital" (*guanliao ziben*), and that of war criminals, while changing some enterprises to state-owned or "public-private partnerships" (*gongsi heying*).[9] Although teahouses, like all other professions, were put under the new government's supervision, their business operations were not influenced much by the government at this time.

The reorganization of the Teahouse Guild was part of the state's effort to change old-style economic organizations into tools of control over all professions. In August 1949, even before the Communists' victory, the Central Committee of the CCP issued "Instructions for Organizing the Association of Industry and Commerce," which ordered that all old chambers of commerce be transformed into the Association of Industry and Commerce (Gongshanglian). In March 1950, the Department for Work in a United Front (Tongzhan bu) pointed out that the Gongshanglian is "an important organization for promoting the united front work" in private-owned industries and commerce, and the CCP, and government, could use it to "unite and educate" businessmen in order to implement government policies and laws. This meant that a transformation within the guilds would be under Gongshanglian supervision. In the process of establishing the Gongshanglian, in many other places guilds were already being reformed. For instance, from the second half of 1949, more than 150 guilds in Beijing were reformed, and by the end of 1952, 132 preparation committees for all kinds of guilds were established there.[10]

In Chengdu, there were several levels of administration for controlling teahouses. The highest was the Bureau of Industry and Commerce (Gongshang ju), and the lowest was the New Teahouse Guild; the Preparations Committee of the Gongshanglian (Gongshanglian chouweihui), established in April 1950, was located in the middle. The Gongshanglian took responsibility for "carrying out government policies" and for "uniting and educating" all businessmen and leading them toward reform. Based on government instructions, the Gongshanglian worked to transform professional organizations in April 1950; and by the end of December the process was completed. The result of such transformation was the following: 151 old guilds plus 24 other occupations that did not have guilds were placed into 81 preparation committees for new guilds. The government claimed that such a move released small business "from the control of feudal guilds." In May 1953, they were again restructured into fifty-six "committees for professional trade groups" (*tongye gonghui weiyuanhui*), and the teahouse profession was combined with hotel businesses, thus becoming known as the "Committee for the Chengdu Hotel and Teahouse Professions of the Gongshanglian" (Chengdu shi gongshangye lianhe hui lüzhan chashe ye tongye weiyuanhui). During the Socialist Transformation Movement from 1953 to 1956 the latter was renamed the Committee of Service Professions of the Gongshanglian in Chengdu. Thus, the demise of the New Teahouse Guild occurred over several years, perhaps somewhat imperceptibly, beginning with the above renamings and restructuring of numerous guilds in 1950, and coming to completion between 1953 and 1956.[11] This suppression of guilds went hand in hand with the government policy that restricted the development of the teahouse business and reduced spaces for public life. The gradual decline in the number of teahouses and their overall business slump was a logical and unavoidable result.

The CCP's overall national policy to reduce the influence of guilds was created in order to keep social organizations from challenging the state's power. The central government pointed out that, despite the guilds' long history in handling relationships within professions, in the past they were controlled by a small group of people and, as the government claimed, were used to suppress middle and small businessmen. Therefore, they were not to be banned but to be transformed completely.[12] Although it was true that in earlier times middle and small businessmen were sometimes suppressed, the issue was largely exaggerated. However, the CCP fully recognized an antistate threat, because guilds had resisted the GMD government.

Under socialism, Chengdu now began the effort to gain control of small businesses such as teahouses, but change was not immediate. In fact, the Communist Party's control and transformation of teahouses were undertaken gradually, beginning with a registration requirement. In June 1950, the government demanded that street vendors register the stalls that lined the streets. Of a total of 7,136 vendor applications, the government approved only 2,481 for long-term business operations and 1,681 for short-term operations, and denied 2,974. After the process was completed, all street vendors had to carry a government-issued license and were allowed to sell their items only in the markets assigned to them; they were prohibited from setting up stalls on heavily traveled streets or blocks.[13]

All shops were required to sign contracts, which are preserved in the Chengdu Municipal Archives. One example is the guarantee signed by the Broad View Tea Balcony (Daguan chalou) in February 1951: "I am Su Bingcheng who operates the Broad View Tea Balcony at 24 North Three Bridges Street [Sanqiao bei jie] and I have obeyed all regulations issued by the government. I confirm that all information in the registration is true. If there are any violations or inaccuracies, I am willing to bear all responsibility." Each teahouse had to have two guarantors, usually business owners (see figure 1.1).[14]

The Chengdu municipal government, working with the departments of industry and commerce, public security, taxation, health, and culture, manipulated every aspect of the teahouse trade and imposed various fines. There were price controls, prohibitions on peddlers, and penalties for "lawless" behavior by patrons; restrictions regarding placement of tables and chairs on sidewalks, management of waiters and waitresses, and performances; bans on gambling and trading gold; and rules on sanitary

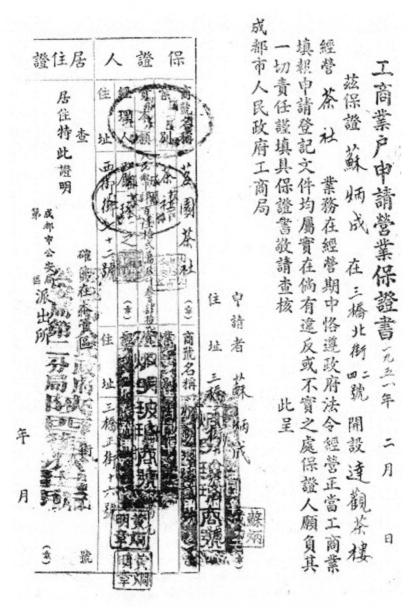

Figure 1.1 Guarantee signed by Broad View Tea Balcony. From Chengdu shi zhengfu gongshang dang'an (CSZGD) 40–65–13.

conditions and inspections for hygiene.[15] While similar measures had been in place during the Republican era, implementation by the Communist government was much more forceful and effective. During the mid-1950s, while implementing public-private partnerships, the local government carried out a "balanced budget policy."[16] Despite these efforts, however, and because of the state's encroaching control and the associated dramatic change in the political and economic environment, teahouses faced a very difficult situation. Indeed, the decline of the teahouse was predictable.

Reorganization of the Teahouse Guild in 1950

After Chengdu's government was taken over by the PLA, the old Teahouse Guild continued to handle the teahouse profession's affairs for eight or nine months. This changed beginning in September 1950, when the Gongshanglian informed all directors, supervising directors, and heads of groups of the Teahouse Guild with membership records to participate in another of their "informal meetings" in order to "exchange ideas for reforming the guild." A few days later, an assembly was held and attended by 408 teahouse keepers. They were divided into five groups to "select candidates for the preparatory committee." Twenty-five members were chosen, and a director and associate director were also selected.[17]

On October 20, 1950, a meeting was held to announce the establishment of the New Teahouse Guild, at which representatives from government offices gave speeches. The Gongshanglian first reported the process by which the New Teahouse Guild was established; then the director of the guild announced the new mission: "To understand government policies and to carry out all government laws and decrees." Not a single word was spoken about protection of professional interests—the most basic function of the pre-1949 guild. Then, Liao Wenchang, former president of the guild, congratulated the establishment of the New Teahouse Guild and apologized for "not serving the teahouses well."[18] This was a hapless apology. In fact, even though the GMD had enforced control over guilds during the War of Resistance, the older Teahouse Guild had still been able to organize teahouses and to fight for their interests.[19] Probably, Liao hoped that the New Teahouse Guild under the new government might actually serve the profession; he surely could not have anticipated the guild's disappearing just a few years later into a vast bureaucratic blend of trade-group committees.

The representative of the Bureau of Industry and Commerce emphasized three points in the October meeting. First, he said that the committee was formed of members who were examined by the bureau carefully, and he accused the old guild of being controlled by a small group. He wanted the new leadership to unite all people in the profession and to pass government policies and laws for all members and receive members' inquiries to the government. Second, he pointed out that members in the old guild did not take care of affairs and hoped that all members now would support the New Teahouse Guild. This statement was obviously not accurate: I have noted, above, the old guild's organizing strength. Third, the most important goal of the New Teahouse Guild was to organize and train members and to inculcate "a better understanding of politics" (*tigao zhengzhi renshi*).[20]

The representative of the Shop Workers' Guild (Dianyuan gonghui) made a speech in which he criticized some teahouse keepers for selling their businesses and firing employees. Actually, such actions resulted from the movement to "clean up bandits and oppose local despots; and reduce rent and return deposits" (*qingfei fanba, jianzu tuiya*). Some Chengdu teahouses were owned by absentee landlords, who used security deposits on leases as their own capital to open a teahouse business. Now that they were under pressure from the government to return some part of that money, they had to close their teahouses and get cash out of them. But the representative was calling it an "illegal action" (*bufa huodong*) when shop owners closed without government approval. He wished members of the guild would work together during this difficult time and observe the principle of "benefiting both proprietors and employees" (*laozi liangli*).[21] In fact, the owners who shut their businesses had no other options, as rural actions were becoming increasingly violent, especially when the Land Revolution swept in like a storm. They had to do whatever was necessary for survival, so they logically abandoned their teahouse businesses for cash.

It is interesting that the same representative acknowledged the economic crisis that confronted small businesses: "Under the GMD reactionary regime, industry and commerce and teahouse businesses were very prosperous. But, after liberation, all businesses have become very depressed." The reasons, he explained, were changes of lifestyle: for example, the way silks, satins, woolens, and cosmetic goods were no longer popular, to the extent that 60 percent of such goods were unsold. "In the past, bureaucratic capital and landlords manipulated markets" and "they basically engaged in speculative businesses," he said. Therefore, he defined prosperity in the past as "false prosperity" (*xujia fanrong*). This assessment is hardly convincing. Until 1950, commerce in Chengdu was dominated by small businesses, and there is no evidence to indicate monopolization and manipulation of markets by so-called "bureaucratic capital and landlords." Actually, any regime change whatsoever would have shaken markets, and any new regime has to devote time to stabilizing society and the economy.

Consumption of certain consumer goods, as listed above, was indeed influenced by political changes, because most purchasers were upper- and middle-class people. When the Communist revolution was unfolding, even though it had not touched them directly, rich people would reduce their consumption of leisure goods. Therefore, such merchandise no longer sold well. Furthermore, the government wanted to transform Chengdu from a "city of consumption" (*xiaofei chengshi*) to a "city of production" (*shengchan chengshi*).[22] In such a transformation, one should not be surprised that government policies emphasized industry but overlooked commerce. Furthermore, in the language of revolutionary discourse, the word "consumption" was quite negative, and the policy to make Chengdu into a city of production turned into a long and arduous process. Only with the reforms after 1979, and after recognition of the multiple functions of cities, did the government start to encourage consumption. The teahouse, as a typical consumption profession, inevitably faced a crisis of survival during the political and economic environment of the 1950s (see figure 1.2).

The same representative had more to say. He talked about relations between owners and laborers, pointing out that "today is a new society," so relations between owners and laborers were different from in the past. According to the representative, all disputes between owners and workers occurred because "proprietors had bad habits fostered in the old society." He asked the members of the New Teahouse Guild to have a discussion with their workers if a dispute occurred, and he criticized some teahouse owners for laying off workers, accusing them of "passing around a rumor" that the government would demolish the teahouse

Figure 1.2 Crowded teahouse in a Chengdu suburb,
September 2015. Author photo.

profession. What happened to the teahouse businesses later proved the
so-called "rumor" to have been not all that groundless. This showed a
sense of crisis in the profession—a lack of confidence toward the regime's
policies concerning small businesses.[23]

During the same meeting, a police representative talked about security. He complained that the regulations issued by the police two months
previously had actually not been carried out, and he hoped that under
the New Teahouse Guild everyone would take responsibility for security,
paying special attention to bandit and secret society activities and reporting them to the police without worries over "personal considerations"
(*qingmian*).[24] Why did he mention "personal considerations"? In the past,
teahouses served all walks of life—the high and low, the powerless and
powerful—and avoided offending those with connections to, or who were
representatives of, government or important associations. All regimes,
from the Qing dynasty to the Nationalist government, demanded that
teahouses report illegal activities, but the teahouses always turned a blind
eye to them because, as small businesses, they could not afford to offend

powerful interests. The new government could not relax these concerns, and it is no surprise that, as in the past, the teahouses were unwilling to carry out the regulations.

From the speeches of this meeting, we can see that the government actually defined what the New Teahouse Guild could do and that the space given for its actions was to be limited. The guild had to be under the leadership of not only the Gongshanglian but all departments of the government. What it could do was simply to carry out government policies. We cannot imagine that it could protect the interests of the profession and its own ability to challenge the government. Being "under the leadership of the people's government" became the only option for guilds in general.[25]

"Under the Leadership of the People's Government"

In the meeting hall of the New Teahouse Guild, slogans on the wall reflected the influence of the state and the impact of politics. This indicates that the guild was being used as a political and ideological tool. We read about "mobilizing mass and political education," "raising members' political awareness," "removing the old in order to build the new," "smashing all feudal factions," "establishing new ideas and a new style of work," "cooperating with the government on economic and constructive plans and instructions," and "developing the economy and flourishing markets." Some slogans demanded that members "get rid of the evil custom of indifference" and "get rid of the sense that 'business is business.'" At this moment, the government did not want to suggest that the old guild had no redeeming features, because it was still useful for the government to control the profession; it thus asked members to "critique the merits that came down from the old guild."[26]

We can find more details about the New Teahouse Guild from the eighteen articles of the "General Regulations of the [New] Teahouse Guild of the Gongshanglian in Chengdu" (Chengdu shi gongshangye lianhe choubeihui chashe tongye gonghui choubei weiyuanhui jianzhang) issued in October 1950. According to these, as soon as the New Teahouse Guild was formally established, the old teahouse guild would "end its activity immediately" and the organization would be taken over by the New

Teahouse Guild. The general regulations assigned the guild eight tasks: (1) explain government policies to members and help the Gongshanglian carry out its policies; (2) provide information about the profession to the Gongshanglian; (3) guide all members in their study of the reformed mentality in order to build new ideas of management; (4) help and guide all members to improve their professional skills in order to enhance production and management; (5) promote all decisions made by the Gongshanglian; (6) take over all properties, archives, accounting records, and registers; (7) investigate and persuade nonmember teahouses to join the New Teahouse Guild; and (8) group all members based on their locations and the nature of their service.[27]

Furthermore, the titles of major positions in the New Teahouse Guild were changed. Its head was now called "director" (*zhuren*) rather than "president" (*lishi zhang*). The size of the board membership was made twice that of the old one. The board of the New Teahouse Guild had twenty-five members, selected from all districts based on discussion and negotiation among the members and approval from the Gongshanglian. Of these, thirteen were on the standing committee, "selected through consultation" (*xieshang tuixuan*), and a director and associate director were chosen by "nominating each other" (*xieshang hutui*). Also, the director and associate director nominated a secretary and an assistant secretary, as well as heads of three specific offices—organization, culture and education, and general affairs; all these were chosen from the members of the standing committee. The New Teahouse Guild held meetings every two weeks, but the standing committee met once a week. The director and associate director could call meetings at any time they deemed necessary.[28]

In the Archive of the Chengdu Guilds for All Professions, I found short biographical notes on the twenty-five New Teahouse Guild members; these tell us about their backgrounds. All were teahouse keepers, and only one was female. The youngest was twenty-one, and the oldest seventy-two.[29] Twenty-four had some level of education—nine had had "private tutors" (*sixue*), five had attended elementary schools, seven middle schools, and one college. Most of them had changed careers, having worked as shop clerks, accountants, government employees, military personnel, chefs, apprentices, peddlers, factory workers, and so on. The person who had been in the teahouse business the longest had done so since

1925, whereas the person who had been there for the shortest amount of time had been in the profession only since 1949. In the column giving data on "political parties," the biographical notes reveal useful information: for nineteen there are no relevant data; two "joined the GMD, collectively"; two "joined the Youth League for the Three People's Principles (Sanqingtuan) and GMD, collectively"; one joined the Gowned Brothers (Paoge, the name of the Sworn Brotherhood Society in Sichuan); and one had "no party affiliation."[30] During the War of Resistance, many young people joined the Youth League and the GMD, especially those in schools; but such memberships became a serious issue concerning "political background." The fact that some who had such backgrounds were still able to be board members of the New Teahouse Guild at the early stage indicates that "bad" backgrounds had not yet become a serious political problem.

In order to effectively control the various entertainments offered at teahouses, the New Teahouse Guild established the "Group for Teahouse Theaters" (Shuchang chazuo zu).[31] I have found three versions of the "General Draft of the New Teahouse Guild's Group for Teahouse Theaters" (Chengdu shi chasheye tongye gonghui choubei weiyuanhui shuchang chazuo zu jianze caoan), which was probably revised several times. According to the latest version, dated November 1950, the goal of the group was "to unite all performers of Chinese folk art, to follow the new movement of literature and art [*xinde wenyi yundong*], and to propagate the heroic stories of people in the revolutionary struggle, and in production and construction." Any teahouse with a stage (sometimes actual raised areas and sometimes a designated floor or table area) could apply for membership in the group, but approval was to be granted by the Bureau of Culture and Education (Wenhua jiaoyu ju). That bureau had a regular meeting once a month, but ad hoc meetings could be called. The general draft defined two rights for members: to nominate and select the head and assistant head of the group, secretaries, and staff, and to discuss and vote on the affairs of the group. The members had two obligations: to suggest ways to improve professional skills, and to pay their membership fees.[32] The fact that it allowed the group to be established indicates that the government recognized the unique ability of teahouse theaters potentially to deliver socialist entertainment and propaganda.

The years from 1950 to 1953 were quite important: the new CCP government was gradually gaining control of urban industry and commerce. The above has shown that teahouses, as small businesses with close ties to the people's daily lives, were increasingly restricted by state power, while the New Teahouse Guild became in some sense a representative of the government, no longer having the nature of pre-1949 guilds that protected the interests of the teahouses. Both locally and nationally, guilds no longer had independence; their older functions were almost completely lost, and they actually became spokespersons for the state concerning the professions. Ultimately, we find no evidence that the post-1949 guilds fought for their own interests. On the contrary, we can see that the New Teahouse Guild put pressure on teahouses so that they carried out state policies that damaged their own interests. The guild existed in name only after the policies of the party were instituted. This situation matched the larger political environment in 1950s China.

The New Teahouse Guild and Economic Life

Although the New Teahouse Guild had a short life, it played an important role in reforming and controlling teahouses. According to its report dated February 1951, the New Teahouse Guild had accomplished five tasks: reforming the old guild and examining members' requests and enhancing relationships between the government and guild members; handling the reelection of the heads of the districts and groups, including the directors of the districts and the heads of the groups; organizing a "Consultative Committee on Labor and Ownership" (Laozi xieshang hui); writing a tax report for the year 1950 and assuming responsibility for collecting professional taxes; and launching a campaign for "winter clothing donations" (*hanyi juankuan*).[33]

A "working plan" of the New Teahouse Guild for its 1951 activities announced seven upcoming tasks for that year: (1) coordinate with the recent reconfiguration of the city's districts and thus reorganize the teahouse owners and managers into large and small groups;[34] (2) register all teahouses after grouping and require all members to register and compile registration records; (3) enhance labor-ownership relations and improve businesses through a policy of "benefiting both proprietors and employees"; (4) investigate business conditions and help overcome difficulties; (5) accept applications for membership; (6) handle procedures of membership confirmation;

and (7), establish the Guiding Committee on Work Tasks (Yewu zhidao wei-yuanhui).[35] In short, the working plan tells us that business registration and labor-owner relations were the focus of the New Teahouse Guild that year. In July 1951, based on instructions from the Chengdu municipal government, the Gongshanglian issued an "urgent announcement" that required all guilds to fill out an "organization registration form" to "obtain legal status." This form collected extensive information, including data about the number of employees, economic situation, capital sources, current business plan, and so on.[36]

Women's liberation was a long-standing mission of the CCP, and thus, as soon as the new government was established, it contacted women who were in the teahouse profession. In July 1950, the Gongshanglian held an informal organizational meeting with women. The Committee of Women's Representatives (Fudaihui) was formed, and certain women were chosen and sent to the Gongshanglian to receive training (the source does not specify what sort).[37] In August, ten were selected as the formal women's representatives, most of them between twenty and thirty years old—the youngest was eighteen and the oldest forty. Except for two who were unidentified, the rest had received at least elementary education, and three even had studied in middle schools. These women had various occupational backgrounds before 1949, such as government employees, nurses, housewives, accountants, and so on. One of them reported her husband as having been a "special agent" of the GMD—he was arrested and later executed. Another woman's husband used to be a member of "superstitious sects and secret societies" (*huimen*).[38] During that time— the early 1950s—the criteria concerning political backgrounds were much less restrictive than those just a few years later, so some women whose husbands had a problem of "background" were selected as representatives nonetheless.

The new government controlled the teahouse profession through the New Teahouse Guild and even penetrated into the management of the teahouses, a goal no other government had ever had. Employment practices were supervised. The Chengdu archives contain three documents about the Broad View Tea Balcony mentioned earlier: a "list of employees," "survey of capital," and "survey of assets and inventory." They are a treasure trove of very rare, detailed data. On September 23, 1951, the Preparations Committee of the Chengdu Teahouse Guild noted that the

Broad View had moved to a new location because of a road-widening project.[39] Another example is the Full Moon Teahouse (Yuekuan chashe), which opened for business in April 1950 but sold only about twenty bowls of tea each day. The owner, in debt and unable to make ends meet, could not pay his employees. Thus, in keeping with the practices of the times that protected workers' interests, he had to "consult with the workers about going out of business," as well as with all other parties involved, such as the union and guild, and sign a "contract for dismissal of employees due to the closing of a business" (*xieye jiegu hetong*). Under such a contract, the employer had to pay unpaid wages as well as a certain amount of additional compensation.[40]

In 1951, the Lucky East Teahouse (Lidong chashe) on Fragrant Herbs Fountain Street (Chaiquan jie) asked permission to close because it could not pay the rent. From the agreement between employer and employees reached in "a democratic manner" (*minzhu de fangshi*), we learn that despite a significant debt—about 12 million yuan—the agreement required the employer to provide workers with "severance pay" (*jiegu fei*).[41] This document reveals important information about teahouses, such as wages (and how they were paid), labor and employer relations, and practices for hiring and firing. From this, we also know that teahouse workers' daily wages were counted up in equivalents of bowls of tea and ranged from ten to twenty-one bowls per day (they were in fact paid in cash in some cases, and in others in rice). In the early 1950s, a bowl of tea was usually sold at about 400 yuan. As in the Republican period, teahouses had to provide meals for workers (see figure 1.3).

In May 1953, the Bureau of Labor in Chengdu required the New Teahouse Guild to report any teahouse that hired without proper permission; and information was collected about the names of employees, their family backgrounds, their relationships with employers, and the dates they were hired and terminated. After such investigation, the guild identified five teahouses that had violated policy. For instance, one teahouse had to hire a man to temporarily replace one of its workers who had injured his foot. In another case, an unemployed man often stayed in a teahouse whose owner was his friend, and sometimes he helped the waiters.[42] It is interesting to see the operational details that the government wanted to control, and the breadth of its supervision. The guild pledged that it would fully investigate any unauthorized employment.[43]

Figure 1.3 Waiter at the Cry of the Crane Teahouse in the
People's Park, June 2003. Author photo.

Such rigorous control matched larger concerns in the political environment, especially as concerned tax collection, which particularly affected teahouse business. The primary purpose of government controls was not to micromanage the teahouses but to monitor their incomes for purposes of tax revenues. However, the CCP and the central government soon felt that such measures were not enough, so they launched the Three Antis and Five Antis, which in Chengdu, to a large extent, targeted small business proprietors.

The New Teahouse Guild and the Three Antis and Five Antis Campaigns

The government's economic policies at this point began to exhibit illogic on several fronts that had to do with the operations and existence of small businesses. On the one hand, in such a political and economic environment small businesses faced problems of sheer survival, so tax revenues inevitably shrank. But on the other hand, as government did eventually expand revenues, its goals and legitimacy slipped. Since it could not reach it goals, the government had to rely on political action, and the Three Antis and the Five Antis Campaigns can be seen as powerful tools.[44] In the past, small businesses had always tried to minimize their tax burden through every conceivable tactic in order merely to survive competition.[45] After the establishment of the Communist government, business practices did not change overnight, and teahouses operated by customary methods. According to an investigation made by the Bureau of Tax Affairs in August 1950 of 120 small shops, "there is not one honest account book," and some even had "two or three fake account books," deemed by the authorities as "an opportunistic custom fostered in the old society."[46] The new socialist state was seemingly not equipped to mold the nature and purpose of small business as quickly and successfully as it would have liked to do.

The new government adopted much tougher and more effective measures to deal with tax evasion than had previous governments. By conducting ideological movements through strong propaganda offensives, the government successfully connected tax payment with patriotism. Based on what is contained in the "Propaganda Outline Concerning Taxation in Chengdu" (Chengdu shi shuiwu xuanchuan gangyao), the government was employing all manner of propaganda in order to "educate" people on the need to pay their taxes. The government claimed that by the end of 1950 many "avid supporters and model taxpayers" had emerged. Through procedures like "investigating dark areas and fixing leaks" (*chahei jilou*), 1,987 cases of "violation" were found, most of which were "revealed" by shop workers. In April 1951, eighty professions participated in the "great mass fervor of collective tax paying." Taxation became highly organized, and a "three-level assessment system" was established: appraisal groups (*pingyi xiaozu*) were the lowest; next were committees for appraisal of the professions (*hangye pingyi weiyuanhui*), one for each profession, organized by guilds; and the highest was the Committee to Promote Taxation (Shuiwu tuijin weiyuanhui). The concrete procedure at the first stage was that the appraisal group gave a primary assessment to decide the level and amount of tax that was pegged for individual teahouses within the group. Then, each committee for appraisal of the professions examined the amounts for its own profession. Finally, each guild compiled amounts of payable taxes into a bound volume (which covered all professions) and sent it to the Committee to Promote Taxation for reexamination and sent notifications on the tax rate to all shops.[47] The government required all shop owners to make a "patriotic pledge" (*aiguo gongyue*) and to guarantee that they would not engage in "false reports, coverups, tax evasions, or defaults." It also demanded that shops keep their original receipts for all expenses and establish account books that followed certain accounting standards.[48] The Communist government, for the first time in Chinese history, entered the internal goings-on of small businesses and changed their management procedures to ensure tax revenue.

The Three Antis Campaign (December 1951 to January 1952) and the Five Antis (February to June 1952) were centrally designed and run, moving like a storm throughout China. They targeted corruption, waste, bribery, and tax evasion, among other things. Some business proprietors committed suicide because of intolerable pressure when the campaigns were at their highest pitch. All owners had to go through four steps: "workers' reports, exposing faults of competitors, confessions, and finally, verification by the work team."[49] The New Teahouse Guild in Chengdu held two mobilization meetings, one for the Three Antis in January 1952 and the other for the Five Antis, in February. Almost all teahouse proprietors attended both meetings. The Gongshanglian demanded that members submit a "confession" and a pledge before February 17. Everyone had to report his or her wrongdoings and was automatically suspected of tax dodging. The director of the guild had to be first to make a confession.[50] The government encouraged people to supply secret information about business owners.

During the campaigns, Song Yi, head of the New Teahouse Guild's General Affairs Office, was found to have misappropriated public funds. Song was a teahouse keeper, thirty-three years old, with a primary school education. He once worked at the Bureau of Tax Collection of the local office of the Nationalist government, and he was also a member of the Gowned Brothers and had a history of misconduct and bribery in the brokering of jobs. Song worked at the office of the New Teahouse Guild for six months, from June to December 1951, and stole public funds. The reason, he claimed, was the financial strain he was under after losing money in his business, and he promised to repay by selling his own house.[51] In April, the court issued a verdict: Song had embezzled over

6 million yuan of patriotic donations to the "War to Resist U.S. Aggression and Aid Korea" and over 2 million yuan of the workers' relief fund and membership fees. He was sentenced to ten months in prison, on top of his pledge to return the entire amount.[52]

Although embezzlement is usually considered to involve those with a degree of power, mere "tax evasion" is generally a common practice, and so it was at this time in China. Many evasion cases were brought out during the Five Antis. As mentioned, tax evasion was often a survival strategy for small businesses, but local governments in the late Qing and Republican periods did not have the means to treat the issue seriously, and in certain circumstances turned a blind eye. But during the CCP's mass movements, infractions came under the spotlight. In Chengdu all teahouses had to report if they had evaded any taxes. According to the report of the Fifth Group of the Fourth District, for instance, of seventeen teahouses in this group, eleven were accused of tax evasion. Amazingly, even very small amounts were reported, including the fee from a barber who used the teahouse for his haircutting business, and from a farmer who harvested human waste from the toilets, and from a peddler who sold pancakes in the teahouse—also a teahouse keeper's finding an iron chain and reselling it for a small amount of money, and an official of the Bureau of Tax Affairs who consumed tea and cigarettes in a teahouse whose accounts he was auditing. In the past, it was a common practice for people who used a teahouse as a location for their own enterprise to pay a small amount to the teahouse. Now, however, even such tiny matters were reported to the government. What is surprising is the government's ability to dig up the relevant details and exercise such thorough control.[53]

The Depression and Teahouse Business

The business depression after 1950 was mainly caused by government policies, which generated a chain reaction: capital and material fell into short supply, sales fell off, bankruptcies increased, and high unemployment occurred. After the two campaigns, "owners of private industry and commerce were seriously discouraged," yet the government did in fact gain more tax revenues in this period. Owners felt threatened by a future filled with unknown challenges. Business for profit was the basic motive for being a shop proprietor, but such a motivation became incompatible with the larger political environment and the revolutionary discourse. Some professions, occupations, and shops could not survive.

The Bureau of Industry and Commerce and the Gongshanglian, for example, actually forced all pawnshops and shops that sold "superstitious items" (*mixin yongpin*), jewels, and antiques and jades to shift to other forms of business. The government also believed that there were too many shops for silk, wool, Western-style suits, ginseng and deer horns, scroll mounting, cosmetics, and cigarettes, and too many photo studios, restaurants, and teahouses; thus it decided to change some shops into other services or to have them sell certain products under government supervision. In August 1952, with cooperation from the Bureau of Industry and Commerce, the General Union, the Gongshanglian, and the Bureau of Labor, the Chengdu Study Committee on Repurposing and Closing Private Businesses (Chengdu shi siying gongshang qiye zhuanxieye yanjiu weiyuanhui) was established.[54] The number of small businesses declined dramatically. In 1950 there were thirty-five thousand workers in private businesses in the East and West Districts of Chengdu, for example; but in 1954, only about ninety-two hundred were left. One account says that "very few" restaurants and teahouses remained, although the actual number cannot be determined.[55]

Many years later, researchers from the Bureau of Tax Affairs revisited the history of the Five Antis Campaign and admitted that although the movement enhanced tax revenues, officials nevertheless had been radical in their approach and "did not follow policies."[56] Another person stated that "in 1952 many shop owners could not understand the Five Antis Campaign, as the leaders of the campaign went to extremes and caused many proprietors to shut down their shops, resulting in shrinking business, sluggish circulation, a depressed market, and a significant decline in tax revenue. The city only collected 20.2 billion yuan in taxes in 1952, almost half the revenue compared with 1951."[57] I would like to argue that it was the political situation and the state's policies that made officials in 1950–1951 pursue such extreme approaches toward small business. After the Five Antis, some small businesses folded, some faced obstacles to survival, and, finally, those that sold merchandise or did business defined as a service for "feudalism" or "capitalism," including teahouses, were required by the government to "change directions or occupations." An even more rapid decline in teahouses and other private businesses came about during the Socialist Transformation, 1953 to 1956.

According to archival records, many teahouses started going out of business beginning in the early 1950s. The high-end Rushing River Teahouse (Zhuojiang chashe) on General Offices Street (Zongfu jie), a crowded commercial area, opened in the late 1940s and was well financed; it had seventeen employees and annual sales of 162,000 bowls of tea. Over time, it became a gathering place for news reporters. By the early 1950s, however, it had accumulated 1.2 million yuan in debt, plus considerable unpaid taxes. In June 1951, the building in which the teahouse operated was sold, so it was unable to renew the lease and was forced into bankruptcy.[58] Some teahouses were forced to relocate, which also hurt them. The Sleeping Stream Teahouse (Zhenliu chashe), a famous Republican-period teahouse in Minor Walled-City Park (Shaocheng gongyuan),[59] is one example. In 1950, it employed nearly thirty people and was highly profitable, but in 1951 the government took over the property the teahouse rented, so the teahouse moved to Long-Lasting Ease Street (Changshun dong jie), where it had to compete with eight other teahouses. Eventually, Sleeping Stream Teahouse had to close.[60]

Many teahouses were driven to extinction sheerly because of politics. The Cry of the Crane Teahouse (Heming chashe) in Minor Walled-City Park had a long history. As a joint partnership, in 1951 it had thirteen investors, more than 47.63 million yuan in fixed capital, and more than 13.55 million yuan in floating capital, with average annual sales of 186,000 bowls of tea. In October of that year, the manager, named Li, was sentenced to death as a "counterrevolutionary," and the government appropriated all the assets, including real estate, funds, materials, appliances, and so on, and changed the ownership from a private partnership to state-owned, under a new name: the People's Teahouse (Renmin chashe). All workers stayed on the job.[61]

The Three Antis and Five Antis Campaigns brought down many teahouses. The successful Near to the Sages Teahouse (Jinsheng chashe) had opened in 1934. It employed sixteen people, but in 1951 the government forced it to move to a remote location, where the business suffered and accrued a 1 million yuan debt. During the two campaigns, an employee reported to the authorities that the owner had hidden four boxes of tea leaves, 150 baskets of charcoal, and some gold and silver; ultimately the teahouse was shut down.[62] This example illustrates that during such campaigns, basic business practices—for example, inventory storage—were deemed criminal. These policies inevitably affected the city's economy.

Occurrences like these were common. Many teahouses went out of business as a result of a combination of factors, including the intense political movements, economic policies, changes in lifestyles, and social trends. It should be noted that because the government did not encourage residents to frequent teahouses, many customers stayed away, making business even more difficult to sustain. Decline also resulted from more specific difficulties. Some shops were closed because the owners had no children who wanted to take over, some because of unresolved property disputes, and so on. On the other hand, the growing urban population and urban expansion led to the establishment of new teahouses in some areas of the city.[63] When famous teahouses began disappearing during the 1950s, many smaller, street-corner teahouses survived. The reason probably is that smaller teahouses drew less attention from the state and were more flexible in adjusting to political and economic change, and therefore could linger in society's cracks. Regardless, they differed little from late Qing and Republican-era teahouses. The lives of the people involved with teahouses, however, changed dramatically. Ultimately, I find no evidence to show that the state particularly tried to save any teahouses or any type of teahouse. That these businesses continued to operate was only because they offered a livelihood for so many, and the state could not simply close them all down. However, the state did open a few new teahouses for "socialist entertainment" (see chapter 2).

Small Business and State Control

The use of mass movements for political control was the new regime's strategy from the beginning. As Julia Strauss points out, "The young PRC's chosen strategy of regime consolidation and establishing socialism was through, first of all, establishing and strengthening the coercive and infrastructural capacities of the party-state, and secondly, launching political campaigns of mobilization."[64] In light of this, the Three Antis and Five Antis Campaigns ostensibly may be seen as having been created not just to solve economic problems, but also to increase the CCP's political control. This was the case not just in Chengdu, but across China. A study of the campaigns in Shanghai shows that so-called "tiger-beating teams" were sent to shops to check bookkeeping and to hold meetings for the purpose of mobilizing the shop workers to report wrongdoing and unlawful conduct. However, the movement quickly expanded and gave workers license to attack and even torture shop owners to the point of suicide, and to demand nationalization of businesses. These actions seriously affected the economy not only in Shanghai but also throughout the country, and many privately owned enterprises went bankrupt. "What had started as an effort to cut government spending and curb inflation turned into a sharp economic recession."[65] Other studies, however, suggest that the Korean War gave the party and the state the opportunity to seize wealth from private citizens, strengthen their own power, legitimize Communist rule, and enhance Mao's ongoing revolution. The CCP broke the promise it made during its revolution, citing the breakout of the Korean War as a reason for "an urgent drive toward state power."[66] The sacrifice of private enterprises was made as a logical step in the CCP's expansion of its political agenda.

Studies of the Three Antis and Five Antis campaigns have basically focused on CCP policies and the capitalists. In his study of the Five Antis Campaign in Shanghai, John Gardner states that "the supreme irony would appear to be that although bourgeois corruption was eliminated successfully by the leadership, corruption within the Party was not."[67] Yet it may be a misunderstanding to assume the campaign's main target was the large-scale capitalists. The case of Chengdu tells us that small-business proprietors were also attacked. It is obvious that the CCP had a remarkable ability to mobilize the masses, as it would say, using a variety of means. From its reorganization of the older guild and the undertaking of the Three Antis and Five Antis campaigns, we can see that the party depended on "activists" (*jiji fenzi*)—workers or shop employees who were politically and ideologically close to the party—to challenge guild leaders and business owners. The activists became a powerful CCP catalyst to accelerate the so-called socialist transformation.

To control guilds and other professional organizations was a continuation of a GMD policy from pre-1949, although the CCP took it much further. As Nara Dillon explains, "The tension between change and continuity in the 1949 revolution is thus extremely complex." Actually, the

CCP "continued to operate many of the corporatist institutions created by the Nationalists," showing that it was "much more effective in gaining the support of the urban elite" than its "supposedly conservative predecessors" had been.[68] However, urban elites soon found themselves in a difficult predicament when they, too, became the subject of government attack.

To a certain extent, it might be a misunderstanding to believe that the CCP changed its policy after 1953 when the "New Democracy," which allowed the existence of capitalism, began its shift to a "Socialist Transformation." In Chengdu, a policy that diminished capitalism actually was carried out as soon as the new urban administration was established in 1950. The decade of the 1950s was complicated, to say the least. As Jeremy Brown and Paul Pickowicz noted in their edited volume on early 1950s China, "Such diversity [i.e., the coexistence of capitalism and socialism] makes it impossible to provide a definitive answer to the question of whether the early 1950s represented a relatively peaceful 'honeymoon' or an ominous foreshadowing of disasters to come, a time of dashed promises and betrayed hopes. The era was many different things for different people in different places."[69] Indeed, in Chengdu, we have seen complexity but with no "honeymoon" period between the socialist state and small businesses. Under the socialist planned economy, the government paid more attention to its obsession with industrialization than to small businesses. Dorothy Solinger found that "under the [state's] plan, the allocation of resources [was] based principally on political decisions, and not on a pricing system."[70] Therefore, money always went first to state-owned enterprises, while private businesses had to fend for themselves. Because small businesses provided a livelihood for many people, the government had to let them continue, albeit with many burdensome new restrictions under which the teahouse, along with other types of business, inevitably declined.

Previous scholarship regarded the late 1950s as the turning point, with economic difficulties caused by new government policies. Kenneth Lieberthal, for example, writes that the CCP faced a transition "from success to crisis."[71] The experiences of small business owners in Chengdu, however, show that this transition actually took place much earlier. From a local perspective, especially in the city of Chengdu, we have seen the early failure of new economic and cultural constructions. Of course, the determination of success or failure depends on one's vantage point. From the position of the CCP and the socialist state, the changes were successful because they achieved their highest priority: control. I do not suggest that they were not concerned with people's livelihoods and economic development, but that these tasks were subservient to a larger political agenda. Many ordinary citizens, especially those who ran small businesses, who suffered under the government's relentless restrictions and interruptions, and who were under constant political pressure, viewed the changes as negative. In this light, the decline of the teahouse industry was in a certain sense inevitable, and was in a direct line with that first civil action taken by the victorious PLA, namely the "takeover" of culture—perceiving small businesses as a commonplace site of culture. As we see next, another target of this sort of control was street-level entertainment, often associated with the teahouse businesses.

2

STATE CONTROL AND THE RISE OF
SOCIALIST ENTERTAINMENT

On December 27, 1949, almost three months after the establishment of the People's Republic of China, Chengdu was taken over by the PLA. The new government's agenda contained thousands of points, many of a critical nature. But one matter it addressed was the control of popular entertainment, which party cadres recognized as an important aspect of daily life.[1] Communist control could not be achieved overnight, however, but required a long-term effort. The Communists adopted policies and methodologies regarding urban administration that differed fundamentally from those of the Nationalists. From 1950 to 1956, the state gradually extended its control, replacing old-fashioned forms of popular entertainment with socialist ones.[2]

In the 1950s, the popular local operas and folk performing arts, generally called *xiqu*, remained as the major entertainment for Chengdu residents, although there were cinemas, cultural centers (*wenhua gong*), and similar facilities. As Bonnie McDougall pointed out, in Chinese culture the performing arts probably reached "a wider audience than any written literature," and therefore they became "objects of serious attention for the cultural authorities."[3] Perry Link also found that "a chief function of Chinese literature and performing arts has been to influence the attitudes, and hence the behavior, of its audience in socially beneficial ways."[4] The new government knew very well that to control popular entertainment was, to a large degree, to control people's minds.

We know little about folk performers' fates in local places after 1949. Bonnie McDougall pointed out in the 1980s that relevant studies had "focused on the biographies of writers and performers, their contribution to intellectual history, the sociopolitical context of their works, and content analyses of works for studies of policy changes."[5] However, two recent books on cultural life in socialist cities help fill in the gap, though still keeping the focus mainly on Shanghai. Jin Jiang's published research, titled *Women Playing Men*, deals with the literary transformation of the early socialist years. Focusing on Yue opera, it explores the impact of the Communist regime on the performing arts and popular entertainment. After 1949, the government made an effort to form Yue opera into a tool of socialist entertainment. Jiang's attitude toward the results of the state's intervention is positive, pointing out that "there should be no question that the PRC state, and the Communist revolution, had a positive impact on the actress's transformation from member of the underclass to full member of society."[6] It is true that when the state added performance troupes to its system of direct propaganda, it in some sense strengthened the overall profile of local entertainment and gave performers job security.

However, in general, popular entertainment paid a profound price. Folk actors brought into the system became tools of propaganda in "service to workers, peasants, and soldiers," and all performances became politically centered. Moreover, even though state recognition ensured survival, those who were excluded lost everything—including their livelihood. Qiliang He's recent book about *pingtan*, a popular form of singing and storytelling in the area of Jiangnan, particularly in Shanghai and Suzhou, shows us a vastly different picture from that given in Jiang's book on Yue opera. He presents details of the impact of the socialist state on entertainment and in particular how *pingtan* artists experienced the sort of post-1949 controls that Chengdu storytellers, balladeers, and other performers did. As he points out, when the Communist Party and its socialist state became "the lone patron and arbiter" of performances, the party would decide what people should watch for their entertainment.[7]

The new government had a broad task—manipulating urban culture generally—through which it worked out its more defined task, namely the establishment of socialist forms of entertainment. Now, for the first time in Chinese history, the state was able to extend its reach into the most minute and emotional aspect of people's lives, changing the content and structure of activities, controlling performers' livelihoods and fates, and manipulating the ideas and values contained in their performances. Here I will discuss three aspects of this state control during the period from 1950 to 1956. First is the process by which the new government took control of major teahouse theaters and troupes and turned them into venues for "revolutionary popular entertainment" and "tools of propaganda and education."[8] Next, the chapter explores why and how the government tried to eliminate the "bench-sitter operas" (*bandeng xi*), locally called by another name—"the drum-beater operas" (*da weigu*). This was a popular entertainment conducted by teahouse patrons themselves, gathering to sing local operas using simple instruments and without makeup or costumes. We see eventually that it could not be removed entirely. Under the government's campaign, what situations did its participants face, and what were those government measures? Finally, based on a thorough investigation of all genres of popular performance in 1955, I show that the government carried out measures to reform performers, many of whom were forced to leave the profession.

The Establishment of New Cultural Organizations

The Communists' control of urban culture began under their post-1949 military administration. On January 1, 1950, only a few days after the PLA entered Chengdu, the Committee for the Takeover of Culture and Education under the Military Control Commission was established.[9] The committee had several offices in charge of different sectors such as literature and art, education, news, and publications. The main mission of its Department of Literature and Art (Wenyi chu) was "to propagandize the CCP's policies and guidelines and to supervise all affairs related to culture and art in the city."[10] On May 17, 1950, the Bureau of Culture and Education in Chengdu (Chengdu wenhua jiaoyu ju) was established, to replace the Committee for the Takeover of Culture and Education.[11] All teahouse theaters, whose performances included Sichuan-style arias or ballads (*qingyin*), bamboo clapper singers (*jinqian ban*, lit. "metal-cash [or coin] clapper"), drum singers (*zhuqin*), dulcimer players (*yangqin*), lotus-leaf singers (*heye*), vocal imitation, and shadow plays, "would be placed under the committee's supervision, regardless of the nature of ownership and political orientation."[12]

In February 1950, the Military Control Commission had sent its representatives to take over the Classic-Mode Peking Opera Society (Zhengsheng jingju she) and the Three Aides (Sanyigong) teahouse theater, even changing their private ownership into a "public-private partnership" (*gongsi heying*). In March, the Working Committee on Theater Reform in Chengdu (Chengdu shi xiqu gaige gongzuo weiyuanhui) was established under the leadership of the Department of Literature and Art and the Union of Western Sichuan Literature and Art Circles (Chuanxi wenxue yishu jie lianhehui), making the Three Aides (Sichuan opera) and the Classic Mode (Peking opera) their examples of experimental theater reform. At first, the Working Committee gave the theaters and troupes "positive guidance" and gave performers "rudimentary knowledge of the New Democratic revolution" (*Xin minzhu zhuyi geming*), a slogan promulgated by the CCP in the early 1950s. The committee also promoted various revolutionary dramas developed in the so-called Liberated Areas.[13]

At that point, the government set out to "popularize" the Three Aides, first by "touching the basis of thought," then "explaining and discussing," and finally, "giving lectures." The process reflected the thorough work of the new government in addressing every step of the policy implementation. Before long, a new play, *A Peasant Takes a Wife* (*Xiao Erhei jiehun*), was performed in Chengdu.[14] The Three Aides was also the first theater to be managed by individuals selected from each committee group. In December 1950 the government renamed it the Chengdu Experimental Sichuan Opera Troupe (Chengdu shi shiyan chuanju yuan) and appointed a director and associate director, a measure that "fundamentally changed the nature of the theater." Soon after, it held performances of *The Emperor and the Prostitute* (*Huangdi yu jinü*), *Kingdom of Heavenly Peace* (*Taiping tianguo*), and other new dramas intended to "lead the theater reform" (see figure 2.1).[15]

Figure 2.1 Sworn Brotherhood Tea Balcony at Wuhou Temple,
June 2003. Author photo.

In May 1951, the Central Government Administrative Council issued "Instructions for Theater Reform" and created the "Three Reforms Policy," which related to "performers, operas, and systems" (*gairen, gaixi, gaizhidu*); this soon was implemented across the nation.[16] The policy of theater reform by the Communists was actually made before the establishment of the PRC, during the developments at Yan'an (1935–1945) and the Civil War period (1945–1949). The CCP decided on a type of theater censorship that had a long history, going back especially to the Ming and Qing periods.[17] In wartime Chengdu, scripts of performances in teahouses required vetting by the Nationalist government for approval, although few theaters followed the regulation.[18] Under the pressure of the Communist regime, "entertainers one after another voluntarily eliminated superstitious content from their shows."[19] In fact, "voluntarily" might not accurately reflect the situation. The performers did not have much choice but to obey the government policy. As Siyuan Liu points out, the so-called theater reform basically came about to enforce censorship. The results were "devastating," because censorship affected "the entire repertoire of hundreds of genres of a nation's popular theatre." The worst impact concerned "the vast majority of plays that could not get approved," or which did not get a chance to be revised, and thus were never shown again.[20]

Some plays, however, were revised and then performed in Chengdu's "reformed" theaters. Performers were organized and sent to the countryside for tours as part of the propaganda disseminated for the land reform movement. The new government investigated more than five hundred entertainers in 145 venues "to get correct information, register them, and issue certificates of performance." In 1950, the Preparations Committee for the Entertainment Reform Association (Qugaihui choubeihui) was created, and two years later the association was formally launched, so that all performers were required to register in it.[21] This requirement was similar to the Nationalist government's earlier policy requiring all teahouses to register with the teahouse guild.[22] Through an intermediary committee, the PRC state did not have to deal directly with large numbers of individuals in the profession but gained efficient and comprehensive control using a professional association. This is also a good example of the CCP's policies having a connection with Nationalist policies in many ways—policies aimed at the control of small business and popular entertainment—although the scale of implementation was quite different between the two regimes.

The Takeover of Major Performing Troupes and Theaters

In Republican-era Chengdu, teahouse theaters used for storytelling and other folk performances were literally termed storytelling sites (*shuchang*). In 1949, when the Communists took over Chengdu, twenty-four teahouse theaters had already held a business license for that purpose, as issued by the GMD government.[23] One of the earliest measures of the new government control over urban culture was the creation of the May Cultural Service Agency (Wuyue wenhua fuwu she) in early 1950, the goal of which was to "cooperate with the government to promote cultural undertakings and improve literacy." The agency became the first organization granted a permit to provide social and cultural services to the public. Initial funding was provided by the West Sichuan Military Control Commission (Chuanxi junguan hui), by some "socially progressive people" (*shehui jinbu renshi*)—a label for those close to the CCP—and shops. The agency opened on May 1, 1951.[24]

Although the May Cultural Service Agency was not owned by the state, it "always put the needs of the government as its highest priority, and to cooperate with the government in promoting literacy," as well as to provide "revolutionary popular entertainment" (*geming de dazhong yule*).[25] The agency's main accomplishment was the establishment of the First Experimental Teahouse Theater (Diyi shiyan shuchang), which offered folk and historical plays as well as new works that reflected real lives and current affairs, and thus drew large audiences. According to one account, the theater "was often full during peak times."[26]

The May Cultural Service Agency also opened the May Theater (Wuyue juyuan) to perform both Peking and Sichuan operas.[27] The provincial government planned to support the agency with property and funds to build a new theater, but this was thwarted by the Three Antis and Five Antis Campaigns. Nevertheless, the agency was able to open the May Cultural Recreation Tea Garden (Wuyue wenyu chayuan), a "place for propaganda and education," which became "the most prosperous teahouse during that time," selling five thousand bowls of tea each day. In addition, it offered more than ten different newspapers, and chess fans formed the May Amateur Chess Group (Wuyue yeyu qiyi zu).[28]

Although the goal of the May Cultural Service Agency was political, it was operated as a business entity, and some people suggested that it could be more profitable if it were managed like the Great World (Da shijie) in Shanghai or Confucius Temple (Fuzi miao) in Nanjing.[29] Despite this, the agency decided to provide a "cultural service" through local performers, and it "supported its cultural tasks by operating as a business with sole responsibility for profits or losses." The Committee for the Affairs of the Agency (Shewu weiyuanhui) was elected by its members, with three subcommittees: cultural and educational, work and management, and routine affairs.[30] With the universal politicization going on at the time, however, being financially responsible for its business apparently violated the principle of state control, and thus did not last long. In 1956, the Bureau of Culture in Chengdu took over the agency and turned it into the Chengdu People's Office of Arts (Chengdu shi qunzhong yishu guan) as a part of its cultural administration.[31] The agency reflected the trends of the moment in China, where local culture was gradually losing uniqueness and was being subsumed by national politics; moreover, old-fashioned popular entertainment was largely replaced by modern socialist propaganda.[32]

With approval from the Chengdu municipal government, the Second Experimental Teahouse Theater (Dier shiyan shuchang) was established in 1952, succeeding the New Chengdu Peking Opera Troupe (Xinrong pingju tuan), a joint-stock company that had been organized in 1950.[33] Later investigation revealed that all its shareholders owned brothels, so its actresses were primarily "sisters who changed their professions," with "sisters" meaning "reformed prostitutes" (*congliang*, lit. "pursuing a better life"), a term used in the pre-PRC period. The troupe survived despite the execution of its owner, Beard Li, a master of "a superstitious sect," and despite a business slump that was a result of the economic downturn. The troupe performed mainly "ballad or aria singing" (*qingchang*), with an occasional Peking opera. As seen in the cadres' documents, some said the performers "were slackers without any discipline" and that their performances were "vulgar and backward."[34]

Later, the troupe moved to the New Chengdu Teahouse (Xinrong chashe) on China Revival Street (Huaxing jie). Soon after, when the government began enforcing a "reform of vagrancy and prostitution," the sisters of the troupe were said to have actively immersed themselves in study and professional training through which they "overcame their wrong ideas." After becoming the Second Experimental Theater, the troupe gained "a new appearance," no longer offering ballad singing but focusing on performances of full-dress Peking operas, which drew more spectators. In 1954, with the government's support, the theater became the New Chengdu Peking Opera Troupe (Xinrong pingju tuan). The government appointed cadres as troupe leaders, trained members in the Communist Party agendas, restructured the organization, established rules, and even lent funds for the purchase of costumes and stage effects. The troupe thus acquired a "new face," thanks to "the government's care" and "new leadership." Later that year, the troupe, guided by the Bureau of Culture in Chengdu, established a "Committee for Troupe Affairs," which laid out regulations for work and meetings and organized subcommittees such as stage management and general affairs. In October 1955, in response to personnel disputes, the Bureau of Culture in Chengdu sent cadres to the troupe to "help make things work" and "elect" new leaders, thus "normalizing" business and training processes.[35]

The Second Experimental Teahouse Theater troupe had sixty-three employees from various backgrounds. Among them, twenty had joined the profession before 1949, making their political backgrounds complex; five were members of "superstitious sects and secret societies"; four were former GMD military personnel; and two belonged to the Gowned Brothers. Ninety percent of the performers were female, with "almost all of the roles played by women," which the government considered "a serious problem for the troupe's development." Regardless, the troupe performed a variety of plays that were "welcomed by the nearby area's residents."[36] For example, *Eighth Sister Yang Sightseeing in Spring (Yang Bajie youchun)* had fifty consecutive performances, and *Mistress Xiang Lin (Xianglin sao)*, thirty. In 1955, "a formal system of rehearsals" was introduced, requiring performers to go through a series of steps—discussing the script, analyzing roles, and practicing the lyrics, tunes, and music—before final rehearsal.[37] The state's new changes and regulations made an ostensibly modern-style profession out of local Chengdu performers who had for generations practiced their profession in old, family-style organizations, with little or no focus on texts and analysis.[38]

Political, literary, and professional studies were the socialists' tools for cultural transformation. In Chengdu before 1954, because of a "lack of leadership," such studies were not carried out, but since the arrival of cadres from the Bureau of Culture in Chengdu in 1955, literary studies were progressing, although professional and political studies had not been added to the agenda. As a result, more than half of the Second Experimental Teahouse Theater employees could read a newspaper and write a simple letter. There was no professional training, however, because of a lack of instructors. Furthermore, two-thirds of the performers were "liberated sisters" *(fanshen jiemei)*, yet they were criticized by the government for "not having changed their old habits" and for "having no passion for learning."[39] In the past, troupes had specific paths for training, including a well-established apprentice system through which a close bond developed between masters and trainees. Such "old habits" would not be changed overnight and actually coexisted within the new training system (see figure 2.2).

A government investigation described the Second Experimental Teahouse Theater troupe's financial management as "chaotic" prior to 1953. A lack

Figure 2.2 Performance at a teahouse, May 2003. Author photo.

of bookkeeping meant that "funds could be abused by managers." In 1954, the Bureau of Culture in Chengdu helped the troupe establish accounting rules, leading to the "beginning of normal management." Business was not good, however, and its members "could barely survive," their futures "having no guarantees at all." In that year, the troupe rented a theater in the People's Commercial Center, funded and owned by the Bureau of Culture in Chengdu.[40]

An investigative report on folk performers and their venues in Chengdu found that the administration and business dealings of the two experimental teahouse theaters were "directly run" by the Bureau of Culture in Chengdu. The report stated that both theaters had "become good examples" of the entertainment profession. Following this development, ballad (aria) singers ended the "objectionable practice of placing orders for certain songs" (*dianchang lougui*) and opened three "performance houses," where they put on "folk-art plays" (*quyi ju*).[41] Thus, just as the new government anticipated, the two experimental teahouse theaters had a major impact on the city's popular entertainment and facilitated the transition from folk amusement to so-called "revolutionary culture." The government's cultural policies were often biased against practices connected to the older popular entertainments, although the CCP always claimed to understand the lower classes best. In fact, its policies perpetuated the kind of discrimination against popular culture that had been a hallmark of the old elite and orthodox values, though now usually under the banner of "revolutionary culture."

Attacks on Personal Amusements

In late-Qing and Republican Chengdu, amateurs who put on "drum-beater" (*da weigu*) or "bench-sitter" operas (*bandeng xi*) were very active in the teahouses. Opera lovers often gathered to sing along with instruments, without makeup and costumes. The participants' humor entertained the other patrons and would increase business for the teahouse. The practice even led some participants into professional careers as entertainers.[42] After the CCP gained control of Chengdu, however, cadres regarded it as grassroots activity, and "a form of the Gowned Brothers' teahouse pastime," or a "form of entertainment among secret societies." This categorization was the fatal blow to the bench-sitters' operas, and as a result, "the activity disappeared along with the destruction of the Gowned Brothers."[43] When the Preparations Committee for the Entertainment Reform Association was established in 1950, some amateurs registered with the government as providers of puppet or shadow shows because bench-sitters' shows were not recognized officially.[44]

In September 1953, however, the bench-sitters' singing of songs from certain operas was revived at a teahouse on South People's Road, and later moved to a teahouse on Purification Street (Chunhua jie). This immediately drew the government's attention because it "brought people together without permission"—the real impetus for the government's antagonism. This was seemingly part of the idea that when all activity must exist only under the leadership of the party and the state, spontaneous, voluntary associations should be prohibited. Based on a 1954 report by the Bureau of Culture in Chengdu, there were thirteen participants "whose backgrounds were very complicated," including folk performers, shop owners, craftsmen, actors, and "old-time amateurs of Sichuan opera," as well as those who "have made a fresh start" after lives as hooligans, prostitutes, and "family members of reactionary military officers."[45] This is another indication of how closely the state watched and analyzed its citizens and their actions.

The government noted that the participants were "not professional actors but used singing as a subsidiary business." As mentioned previously, the bench-sitter players traditionally sought amusement; but according to the above-mentioned 1954 report, after the revival of the activity they tended to become professionals. The amateur players began to "run the business" in the evening, their "drums and gongs making loud noises." The report accused the performances of being "unprofessional," "arbitrary," and appealing to "vulgar tastes" (*diji quwei*) to "draw more audience members and earn more money."[46] Performers were accused of singing songs that "defamed historical heroes." Another investigation, specifically of bench-sitter opera in 1955, criticized the "unrevised, old scripts" and "obscene and vulgar" (*xialiu yongsu*) performances that "have a bad influence on the populace."[47] Although the Preparations Committee persuaded them to stop performing, they eventually continued doing so, and gained even more fans and drew professional actors into the group. They performed in many teahouses, their popularity growing by letting the audience request songs and join in on "lascivious" lyrics. One teahouse owner and seven other residents tried unsuccessfully to register their bench-sitter opera business with the government under the name "Sichuan Opera Residential Troupe" (*jumin chuanju tuan*). This was an example of the socialist state's inability to suppress entirely the popular culture of Chengdu— a culture that it was criticizing as obscene and vulgar. It shows the strength of folk tradition to endure despite the overweening apparatus of state control.

Class struggle had been a major focus of the CCP since 1949, and one of its early policies was to conduct a class analysis. According to the same investigative report on bench-sitter opera, by May 1955, twelve teahouses offered bench-sitter operas, and eighty-six people (sixty men and twenty-six women) made a living this way. Thirty of those (35 percent of the total) were housewives, shop workers, craftsmen, hawkers, and other members of the urban lower class or in "superstitious occupations" (*mixin zhiye*); twenty (23 percent) were merchants in small or medium-size businesses; seventeen (20 percent) were former hobos or prostitutes; eleven (13 percent) were landlords, servicemen, and policemen; and eight (9 percent) were unemployed actors from the Sichuan opera. In addition, their political backgrounds were found to be "very complex." Twelve were secret agents of some type, nineteen were members (four being masters) of the Gowned Brothers; three were heads of *jia* in the *baojia* (a local security system), two were members of the GMD, one was in the Youth League of the Three People's Principles, one was in the Yiguandao (a religious sect categorized as a "counterrevolutionary organization" after 1949), and one was a drug dealer.[48] People's undesirable backgrounds provided the authorities with more than enough ammunition to attack and persecute.

Ultimately the performers were put into one of three categories based on the party's official criteria. Twenty-three of the performers with very complex backgrounds were accused of "the worst influence on the public" and using "the ugliest content and images." The second category, also with twenty-three actors, was for those who gave performances formerly seen as "chaotic" and "unhealthy" but now "improved" following criticism in local newspapers. The third category, numbering forty, were performers in operas named in programs "posted on placards" (*guapai yanchang*) at various teahouses; the players received "fewer negative comments from the audience" because they "seldom added lyrics arbitrarily," "the titles matched the content" of the opera, and no complaints were received from nearby residents. The 1955 investigation concluded that the bench-sitter operas should not exist "in professional form in teahouses," even going so far as to claim that the practice "had never existed in the old society." Furthermore, the loud drums and gongs "affect public order," and the "unhealthy" topics "poison people." Of the participants, thirty-four had other ways of earning a living and did not rely on their performances, and so the government favored "proper and positive measures to gradually prohibit this activity."

Half a year later, however, bench-sitter singing became more popular, spreading from twelve teahouses to fourteen, with the number of participants increasing from 86 to 166. This led the Bureau of Culture in Chengdu to issue a report on the current distribution of these operas in late 1955. This particular report stated that "no concrete measures had been taken to enforce the decision to eliminate these activities."[49] Furthermore, productions became more elaborate: Makeup and costumes were being used, and programs contained "much superstitious poison" and "obscene dialogue." According to the report, "some backward audience members said they want to see such operas so they have to go to these teahouses, where the price is low and the setting is comfortable." It would seem, then, that some people at the time embraced the bench-sitter opera style, especially given the relative lack of other cultural offerings. Yet another report noted that because these operas were a "bad influence on the populace," residents "appealed to the police one after another to expel them." Such opposing assessments probably reflect either residents' differing opinions, or the latter report simply intended to support the government's position by exaggerating the opera's negative aspects.[50] Ultimately, all these reports were made by cadres of the Bureau of Culture, whose main drive as administrators of programs was to eliminate the targeted activities that came under their policy of banning non-state-approved voluntary performances. Administrators' plans, though, did not always succeed.

The above-mentioned 1955 report of the bureau concerning the distribution of bench-sitter operas also acknowledged that the makeup and costumes were introduced by numerous performers who lost their jobs elsewhere and then came to Chengdu. The bureau also explored other issues, such as making program booklets available to the audience for one-tenth to one-fifth yuan per song. In addition, because most performers were women, they were accused of "taking opportunities to seduce customers," even to the point of sexual contact. The Bureau of Culture noted bitterly that the local police refused to get involved.[51]

The bureau mentioned that some troupe organizers were connected to the local government. For example, the "Workers and Peasants Troupe" (Gongnong jutuan) claimed to have been organized by a district government of the Chengdu suburb of Jianyang County; its members primarily were former itinerant entertainers who performed during winter and summer, when farmwork was slack, and were dismissed during the planting and harvesting seasons of spring and autumn using "departure certificates," which were, the investigators complained, "illegally issued" by the county or district governments. The report accused some performers of "trapping youngsters" to keep them from school and seducing peasants to "leave the fields." In fact, it was a long practice among peasants in rural Sichuan to find other occupations as tradesmen or itinerant performers during the slow seasons. Therefore, lower-level officials simply were upholding a well-entrenched custom, despite the government's attempts to roll it back.[52]

The bureau moreover acknowledged that after 1950, when many troupes were involuntarily dismissed, many of their members "did not get proper settlements" and were forced from Chengdu back to their home-towns, where, without a way to earn money, many "became vagrants." Some managed to return to Chengdu and join the "illegal troupes." Either way, it is clear that many participants in bench-sitter opera had no other options for survival. The "costumed rehearsal" was a way to draw more audience members, bringing their average daily earnings to between eight-tenths and one yuan, which was sufficient for living. The growing num-ber of teahouses involved in this business attracted increasing numbers of entertainers and amateur players to Chengdu, making it even more difficult for the party to solve its perceived problem.[53] Thus, in the data just examined, we have seen that a state's aim for control—namely the party's grasp at local culture—could not bring about utter domination of certain of the culture's aspects, especially when they satisfied deep needs for personal and group entertainment. Thus the power to resist the state did exist, even if in an indirect and unorganized way.

Eliminating Bench-Sitter Opera

The state under Early Socialism did not give up in this case. On Janu-ary 28, 1954, the Bureau of Culture in Chengdu further proposed a mea-sure that would eliminate the bench sitters, claiming that "bench-sitter opera is not a proper folk art, has no future, and could never become a tool of propaganda and education." The bureau also pointed out that bench-sitter opera's growing popularity hindered the development of "authentic folk performances." This, it claimed, gave "former landlords and Gowned Brothers a way to avoid physical labor," which should not be allowed. A subsequent investigation found that the majority of par-ticipants were not in the Gowned Brothers, but this provided the govern-ment a convenient justification for its actions. The bureau decided on two measures. The municipal government first asked all district governments "to prohibit bench-sitter operas in their areas" and "to refuse to prop-erly register the actors," and then prohibited all guilds from performing such shows and operating this type of business in teahouses or other pub-lic places.[54]

On May 8, 1955, the Bureau of Culture devised a three-stage strategy. First, the municipal government would make district committees of the Bureau of Culture in Chengdu, neighborhood offices, and local police stations responsible for enforcing the prohibition against the bench-sitters' performances. Second, the government should deal with performers according to their respective situations: those who were unemployed were allowed to perform "good songs," although they had to gradually reduce the amount of time dedicated to performing and eventually find other livelihoods. Those who already had other prospects were to be persuaded to "leave this business and look for other work." Those who used the opera as a "cover" for "prostitution, blackmail, and other illegal activities" were banished immediately. Third, the government would use "positive guidance" with the twelve teahouses where bench-sitter operas were performed and would meet with the "operators" to point out the problems.[55]

For reasons that are unknown, however, the Chengdu municipal government did not take action until six months later. On February 2, 1956, it issued "Instructions for Restricting Bench-Sitter Sichuan Opera," based on three new measures of the Bureau of Culture and instructing the district governments and Bureaus of Culture, Public Security, Civil Affairs, and Industrial and Commercial Administration to "quickly stop the continuous development of this opera form, a harmful phenomenon."[56] With this, the first of the initiative's three stages finally was implemented.

To begin stage one, a meeting of the "bench-sitter operators" was held for "education" regarding the "blindness" (*mangmu xing*) and "bad influence" of their activities. Participants were forbidden to promote the opera or use makeup or special costumes, a move intended to push it back into amateur status. According to the report "Dealing with Bench-Sitter Opera" (Chuli weigu baogao) of March 1956, this met with "general resistance." Teahouse managers used all kinds of excuses to justify postponing implementation. Their purpose, the report assumed, was to "get through the Spring Festival and then split up and move to the suburbs to continue their performances." Regardless, the government was determined to end the shows immediately and sent cadres to all teahouse theaters to make business "difficult" and force those involved to "reconsider their future livelihood." On February 9, 1956, the Bureau of Culture and the Bureau of Industry and Commerce held a meeting of teahouse managers and announced that no teahouses could host this entertainment without permission. While current players could continue performing until any general action was taken, the report observed that the ban on makeup and costumes made the operas so "unprofitable" that managers were ending them abruptly.[57]

A working team set up by the government placed all performers into six categories (A to F) that received differential treatment. Category A included thirty-three people who had made a living as performers for many years and who were accused of no serious wrongdoing but had no other way to earn their living. They were given permission to continue as performers, but they had to join a professional troupe. Category B included forty-three unemployed actors who had no other means of earning a living; they were allowed to continue performing temporarily, and their registrations were to be transferred to the local government office nearest their residence, which would help them find other jobs. Category C included twenty-four young, unemployed troupe apprentices, who were temporarily allowed to perform while awaiting arrangements for new jobs. Category D comprised sixty-one individuals, the largest group, many of whom were housewife-amateurs; they were required to stop performing immediately.[58] Category E included forty-three performers, who were to be sent back to their hometowns to find other work, with their transportation funded by the Bureau of Civil Affairs if necessary. In category F there were twenty-one elderly or disabled people, to be "taken in for relief" and "reformed." The situations for another seventeen people were unclear; the working team would investigate them further.[59]

In the second stage, on February 18, in an action that the report claimed received "unanimous support," the authorities called more than thirty performers and managers to a meeting to "educate" them and convince them that bench-sitter opera was "not a legitimate way to make a living." Eight were selected as members of a "rectification group" (*zhengdun xiaozu*), visiting every teahouse theater to persuade performers to go back to their hometowns or, at a minimum, stop performing. The group provided daily progress reports and "played a significant role in this task." Some performers, who had little recourse against the powerful state machine, accepted this fate and left the city.[60] Even if the endeavor did receive "unanimous support," it was simply a reflection of helplessness in the face of an inflexible outcome.

On February 20, the "rectification group" met with all performers and announced several new measures. The discussion "had good results," with some "expressing a desire to give up the business." According to the report, several women stated a wish to return to their previous occupations as housewives, while others "recognized that they were wrong" to have believed both that performing signaled an enjoyable career, and that "they were no longer miserable at home." February 21 was the deadline: the group informed those leaving Chengdu to finalize their plans and issued a final mandate to those who continued to perform. By February 24, five teahouses were "unable to operate business" because they lost most of their customers without bench-sitter operas, thus driving even more performers from the city.[61]

Throughout all this, the ongoing national political environment was colored by the movement of "Socialist Transformation": folk performers in Chengdu generally were sacrificed for the furtherance of "revolutionary culture" (see figure 2.3).

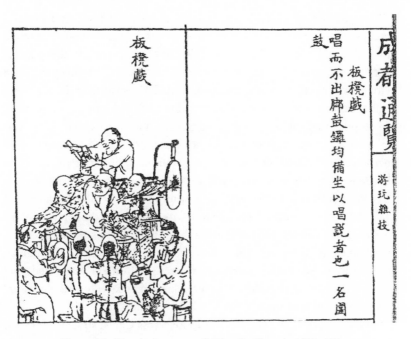

Figure 2.3 "Bench-sitter opera." From Fu Chongju 1910, 120.

Reform of Bench-Sitter Opera

In stage three of the restriction of the bench-sitter amateurs, the above measures were all implemented according to the government's plans. By the end of February 1956, the government rectification group, in an effort to ensure "gradual reduction in the number of locations for bench-sitter operas," transferred the files on all performers to neighborhood offices tasked with finding them jobs.[62] On March 1, the rectification group implemented a final push in dealing with these performers; the group harshly criticized the neighborhood offices for a "wait-and-see" attitude. On March 4, the rectification group divided all permitted actors into six troupes that it would allow to continue, and the Bureau of Culture put an end to all other bench-sitter performances in teahouses. The next day, the six new troupes began performing in six teahouses. Under the new rule, if any of these troupes became too small to perform, it would be disbanded and its players redistributed to other troupes, thereby causing troupes to become defunct through attrition rather than through outright prohibition.[63]

The Bureau of Culture concluded that "the mission was successful because the instructions from the authorities were clear, all offices worked together, and the populace was fully motivated toward the policy." Between February 7 and March 4, 1956, all "illegal," "temporary," and "itinerant" troupes were disbanded, with 242 performers in seventeen teahouses reassigned based on their "individual situations." Among them, 74 stopped performing, 50 returned to their hometowns, and only 1 was taken in by the police (*shourong*), for a total of 125 (52 percent of all participants).[64] Another 36, however, were allowed to remain in the business. Fifty-five received permission to perform temporarily, and 26 received permission to perform while waiting for new jobs, for a total of 117 (48 percent of the total). The numbers differ from those given by the working team mentioned previously; the numbers here are higher, except the "taken in" category, which dropped from 21 to just 1. The Bureau of Culture closed eleven teahouses where bench-sitters performed, and 117 performers were assigned to the remaining six teahouses that were still allowed to host them.[65]

Surviving actors in Chengdu, like those across China, struggled for their livelihoods. In 1956, the *Opera News* (*Xiju bao*)—an official semimonthly magazine—published a letter by actor Huang Zhenyuan, titled "Please Listen to Our Appeal," which reflected on this predicament. Huang called for "concern for the lives of performing artists and respect for their work" and stated that performers, the majority of whom were in private troupes, worked very hard "to please audiences and play a positive role in society." The author stated that in recent years, "we have not paid enough attention to the plight of the hundreds of thousands of performing artists" at a time when business was in steep decline. While prominent actors earned about thirty yuan monthly, the majority earned seventeen to eighteen yuan, with a considerable number—their families' sole support— surviving on as little as ten yuan. Huang mentioned that troupes had no means for housing or caring for performers who were elderly, in poor health, or otherwise unable to perform, leaving them "anxious and helpless," along with their families, many of whom traveled with the troupe and lived backstage.[66]

Compounding the situation, according to Huang, performances often faced the problem of being subject to "unreasonable interference" by the government in the towns where they toured. Local institutions had no respect for itinerant actors and could arbitrarily command them to entertain officials without compensation, or could simply disrupt their performances. Troupes that did not perfectly navigate the tricky waters of public relations could face "unexpected calamities," part of what Huang called the "outrageous attitude" of the ruling class of the "old society." He noted that despite performing an average of four hundred to five hundred shows annually, actors received only three to five months' worth of compensation each year between 1952 and 1956. There were other obstacles: Huang complained about the time his own troupe was scheduled to perform during the first lunar month—peak season—only to find that the government had taken for its own purposes the same facility they had reserved, thus delaying the performances for ten days. Without a stage, the troupe was forced to seek audiences in much less profitable rural and mountainous regions.

That Huang's letter could even be printed was due to the so-called Hundred Flowers Campaign, a short period of false "free speech" in 1956, and the fact that intellectuals' opinions were of intense concern. An editorial comment on the letter noted that while the central government's Ministry of Culture had recently focused on these issues and put measures in place to address them, implementation would be the sole purview of the cultural institutions that were part of local governments; and these measures would affect hundreds of thousands of performing artists nationwide, inevitably altering the "development of theater arts in the future." The editorial also emphasized that some troupes needed reformation simply because of the poor quality of their performances and staff. Finally, it argued that the government should protect the legitimate rights and interests of performing artists, correct previous wrongdoings, and educate its cadres to respect these performers and their work.[67]

The affected performers were unfortunate, but luckier than those forcibly evicted from the profession, as described previously, in that they could at least openly communicate their plight. This advantage turned out to be short-lived, however. In May 1957, during the Hundred Flowers Campaign, the Chengdu Municipal Party Committee hosted an informal discussion with non-party representatives of the performers and solicited their views on the CCP. Some participants complained that they did not have regular venues and had to go to teahouses or other public places, where they were often rejected and marginalized. The mayor immediately instructed the relevant departments to solve this problem.[68] That such a complaint from local performing artists could be broadcast like this was only because it occurred during the Hundred Flowers, in which the CCP solicited people's criticisms of the party. In other circumstances this would not have received public disclosure, given the party's tight control of media. Unfortunately, the subsequent Anti-rightist Movement suppressed all the discontent that had emerged. Those who responded to the CCP's previous invitation and criticized the party were dubbed "rightists," and many were dismissed from their jobs or even sent to labor camps. Although some actors could still make a living through their craft, self-preservation in this brutal political environment required that they express no discontent.[69]

The Socialist Transformation of Popular Entertainment

The socialist state was heavily committed to make great efforts to transform everyday culture in public establishments into material for "revolutionary propaganda." In 1955, the national Ministry of Culture issued "instructions on enhancing leadership and management of professional folk performance troupes." Based on those instructions, the Bureau of Culture in Sichuan made a "working plan for cultural affairs." Then the Bureau of Culture in Chengdu carried out a full-scale investigation of professional troupes and folk performers in the city from August through November 1955, for the purpose of guiding "politics and minds" and for completing the "socialist transformation" of popular professional troupes and folk performers so that they might "play a role in socialist construction." Another purpose was for the bureau to know all about the situation of folk performers and the places of performance in order to "enhance leadership and management" and "restrain unguided performances." As a result, all forms of folk performances were investigated.[70]

The cadres at the Bureau of Culture's Division of Opera and Folk Arts (Wenhua ju xiquke), along with a few from district-level offices, handled most of the investigation. A working team was put together to survey popular performance troupes. The team visited each one and from it recruited three to five "active and reliable" troupe members. The Bureau of Public Security was asked to determine each of these actors' political views and background. All recruited troupe members met for four days to become acquainted with the purpose, methodologies, and policies for the reform of the troupes' presentations. Although the bureau's team was advised not to interfere with troupes' regularly scheduled performances, the team members were asked to report any "hidden counterrevolutionaries or other bad elements," which would trigger involvement by the Bureau of Public Security and related departments. The cadre investigators in general relied on "the masses" and on the close relationships with the embedded "activists" in the troupes. They also placed a certain tactical value in manipulating performers' "minds and lifestyles" and stated that "public criticism" or "self-criticism" should not be used, but instead they could use education through "positive reinforcement." This kind of thinking emerged from the belief that actors were backward and susceptible to moderate psychological measures. The Bureau of Culture also enforced "firmly established leadership" through a decision-making process of "asking for instructions and reporting to superiors."[71]

The investigation had three aspects: "proliferate, educate, and mobilize the masses."[72] From its outlines, as drawn by the Chengdu Municipal Bureau of Culture, we know that the government wanted to find

out about nearly every aspect of work and life in the troupes: historical background, organizational structure, personnel, information about
performances, professional training, finances, performance venues, and
overall environment.[73] The report also tells us that there were 405 folk
performers and 105 venues in the Eastern, Western, and River View
(Wangjiang) Districts of Chengdu. Performances included thirteen folk
forms: bamboo clapper singing, lotus singing, flower drum, storytelling,
bamboo dulcimer singing, drum singing, cross-talk (two actors performing comic stories), vocal imitation, ballad singing, Peking opera singing,
puppet shows, magic, and shadow plays.[74] An almost identical list was
provided by the Bureau of Culture and Education in Chengdu on May 17,
1950, mentioned previously. This may imply that after five years, such
popular forms of entertainment survived despite the constant control of
the state. The report detailed the political backgrounds of the performers,
and a high percentage were said to have "political problems." Of the 405
performers, 219 joined the profession before 1949, and 186 after 1949.[75]
Eighty-eight of the 186 had difficulty making a living: they included the
unemployed "urban poor," handworkers, salesclerks, housewives, the
self-employed, and students. Sixty-one were former landlords, policemen,
government employees, and members of "reactionary" political parties.
And finally, thirty-seven were considered the "scum of society" (*shehui
zhazi*), engaged in superstitious professions, and prostitutes from the old
society. Some had sufficient skills to earn a living as performers, while
others did not.[76] The second and third group—those with "political problems" plus those defined as "scum"—made up about a half of the total.[77]

In this profession, 171 people (42 percent) had "political problems,"
and the general assessment was that "most are bad elements that infiltrated the folk performing profession; only a tiny fraction were folk performers prior to 1949. Their minds and lifestyle are generally no good;
they deliberately spread dissatisfaction and carry out secret activities."
One example is a cross-talk actor named Zhang, who had "a background
of serving the old government," "a close relationship" with high-ranking
military officers in the GMD, and who once "smuggled goods from Hong
Kong using military planes." In 1952, he "infiltrated the folk performing
profession and pretended to be an activist supporting the government"
but was arrested because of "political problems."[78] Clearly, Zhang's
major trouble, as far as can be ascertained from this report, came from his

background and not because of any illegal conduct after 1949, a situation that underscores how the CCP essentialized this notion of "background" determining one's fate under the new regime.

Of the 405 total just mentioned, 117 (or 29 percent) in fact were storytellers, and of those, 43 had joined the profession after 1949. The next-largest group was ballad singers, totaling 113 (28 percent). Unlike the storytellers, they were mostly female and, interestingly, had taken up the craft after 1949. The report accused some of "having evil lifestyles as prostitutes who used their singing to defraud." While their incomes varied, most could support themselves.[79] The next group in numbers was bamboo dulcimer singers and dulcimer singers, with seventy-three (18 percent); most of them were elderly blind men with a long history of performing, and with a low literacy rate. They found it difficult to earn a living wage. The fourth group, with forty-six (11 percent), were performers of puppet and shadow plays, most of whom were elderly, with experience prior to 1949, and now "barely keeping up a liveli-hood." The fifth group numbered forty-one (or 16 percent): they were bamboo clappers, lotus singers, and flower drum singers, most of whom had joined the profession before 1949 and had relatively good incomes. Those who performed big-drum singing, cross-talking, and vocal imita-tion belonged to the final group, with eleven people total (just under 3 percent), most of whom entered the business before 1949 and enjoyed "relatively good income and stable lives."[80] From this, we can see that, with the exception of storytelling and ballad singing, all forms of folk performance stopped developing after 1949, and artists faced significant obstacles in making a living.

Venues for these genres of folk performance totaled 145, falling into three categories. First of all were the two "experimental theaters" men-tioned earlier in this chapter. The second type was the 132 teahouses, and the third was 11 storytelling sheds (*shupeng*).[81] It seems also that 165 shows per day, of the various arts, were available, and Chengdu residents had a wide array of offerings until the mid-1950s. We do not know the numbers (or average) of attendees per show, but perhaps it was quite large, given that folk performances were the most basic form for entertainment.

The Bureau of Culture's investigation uncovered three major problems in the world of folk performers. First was the lack of orderly planning and uncontrolled growth that cadres associated with the near doubling of the number of performers from 219 to 405 between the years 1950 and 1955. Because the performers were scattered and itinerant, as well as "only loosely supervised and educated," the bureau claimed that it "had not recognized the problem of these performers and had not carried out an effective way to control their development; and did not conduct careful investigations." The Entertainment Reform Association was established in 1952 but was not well organized and could not play a role in "helping the government unite and educate folk performers." In April 1956, the Bureau of Culture held the first meeting of all folk performers to "guide them to change their performances." "A lack of management and education of these people" persisted, however, it was claimed.[82] However, the claim that the number of performers had "doubled" is arguable. Based on the investigation, 219 performers joined the profession before 1950, but we should not assume there were only 219 people total, because many changed careers after 1950, as discussed before. Many were forced to leave the profession when troupes were reorganized and numerous teahouses closed down beginning in 1950. The numbers should be understood in this way: by 1956, of the large number of folk performers who had been in the profession before 1950, only 219 remained.

The second of the three perceived problems had to do with "careless talking and singing" (*luanshuo luanchang*) and "dirty performances." The bureau pointed out that performers lacked education and management, creating "serious chaos" in the profession that was in part a result of the tone of "licentiousness and supernatural," especially in the genres of storytelling, ballads, and bamboo clappers. Performers were accused of using "lascivious lyrics" (*yinci*), such as found in the ballad "Eighteen Touches" ("Shiba mo").[83] Other examples were found in "The Broken Bridge" ("Duanqiao"), for which actors changed the lyrics from "entering the sedan chair by holding the lady's hand" to "pulling the lady into my clutch," while they showed "all kinds of ugly expressions" for the audience's amusement (see figure 2.4).[84]

The bureau thought that the performances generally had a negative influence on young people. In one example, after watching a story about a legendary warrior, a young student lay on the ground in front of an oncoming car to test his belief in a protective "gold cover and iron garment" that fended off knives, guns, and moving vehicles. Furthermore,

Figure 2.4 "Singing with the Daoist instrument." Fu Chongju 1910, 120.

students skipped classes to watch stories about ghosts and superstitions.[85] The bureau's, and in fact the state's, concern over slightly flirtatious innuendos in lyrics and students' skipping classes to attend storytelling seems overly prudish. The same might be said of so-called magic, and people's beliefs about these powers: it was simply a widespread condition, as seen in the example of the Boxers in 1900. By this point in time, "superstition" had become a well-utilized topic in the state's many pronouncements that corrected and warned about popular culture and that did much to hem in the movement and speech of everyday people in their public lives.

The third problem discussed in the report of the bureau had to do with "bad lifestyles" (*buliang zuofeng*). It was noted that some performers "forced audiences to select and pay for songs from the program list" (the same problem that had been addressed in a previous report), and they engaged in "sleeping around" and "blackmail." Some performers, based on the report, were punished under the laws for insulting women, rape, drug trafficking, fraud, and bribery. A certain bamboo clapper was sentenced to death during the 1956 "campaign against hooligans and bandits" under the charge of insulting more than thirty women. A ballad singer was accused of singing "lascivious lyrics," having sexual relationships with three men, and swindling money. "Whenever she found out that an audience member was rich," the report stated, "she would seduce him at restaurants and hotels until he was out of money."[86] Of course, illegal conduct like this, coupled with governmental prejudice, would have damaged the profession's overall reputation, yet it is also worth noting that these "illegal" acts were often exaggerated and unclearly stated by the government.

The Bureau of Culture, based on its 1955 report, now actually created an ordered system for the profession. The municipal government notified the offices of all districts and the Bureau of Public Security that henceforth neighborhood offices and police substations would be held accountable for the actions of folk performers, putting an end to what the government had earlier announced as "uncontrolled growth." Prospective performers had to receive approval from their district office and report to the Bureau of Culture. Those deemed skilled, and whose households were registered in the city, were issued a "permit for folk performance." Many were dissuaded from becoming entertainers, and those who had no other means of support received a "temporary permit" but eventually were forced out, as were prostitutes, beggars, and the like.[87]

The bureau furthermore went about "improving the subjects of stories and songs" and trying to eliminate "toxic" programs, those that were "pornographic," "superstitious," and "insulting to the working class." These included, among others, *Stories of Jigong* (*Jigong zhuan*), *The Picture of Ten Beauties* (*Shimei tu*), *Missing the Scholar* (*Si xiucai*), and *Eighteen Touches*.[88] Programs that were slightly problematic but "not very harmful" were allowed to continue while being revised. The Bureau of Culture also required entertainers to register their programs and revise them collectively. After that, the Compiling Group for Folksong Performers (Quyi yiren bianxie zu), supervised by cadres in the relevant government departments, reviewed and made any necessary changes. Programs that conformed too closely to old styles were officially banned, while new ones were promoted and performed at the two experimental theaters, thus being examples to the rest of the venues. Performers were required to give a small-scale "model show" (*guanmo*) monthly and a full performance quarterly so that their counterparts could learn the parts.[89] In addition, the Compiling Group organized folk performers to revise old programs as well as write new works, all to be performed in the two experimental theaters.

Finally, the bureau tried to "strengthen folk performers' political and professional education." A "core learning group" was established for the weekly study of political events and professional policies, and its members in turn coached the other groups. The government arranged political study sessions according to its "opera and folk performers' study plan"; the latter included a basic overview of literary and art criticism and theory, and policies for opera reform.[90] This so-called political study was an important means of intellectual manipulation by the CCP. By the nature of their vocation, folk performers were a very loose conglomeration, and such intervention surely had a significant effect in controlling them.

The Socialist State and Cultural Transformation

The new state under the Communists after 1949 played an unprecedented role in people's cultural recreation, as well as other aspects of life. In the past, people had often resisted efforts by elites and the state to control them, and this kind of resistance shows up even through the 1950s. But, comparatively speaking, it became quite diminished in the face of the strongest state in Chinese history. "Bench-sitter opera" disappeared quickly after 1950, although it sprang back from 1954 to 1956, and forms of folk entertainment faced insurmountable odds under various attacks by the state. The fate of the performers and their arts, after 1949, was the same as that experienced by many forms of popular culture and entertainment that were not considered by cadre groups as "revolutionary literature and art" (*geming wenyi*) or socialist propaganda.

During this period, the CCP and the government made a great effort to promote broad-based cultural movements that represented certain revolutionary ideologies they could easily manipulate. Old-style genres, especially those that appeared on streets and in teahouses—in closest proximity to ordinary people's daily lives—suffered from all kinds of restrictions.

Communist revolutionary culture emerged from rural regions, especially the "liberated areas" where people's daily lives were highly organized by the Communists, and popular entertainment often became subsumed into mass mobilization efforts. Some events drew as many as one or two thousand participants. When David Holm studied *yangge* (lit., "rice-sprout song"), he found that it had been introduced for propaganda purposes in 1942 and that the CCP's power extended to the lowest denominators at the grassroots level, even into the smallest villages. *Yangge* was basically a North China integration of dance, song, and various acts performed by villagers. The party's appropriation of it marked a new direction in establishing a revolutionary culture through public celebrations and mass events. In the liberated areas, this was "a very rapid development, as the Party intensified its efforts to penetrate village society, of a range of new rituals and ritual-like observances designed to involve the masses as participants in public life and to give expression to the values of New Democracy."[91] John Gardner's study of early 1950 Shanghai noted that the CCP had created "a high degree of organizational skill in an agrarian environment, and by 1949 it appears to have enjoyed considerable legitimate support in rural China," but, writing close to that time, he still questioned whether "it could handle the task of controlling the relatively sophisticated and functionally diffuse urban sector of society."[92] Brian DeMare's new study of CCP drama troupes, *Mao's Cultural Army*, deals with propaganda teams in rural areas and reveals the importance of performing arts for the success of the Communist revolution.[93]

With the Communists' victory, the "red" revolutionary culture transferred from the countryside into the city, where such a culture did not have similar roots. There, in public life and urban spaces, what the CCP accomplished was basically successful, from its perspective, but it sacrificed a rich urban culture: the socialist state actively sought to diminish the extant culture. Its culture administrators, so to speak, did not have a clear idea how to transform the culture of the cities into something socialist, and continually sought out solutions. They depended more on their experience with rural culture and propaganda than on their more limited exposure to centuries of urban performing arts. Their priority had been to transform pre-1949 local culture into something that could serve their agenda and to make it a product of the state's control of people's leisure time for purposes of indoctrination.

But the situation is even more complex than that. We should understand that so-called revolutionary culture, while a creation of the Communist movement, actually had some roots in Chinese traditions. To transform those customary practices into new ones was in some sense and to some degree a nationwide trend, as seen in Wai-fong Loh's study of the film *Liu Sanjie*. Liu's story can be traced back as far as the Ming dynasty, and during the twentieth century, scholars collected the rich oral materials about Liu's life. But after 1950, films often were infused with the theme of class struggle, and the film *Liu Sanjie* was no exception: "Liu is a firewood-cutter who attacks the rich landlords through her songs."[94] Such an iconic theme serves as an example of how traditional stories were converted to serve revolutionary ideals. According to a study of "revolutionary songs" by Isabel Wong, "The use of music as a social, political, and educational tool, as advocated by Chinese Marxists, is not alien to traditional Chinese thinking." It was actually a serious concern of governments ever since the Western Han dynasty (206 BCE–9 CE). In this sense, ritual offices at dynastic courts incorporated faraway, or ethnically non-Han, or even cult music and dance to demonstrate the emperor's sway over "all under heaven" and bolster legitimacy; in this sense, changes in the music would sometimes be instituted to indicate ideological concerns.[95] It is possible, then, to say that the Communists adopted a practice of those ancient political elites, whom they saw as having educated and enlightened the masses.[96] The important point is that no previous regime had succeeded in reaching the scale and depth of control of culture (or even intended to do so) as did the Chinese Communists. It is interesting, based on Wong's study, to note that revolutionary songs also had connections with heterodox or subversive movements, such as the Taiping Rebellion. A comparison of the Taiping songs with those of the PRC reveals "many similarities between the contents, style of language, titles and use of metaphors of these two bodies of texts."[97] We thus see that the cultural policies of China's Early Socialism had a complex, early origin that was skillfully manipulated by the new regime. It is worth mentioning, as well, that there were other roots of Early Socialism's urge to manipulate culture—in particular the Soviet model of the politicization of culture, from fine arts and music to urban lifestyles and urban planning.[98] Stalinist modernization programs were consistently apparent to Chinese cadres up until the mid-1950s, when China outwardly broke with the USSR.

Actually, the period from the 1950s to the early 1960s was a time when both the revolutionary and the older folk performances coexisted. This was regarded by Bonnie McDougall as "the tendency toward cultural diversity that undermined the national goal of a unitary mass culture." However, the old forms were "highly popular at different audience levels but highly resistant to revolutionary modernization." For example, modern drama was "patronized almost exclusively by the urban intelligentsia and obviously designed to transmit a modern revolutionary content."[99] However, what we see from the Chengdu example was not "the tendency toward cultural diversity," but just the opposite: a tendency toward uniformity. This phenomenon underscores the long process that the decline of older local cultures and the encroachment of radical revolutionary culture required, from the early 1950s to the mid-1960s. Of course, some scholars might argue that the socialist state might not have had enough power to control all entertainment, so people still had significant space in which to conduct activities and amusements; and we saw examples of that. It is also true that even the strongest state, especially within the massive territory of China, would miss some areas and could not control every nook and cranny. An example is bench-sitter opera, as described in this chapter. It could not be kept down completely, despite all the attempts. Nonetheless, I am arguing that we should recognize the tremendous capability of the CCP to control people with power that reached even the lowest, most spontaneous and individualistic, places in society, an achievement not matched by any other regime. From the facts about literature and performances in the early PRC provided in the volume edited by Bonnie McDougall, we can see that the cultural transformation of this period "could be carried out in three ways: by controlling authors, by controlling their work, or by controlling their audiences," and "authors and also performers became state functionaries under Party or other control, so that their intellectual and artistic autonomy could be undermined by political demands."[100] Her edited volume provides excellent case studies of the experiences of well-known intellectuals, writers, and artists under Mao. However, such studies usually do not venture much into the stories of ordinary entertainers, performers, and folk artists at the street or neighborhood levels—details brought out in this chapter.

3

The Decline of Public Life
under Mao's Rule

From the late Qing to the Republic, the teahouse was the most important public space and a facilitator of daily life in Chengdu. In 1949, after
the Communist revolutionaries claimed victory, they not only established
a completely different political system but also fundamentally reshaped
economic and social structures: the changes in daily life were unprecedented.[1] This chapter looks at the changes in public life in the newly
socialist Chengdu; it underscores how the Communist government not
only determined the fate of the teahouse but also transformed all public
life.[2] The teahouse industry and public life are tightly related, and for this
reason the chapter also explores how the government's policies to control
small businesses caused teahouse business to decline.

While urban residents in the 1950s and 1960s could pursue those
aspects of their daily lives that had to do with the teahouse, the very existence of leisure pursuits in teahouses was an idea that seriously conflicted
with the state's modernist-aimed agenda to construct a new, industrial
city. In a time when class struggle was emphasized, teahouses became an

arena for political campaigns; and as the government increasingly disrupted life in public spaces, residents had increasingly fewer opportunities to take advantage of the teahouse.[3] During the radical 1960s and 1970s, with the exception of political rallies organized or approved by the government, the spaces for public life were very limited. All remaining theaters, cinemas, and similar venues were simply domains of political propaganda, where people received "political education" designed by the CCP. People increasingly stayed in their homes, where they felt safer to express themselves, instead of going into public spaces to seek and participate in information and sociality. Teahouses would dwindle in number virtually overnight during the radical revolutionary wave of the Cultural Revolution (1966–1976), when a careless remark could lead to grim repercussions. People avoided public life and political talk in public, even in some circumstances in their homes: it was not uncommon that words spoken or things cherished in homes became known to unruly Red Guard agitators, who would persecute members of such families. This decade was the nadir of the teahouse and public life in China in the twentieth century. While the government could not realistically forbid the very existence of teahouses, given their important urban role, it could—and certainly did—make the survival of the industry exceedingly difficult, both logistically and politically.

Teahouse Life in the 1950s

Ma Shitu, an elderly revolutionary, recalled that after the new government was established, the teahouse became thought of as a place of unseen filth and idleness:

> Since they were not places where the revolution could be supported, we had to firmly eliminate them. Therefore, many teahouses were closed. Although people disliked this inconvenience, they could not do anything about it except offer unconditional obedience. In fact, some insightful people believed that we could have the benefits of teahouses without the detriments. Of course, the bad elements would be completely eliminated, but the teahouse could be used as a center of cultural activities and a place for propaganda and popular education. These voices were not heard by the authorities. Therefore, teahouses almost disappeared off Sichuan's very earth.[4]

Such an attitude about carriers of social ills did not originate with China's Communist cadres, but began among progressives throughout China from the early twentieth century as a set of ideas that blamed certain aspects of popular culture for hindering modernization and Westernization. The Communists carried this forward by claiming that teahouses represented "backward," "unhealthy," and "time wasting" elements but launched their attacks more furiously than ever before in Chinese history. Although Ma's statement that teahouses "almost disappeared off Sichuan's very earth" might be an exaggeration, their number was indeed greatly reduced. As a large city, Chengdu was subjected to tighter control by the state and thus felt a stronger political impact, making the disappearance of teahouses there much swifter than in rural market towns. According to Regina Abrami's study, nonresidents of Chengdu could not get business licenses. Furthermore, shop owners and regular marketplace vendors were required to renew their licenses annually. Thus, "cadres from the Bureau of Industrial and Commercial Management had enormous power to define the size and scope of legitimate private trade."[5]

After 1949, teahouse-related topics started to drop out of the usual stream of documents, such as local newspapers. Partly this was because under socialism, government-run local newspapers paid scant attention to teahouses (in contrast to the coverage in the Republican era). What articles that were published and that still exist were sheer propaganda. In 1956, for instance, a *Chengdu Daily* story titled "A Teahouse Worker Is Not Afraid of Difficulties" described how a stove keeper named Long Senrong in the Brocade Spring Teahouse (Jinchun chashe) contributed to a "worker competition" by using sawdust as a substitute for coal, which saved 120 *jin* (1 *jin* is about 1.1 pounds) of coal daily, or over 43,000 *jin* annually. He also helped thirteen other teahouses retrofit their stoves for this purpose.[6] Some memoirs provide other useful perspectives. One man (whose sparse childhood included earning coins for picking up cigarette butts from a teahouse floor) recalled that his father, after being labeled a "rightist" during the Anti-rightist Campaign of 1957, was sent to work as a stove keeper at a teahouse that had only four tables. After the last patron left at night, they put the tables together to make a bed. He and other workers would be awakened each morning by the old men who came for their "early tea" (*zaocha*).[7]

A regime change can be accomplished quickly, but the associated lifestyle and cultural transformations take much longer. Frequenting teahouses was a habit ingrained in Chinese culture for over a thousand years, and it continued as part of daily life despite the political upheaval under the first decade of Communist rule, when the teahouse industry was suppressed. Public life was very much observed and supervised by the state, especially by lower-level representatives such as police officers working out of substations (*paichu suo*), neighborhood offices (*jiedao banshichu*), and members of residential committees (*jumin weiyuanhui*), to whom patrons who seemed outside of socialist ideology and morality would be reported, often with dire consequences.

An elderly man recollected the Abundant Virtue Teahouse (Desheng chaguan) on West Imperial Street (Xiyu jie), which had a spacious entrance hall; the front of the teahouse was designated for first-time guests and the rear for regulars. It opened in the early 1950s and enjoyed a booming business from the start. The teahouse offered cross-talkers every night, performed by Chengdu's best-loved comedians. Shows were rarely updated, however, so business gradually dwindled, and later on cross-talk was replaced by bamboo dulcimers. In addition, there was a popular actor there named Yang, who could sing a complete version of *Ci Yun's Revenge* (*Ci Yun zouguo*). His performance was extremely touching, and the audience would grow anxious or sad along with the fictional characters. During intermission, as Yang took a catnap, smoked, drank, and otherwise relaxed and prepared for the next segment of the story, his wife collected money from the audience.[8]

Another teahouse-goer, named A Nian, describes how in the 1950s his father often took him to a corner teahouse at night to hear storytelling, and he became acquainted with several boys who picked up cigarette butts. When the teahouse was packed, he was able to acquire enough butts to keep his father smoking for two or three days. Later, his family moved downtown, next to a teahouse, where several times a day he purchased boiling water for his grandfather's tea—a favorite activity that gave him a chance to have fun. When he lingered too long, he always made excuses about the water not being ready or having to wait while other customers were served. His grandfather knew that, in fact, he was caught up watching fortune-tellers, musicians, magicians, and eating from food vendors. He admitted that "if I entered, I could not walk out without staying very long. It was the pleasure palace of my childhood, and today's nightclubs or karaoke halls have never been as exciting."[9]

The noted writer Huang Shang liked to frequent all kinds of teahouses in Chengdu, large and small, such as those by the river in the People's Park, tea balconies on Warm Spring Road (Chunxi lu), and the Three Laurels Tea Garden (Sangui chayuan) located in a renovated garden. He said that teahouses in 1950s Chengdu held interest for people, and that anyone who entered "would naturally get accustomed to the Chengdu lifestyle." Huang described how folk performers sang a variety of songs and told many kinds of stories in the teahouse. Tobacco sellers rented out bamboo smoking pipes that were four to five Chinese feet in length— so long that customers had to rely on the salesman to light the tobacco. Numerous peddlers moved between tables and behind seats, selling melon seeds and peanuts. Shoemakers made a living there as well, as did vendors who rented out comic books.[10] This long-established way of life flourished from the late Qing to the Republic, and persisted even after the Communist revolution (see figure 3.1).

Figure 3.1 Teahouse occupying a sidewalk in a Chengdu suburb, September 2015. Author photo.

Another elderly Chengdu resident, Zhang Xiande, noted that most teahouses in the 1950s were located on street corners, along riverbanks, at the ends of bridges, or in parks. Those in commercial areas were high-end and elegant, but those that typified the Chengdu teahouse best were found on street corners. Zhang said that "Let's go to the teahouse on the corner" was probably the most frequently uttered phrase in Chengdu at the time. In addition, waiters—so-called experts of tea (*cha boshi*)—proudly inherited their predecessors' professionalism, skill, and quickness, which led to good relationships with patrons.[11]

Zhang also recalled that the street where he once lived had two medium-size teahouses: the Ten–Thousand-Flowers Balcony Teahouse (Wanhualou chashe) and the Hundred-Flowers Teahouse (Baihua chashe). The former, which closed in the early 1960s, was a street-front house with two floors plus tables and chairs on the sidewalk, and could accommodate more than one hundred customers. The Hundred Flowers could hold dozens of patrons and was often very crowded, especially during bench-sitter operas and storytelling. The government tried to restrict this form of opera but was not entirely successful.[12] Storytelling more often occurred at night, rather than the afternoon. Popular programs were *The Legend of Yue Fei (Shuo Yue)*, *Water Margin (Shuihu)*, *Romance of the Three Kingdoms (Sanguo yanyi)*, *Ghost Stories (Liaozhai)*, and *The Story of Monk Jigong (Jigong zhuan)*.[13] Despite the Communist government's best efforts, these popular programs endured to a remarkable degree. However, with the increasing radicalization of politics during the Socialist Education Movement (Shehui zhuyi jiaoyu yundong) from the early 1960s until the eve of the Cultural Revolution, storytellers had to closely follow politics and perform only revolutionary stories such as *Lin Zexu Bans Opium (Lin Zexu jinyan)* and *The Fighting Squad behind Enemy Lines (Dihou wugongdui)*. The Hundred-Flowers Teahouse operated until the Cultural Revolution.[14]

In many people's memories, teahouse life was still in evidence even in the worst periods of Early Socialism. Mr. Huang was born in 1956 and lived on East Great Street for many years. He recalled the teahouse next door, whose activities he often watched through a hole in the wall. Until the eve of the Cultural Revolution, there were still puppet shows, "Daoist zither playing" (*da daoqin*), and long, smoking water-pipes. During summer, several people, including his brother, earned money

Figure 3.2 Old man showing off his trick outside a teahouse in a Chengdu suburb, September 2015. Author photo.

by operating a giant ceiling fan that turned by pulling a rope connected to the blades.[15] One teahouse patron recalled that during the 1950s a colleague of hers went to the teahouse for early tea at five o'clock every morning. When he became a father, he brought his baby to the teahouse, even in winter. He would return home for breakfast and then head to work. Even after moving many miles from the teahouse, he continued to go there by bus.[16] This indicates the attraction and importance of teahouse life (see figure 3.2).

The relationship between the folk performer and the teahouse was simple; generally, all a performer had to do was enter an arrangement with the owner regarding programs and showtimes. The teahouse and the performer collected money for tea and for the show separately. However, performances that required several participants, such as shadow plays and folk dramas, had also to contribute to rent, electricity, and other costs. Performances were always in the afternoon and night. A government report in 1955 stated that, among all folk performers, 54 percent were storytellers, while bamboo clapper singers, lotus singers, bamboo dulcimer singers, and dulcimer singers together accounted for 33 percent. Puppet shows and shadow plays were performed only once per day. The report claimed that the plays and operas were "unrevised" and had "old, toxic words" that could simply "attract more viewers, and performers made their living by resorting to dirty and vulgar actions" (*xialiu yongsu*). The report also acknowledged, however, that some actors had revised their conventional approaches to reflect "today's lives."[17]

Storytelling "sheds" were another type of venue where customers could spend an entire day watching storytelling and other folk performances. The sheds were crude structures on the outskirts of the city, and the customers as well as performers were mostly low-income, low-status peasants. The same 1955 report said that the performers spoke and acted carelessly on stage, their "lascivious" routines exerting a "bad influence" on the "masses." It accused the performers of "bad lifestyles" and having connections to "hooligans and thieves." A bamboo clapper and four ballad singers were arrested and sent to a labor camp for "prostitution, thievery, and fraud."[18] Ignored by previous governments, the sheds now drew close scrutiny.

The long debate over admitting women into teahouses grew during the first half of the twentieth century and gradually was resolved in their favor.[19] Well into the 1950s, however, teahouses remained very much a masculine world, and women—especially young women and students—who frequented them were harshly criticized, whereas middle-aged and elderly women received more tolerance. Customers' attire and appearance also reflected the changing times, as Mao suits became more popular than long gowns. It also became fashionable to place pens in one's chest pocket as clues to one's identity: "a young pupil has a pen; a middle school student, two pens; and a college student, three pens."[20]

Some "old-school patrons" were said to have "first-class permanence" in teahouses and were "nailed to their seats" for hours on end: it was a home away from home. For them, going to the teahouse was not about tea or even playing chess and listening to opera, but the "special atmosphere." They came to the teahouse early in the morning, bought a bowl of tea, and read newspapers for a few hours, draping a newspaper over their faces if they felt like napping. As Zhang Xiande noted, "Ever since childhood, I have seen all kinds of characters in the teahouse, many of whom had some special quality that made them interesting." The ones he found most

Figure 3.3 A group of elderly men in a teahouse in a Chengdu suburb, September 2015. Author photo.

impressive, however, were those who could stay in their seats for an entire day like a "Zen Buddhist monk," in meditation or withdrawal. Some may have thought such people offered nothing to the atmosphere, but, Zhang believed, some might have been hermits who lent an air of mystery, symbols of Chengdu who fully embraced the city's unique focus on leisure and distinguished themselves as true local types (see figure 3.3).[21]

Well-known intellectuals such as Meng Wentong, a Sichuan University history professor, joined the ordinary citizens as a teahouse regular. He did not give tests to his students in the classroom, but at a teahouse in Riverview Park next to the university. Students went there in small groups to take exams, and Meng paid for their tea. In addition, his method of testing was unorthodox in that instead of asking his students questions, they asked him. He judged their academic progress by the quality of their questions. If a student asked a particularly good question, Meng would smile and comment, all while smoking a long pipe. If any student needed extra tutoring, he would invite the student to the teahouse next door to his home, "to discuss things, while drinking tea, that you would never hear in the classroom."[22] Because Professor Meng was doing this during the repressive period of Early Socialism in Chengdu, it stands out as a continuity of the free practice at universities that existed during the Republican period. It tells us that although the government increasingly enforced its control on all fronts, professors still could have some liberties in the public space. Ironically, such a way of teaching would not be permitted in today's universities, which are run with heavy bureaucratic management.

Thus we see that the teahouse remained popular for a considerable period under the CCP regime. Until the eve of the Cultural Revolution, people in Chengdu enjoyed themselves there, despite increasing anti-teahouse sentiment from the government and in the overall political discourse. Soon, this picture would change. The Cultural Revolution would deal teahouses a serious blow, causing them and other elements of voluntary public life to nearly disappear. Public life in Chengdu reached its lowest point.

Contradictions in the Mixture of Industrial Development and Teahouse Life

Historically, Chengdu was built on commerce and handicraft industries. *People's Daily* in 1954 published an article titled "The Way Out for Craftsmen in Chengdu" (Chengdu shougongye zhe de chulu), which underscored a special relationship between small-time craftsmen and teahouses. The article noted that "dealing with exploitation by middlemen" was the most painful issue for craftsmen. Apart from the small number who had their own shops, to make sales most had to rely on brokers, who worked out of public view in backstreets and alleyways. In slack seasons, various craftsmen sold products to merchants or to "bottom shops" (*ditang*), namely, buyers in teahouses who offered rock-bottom prices to desperate craftsmen. For example, the Great Ambition Teahouse (Yuanda chaguan) on Leather Shop Street (Pifang jie) was a "bottom shop" for leather shoes. Shoemakers brought shoes there, and the brokers would appear uninterested. Finally, they would examine the shoes, criticize for flaws, and offer the lowest possible price.[23]

The same article revealed the general state of the economy in Chengdu. The government described Chengdu as "a famous handicraft city, with streets lined with handicraft shops" clustered by type. For example, tanning workshops were concentrated on Leather Shop Street and wooden goods in Cookware Alley (Luoguo xiang). Handicrafts in the early 1950s, it was pointed out, accounted for 98 percent of Chengdu's industrial establishments, 74 percent of the total number of employed people, and 41 percent of total industrial output. There were ninety-six handicraft professions, including brick masons, tilers, and others related to construction materials and equipment; makers of harnesses and iron and wooden farming implements; and suppliers of industrial raw materials, as well as all kinds of jobs related to the production of furniture and other household necessities, for a total of more than ninety-five hundred kinds of products.[24] Under the new government crackdown, however, handicraft sales became more difficult and gradually gave way to the rise of large-scale heavy industries.

After 1949, to frequent teahouses was increasingly considered a negative social activity, so the decline of the teahouse was regarded as evidence of social progress. In 1956, Zhang Yan described his two visits to the city, before and after 1949, in a long *People's Daily* essay, "Back to Chengdu." During his first visit at the end of 1946, soon after the Japanese surrender, Zhang observed people loafing in teahouses, and he left Chengdu disappointed. Upon his return in 1956, the city gave him "a first impression of being brand new," but he was able to relate this new city to the old Chengdu.[25] Zhang thought that the city's most prominent change was its roads. Just six years after the Communists' takeover, the government had renovated more than one hundred kilometers of roads, and almost all the main streets were asphalt or cement, many having been widened from twelve meters to twenty meters. Medians with flower beds, hibiscus bushes, and sycamores were added to a few major roads. Zhang said that the most dramatic change was in the area of the old Imperial City (Huangcheng), formerly a "famous slum, full of broken streets and alleys, smelly and dirty, with mud everywhere, next to a mountain of garbage that had accumulated over decades." Now, however, the entrance to the Imperial City featured a wide asphalt street, called People's Road South (Renmin nanlu), where celebrations were held on International Labor Day (May 1) and National Day (October 1). Yet it should be mentioned that the road construction caused many street-corner teahouses to be removed, never to be reopened.

Zhang went on to praise the achievement of having replaced mountains of garbage with a stadium that could hold thirty thousand people. Also, the smelly Imperial River had been broadened and deepened, allowing a flow of clean water into the city. There also was tremendous construction beneath the roads. Less than two months after the takeover, the government dealt with the sewer system, the top concern of residents throughout the city. Nearly one hundred thousand people helped clean the city's rivers and the drainage system and built a new, concrete sewer system that could serve two hundred thousand inhabitants—one of the major, early successes for the government.[26] Chengdu frequently suffered from serious flooding during the Republican period, but the new government solved this problem within a short time.[27]

While Zhang did not focus on teahouses per se, he expounded on Chengdu's new, "progressive" image and undoubtedly considered any remaining teahouses to be associated with old, "negative" characteristics—in line with the general trend, as mentioned earlier, for elites (now cadres and journalists) to characterize teahouses as breeding grounds for social and political problems. He saw Chengdu's rising "forest of smoking chimneys and water towers" as the beginning of its transformation into a "future industrial city," incompatible with teahouses. Chengdu was a conventional consumption city, and the CCP included it in its ambitious plan for the establishment of industrial cities. In the office of the Commission of Urban Construction, Zhang saw a huge blueprint of Chengdu and noted it was anticipated that by 1962 the whole city would be "factories rising up level upon level." In its ten-to-twenty-square-kilometer center, chimneys and high buildings would be "as dense as forests." Beyond twenty kilometers would be "workers' towns" (*gongren zhen*), "like satellites defending this huge, socialist, industrial city."[28] This was obviously a complete departure from the city's accustomed economy and consumption habits, and public spaces for everyday life such as teahouses hardly found a place in an aggressive "socialist construction" that had many aspects to it of Maoist modernization campaigns. Zhang's report precisely reflected the government's nationwide policy regarding the urban economy. As Ying-mao Kau found, "Since it assumed power in 1949, the new Communist leadership in China has given priority to modernization and industrialization among its major national goals."[29] Such policies reflect the intense mood of the party at that time toward a much-desired industrialization that party leaders thought would quickly transform China into a strong nation.

Teahouses faced another sort of difficulty, one shared by all small businesses. After the socialist transformation from 1953 to 1956, the government required all shops to renew their licenses, but it denied many applications.[30] In 1957, only 3,598 Chengdu shops were granted registrations; of these, 2,393 were public-private, small-trade partnerships, and 2,211 were businesses operating from households.[31] According to a table on handicraft production and the development of the socialist transformation of Chengdu, in 1949 there were 10,997 handicraft households, employing 31,427 people, but the number was reduced to 1,825 households in 1956, after most had been turned into "organized units," usually called "collective ownerships" (*jiti suoyou zhi*), for example, street factories (*jiedao gongchang*) and collaborative shops (*hezuo shangdian*).[32] In January 1957, on the eve of the Great Leap Forward campaign, the city had a total of 438 teahouses, plus 26 "tiger stoves" (places where hot or boiling water was sold on a take-out basis), further dropping the number about a quarter, from 541 in 1951. The number of employees dropped from 3,885 in 1951 to 2,128 in 1957, a decrease of 45 percent.[33] In a significant shift, some teahouses became state-owned enterprises, which had never before existed.

This campaign reached its zenith in 1958 as part of the Great Leap Forward, when collectives replaced families and private life; as a result, voluntary public life diminished and new problems arose when almost everything in life became collective.[34] There is very little information about teahouses in Chengdu at this time. According to some accounts on the Great Famine of the late 1950s and early 1960s, Mao arrived in Chengdu on March 4, 1958. He toured the city the next day accompanied by the head of the Provincial Committee of the CCP. When Mao saw the city wall, he said, "The city wall in Beijing has been dismantled. This wall not only does not look good but also blocks traffic, which makes it difficult to come in and go out of the city. The city wall represents backwardness. Therefore, it is progress to dismantle it." Sometime that year, the Chengdu city wall was gone. During the same tour, from the window of the car, Mao found a unique urban landscape: many teahouses. Mao believed that it was a waste to spend too much money on drinking tea in a teahouse and expressed criticism. "The head understood what Mao meant, and teahouses disappeared immediately."[35] Although there are no official records to corroborate it, such a criticism definitely matches Mao's basic understanding of cities and city life. In his mind, the teahouse, like the city wall, represented the past—something to be abandoned.

Teahouses, however, would not be gone easily. An article in *People's Daily* in December 1958 with the headline "To Make Commune Life Colorful, Pi County Maintains and Improves Restaurants, Wine Shops, and Teahouses" describes how the government of the Chengdu outskirts sought to better manage its dining halls, adjust its policies to better meet people's multifaceted needs, and enrich life overall. The article stated that Pi County achieved its goal: more than forty thousand farming households had their meals in communal dining halls. Because these could not meet everyone's needs, the county party committee decided to allow peasants to keep cookstoves and allowed restaurants, wine shops, teahouses, and tofu shops to remain in business. Teahouses "facilitated tea-drinking for farmers" and offered magazines, newspapers and performances as part of the rural "cultural paradise" (*wenhua leyuan*) (see figure 3.4).[36]

Figure 3.4 A suburban Chengdu teahouse, July 2003. Author photo.

The radical policy during the Great Leap Forward that nearly eradicated teahouses eventually had to be relaxed. Although we do not know if this was in response to peasants' complaints, it shows that even in the most intense part of this campaign, teahouses to a certain extent managed to survive. It is important to note that Pi County played an important role in the Great Leap Forward. In March 1958, the Politburo of the CCP Central Committee held a meeting in Chengdu to prepare for the full-scale launch, during which Chairman Mao visited Pi County and set the tone for the movement.[37] Despite its radical nature, however, the Great Leap Forward could not destroy the teahouses: they were too embedded in the local culture.

Politics and Class Struggle in the Teahouse

At first glance, teahouses after 1950 differed little from those in the Republican era, but the political world that had entered them grew increasingly intense.[38] The street-side entrances to most street-corner teahouses, as in the past, were secured with removable wooden boards that were taken down one by one when the teahouse opened, and the rooms contained bamboo chairs and low, square tables on which lidded tea bowls were placed. A significant change, however, was that the public notices on the wall saying "Do Not Talk about National Affairs" were replaced by posters obligating customers to "praise the Communist Party," as well as "slogans of the new society." Before 1949, relatively educated teahouse owners had decorated wall spaces with elegant poems or insightful phrases. After 1949, however, with one political movement following another, teahouse walls and posts were overtaken by government posters, documents, and notifications, another reminder that one could not escape the state and its politics.

Many teahouse owners and workers came from the type of loosely organized secret society known as Gowned Brothers and naturally became objects of attack by the new regime. According to the 1955 registration lists for the Sichuan opera troupe at the Garden of Ease Teahouse (Suiyuan chashe), the teahouse had twelve employees (only one of whom was female); in the column of the list for "participants in enemy organizations," three had left the question blank, one wrote "private school for four years," and the rest—that is, almost two-thirds—stated "no political party but membership in the Gowned Brothers."[39] In fact, many folk performers had joined what were being deemed as "reactionary organizations" like the Gowned Brothers, the GMD, or the Three Principles Youth League to ensure their very survival during the chaotic period.

The Hundred Flowers and Anti-rightist Campaigns in the late 1950s profoundly affected teahouse commerce and culture. In previous scholarship, the policies of these campaigns were thought to have been aimed only at intellectuals, but archival data show that even commoners such as small traders were caught up.[40] Based on the registration forms for "rectified learning among mainstays of the industrial and commercial sectors," the "political identity" of manager Ma of the Whistling Song Teahouse (Yinxiao chashe) was that of a member of the "Democratic National Construction Party," with a "middle leftist" (*zhongzuo*) "political attitude." The archival reports of opinions from a variety of persons that were expressed during the Hundred Flowers included business owners' thoughts on current policies. Some expressed dissatisfaction in a moderate way: for example, "I think our wages have actually been reduced under the wage reform, which violates the principle of keeping wages constant," and "the union does not educate workers but focuses only on class stratification." There are materials containing secret exposures, in which someone noted Ma's complaints that "the government does not pay attention to private business owners."[41] From these, we can see that the government kept careful watch over words and deeds, and its control was much tighter than ever before. People soon realized that they had to be active participants in whichever political movement came along, but nonetheless keep their mouths shut to avoid trouble. (Later in this chapter, in the story of a Mr. Jiang, we have a good example of the danger people faced because of conversations in the teahouse.)

Some people were classified as "counter-socialist elements" simply because of their past experiences or the content of the plays or songs they performed. For example, a certain Mr. Luo was born poor, and he eventually became a storyteller. In 1949, he joined the Gowned Brothers and then became an officer in the Anti-Communist National Salvation Army (Fan gong jiuguo jun). Because he turned himself in and "made a fresh start," he was not put under surveillance. Later, someone accused Luo of being a GMD secret agent, but according to "Document of Counter-Socialist

Element Luo," dated to 1958, the allegation was of "unknown origin." Luo continued to make a living as a storyteller and joined a folk performance troupe in 1953 but was expelled in 1955 for "fornication." He then went to Tibet and elsewhere, "profiting" by making 7,000 to 8,000 yuan as a storyteller. He returned to the troupe in 1957.[42] During the Anti-rightist Movement, Luo was identified as a "counter-socialist element." The reason, according to the 1958 document, was simply that he had criticized some aspects of society in his writings and shows. Charges against him included the following:

- "Writing reactionary stories and opposing the CCP's leadership." During the Hundred Flowers, Luo reconfigured the one-act satire *The Headman's Clothes* (*Shouzhang de yiguan*) into a storytelling program. For this he was accused of "demonizing party cadres and attacking party leadership" in a section of his performance that said "They flatter their superiors but make a show of authority to their inferiors. When their superiors want to smoke, they quickly get lights for them; when they want to have tea, they rush to pour boiling water; and when they cough, they quickly get a spittoon. But when it comes to the people's primary concerns, they do not care. Their only concern is the impression they give their superiors."

- "Slandering the reform policies regarding performers and pitting people against the party." This, indeed, is a very serious accusation, one that, according to the document, was based on his comments during the Hundred Flowers policy, namely, that "the folk performance reform has problems" and that "implementation of the ban on superstitious and pornographic programs has gone too far." He noted that officials banned programs without telling why, and some performers suffered persecution and some "committed suicide." He brought up the previous discrimination against folk performers and asked, "Why does the new society still despise us?"

- "Telling bad and toxic stories." The document claimed that Luo had consistently performed "bad" stories that had a "bad influence," "without review by his superiors."

- "Fabricating facts in order to mislead." The document stated that after visiting Tibet in 1957, Luo told others about the carnage of the PLA's suppression of uprisings that year, in which "bodies were piled high like a mountain." He also described how "tens of thousands of people wanted to take back Lhasa, but the PLA warned them that they would blow up the Potala Palace if they rioted." Another anecdote was that once when he was in a movie theater, "someone in the audience fired a gun and killed several people on the spot."

- "Immoral behavior and fornication." The document revealed that before 1949, Luo liked to visit brothels and was addicted to gambling. After remarrying following a 1955 divorce, he toured for the People's Liberation Army and was accused of having a "suspicious relationship" (*aimei guanxi*) with an actress.[43]

Luo's alleged "counter-socialist" words and deeds were from our point of view trivial: criticizing policies, carrying on with a woman, and making rumors. During the 1950s, however, as social and economic life became increasingly politicized, trivial things added up to serious "crimes" if one were categorized as "counter-socialist." Some managers and performers were expelled from teahouses, some had to close their businesses, and some were even arrested as counterrevolutionaries. Luo's criticisms have in fact been proven correct in hindsight, and the situations he described are still common in China today. From a contemporary perspective, he was a man who had independent thoughts and the courage to criticize authorities, but during that radical age, this made him a criminal. As Perry Link points out, under the socialist state, political satire was a dangerous business, even when performers' motivations were patriotic.[44] The government continued its more specific attacks on small-business owners and teahouse performers and managers into the 1960s, except for short periods of recovery under Liu Shaoqi's retrenchment.[45]

Luo's fate may reflect the experiences of a great number of performers who had had brushes with the law and whose sole objective was to live and work under the new system, with no intention of opposing the party or government. Perry Link notes as well, in his study of the whimsical and satirical genre of cross-talkers, that performers wanted to use a satirical approach to explore the mistakes of the cadres, the superiors, and the government as a way to help improve their new society; but they did not understand the danger. He uses the metaphor of "crocodile birds," which pluck food residue from crocodiles' mouths and help crocodiles clean their teeth, all the while making themselves vulnerable to being eaten.[46] If a performer were careless in speech or behavior, he would find himself in a dangerous situation.

Folk Performance in the Early 1960s

In the early 1960s under Liu Shaoqi's relaxed policies, folk perform-ers in Chengdu began returning to their craft following both the famine of 1959–1961 and the massive political movements of the late 1950s. Under the specific Liu policy of the "Three Selves and One Guarantee," people had a little more freedom and could recover their small busi-nesses.[47] Teahouse owners were quick to take advantage of this oppor-tunity, which in turn provided a platform for the resurgence of popular entertainment. Party cadres noticed this and reacted. As described in the "Work Plan for the Investigation, Management, and Disposition of Itin-erant Folk Performers" issued in December 1962 by the Chengdu Bureau of Culture, there was a trend of growing numbers of itinerant entertain-ers who performed "unhealthy programs." In fact, the Bureau of Cul-ture overreacted. The presence of sixty entertainers in a city of more than a million residents hardly constituted a tidal wave. This number was much lower than the total of 405 in 1955, and greatly reduced from the Republican era.[48]

Nevertheless, the government decided to register and strengthen its oversight of this group: it would organize them, limit their growth in number, "improve their minds," and transform them into servants for socialist propaganda. The principle behind the government's handling of this matter was to treat entertainers differently based on their situations. "Real performing artists" (i.e., registered entertainers) who did not have another suitable career were issued a temporary performing permit to perform only in assigned places. Those who had another form of employ-ment in 1958 were denied permits and forced to make a living elsewhere. Amateur, part-time entertainers were eliminated immediately. Performers who were allowed to continue were made to study regularly to "improve their thinking and understanding."[49] We can see many similarities with the measures carried out in the mid-1950s concerning bench-sitter opera, as discussed in chapter 2.

Based on the December 1962 work plan, there were a total sixty per-formers, falling into the same categories that were commonly deployed in statistical surveys: twenty-eight storytellers, twelve bamboo clapper singers, five pure singers, four bamboo dulcimer singers, four lotus sing-ers, three flower-drum singers, three magicians, and one plate singer (who beat rhythms on a plate while singing). The main reason for the increase at that time was that those who had arranged for other jobs in 1958 left their positions after the Great Leap Forward campaign caused closure or worker reductions at many factories. The descriptions noted that some of these performers had "complicated backgrounds" as former secret agents, reactionary officers, and rightists. Most were forty to fifty years old, traveling between teahouses to make a living without access to a permanent stage. They performed once or twice a day and tried to accommodate "lowbrow tastes" to ensure larger audiences and incomes. They earned generally three to five yuan per day; the lowest was one yuan, while the highest, more than ten yuan. Some top earners, the report said, enjoyed "lives of luxury."[50]

On January 12, 1963, the Bureau of Culture, the Bureau of Public Security, and the Second Bureau of Commerce jointly enacted "instructions on strengthening the management of itinerant performing folk artists" in response to the "rapid growth" of this group. The instructions noted that "the performances were mostly good, and politically healthy, playing a positive role in publicizing the party's principles and policies and encouraging people's enthusiasm for work. They have appropriately met most of the people's needs for culture and entertainment."[51] In July 1964, the Bureau of Culture issued a notification requiring teahouse workers to assist the government in "firmly stopping performing folk artists who present bad stories"; it was necessary because of the considerable number of itinerants who gave "unhealthy programs" and did not obtain government approval. Teahouse owners and employees were required to actively support "modern programs" and oppose "superstitious, obscene, and absurd performances."[52] Apparently, the definitions of these terms were decided by officials who had clearly negative attitudes toward folk genres and a tendency to discriminate against those performers. Why, in early 1963, did the bureau seem to have no problem with folk performers, but in mid-1964 it turned negative? This switch actually reflects the nationwide change in political climate. After the Great Famine, Mao's radical policy was replaced by Liu Shaoqi's more realistic one, which not only gave more space for economic recovery but also exerted less control of people's daily lives. However, beginning in mid-1963, Mao launched the "Socialist Education Movement" (Shehui zhuyi jiaoyu yundong) and ended the short, relatively free period.

Popular entertainment in any culture as a rule will, in the long run, remain vital.[53] In China, especially in Chengdu, the performers returned to the teahouse stages after the Great Famine, as mentioned. What is of note in this case is that their programs were predominantly traditional, in defiance of the government's great effort after 1949 to establish "socialist entertainment" that could do away with "superstition" and "pornography" and any efforts to discredit the "party's principles and policies"—the terminology most often used by government officials, elites, and others who spearheaded reformist and revolutionary discourse throughout the second half of the twentieth century. Despite the state's harshest efforts, the older, well-known programs could not be eliminated entirely. That came only later, via the Cultural Revolution, the "revolutionary culture" that ultimately usurped all public spaces and stages.

Survival through the Radical Years

Few records about teahouses during the 1960s remain, mostly because teahouses' role in daily life and importance to the city's economy shrank dramatically, but we can glean information from statistics about businesses in Chengdu. Despite government control, small trades managed to survive—although unofficial and illegal. In the early 1960s, for example, the traders in Chinese medicine had set up their regular market at the city's northern train station, where they conducted inter-province trade in commodities. One unspecified report showed over five thousand long-distance traders going there daily in the early 1960s. Teahouses also resumed their role in the economy as "stores of market information, brokering deals between buyers and sellers." Traders of Chinese medicine operated illegally in two teahouses, which were shut down during the Cultural Revolution. Then, the trade moved to the teahouses outside the northern train station; one such was the Red Flag Teahouse, a cooperatively owned establishment near the train station. Another man opened the Blue Dragon (Qinglong) Teahouse as a competitor, starting the so-called teahouse war.[54]

In 1962, the Chengdu municipal government restored the certification and licensing requirements for all industrial and commercial enterprises and for those private businesses involved with commodity production, transportation, food and drink, personal services, culture, and entertainment. No business was allowed to operate without a license. The total of state-owned and jointly owned industrial and commercial enterprises was only 6,006. But by 1964, the figure dropped to just 1,065, including 113 food-related businesses. At the same time, of 1,622 collectively owned enterprises, 196 were food-related, including teahouses (which were no longer a separate category for registration purposes).[55]

My research fortunately encountered statistics in the city's archives pertaining to teahouses on the eve of the Cultural Revolution. The "Registration of Industrial and Commercial Enterprises" of March 1966 states that Chengdu had 167 teahouses, which employed 1,395 people and had a total capital of 228,124 yuan, "reserve funds" (*gongji jin*) of 192,455 yuan, and "public welfare funds" (*gongyi jin*) of 29,260 yuan.[56] Also, according to the business registration of the West City District on March 15, 1966, there were eighteen "cooperative teahouses" (*hezuo chashe*), which had sixty branches and employed 429 people with a total capital of 91,057 yuan, reserve funds of 84,171 yuan, and public welfare funds of 10,273 yuan. These teahouses were all collectively owned.[57] This tells us that on the eve of the Cultural Revolution, the number of teahouses in Chengdu had gone from more than 600 in 1949 to 167, with a corresponding decrease in the number of employees— from 3,885 in 1951 (see above) to only 1,395 in 1966, a decline of two-thirds.[58]

Despite the best efforts of those driving the "revolutionary lifestyle," teahouses continued to play a role in people's daily lives. References in newspapers and official documents dwindled to almost nothing, but information is found in unofficial sources such as memoirs and diaries. For example, Ma Shitu, mentioned earlier, who was once deputy director of the Department of Propaganda of the CCP committee in Sichuan, recalled that when Zhu De, PLA marshal and chairman of the People's Congress, came to Chengdu in the early 1960s, he wanted to drink tea from a customary three-piece tea set (bowl, lid, and saucer), but none was available. Tea drinking in teahouses was called "drinking lidded-bowl tea" (*he gaiwan cha*). The saucer was used to cradle the bowl underneath and prevent spills. The lid that covered the bowl was used to keep the water hot, and also, when tipped downward, it stirred the tea leaves and kept the leaves in place when drinking. Zhu, a native of the province, criticized the city for wrongly closing down teahouses and abandoning a bit of material culture with which he was familiar.[59]

In the spring of 1963, historian Xie Guozhen of the Chinese Academy of Science was invited by Professor Xu Zhongshu, chair of the History Department of Sichuan University, to deliver a series of lectures. Xie noted in his diary that the first thing he noticed about Chengdu was the prevalence of teahouses filled with working people sitting in bamboo chairs at low, wooden tables, sipping tea and relaxing. For the next three weeks or so, he described numerous teahouse visits in his diary: meeting friends, preparing his lecture notes, listening to the bench-sitters' performances, and watching other shows.[60] Xie's diary reflects the "real" Chengdu and the texture of the city's intellectual life, which apparently could be found in a public space that could appeal to professors; and this was only three years before the Cultural Revolution. We have here another piece of evidence of the embedded vitality of the teahouse in everyday life, despite the negative environment in these years of Early Socialism.

But just as in the Republican era, teahouse life contained hidden dangers, namely the trouble that resulted from conversations about politics. In fact, under the previous GMD government, secret agents of the police would go to a teahouse to collect intelligence; they could arrest anyone who criticized the government and could force a teahouse to close if it faced such an accusation. That was why there was a public notice "Do Not Talk about National Affairs" (*xiutan guoshi*) on the wall in almost all teahouses.[61] A similar danger existed after 1949. For example, Mr. Jiang, a bank employee categorized as a "bad element" after 1949, frequented teahouses. In 1966, based solely on secret reports by his fellow teahouse-goers, Jiang was charged with critical attacks against the following: Chairman Mao (because he criticized his "cult of personality"); the "Three Red Flags" (Sanmian hongqi), because he talked about the widespread starvation of the "Three Bad Years"; and domestic and foreign policies. After being publicly denounced, he was arrested and spent eight years in a labor camp.[62] Jiang was one of many who paid a high price for statements uttered in a teahouse.

As soon as the Cultural Revolution was launched in 1966, teahouses became easily associated with the "old way of life" and thus an obvious target of attack.[63] Under the powerful "Breaking up the 'Four Olds' Campaign," to patronize teahouses was considered a "bad habit of the old society," and teahouses were regarded as filthy gathering places for "class dissidents" (*jieji yiji fengzi*) and "backward masses" (*luohou qunzhong*). Teahouses were forcibly closed; some disappeared, and some were transformed into "tiger stoves"—not public sites but places only for buying hot water. The tiger stoves were not as plentiful as teahouses; there was only about one for every three or four streets.[64]

Jung Chang recalled in her famous autobiography, *Wild Swans*, how teahouses were forcibly closed in Chengdu at the beginning of the Cultural Revolution. At the time, she and two dozen other students, most of whom were Red Guards, went to a teahouse to shout: "Pack up! Pack up! Don't linger in this bourgeois place!" A boy even jerked a paper chessboard off a table, sending the wooden pieces flying to the ground while he shouted, "No more chess! Don't you know it is a bourgeois habit?" He later threw a handful of the pieces into the river. A few students attached slogans to the teahouse walls. Some demanded that the manager shut the teahouse down. They chased many patrons away.[65]

By this time, street politics in Chengdu had reached an extreme, with a variety of factions of mass organizations each pressing its own power and expressing loyalty to Mao in public places. The so-called Black Five Elements (Hei wulei)—landlords, rich peasants, counterrevolutionaries, bad elements, and rightists—were denounced, humiliated, and paraded through the streets while Red Guard propaganda teams performed the "loyalty dance" and other revolutionary activities. Eventually, street violence escalated into full-scale street wars, complete with public executions among factions of the mass organizations of armed workers and the Red Guard. "Big character posters" were pasted everywhere: streets, parks, schools, factories, and government offices. Since all schools were closed for the "revolution," local youths had nothing to occupy their time but loitering on the streets. The entire nation fell into a state of frenzy. How could such a world accommodate the simple pleasures offered by the teahouse?[66]

I can give only a very brief sketch of teahouses during the Cultural Revolution, because there is little material evidence, a situation caused not only by the precipitous decline in the number of teahouses under such a radical political environment and the attacks by the Red Guard, but also by the accompanying overall diminishment of the role of the teahouse as a staple of everyday life and the dearth of descriptions of teahouse life in the news media, given the perception by radical leftists that teahouses reflected a "feudal" and "backward" lifestyle. During the early stage of the Cultural Revolution, cultural and recreational life, as sociologist Martin Whyte stresses, was "impoverish[ed]." People were required "to participate in a narrow range of activities over and over again, the most dramatic case being the repetitiously performed model revolutionary operas."[67] Later during the Cultural Revolution people did have a little more choice of cultural diversion, but this consisted almost entirely of "revolutionary," "political," or "educational" shows, not any for entertainment and leisure.

Yet it is not surprising that some can recall their experience in the Cultural Revolution without exhibiting very much stress or anxiety. Whyte offers an explanation: "For many urban young people this was an exhilarating time, at least initially. Instead of being locked into a tight competition to try and secure future opportunities in the urban job hierarchy, they found themselves called to act on a larger and more important stage as the vanguards in a new revolution."[68] They might have simply enjoyed some innocent loosening of restraints, but instead many lost their only opportunity to get an education, and we know that many people were killed in the widespread violence. Today, as the generation of the Red Guard has dominated CCP leadership and areas of the economy, education, and the military, people are still debating how and to what extent the Cultural Revolution impacted and changed their lives forever.[69]

I would like to emphasize that to evaluate public life during the Cultural Revolution requires us to look not just at the main trends but also the exceptions that illustrate them. Of course, despite the times, people still conducted their daily lives and still sought entertainment, but faced many more (and unique) difficulties than previously. Public life became dangerous. "In the early period of the Cultural Revolution people were in danger of being stopped on the street and having their hair cut or their clothing torn if they were not wearing the proper proletarian style."[70] Chaos reigned, and violence spread. Public life was more controlled than private life, where state power faced limitations, but the state remained ever watchful. There are countless examples of residents whose homes were invaded without provocation by those who ostensibly were involved with street or neighborhood watches. There is no question people did not have basic freedoms and did not feel safe in their conduct in spheres of

Figure 3.5 An old teahouse in a Chengdu suburb, September 2015. Traces of
the Cultural Revolution still remain on the wall, where we see the slogan
"Long Live Chairman Mao." Author photo.

public life. As a result, the space allotted for public life grew increasingly
small. Although people appeared in public and undertook daily tasks
there, and had many chances to watch revolutionary dances and songs
performed on the street or parades for ersatz celebrations of "revolutionary victory" or "victory of Maoist Thought," or Mao's birthday, this was
but a hollow and corrupt shell of the type of public life I defined in the
introduction (see figure 3.5).

During the late 1960s, in what has been termed the middle period of
the Cultural Revolution, teahouses, especially those in parks, experienced
something of a revival because they served as rest stops—a useful purpose,
given the insults to public life. Of course, many basic functions had to be
changed: for example, instead of being served by waiters, guests had to
stand in line to get boiling water from a barrel. The bamboo chairs with
arms were replaced by stools, so that lingering became uncomfortable.
This made teahouses lose some of their appeal.[71] Beyond physical accou-
trements, the teahouse atmosphere became very tense. Various public

notices and prohibitions by the "people's security group" (*renbao zu*) and "mass dictatorship group" (*qunzhuan zu*) were pasted at entrances or on counters.[72] The state, while powerful in its effort to control every aspect of society, inevitably missed some spots. For example, fortune-tellers still conducted their business in the teahouse, albeit secretly. Hawkers found a way to sell their goods in teahouses, despite strict prohibitions. Beggars, seen as causing socialism to "lose face" and thus forbidden in public places, also continued their presence there.[73] But in general, the numbers shrank to the point that this old, useful way of public life in public spaces could no longer play an important role in people's everyday lives. All this would change virtually overnight with Mao's death and the fall of the "Gang of Four" in 1976.

Part II

THE RETURN OF PUBLIC LIFE, 1977–2000

Mao's death and the arrest of the "Gang of Four" in 1976 ushered China into a new era. Deng Xiaoping's reforms and opening-up policy completely changed the face of socialist China, not only in the broad areas of politics, economics, and culture, but also in everyday life, in which people gained certain freedoms. Indeed, from 1977 to 2000, the focus of the nation was on the economy and its development. Although the CCP no longer held mass political movements, politics still, however, was not entirely divorced from cultural and social life, and the party firmly kept to the principle of "socialism with Chinese characteristics." The period from 1979 to 1989 is regarded as having been the freest time for ideologies under the Communist regime; people experienced relatively more freedom in thought, social activities, and political involvements. During the late 1970s and 1980s, along with economic reforms such as the creation of the Special Economic Zone, encouragement of international trade, arrival of foreign investments, and the notion of "citizens' engaging in business," there were ideological and political struggles as well. The latter included the "Democracy Wall," the "Bourgeois Liberalization," and the "June Fourth Movement," and these became hot topics in the teahouses. During the 1990s, Western-style stock markets opened, migrant peasant workers flooded into the cities, state-owned factories laid off workers, and local governments everywhere undertook, for better or worse, land clearance and new construction. Along with these changes, public life flourished in China, and in Chengdu as well. As before, we are able to detect the impact on people in Chengdu through the microcosmic elements of the city—the teahouses.

The following three chapters show the recovery and flourishing of teahouses and public life during the post-Mao reforms and the opening-up policies. We will find how the teahouses adopted to the new environment and offered space for a variety of social groups, such as writers, amateur performers, and retirees. Subsequently, we come to understand how teahouses could provide livelihoods for large numbers of migrant workers, who enriched public life with their services. Public entertainment could cause conflicts, and we witness this through a vastly popular pastime—mahjong. The game inspired a national debate over "healthy entertainment" and the city's image, and it gives us the opportunity to observe how a local issue reflected a national problem and to what extent people's public lives were changed, or not changed, under the wave of commercialization and globalization.

4

The Resurgence of Teahouses in the Reform Era

The post-Mao reforms fundamentally changed China and provided environments in which teahouses revived and expanded the overall size of their operations.[1] The reforms encouraged people to "exercise initiative and make money, all of which made them less receptive to communist ideology."[2] China's political decisions, from the highest levels, created a type of business environment conducive to small businesses. In 1987 a certain "theory of the preliminary stage of socialism" removed the ideological obstacle to private ownership, and in 1999 an amendment to the constitution granted private businesses equal legal status with the state and collective sectors; these further enhanced China's new markets.

Small businesses sprouted up immediately. By 1996, the retail sector accounted for about 9.2 million very small (one- and two-person) retail shops, of which about 7.8 million were privately owned; about 1.2 million were collectively owned, with an average of six employees each, and accounting for about 28 percent of total sales.[3] But we should be aware of the realities at the time: China did not have a real "market economy."

As Dorothy Solinger points out, "In consequence, the ostensible 'marketizing' of the Chinese economy has resulted in the creation of a 'market system' wherein much economic exchange paradoxically continues to be structured along lines very similar to those that existed under a more centrally planned economy."[4] However, small businesses depended least on the centrally planned economy, and as the latter weakened, teahouses grew in number and in their variety of services. Similarly, as the political chains concerning aspects of everyday life loosened, people increasingly turned to making money and increasing their material quality of life. Growing leniency in the political and economic spheres and the restoration of public life and its relevant infrastructure brought to Chengdu the return of its teahouses—the perennially significant landmarks.[5] To some extent, the renewal of the teahouse business was the best indicator of private enterprise's expansion.

To open a teahouse during the Reform Era was easier to do than ever before. In the Republican period, the Teahouse Guild had tightly controlled the total number of teahouses to avoid serious competition within the trade—and even controlled the price of tea.[6] In the post-Mao period of reform, as long as a person had sufficient capital, he or she simply applied for and received a license. Furthermore, unlike other industries, a teahouse required minimal investments: a rented room, a stove to boil water, and some tables, chairs, and tea bowls. In smaller teahouses, one person could handle everything as manager, waiter, and stove keeper. Of course, the upscale teahouses that started to appear required much larger investments. Before long, Chengdu had more teahouses than at the peak of the Republican era.[7] As a result, business became much more competitive.

During the period being discussed here, street-corner teahouses began to coexist with high-end tea balconies, each one serving different social groups and providing different functions. Their management and operation were virtually the same as in the first half of the twentieth century, except for the lack of a guild.[8] The teahouse, as a small business, had its own way of operating. On the one hand, it had to follow the country's overall economic trends; on the other hand, it had strong and unique geographical components.[9] Unlike in the Republican and Early Socialist periods, and with the ending by the mid-1950s of the New Teahouse Guild along with other guilds (see chapter 1), there was now no guild in Chengdu to control the number of teahouses, so they increased substantially. There were few barriers anymore to entering the business: anyone who went through the easy license and registration process could open up shop. Licensing documents were issued by different government agencies in Chengdu, namely the Bureau of Commerce, the Bureau of Industrial and Commercial Administration, and the Bureau of Sanitation. They generally required basic information, such as the address and name of the owner, type of services offered, and a period of time.[10] But there were also a large number of unregistered teahouses, operating as "neighborhood centers," "internal services," and so on, plus many located in small alleys and areas adjoining the city and countryside. All of them enjoyed a free ride during this golden time for small business.

The Revival of Chengdu's Teahouses

At the end of 1979, in Chengdu there were 2,318 households that engaged in "privately owned businesses"; a year later, the number had risen to 7,242; and by 1982 it reached 16,659. As the government further relaxed restrictions from 1983 to 1985, any resident who met minimum qualifications was able to obtain a business license. Quickly, a trend emerged in which "all citizens were involved in business" (*quanmin jingshang*). Thus, by the end of 1985, the number of household businesses reached 123,901. While there was a slight downward trend in 1986 and 1989, by the end of 1989, 155,675 households in Chengdu owned businesses, counting for 69 percent of the total of 224,225 businesses. The 1989 end-of-year tally of industrial and commercial registrations lists six items under the category "services for residents": travel, hotels, barbers, bath houses, laundries, and photography—but no teahouses. However, the category named "public food and drink businesses" (*gonggong yinshi ye*) had 5,226 firms engaging 43,166 employees. It is in this category that I assume teahouses were included.[11] It is worth mentioning that although the June Fourth Movement was an incident that profoundly changed politics in China as well as Chengdu, it did not induce a change in teahouse life. Small businesses continued to grow in number after 1989, especially after Deng Xiaoping's Southern Tour.[12]

The private business boom in the 1980s energized teahouses.[13] In 1984, even the *People's Daily* was filled with praise: "'Teahouses, Teahouses': people now talk about them. [But GMD] reactionaries were afraid of teahouses, and during the War of Resistance against the Japanese, big signs were pasted on the walls of teahouses in Chongqing, with the warning, 'Do Not Talk about National Affairs.' The 'Gang of Four' were also afraid of teahouses, so that when the Gang were at the peak of their power, teahouses were forced to shut down."[14]

In fact, the policy toward these public spaces held by the post-1949 Communist regime differed little from that of the Nationalists before them. Both the GMD and the CCP held a negative attitude toward teahouses, but the Communists implemented much more effective control. Here, the *People's Daily*'s blaming the Gang of Four for the demise of teahouses was clearly inaccurate. As discussed in previous chapters, the decline of the teahouse and the shrinking of public spaces were caused by the broader post-1949 political environment. The public notice "Do Not Talk about National Affairs" posted by teahouses in the Republican era was never found there under socialism. Under Mao's rule, the posting of such messages was seen as evidence of a certain kind of muted resistance concerning the very lack of freedom of speech, and so they became forbidden.

When the author of the 1984 *People's Daily* article arrived in Chengdu, he saw that teahouses "may not have rebounded back to their original scale" but that any sort of resurgence reflected "the country's peace and order, and highly democratic environment." This is indeed an accurate observation of the teahouse as microcosm of the changes in the larger society, reflecting the wholesale positive expectation that people had for a new era (although it should be added that the teahouse has never become a "highly democratic environment"). Of particular note was his comment that, as "increasingly more cadres retire, they will get tired of staying at home. So, they can go to the teahouse for fresh air and to hear people's views that they cannot get from official meetings. Wouldn't it be great if they could learn the pros and cons of the policies from listening to conversations? Times have changed, so have today's teahouses."[15] The author was also correct that no other places were better than the teahouse for finding out people's opinions. It is interesting to compare this article with the *People's Daily* article cited in chapter 3. We can see that with political changes, the newspaper that represented directly the official voice of the CCP and the central government had changed its attitude toward the teahouse, and this naturally boosted the increase in numbers of teahouses.

Around 1990, however, the number of street-corner teahouses in the small streets and back alleys decreased dramatically because of the large-scale demolition and reconstruction of Chengdu's urban landscape. Yet by the mid-1990s, these lower-level teahouses reclaimed their market share relative to middle- and high-level teahouses. Each of the three levels had several hundred teahouses, targeting different clientele. Furthermore, a large number of "mahjong houses" (*majiang guan*) had opened by this time. Thus, as the consensus grew that street-corner teahouses were too shabby, dirty, and noisy, they tried to attract more patrons by adding video shows. The mid-level teahouses were comfortable and clean, providing good service, a variety of tea, elegant tables and chairs, and decor, and they continued to draw customers.[16]

Chengdu's teahouses left a deep impression on foreigners who went there following China's opening. In his book on Chengdu, the Japanese scholar Naitō Rishin vividly describes teahouses, especially those in parks, which were constantly overflowing with patrons sipping tea, eating various snacks, and chatting about everything from gossip to politics. Naitō believed that Chengdu retained the well-known earlier lifestyles, with the teahouse as an important element.[17] Similarly, Takeuchi Minoru, a professor at Kyoto University, took an opportunity to satisfy his older wish to visit a teahouse in Chengdu. While there, he went to a teahouse at the Bronze Ram Temple (Qingyang gong). Although it had more than one hundred tables, he could not find a seat. He then went to Hundred Flowers Pond Park (Baihua tan) and found a teahouse at the corner of the main entrance, where nearly all of the more than thirty tables were filled. Takeuchi observed that the teahouse "seems like a club for old people in this area." A group of men and women occupied five or six tables, chatting as if holding an informal meeting. The open courtyard held another two or three groups of patrons.[18]

Takeuchi came to the conclusion that "because people in Chengdu are in love with their teahouses, the traditional teahouse is not extinct in China." In addition, he remarked that the teahouses that Lao She described as a symbol of old Beijing had been replaced with a "big-bowl tea culture," the kind of tea business at the sides of streets, for quick consumption. Although teahouses were plentiful elsewhere across China, most were well-decorated, luxurious, and sophisticated facilities, featuring women performing tea ceremonies and tea arts—and they were also expensive. "As for the atmosphere and fun of the old teahouse, nothing is left," Takeuchi lamented. Chengdu, however, was different. "Although there are high-end, luxury teahouses, designed for rich people's ostentatious lifestyles, there are also a lot of rustic teahouses for ordinary citizens." Most of those were in small alleys, or other humble locations such as street-shop houses or riverside bamboo sheds. Some were under a canopy of trees, with a few square tables, a dozen bamboo chairs, plus a stove, large iron pots or copper kettles, and three-piece tea bowls. Takeuchi wrote that these had "become a happy oasis for urban commoners."[19] He believed that the solid, grassroots foundation of teahouse culture in Chengdu made this sustainable.

The functions of teahouses under the reforms of Late Socialism generally differed little from those in the past. Old-style street-corner teahouses, upscale tea balconies, and tea gardens in parks and temples had a long history. One new function did emerge—namely, the below-street-level teahouse-qua-video-room, which became very popular in the 1980s and 1990s. But these went out of business with the addition of dozens of television channels in private homes, the appearance of VCRs and DVDs, and finally the U.S. pressure to enforce intellectual property rights internationally and the subsequent government crackdown on digital products.

The Human Scene in Street-Corner Teahouses

Street-corner teahouses, which, as discussed earlier, were the smallest and least well-appointed, were Chengdu's most common public space for ordinary residents. They usually were one or two rooms with fewer than a dozen tables. They typically opened directly onto the street, with an entrance that was closed and opened with a rolling screen or with several removable wooden planks. This arrangement was very convenient for customers. When the teahouse became overcrowded, people very easily moved tables and chairs out onto the sidewalk or whatever surface was there. My fieldwork indicates that elderly people shopping for vegetables made frequent stops at teahouses. They would drink tea, chat with friends, and peel the outer layers of their produce before proceeding home.

Teahouses were especially concentrated in the Wide and Narrow Alleys district. In the early 2000s, this district was the subject of conservation

Figure 4.1. A shabby teahouse on Broad Ally, June 2003. Author photo.

and rebuilding plans to create a historical zone.[20] On the wall of a shabby teahouse on Wide Alley, a note was written in both Chinese and English: "Tea at one yuan" (see figure 4.1). Foreign travelers stayed at the Hotel International nearby, and this street-corner teahouse sought to lure them in. Walking a bit farther, one could see a teahouse called the Eight Banners Tea Garden (Baqi chayuan), a name obviously adopted in homage to the area's history as part of the old Manchu inner walled city.[21] The teahouse was attractive and elegantly decorated but had few customers. Several steps farther, in the same district, was a very small teahouse, with tables and chairs placed on the sidewalk under the shade of trees. In addition, a plastic shed protected customers from the elements, and they played mahjong as pedestrians stood around watching.[22]

My fieldwork in the summer of 2000 led to an observation of one of the lower-level type of teahouse, named Gathered Happiness Teahouse (Jile chaguan), and to the views of its owner-keeper.[23] The teahouse was on Buddhist Monk Street (Heshang jie), behind the Great Benevolence Temple (Daci si), in an area used as a farmers' market. The teahouse was very small; it had only six tables—four inside and two on the sidewalk—and about thirty to forty bamboo armchairs. It appeared generally old and lacking attention, with a stove in the inner room where the keeper lived. A cup of tea cost from one to five yuan, with the cheapest one being a jasmine tea. The keeper and his wife, both of whom came from a rural area, rented the teahouse from the building owner at a few hundred yuan per month. In an interview, the keeper claimed that opening it had required capital of 6,000 to 7,000 yuan. Across the street were two or three tables with a dozen plastic chairs and a big Chinese *cha* (tea) character on the wall, but those things belonged to a teahouse that had opened a few months earlier and was operating without a license and thus not paying taxes. The keeper said that the business of the illegal teahouse was low: it could not compete with his teahouse, which had had six to seven years of history; and furthermore the reason the authorities did not deal with this violation was that they probably did not know about it or assumed the tables and chairs belonged to his teahouse.

Tradespeople were present at many different times. A constant presence was a young man looking like someone from the country. He ran a bike repair stall in front of the teahouse. Teahouse keepers often charged for setting up stalls outside the door, generally about two yuan per day, but in some cases less. A shoe polisher carrying a toolbox came by, and the owner-keeper asked how much he charged. Later, when a female customer saw a rural-looking man carrying two baskets of peaches, she tried unsuccessfully to negotiate a good deal for them. When a rice peddler passed by, the wife of the keeper asked about his price. Nearby residents bought boiling water at 0.5 yuan (50 cents) per thermos, which were each about a gallon. Although business at the Gathered Happiness was not great, there was always a customer or two. The owner-keeper, who was also the waiter, stated that some were repeat customers. The teahouse was open from 6:30 a.m. until midnight. Every morning, more than a dozen regulars came to the teahouse, most of whom, before their retirement, had worked together at the same factory. They had a rotation system, taking turns buying tea for the whole group. The teahouse charged them only eighty cents per cup. There were other regular groups as well.[24]

Even observations of casual life at the street level tell much about a teahouse and the people associated with it, such as its customers, peddlers, the teahouse keeper, and his wife. We get a sense of everyday life as experienced in an alley-side small teahouse and the close relationships that wound themselves around the teahouse itself and its neighbors and passersby. From that vantage, we see people from all walks of life who depend on each other in many different ways. It was also very interesting to watch how the young migrant couple's work and daily life were seamlessly merged, with no boundary between their living place and business space. Their family life was on full display right before customers' eyes, even if few took notice. In all these ways, the street, teahouse, and people were connected, and from out of this connection public and private spaces emerged conterminously. Such fluid usage of space no doubt helped to increase family coherence and business in the backstreets of an otherwise crowded and prosperous city.[25]

Another small, lower-level of establishment recorded in the fieldwork was the Cloudy Sea Teahouse (Yunhai chaguan) on Three Sages Street (Sansheng jie). It had only six tables—four inside and two just outside the door; these were covered with tablecloths and a bag hung on each side, obviously for gambling money. The owner-keeper was a woman about twenty years old, wearing a blouse, black skirt, and sandals. She rented the space for six months for 10,000 yuan. She said business had been okay: after deducting about 1,500 yuan for rent, more than 100 for taxes, and other expenses, she netted about 1,000 yuan (plus several hundred extra from a public phone service). A sign at the door read, "This teahouse is for sale." She said that more than ten people had inquired, but all believed the price of 14,000 yuan, which she had paid the previous year, was too high. The price covered just the equipment—tables, chairs, stove, television, cups, and bowls—but not the rent.[26]

On a particular day at the Cloudy Sea, one could observe a young man who worked in the drugstore two doors down; between his own customers he would constantly return to drink his tea. Other people concentrated on a televised soccer match. An old man holding newspapers entered and sat by the door. He bought a cup of two-yuan tea and read for forty to fifty minutes, then left. Suddenly, the teahouse keeper spoke loudly: "Sister Wang, do you need help?" She then went outside to help the keeper of a record store move a refrigerator to the sidewalk between the store and the teahouse. Sister Wang needed it to sell cold drinks, and after she opened for business she took tea at the teahouse, sat at a table on the sidewalk, and chatted with the keeper. Several shops were within view across the street: four or five restaurants, two hair salons, and a small clinic. The restaurant workers moved tables and chairs onto the sidewalk in preparation for opening. For almost an hour, only one person entered the teahouse—an old woman carrying a bag of vegetables. She sat and sorted through her produce but did not buy any tea.[27]

Consider also a certain "refreshment bar" (*shuiba*) called Nostalgia Teahouse (Wangri qinghuai chafang) near the Sichuan Provincial Archives on Flower Arch Street (Huapaifang jie). This is an example of a new type of teahouse that sold fruit juices and other beverages in addition to tea. The landlord of the structure housing the teahouse was the Sichuan Provincial Archives, which charged 1,000 yuan per month; and the teahouse proprietor spent more than 300 yuan for the business license and 400 to 500 for the sanitation license, which required that all cups be washed, rinsed, and disinfected. Altogether, she had invested 20,000 to 30,000 yuan on the venture. It had only three tables and twelve chairs. The counter was at the entrance, and it displayed beverages, fruits, and teas in a glass booth. It used an electric stove to boil water. A variety of iced tea was sold at six to seven yuan per cup, while hot tea was five to ten yuan. The room was small but elegant, with flowers in vases on two of the tables and a comfortable temperature, thanks to air conditioning. Just outside was a busy, main street, and the teahouse had been open for only about two weeks. The owner, a woman of about forty to forty-five, told me that costs were higher than at some other teahouses because they used bottled water, not tap water, and the air conditioner was always on. Still, she considered her teahouse to be of the lower type. The shop did not have a door to keep the cool air inside, which wasted electricity, and she said that a door would make people think it was a high-class teahouse, and they would hesitate to come in. This, even though the prices of all drinks were posted on boards just outside.

One of the reasons for going into the business, the owner said, was to help with her daughter's college expenses, which cost "too much" (about 6,000 yuan annually for tuition and lodging, and more than 10,000 yuan to cover her other expenses). She complained that her daughter was spoiled and wasted time at Internet cafés. Thus the owner needed a higher income than the 200 to 300 yuan she had previously earned each month as a government office worker. She had used her compensation from being laid off at the office job in order to open the teahouse. She estimated that she would lose money if sales were less than 4,500 yuan per month, and business so far had been mediocre, at best bringing in about 3,000. In addition to rent, she paid out more than 1,000 yuan on salaries, meals for her workers, water, electricity, and supplies. The location was not ideal, she said, because most of the people moving through the area were migrant workers, who preferred Coca-Cola over fruit juice. She compared her relatively humble location to the eight refreshment bars on Warm Spring Road—one of the most prosperous areas in Chengdu—with each earning 400 yuan per day, or 12,000 yuan per month, against 4,000 yuan per month in rent. She had chosen her location because there were no other refreshment bars nearby. She expected increasing numbers of regular customers, especially young people, as time went on. Business was better at night, when people tended to order to-go, which was beneficial, since the place had only a few tables.[28]

To sum up, the lower sort of teahouse, namely, the street-corner teahouses, attracted loyal customers who required participation in public life in public spaces but could afford only cheap tea. Of course, the teahouse was not the only place for public life: many other public places served this function. For example, Ann Veeck's study of food markets shows that they were, and are, important venues that served as "hubs of socially significant activities."[29] Similar functions are currently being provided by fast food restaurants, dance halls, bowling alleys, and parks.[30]

The Rise of Mid- and High-Level Tea Balconies

In the 1990s, Chengdu experienced broad economic development, which included real estate clearance and buildup. These brought higher-salaried inhabitants, who in turn sparked a rise in the numbers of mid-level and upscale tea balconies. By 2000, there were about eight hundred tea balconies in the city; over a dozen were located by the Funan River. Many large-scale and well-appointed tea balconies were concentrated in the area within the Second Ring Road (Erhuang lu) of the western part of the city. According to a business survey, almost all the latter were establishments of more than one thousand square meters, with some more than twice that. Most customers were middle age or younger, gathering for business meetings or parties, or were young couples meeting outside their homes. Some spent time there simply to read, write, or make phone calls in a climate-controlled environment. Unlike old-style teahouses, such tea balconies did not provide storytelling, operas, or other entertainment beyond soft background music or piano playing, which aimed for a quietude that respected customers' privacy. Strangers in the lower-level type teahouses shared tables and talked to each other, but customers in the fancier places rarely communicated with each other, a quality that kept away fans of the old style of teahouses.[31] However, in the street-corner teahouses and teahouses in parks, the bench-sitter operas still were performed (as discussed in chapter 5), mostly by retired people; and in some humble teahouses local song styles and cross-talkers and the like were still heard.

Prices in the upper establishments were several times those at street-corner counterparts; now, the least expensive cup cost more than ten yuan, going up toward several dozen yuan. One balcony teahouse owner stated that he had to charge higher prices to recoup the 300,000 to 400,000 yuan he spent on renovation and to cover increases in the cost of water and electricity.[32] One new balcony establishment, fifteen hundred square meters large, was decorated by a famous designer and had furniture imported from Hong Kong. It had central air conditioning and more than a dozen luxurious private rooms, for a total investment of more than 8 million yuan. At another place, consisting of a thousand square meters, more than 2 million yuan was invested in remodeling, decor, and equipment. The owners believed that first-class facilities and service would carry them past their competition.[33]

A newspaper article about western Chengdu's upscale tea balconies situated inside the Second Ring Road noted that the optimism and confidence of owners were based on several factors. First, the area had ten new high-end subdivisions, with high-income residents. Second, there were quite a few successful, large restaurants nearby, attracting diners who would want to continue their evening together at a teahouse. Third, major road improvements made transportation from other parts of the city much easier. The owners said that they experienced little threat of competition, despite the high concentration of similar businesses in the area. One teahouse, for example, achieved sales of 8,000 yuan per day but had not yet reached full capacity. Private rooms were popular, with the lower priced at about 38 to 88 yuan per hour, and the more luxurious ones at 280 to 480 yuan per hour. To attract customers, most of these new teahouses had to lower their prices by 40 to 50 percent. Some market analysts warned that the supply of teahouses outstripped demand, while others had a more optimistic outlook.[34]

The high-end teahouses had different methods of operation. One of Chengdu's most luxurious teahouses at the time was the Sentosa (Shengtaosha). It offered valet parking service and shop-boys to hold umbrellas or help passengers from their cars. The teahouse was opened in 1996 on the second floor but grew to occupy the third and fourth floors as well, with the tea hall, private rooms, and on top a Western-style restaurant. A cup of tea ranged from 28 to more than 100 yuan. The private rooms had different décors and ranged in price from 180 to 600 yuan per hour, the tea not included. In addition, there was a buffet at 48 yuan per person. The total investment in the teahouse was 40 to 50 million yuan, which had been recouped by 2000. According to the manager, Sentosa had about three hundred customers each day, about one-third of whom were families and two-thirds businessmen and government officials. In one case, a party of five ordered three cups of tea (at 88 yuan each), two cups of coffee, and a tea with milk, plus a plate of fruit—for a total of more than 400 yuan. On the second floor, where the private rooms were, all the waiters were boys, and on the third floor, in the restaurant, all were girls. The establishment had a separate smoking room, but mahjong was not allowed.[35]

The rise of Sentosa reflected a new commercial culture emerging in this inland city, in which people with higher living standards were seeking higher-quality service and luxury. This included a rise in bookings by businessmen for places at which to entertain officials. In a sense, like other cities around the world, Chengdu experienced circular, self-serving planning—that is, when planning the city's makeover, planners made sure to include expensive venues for plush future meetings at which they might plan for yet more urban overhauls. The manager was noted as saying that he hosted many important officials, superstars, and other well-known people. That is why the private rooms always were under high demand: patrons wanted privacy in, ironically, a conventionally public and relatively informal place.

If Sentosa was the most Westernized of teahouses, the Prosperity Ancient Teahouse (Shunxing lao chaguan) was the opposite, deliberately emphasizing Chinese roots. It was located in the Chengdu Convention and Exhibition Center (Chengdu huizhan zhongxin) and decorated in the style of an old-fashioned teahouse, divided into three parts. The exterior was surrounded by a circular wall, engraved with scenes from Sichuan folklore, which attracted visitors. The interior had two parts: an inner teahouse with a theater where customers watched live, local operas, having their tea at ancient-style wood tables and chairs, and a courtyard tea garden and restaurant with bamboo trees and a few examples of privately purchased antique furniture, but mostly furniture manufactured in Beijing. Its prices were steep, which was part of the reason why, when observed, there were few patrons. An employee offered the opinion that renovation, interior design, and furniture cost five to six million yuan. The convention center owned the unprofitable teahouse and managed to keep it afloat even though it did not pay rent. About four hundred to five hundred bowls of tea were sold each day, and thirty to forty *jin* (about thirty-three to forty-four pounds) of tea leaves were used each month. To break even, the teahouse required 22,000 yuan in sales each day. Observing the establishment three years later, once again there were few patrons (in midafternoon) in such a large venue, which could serve over one thousand customers. Two things contributed to this problem: first was the ongoing SARS epidemic; and the other was a general habit of Chengdu residents, who made a point to go see new venues but rarely returned once their curiosity was satisfied.[36]

The emergence of mid- and high-level tea balconies seems to have reflected the new type of Chengdu residents whose living standards, similar to those of most of urban China, had risen sharply. The preferred business model now featured teahouses that served food, thus combining teahouse and restaurant, especially in the high-end venues. This change also reflected the flexibility of Chengdu teahouses: they could quickly adopt new business patterns to meet people's needs. They guarded patrons' privacy far more than the old-style street-corner teahouses, but their high prices and rarefied atmosphere pushed many to other venues, such as teahouses in parks and temples.

Teahouses in Parks and Temples

In Chengdu, every park and temple eventually became the site of at least one teahouse. In fact, the teahouse, and not the park or temple, became the destination for many because of the ambiance and large spaces. If friends planned to visit a park or temple, they would meet in the teahouse. The Ties of Loyalty Tea Balcony (Jieyi lou) at the Wuhou Temple (Wuhou ci) had excellent facilities, including a courtyard and a stage for opera. My notes show that tea prices ranged from five to thirty yuan per cup. The water was boiled on an electric stove but prepared in the old-fashioned way. A waitress stated that until the SARS scare, there were performances every day. An earwax picker was observed, about thirty years of age; his services cost ten yuan. He said he was a migrant worker and had been doing this work for more than three years.[37]

The People's Park, located in the center of the city, was the most popular place for the retired and elderly. To the right of the entrance was the Garden Tea Stand (Huayuan chazuo), with a sign at the door stating that people could stay the whole day for ten yuan and play chess and cards, drink tea, and have lunch. Inside, a craftswoman made animal figurines out of melted red sugar, attracting many children. Customers could spin the "wheel of fortune" to try to win treats (see figure 4.2). But the largest teahouse in the park was Cry of the Crane Teahouse (Heming chashe), an old, open-air facility with a long history, whose prices ranged from five to thirty yuan.[38]

Figure 4.2. A craftswoman forms melted red sugar into animal figurines, June 2003. Author photo.

The teahouses along the Funan River were always crowded because of the shady, cool willow trees and the beautiful scenery. My 2000 fieldwork took me to one of these. A bowl of tea was five yuan, and the waiter served it along with a thermos bottle—so that customers could make their own refills. Most of the customers were young men and women; some obviously were lovers. There were businessmen there as well, discussing business while drinking tea. Surveys could be conducted there. One survey taker, a college student, said that a few thousand responses had been completed, and he had gotten more than thirty responses of the sixty that were his daily quota. The survey was being done for his professor. The questions in it were mostly multiple-choice and concerned marketing: "What is the most important factor you consider when buying a car: (a) quality of the car; (b) economical to drive; (c) purchase price; (d) appearance."[39] I personally responded that I was not familiar with cars, and others expressed the same concern. But the student said that it didn't matter: people could fill out the survey answers in whatever way they wanted.[40] The contrast here with the old teahouses was stark in regard to the way information was passed and gathered and what kind of information it was. Now, long past Mao's Early Socialism, the teahouse was a site for gathering opinions that were neither political nor truly public, but were commercial information that was not even accurate.

In Chengdu, almost all monasteries operate a teahouse. The Great Benevolence Temple (Daci si) had the popular and well-known Museum Tea Garden (Wenbo chayuan) operated by the Museum Art and Tourism Company (Wenbo yishu lüyou gongsi). In 1992, the company opened a teahouse, restaurant, and snack shop in the temple courtyard, which attracted groups from many organizations. The teahouse was convenient for business meetings, for leisure, or both. A customer could buy a cup of tea for three to five yuan and stay in the same seat the entire day, no matter how many times the waiter replenished the hot water. Daily sales amounted to eight hundred to nine hundred bowls.[41] From 1994 to 1996, when business was at its highest point, more than a thousand bowls of tea were sold daily.[42] The manager, Jiang, herself divided one *jin* (about 1.1 pound) of tea leaves into 140 bowls.[43] There were eight other employees: six waiters and two at the counter. Each waiter had his own area and was in charge of his own pile of bowls on the counter, clearly indicating how many each sold (see figure 4.3).

Figure 4.3. The Museum Tea Garden, May 2003. The yellow poster says,
"Jieda medical equipment serves you for free for your good health,"
indicating that doctors provided service there. Author photo.

Before closing each evening, the waiters settled accounts with Jiang.
According to her, the Museum Tea Garden was run like a family business.
Her husband was now in charge of procurement, after a previous case of an
employee caught cheating by submitting fake receipts for amounts higher
than the actual purchase amounts. The person who sold snacks was also
a relative. But the teahouse had many financial responsibilities because
some employees of the Museum Art and Tourism Company, including a
cashier, accountant, office director, and assistant to the general manager,
were paid by the teahouse although they did not work for the teahouse—
perhaps an indication of tricky bookkeeping. In its early years, the teahouse
prospered; and now daily sales reached 3,000 yuan, with seats often filled
by ten o'clock in the morning. In 1998, however, business began to falter
because of increased competition, among other factors. Furthermore, the
teahouse was in the open air, with the obvious problems of such an operation.[44] My field observations found that the financial situation there was
not all that bleak, largely because of the "gray market" in which vendors

paid the teahouse to use space to sell goods such as books, paintings, and other crafts, and often they drank tea when they had no customers (similar to what occurred at Gathered Happiness, mentioned above). In addition, some Chinese medicine doctors began offering services at the teahouse.[45]

Another teahouse in the Great Benevolence Temple compound was the Great Benevolence Estate Tea Garden (Dacizhuang chayuan) near the main gate. A wooden sign just inside the entrance to the temple advertised, "Have fun for the whole day, with a meal and tea for ten to fifteen yuan." The establishment had an arched gate and a courtyard with a small pond, in the middle of which a pavilion was built. A waitress noted that the pond was stocked by fish vendors every day and thus provided the fish for customers' meals. There was a pretty walkway covered with ivy, and eight or nine mahjong tables. A dining room contained five or six large round tables, and it was crowded on occasion. The same waitress remarked that the price of ten to fifteen yuan for both tea and a meal was low, and thus profits were low—and it was a great deal of work for employees, nonetheless.[46]

Teahouses in temples were hardly associated with religious practice. From the viewpoint of the teahouse, the temple was nothing more than a strategic business location with a solid customer base. Also, China's temples made a good fit with the teahouses, since the temples functioned as spaces for public gatherings and entertainment, creating a solid intertwining of religious and secular lifestyles. Ultimately, both the teahouse and religious public spaces survived the Communists' radical revolution.

The Emergence of Multifunctional Teahouses

The commercial aspects of teahouse culture have always been sustained by adapting to changes in the society and the economy. One strategy was to provide services that met other needs in addition to tea and a place to drink it. Some gradually expanded to include video screens, lodging, and foot massage.

Teahouse as Video Room

The growing popularity of the videocassette recorder in the 1980s and videocassette disc players in the 1990s made films and dramas from Hong Kong and Taiwan (especially those involving the martial arts) very

Figure 4.4. Video room in a street under construction, June 2003. Author photo.

popular in mainland China. To attract customers, many of the humble type of teahouse showed videos, and gradually this became their major business, thus transforming them to "video rooms" (see figure 4.4). The customers were mostly teenagers, migrant laborers, and peasant workers.[47] Unlike old-style teahouses, where chairs were placed around tables, these rooms had bamboo chairs arranged in rows, theater style, so the audience faced the front of the room to watch videos. At night, these places were packed with customers, especially migrant workers, who did not have family nearby and needed to occupy themselves after working. In the 1990s, five yuan was enough for tea plus an entire day of videos.[48]

By 2000 there were still many such teahouse / video rooms, such as the Bruce Lee Video/Poker Teahouse (Li Xiaolong luxiang pai cha) near the rear of the Chengdu Municipal Archives. This teahouse was in poor condition, under a bamboo shed roof, from which was hung a banner with the Chinese character *cha*. At that time, a large wooden board stood outside, on which color photos of VCD covers were pasted so customers could easily identify the programs they wanted to watch. Four people were playing mahjong at the gate, one of whom was the teahouse keeper, a middle-aged woman. A cup of tea plus videos cost only one yuan. The interior was small and dim, with an aisle down the middle, three chairs on each side, in five rows to accommodate a total of thirty patrons. Two small, round stools in each row were used as tables. Only five or six customers, men who appeared to be twenty to thirty years old, were watching a Hong Kong movie. From their accent, they were likely migrant laborers. More than one hundred printed covers from VCDs were posted on the wall, mostly of Hong Kong, Taiwan, and U.S. action movies, such as those starring Bruce Lee (whom this teahouse specifically honored), Jackie Chan, and Arnold Schwarzenegger.[49]

At another teahouse / video room, which sat at a highway junction, a sign at the street entrance had an arrow pointing to where one could enter a large, dim room on the upper level of a house. There were six rows of chairs, with small, long tea tables between each row. Four chairs were on each side of the aisle, to hold about fifty customers. A large-screen television was at the front of the room. On an early afternoon I noted that there was no one in the large room, but some people were playing mahjong in a smaller room. The admission charge was only one yuan, and the quality of tea was poor. The keeper said that her customers were mainly students from the cooking school across the street, now closed for summer break. Generally, she would show videos as long as there were six to seven people, but she often had more than twenty customers. The profit margin was slim, she said. The monthly rent was more than 1,000 yuan for the big room and several hundred for the smaller one.[50]

The emergence of these video teahouses reflected an important transition that was caused basically by new entertainment technology. It seems that television sets and videocassette players replaced performances by local opera actors and folk performing artists, thus amounting to probably the most thorough change since antiquity—from actors on a stage, to machines at the front. Costs were consequently lowered, and the scheduling of shows became more flexible. In the past, the teahouses that were able to provide local operas were those that had sizable space or enough audience, but now even the smallest teahouses could afford to offer entertainment to fewer patrons and capture return customers because of the vast variety of offerings. In this way, large numbers of migrants and urban poor found pastime activities in a rapidly Westernizing city.

Teahouse as Foot-Soaking and Massage Venue

Traditionally, teahouses had sought every opportunity to meet people's needs through a variety of services. In Narrow Alley, a large teahouse was called the Old Alley (Lao xiangzi). Hexagonal lanterns hung at the gate, and on each side was the Chinese *cha* character. Two stone lions stood on each side of the gate. A big board was placed to the left side of the gate, reading "Thanks to our Customers at the Grand Opening." The board had information about the many services available, such as chess and poker in private rooms at ten yuan per hour for a small room, sixteen yuan for the medium-size room, and twenty yuan for the large room; a foot soak and massage using Chinese medicine cost twenty-five yuan for seventy minutes, or thirty yuan for eighty minutes with Tibetan-style fragrant milk. The teahouse also served food. Two waitresses in red uniforms greeted guests at the gate. A girl in a white shirt who probably was the head waitress told me that the teahouse had opened a few months earlier and was not well known. Walking inside, one encountered a garden with a small bridge and a room with glass walls, in which several people were drinking tea, chatting, or reading newspapers. Upstairs were many private rooms, the largest costing 400 yuan per day, tea not included.[51]

Teahouse as Lodging Venue

Some teahouses also provided lodging. My fieldwork recorded opinions about this: one teahouse patron explained that, to save money, some travelers would go to a twenty-four-hour teahouse, filling the hours with a foot massage and a bowl of tea for a few yuan. At ten yuan per hour, an entire night of foot pampering and tea, napping on a chaise-longue type of chair, cost less than a hotel room.[52]

A hotel on Flower Arch Street also functioned as a teahouse, and a fine one at that. One could see some guest rooms from the hallway, but these looked cheap. Apparently, the owner, a woman, also filled the role of waitress. A patron bought a cup of tea and received a small plate of toasted sunflower seeds for no extra charge. Patrons could listen to her talk with acquaintances. First, she discussed taking two recently hired women to the hospital for their mandatory health exams to make sure they were not carrying any lung, skin, or other contagious diseases. Then she talked about her "problem" son, who was about to graduate from elementary school and who liked eating and drinking more than studying. She said she tried very hard to make him understand the difference between right and wrong. From her story, it is possible to understand more fully the issues an ordinary female shopkeeper faced at work and home, and how she handled them.[53]

We should note that regulations generally did not actually allow a teahouse to operate other kinds of business such as a hotel, because the government needed to control businesses individually. Every hotel had to register customers' identity cards, but teahouses did not. Yet, because most teahouses were small, and the government could not oversee all these small businesses, a space grew up for them to expand their operations. The flourishing of new choices, the expansion of teahouse spaces, and the way teahouses could take advantage of the bureaucratic state's inability to keep up all point to a fortuitous growth in public spaces and public life per se. This happened as an indirect benefit of the new direction of the state, and was carried out from the bottom, not as a top-down policy. Urban culture in Chengdu, now positively affected by such expansions and choices, could only benefit.

Market Teahouses

In the 1980s, Deng Xiaoping initiated the nation's transition from a planned economy to a market economy. Unlike the state-owned enterprises whose production materials were guaranteed, non-state-owned businesses had to secure materials through the market, and many materials, such as coal, steel, and wood, as well as certain equipment, were in short supply.[54] At this time, the teahouse embraced its pre-1949 function as a marketplace for peddlers and merchants. According to a 1984 *People's Daily* article, teahouses became a place for "discussing business and passing around information" in the city's rapidly developing market economy. A reporter said that after being in a teahouse "for just a little while," he got all kinds of information on the price of fish and vegetables not only for that neighborhood but for different market niches, regions, and cities.[55] Some teahouses actually became hubs of trade and market transactions for steel, cement, and other production materials, and even automobiles. In 1984, to meet economic needs, the Production Material Service Company in Chengdu opened a trading market, the "Regular Trading of Production Materials on Friday," in the Cry of the Crane Teahouse. For some years, until the government shut down such practices, this teahouse was busy every Friday morning as merchants, manufacturers, and suppliers conducted business.[56]

The most famous market for this purpose was the tea garden in the stadium in North City known as the Friday Tea Club (Zhouwu chahui), which, although remaining privately owned, became the "Chengdu Regular Market for Production Materials." This teahouse took up about three hundred square meters and was crowded with people not only from Chengdu but from other counties and provinces interested in buying and selling raw goods. Hundreds of flyers with information on the materials or prospective buyers and sellers hung from the tabletops. People walked the aisles looking at products and sat at the tables to negotiate terms. By 1987, several hundred enterprises, each paying a few dozen yuan per year, became members, and the deals conducted in the first three quarters of 1987 reached over 200 million yuan. This teahouse market operated for several years.[57]

Many buyers, especially from small companies, did not need to travel far to find suppliers but went straight to the market teahouse. When her company urgently needed two tons of a certain type of rolled steel, a young woman found what she needed right away. In addition, salesmen from villages dozens of miles from Chengdu came for their small factories and companies. A young buyer claimed that he got business done each time he attended. "It is the most convenient place for making small business transactions," he said. It is interesting that some of these buyers and sellers became middlemen for large, state-owned enterprises because they had more connections and had a great deal of information from a variety of channels. They would receive a service fee of something under 1 percent for each transaction. The reputation of this market was good: people trusted the honesty of participants, and there were no cases of cheating. One particular businessman said, "We all have tried to build our reputations over the long run and will not risk damaging them over profit." These factors led the Chengdu branch of the Association of National Economic Information Networks to consider conducting its business of disseminating information about supply and demand trends via telex from this location.[58]

Teahouses also became de facto offices for owners of many of the so-called "briefcase companies" (*pibao gongsi*) that sprang up during the 1980s, when "all citizens were engaged in business." This was the moniker for individuals who worked for themselves, without office space or employees, and carried briefcases around the city, looking for business. They naturally ended up at teahouses. Even those who had offices liked to discuss business in a teahouse. He Xiaozhu, a writer who at the time ran a company, stated that he left his office and met clients at the teahouse, where he felt more relaxed and evenly matched with his business counterparts. Every morning, office-bound business managers would drive to work, take care of paperwork, meet with employees, but then leave for the teahouse, where they would read newspapers and handle business via cell phone. At noon, they would buy noodles or the like, nap on comfortable rattan sofas, and later perhaps meet with more clients. Access to fax machines or the Internet was rarely a problem, since upscale teahouses usually provided those services. If these teahouse patrons did not have any business to conduct, they might play mahjong with a few friends, and the winner would treat the rest for dinner.[59]

As during the Republican period, teahouses became the headquarters of economic organizations. Since many people from outside Sichuan did business in Chengdu, by the 1990s nearly a dozen native-place merchant associations had been established and conducted their activities in Chengdu. People from Wenzhou, in Zhejiang Province, for example, who were well-known for their business talent, were very successful in Chengdu and established the Wenzhou Association. As was the case before 1949, these associations often did not have their own place for activities but adopted teahouses as their headquarters.[60]

In summary, we have seen how the teahouse as a public space not only accommodated relaxation and entertainment, but also functioned as a marketplace and as a business office. To a certain extent, the teahouse contributed to China's economic transformation and decentralization by providing low-cost, suitable venues for a rapidly growing number of entrepreneurs, representing both private firms and municipalities, to gather information and contacts. In some places, the Chengdu government had to build some infrastructure to promote market development. The teahouse, with in some sense its own preexisting infrastructure, found a new use. Even as politics, the economy, society, and culture changed through the twentieth century, and with the emergence of many other public spaces and improvements in business technology and facilities, the market function of the teahouse was never replaced. Furthermore, teahouses prospered as they grew in size and number, gaining highly professional management and organization.

Encountering the Pressures of Competition and Nature

With growing demand for the sort of multifunctional public spaces described above, teahouses increased in number and consequently faced more competition. In order to attract more customers, many teahouses created plush environments. William Whyte pointed out that "the best way to handle the problem of undesirables is to make a place attractive to everyone else."[61] His message was about how to construct the desired plushness, but what was unstated was the result—higher prices. A newspaper reporter covered this topic in a 2000 article titled "Open Air Teahouses Taking Business from Teahouse Balconies." The reporter spent a summer afternoon in a large and expensive teahouse along the Funan River, with 110 tables and 400 chairs, and prices ranging from five to twenty yuan. A worker told the reporter that business had been good in the previous year, when patrons bought their expensive tea, but they spent less as the economy stagnated. The teahouse employed twenty-two workers and paid for uniforms, food, and lodging, plus a new pair of shoes every forty days. The reporter estimated that the teahouse averaged about five hundred patrons per day. One afternoon, the reporter went to an elegant tea balcony, and although signs advertised sales of 25 percent off regular prices, he did not see a single customer between 3 and 5 p.m., and only eight customers between 6 and 9:30. The reporter also mentioned a seven-hundred-square-meter tea balcony that opened in March 2000 after an investment of 5 million yuan, but which closed just six months later.[62] The plush teahouses seem to have been relatively more affected directly and sharply by the overall economy and living standards than were the street-corner establishments.

In order to increase revenues, different teahouses used different approaches to participating in Chengdu's emerging consumer culture. As competition intensified, teahouses increasingly focused on image and publicity. In 2003, the first "teahouse image" contest was held. In addition to the selection of a "Miss Tea" (*chahua*), there was a contest in which more than fifty people competed in the "tea arts" (*chayi*)—essentially pouring.[63] In this event, a young boy and girl demonstrated a style called "Farewell, My Concubine" (*Bawang bieji*).[64] The girl bent over backwards, placing a tea bowl on her midriff while the boy poured boiling water from a long-mouth tea kettle from three feet away. Not a single drop landed outside the bowl, and the judges compared it to "a stream flowing from a high mountain."[65] The Association of Tea Culture in Sichuan organized a tea-tasting contest in Chengdu that tested skills in identifying tea varieties, pouring boiling water, and knowledge of tea. The winner, a young manager of a teahouse, was proclaimed the "number one tea drinker" (*diyi chake*).[66] These kinds of marketing ploys could even lightly cross boundaries with local culture. In November 2003, in front of the Blue Bamboo Leaves Teahouse (Zhuyeqing chafang) on Zither Platform Road (Qintai lu), two nine-year-old twins, another boy-and-girl team, who claimed to be descendants of the Emei Faction of Tea Art (Emei pai chayi), demonstrated their skills. Accompanied by the ancient Chinese song "Water Flowing from the High Mountain" (Gaoshan liushui), and wearing white silk outfits and black cotton shoes, they performed the "dance of the dragon and phoenix." Crouching on the ground and using big kettles that they held above their heads, they poured boiling water into twenty bowls behind their backs, to much applause from a crowd.[67]

Weather, like the trends in competition and marketing, had a considerable effect on the teahouse business. This was the topic of an article with the headline "Teahouses in Chengdu Depend on Weather." We learn that a businessman rented a four-hundred-square-meter space on the second floor of a building near the River View Park at 20,000 yuan per month and spent 800,000 yuan on remodeling and design, adding six small, private rooms and hiring two pretty girls to greet customers at the entrance gate. However, sales were not sufficient to cover costs. He thought it might be a problem with this facility, so he added spaces for karaoke, chess, and card games, and hired a teacher from a public relations school to coach his eighteen waitresses about demeanor and appearance. But the temperature outside was dropping, and so was business. Even lowering the price for a whole day's activities to just five yuan did not attract customers, nor did the seven-day May holiday, nor the adding of food, games, and foot massage.[68] When the weather warmed, however, the teahouses that were virtually empty in mid-May 2000 were overflowing by the end of that month with customers seeking air-conditioning. Some teahouses advertised their air conditioning. The reporter also visited a tea balcony near River View Park and could not believe his eyes: business was booming there, as well. He learned from one interviewee that business was on a weather roller coaster: "Before May 15, we saw fewer than twenty customers a day, but after May 15, and especially after May 19, we had

Figure 4.5. Elderly teahouse-goers playing cards, Chengdu suburb, September 2015. Author photo.

six times that many. But, I am still not happy"—expressing worry about the chance aspect of seasonal business.[69]

Competitions were undoubtedly commercial activities, but at the same time they promoted teahouse culture and offered popular entertainment. They indicate to us that the teahouse was once again adapting to radically new social, cultural, and economic environments and was using new business strategies that contributed to survival and even to increased opportunities to earn money and support families and lifestyles. Today's teahouses are different from those in the past, but their appeal as a kind of democratic public space with convenient services remains largely unchanged. Other uses of public space have emerged to compete for people's time and resources, but they have not replaced the centrality of the teahouse in everyday life. The promotion of teahouse culture at this time fit perfectly into the new, and pressure-filled, business parameters (see figure 4.5).

The State, the Market, and the Teahouse after the Reforms

At the beginning of Late Socialism and the accompanying reforms, the state weakened its influence on small businesses because of the new political environment. In the introduction, I offered an overall way of viewing the major difference between Early and Later Socialism: they went in two different directions strategically. The former built up centralization and state power, and the latter let all that loosen. This view helps us to understand why small businesses in the reform era felt relieved and able more quickly to take business decisions and start enterprises. Writing about this transition period, Kenneth Lieberthal stated that "the state no longer provides a moral compass for the population. Indeed, one of the striking features of contemporary Chinese society is the growth of non-state sources of moral authority and spiritual well-being."[70] But this does not mean that in the area of business the state was totally absent from a general involvement with practices and operations. In fact, it continued to affect businesses, but in a different way. Anthropologist Ole Bruun investigated small business in Chengdu during the period 1987–1991. These years were yet another important transitional period in post-Mao China, going from the most open decade under the socialist state to a resurgence of state control after the June Fourth Movement in 1989. Bruun found that in Chengdu, businessmen tried hard to establish good relationships with state offices in order to ensure better profits. They had to face various authorities concerning licenses and taxes. The tax bureau, for example, forced owners to estimate the profits of their competitors. Some small businessmen would use illicit methods, such as false registration of a private business as a "collective," to avoid taxes. Bruun's study revealed corruption in general as a serious problem, and often one that could not be overcome. In the early 1990s an estimated average life of a small business in Chengdu was four to five years, but 25 percent survived less than two years, while only 20 percent lasted over ten years.[71] All of this reflects a quite different kind of state roadblock that had to be overcome, certainly nothing like the state controls under Early Socialism.

Overcoming officialdom and working around the many changes at national and local levels, therefore, could be perceived as part of the normal process of doing business. One reason for the new vitality was the continuing expansion of consumer culture and markets throughout China. The expansion was in part impelled by the democratic movements of the 1980s, pressure arising from the push for "all people to engage in business," as well as by mass migration of workers into the large cities, the reorganization of state-owned enterprises, city reconstruction projects, and so on. During the 1980s, "the market acted like a giant magnet drawing people into [it] headlong," influencing their "plunge into the sea of commerce" (*xiahai*).[72] When we turn our thoughts to the teahouse, and especially the Chengdu teahouse, the rather ordinary folk who opened a teahouse were making a prudent choice, given that many lacked access to large amounts of capital but could afford to run a small, plain operation. Moreover, those with access to higher finance could invest in the large, high-end tea balconies that sprouted with the complex but powerful wave of development.

5

URBAN RESIDENTS AND MIGRANT WORKERS IN PUBLIC LIFE

The market economy brought significant changes to everyday life, the urban landscape, and all aspects of culture. As Deborah Davis noted, "By the mid-1990s, higher incomes and new retail markets had reduced the obligations on the workplace to satisfy consumer demands." Hawkers filled the streets, and markets sold all kinds of food and mundane items. "Private restaurateurs or subcontractors (*chengbao*) replaced workplace canteens, and a largely commercialized entertainment industry multiplied opportunities for individuals to relax or conduct business in the unofficial world, away from work."[1] People became increasingly dependent on markets and public spaces, where they conducted business, exchanged information, and engaged in social life in an enriched commercial culture.[2] The teahouse once again met these needs and played an important role in the consumer revolution.

There was another kind of "people" seeking public spaces. This was the "floating population" of migrant workers from rural areas—steadily growing in numbers. In certain ways, teahouses became even more important to them than to Chengdu's residents. The migrants provided many services for teahouses, and at the same time they were becoming customers when they were not working in factories, construction, and other jobs. Most did not have family with them and thus rented cheap and unpleasant places; teahouses offered a space for their breaks, for meeting friends, job searches, and sheer leisure. They came to the city to earn a living but did not share the same rights as the official urban residents. Even though government policies were less controlling than in the past, and made it possible for farmworkers to gain temporary status in cities, nonetheless "the household registration system (*hukou*) continue[d] to play a powerful role in shaping rural migrants' experiences, social identity, and sense of belonging in the city."[3] Li Zhang's book *Strangers in the City* is a good study of the "floating population," but her focus is "petty capitalists," not peasant laborers. Teahouse workers were mostly peasant migrant laborers. Zhang explains the Beijing municipal government's great effort to control "Zhejiang village" as an exercise in official "late-socialist urban aesthetics."[4] In Chengdu, the municipal government held a similar notion, namely, that the "floating population" affected urban management, security, and even image, consequently causing the city to impose restrictions. Still, peasant laborers in Chengdu had relatively better experiences than elsewhere because they were scattered, including in teahouses, and were much less visible than were their Beijing counterparts.

For leisure and entertainment, the teahouse was relatively accommodating and inexpensive; it was the most convenient place for social interactions among the elderly and business dealings among the young. As in the past, it served as a marketplace, which reflected the flux of the world outside. Therefore, teahouse life in the 1980s and 1990s was part of the renaissance in public life under Late Socialism, interwoven with the growing complexity of society and consumer culture. In the new world all around, teahouses still held on to customary uses and features, and even today they continue to flourish in modern, urban Chengdu.

Unlike in the period between 1950 and the 1970s, teahouses under the reforms and the opening up no longer served the party as propaganda hubs. Pushing this change along was, of course, the emergence of media such as newspapers, television, and, more recently, the Internet, all of which assumed much of this propaganda function for the CCP and the government. Consequently, the teahouse became politically insignificant, and in general reverted to its role as a place for authentic leisure and entertainment. Yet people could now also openly express cynicism toward politics and even criticize the government.[5] Although the state tried to suppress such speech, its ability to identify and punish transgressors extended only as far as printed publications; it lacked mechanisms for monitoring spoken conversations in teahouses or, until recently, posts on the Internet.

This chapter makes the case that when teahouses mushroomed, newly liberated people, including the mass of nonregistered migrants, returned to urban, public spaces, and the recovery of the teahouse was even a catalyst for the resurgence of public life more broadly. In the Mao era, and especially during the Cultural Revolution, people had withdrawn from public arenas and occupied only their private places, where they felt safe to speak their minds. The post-Mao reforms created a relatively more open political environment that improved public life. In the teahouse, all kinds of people started to enjoy public life, and the teahouse once again became the most important place for socialization, no matter of what age, gender, occupation, or level of education.[6]

Gathering for Common Interests and Socialization

Teahouse culture was so intrinsic to Chengdu that some residents considered it the city's primary distinguishing feature and even "the most accurate measure of real Chengdu people."[7] A survey found that 2.9 percent of Chengdu residents went to teahouses every day, 10.3 percent went once a week, 13.5 percent twice a week, and 8.5 percent twice a month. In addition, a large number of the so-called floating population depended heavily on teahouses; one estimate believes that more than 200,000 people in Chengdu patronized teahouses each day.[8] This number is not surprising, given that an estimated 100,000 to 140,000 people visited teahouses daily during the Republican period.[9]

As the patrons swelled in number, the usual rich variety of teahouse functions was reestablished. The teahouse easily resumed its role as club, a place where friends and acquaintances shared interests.[10] Some specialty teahouses became chess gardens (perhaps six or seven in Chengdu). The largest was located on Provincial Commander Street (Tidu jie), a prosperous area. It had a spacious lobby, where customers—mainly young workers, retirees, teachers, and cadres—drank tea and played or watched others play chess. It hosted chess competitions, for which tickets were sold, and its "500 seats were packed almost every day."[11] Some rich women in Chengdu visited their clubs all day long. They went to the beauty salon in the morning, visited a teahouse at noon, and spent nights at a mahjong house, turning their lives into "just a three-point line."[12]

As before, the teahouse was often a place for personal communication, sometimes providing a neutral venue for first dates, or as a vehicle for long-married couples.[13] When one thirty-five-year-old woman described her daily life, she constantly mentioned the teahouse, where she found her true love.[14] Beginning in the early 1980s, a certain Mr. Cui and his then-wife frequented teahouses: first one near the People's Park, and in later years they tried out others. They often brought their grandson, who spent much of his childhood, from age three to ten, in the teahouse. Mr. Cui was a songwriter and preferred to work in the teahouse, where crowds and noise served as an inspiration. He and friends frequented a teahouse by the Funan River, where he befriended a waitress who was almost the same age as his eldest daughter, and recently divorced. She was not well educated, and her handwriting was "awful," so he taught her calligraphy. Their relationship turned romantic, and after he divorced, they lived together.[15]

Chengdu's teahouses adapted to all kinds of needs. Some, especially those in parks, became veritable marriage agencies. A good example is the People's Park, a popular spot for older Chengdu residents to get together and discuss their children's marital problems. This teahouse established a calendar for dates, an activity that over time grew to attract between three hundred and four hundred matchmaking parents to its relatively small space each Wednesday and Friday afternoon. Parents first asked another parent if he or she was seeking a male or female, found out the preferred age and zodiac sign, and might then proceed to the stage of photos and contact information. A sixty-year-old woman said that her daughter was twenty-nine years old and worked in the post office, but although she would make an excellent wife, she did not necessarily pursue romance. Disturbed about this, the mother went to the teahouse to seek a match for her daughter. The advantage of this method was that parents could gain information directly and bypass the professional marriage intermediaries.[16]

The teahouse was a gathering spot for the literati. Writer He Xiaozhu said he first visited Chengdu and its teahouses in 1983; he usually went to those in parks and then those just off main streets. At the time, telephones were not widely available, so he often met his friends—mostly poets—by bicycling to their homes, calling to them from the sidewalk, then going together to a street-corner teahouse to spend half the day.[17] Writers started making teahouses into regular gathering places. In the mid-1990s, the Ming Qing Tea Balcony (Ming Qing chalou) became their favorite "living room, drawing room, editorial office, chess house, love cabin, and café." Some best-selling books were actually drafted there. Some of the plots in He's first long novel had this teahouse as a backdrop, and he wrote a short story titled "The Ming Qing Teahouse."[18] According to poet Zhai Yongming, there was a group of writers who "slept until noon and then played poker in the Fragrant Kitchen Tea Balcony (Xiangji chu chalou) the whole afternoon."[19] The writer Wang Yue did not drink tea, but he loved to spend time in teahouses. Managers and waiters knew him well, and as soon as they saw him, they would say, "Here comes the fat guy again" and then pour his bowl of plain, boiling water. Wang was drawing inspiration for his characters by listening to and observing customers. He declared himself an "old teahouse-goer" and wrote a book titled *Old Teahouse-Goer's Gossip (Lao chake xianhua)*. His friends and colleagues would tease: "Watch what you say, or the old teahouse-goer will write you into his next book."[20] The Museum Tea Garden in the Great Benevolence Temple (as described in chapter 4) had more than one writer as a regular. The staff knew their favorite seats. Liu Shahe was there every Wednesday morning, until noon. Che Fu met friends regularly, until he was eighty. This routine was fostered in childhood, when he used to follow his father to the teahouses.[21]

The "Old Houses" (Laowu) area outside Sichuan University had dozens of teahouses and five or six bars where young writers and artists liked to gather. The area was actually named Bacon Road (after the British philosopher Roger Bacon) and became even more famous after several columnists wrote about the teahouse life there. To outsiders, Bacon Road seemed like the "real Chengdu," and they patronized the area until it was razed for reconstruction.[22] You Ye recalled that their favorite teahouse was the largest of all. Whenever a soccer game was shown on television, the teahouse would be overcrowded. Patrons could buy tea at two yuan and a glass of wine at three yuan, easily killing an entire afternoon and evening by reading newspapers, playing chess, sunbathing, people watching, and napping. Ye said the teahouse "basically became part of our lives." Later, it was divided into two—half for the teahouse, and half for a bar. This made the teahouse side so crowded that Ye and his friends patronized a quieter place, under trees, instead.[23]

The South Wind Tea Balcony (Nanfeng chalou) on Red Star Road (Hongxing lu), near the *Sichuan Daily* offices, became popular with Chengdu journalists, to the extent that "lazy" reporters would gather information there rather than getting into the field.[24] The Great Benevolence Temple also was associated with news organizations, such as the *Sichuan Daily*, the *Chengdu Daily*, the *Chengdu Business Daily*, and the *Chengdu Evening News*; reporters and editors not only drank tea and exchanged information, but sometimes even held editorial meetings there. This occurred as well at the Museum Tea Garden.[25]

Teahouses in post-Mao China, as during the Republican era, played a role as hubs of various kinds of information. Although this function was weakened under Mao's regime, it quickly came back as soon as the government loosened its control. Even after many modern media had sprung up, including newspapers, television, and the Internet, teahouses were still able to be a source of information for many kinds of people. As before, they were not only places for writers to socialize, but also could inspire topics and material for their works.

Teahouses and Entertainment

The revival of the teahouse satisfied the desire of many for entertainment, and different forms of entertainment fed into the liveliness of the teahouse.[26] The Joy Tea Garden (Yuelai chayuan) was the oldest teahouse in Chengdu, but during the 1960s and 1970s it became the Brocade River Theater (Jinjiang juchang). The theater was expanded in 1984 with the restoration of the old name—Joy Tea Garden—and the addition of a guesthouse, dance hall, shop, restaurant, and film and video screening capabilities. Members of the Association of Sichuan Opera Amateurs (Chuanju wanyou xiehui) rehearsed there every Friday. In the 1990s, the establishment was again renamed, now becoming the Center of

Sichuan Opera Performing Arts in Chengdu (Chengdu shi chuanju yishu zhongxin). After so many transformations, the appeal of the Joy Tea Garden as an old-style teahouse was lost. The new Joy Tea Garden, now as a part of the renamed center, had two stories: a ground floor furnished in the old style with decorative couplets on plaques, and a stage in the center, where the Chengdu Sichuan Opera Troupe drew big crowds every Saturday afternoon. The second floor was turned into high-end, luxury private rooms, much more expensive than the first level. After the renovation, the price of tea went up, driving some older patrons to other places.[27]

Storytelling was one of the most popular entertainment genres. Like stage actors, storytellers used techniques such as clear speech, concise phrasing, rich facial expressions, and dramatic gestures to draw the audience's attention. They sat on tall chairs and told ancient stories in the Sichuan dialect, using only two simple props—a painted folding fan and a carved wooden block, called a "waking up wooden block" (*jingtang mu*). Both enhanced the dramatic effect, as a beautiful girl, for example, could be shown with the fan, and a brutal emperor or righteous man with the block. Storytellers usually performed at the street-corner teahouses in remote alleys; each of them could perform at least five classic stories, which had very elaborate and complicated plot twists. At two hours per day, the longest story could take three months to finish. Almost all the stories ended happily, with good triumphing over evil.[28]

One foreign writer, as written about in a Chinese study of "old Chengdu," described a teahouse as being filled with "old flavors and smoke," as elderly audience members smoked long tobacco pipes and sipped tea from lidded bowls. "The uttering of sighs was the only hint of sound." Although they were "almost as familiar with the story as the storyteller," the audience members never tired of listening. The elderly patrons were generally not wealthy, and most were retired people. Listening to stories with their friends was far preferable to long days alone in their small homes. The foreigner also noted there were more than seventy people in the audience and that their average age was about seventy, but there were only two old women. Interestingly, the storyteller was relatively young, in his thirties and still wearing the blue uniform from his factory job during the day.[29]

In her novel *Sunset Red* (*Jidu xiyang hong*), Qiong Yao describes teahouses in Sichuan, but she said that all she knew about them came from listening to her friends' conversations. In the late 1980s, when she visited Chengdu and her childhood home on Summer Stockings Street (Shuwa jie) in search of her "roots," she could not locate the home's courtyard. She went to a teahouse, but what she found was much different from what she expected: it was located in an alley in the commercial area, "like an old school auditorium," and crowded, mostly with elderly patrons. The stage was in the front part of the hall, and benches were placed in rows, with the tea bowls placed on wooden tables. According to Qiong, the performances were excellent and included Sichuan opera, lotus singing, satirical plays, drums, and bamboo clapper singing. Many people also watched from outside the teahouse.[30]

Quite a few teahouses became locations for self-devised entertainments. Consider the case of the Museum Tea Garden in the Great Benevolence Temple. It was a big establishment; there were three large, ancient-style halls and three courtyards, with wooden tables and bamboo armchairs, both inside and under the eaves outside, with shade from the big trees. Occupying half of the first hall was a store that sold Chinese paintings and antiques, and the other half was the teahouse. In the second hall, the chairs were placed in rows, unlike the usual practice of putting them around circular tables. All the patrons were elderly, and most were women. On a red banner hanging on a pole was written, "Chengdu Activity Center for Elder Sports" (Chengdu laonian tixie huodong zhongxin).[31] This teahouse exemplifies how the revival of teahouse life ushered in the revival of bench-sitter opera, which had been prohibited since the 1950s (see chapter 2). The stage there supported many such performances, whose large audiences bought tea for two to three yuan and watched the performances for free. Two main groups performed there: the Association of Amateur Players (Wanyou xiehui) performed on Friday afternoons, and the Sichuan Harmonies Zither Society (Shusheng qinshe) on Sunday afternoons. The stage was in the backyard hall, which had been added to the teahouse.[32] The programs were mainly Sichuan operas. A sign above the stage read "Performance of the Sichuan Harmonies Zither Society" (Shusheng qinshe yanchang hui), and another sign offstage read "Association of Amateur Singers of Sichuan Opera in Chengdu" (Chengdu shi chuanju wanyou xiehui) (see figure 5.1).[33]

Some of these associations were very active and had regular teahouses for their venues. A teahouse on the Victorious Lower Street (Desheng xiajie),

Figure 5.1 The stage of the Museum Tea Garden at Great Benevolent Temple, July 2000. Author photo.

though shabby, hosted many amateur performers over the span of a decade. One was Lin Zuoyuan, a man in his sixties. Lin's father used to work at the Joy.Tea Garden, and Lin's mother often took him there as a child. He later went there by himself, often sneaking inside to watch a show. Over time, he became familiar with the actors. He became a dedicated fan of Sichuan opera, his only hobby throughout life. In 1958, he was a member of an amateur Sichuan opera troupe and often played at a cultural center on Private Academy Street South (Shuyuan nanjie). During the Cultural Revolution, he sometimes found the prohibition against singing unbearable, and would ride a bike to a field outside the city to practice in solitude. In the post-Mao era, he moved from teahouse to teahouse to sing. After retiring in 1995, he joined an amateur society, and played and sang.[34]

Togetherness Joy (Tongle), established in 1985, and was one of the earliest of these amateur societies, ultimately settling in the New China Tea Garden after moving from teahouse to teahouse. Every Tuesday, Thursday, and Saturday afternoon, members performed there, the sounds of their drums, gongs, and voices filling the neighborhood. They drew in customers, so the teahouse built them a simple stage and shelter, into which more than one hundred audience members crowded, with waiters often having to add chairs. The waiters treated the customers very well. Although the teahouse was located in a narrow alley and was in poor condition, fans traveled considerable distances to attend performances, which were held three times a week. One blind old woman was carried by her husband on his bicycle in the morning, after which the old couple had lunch in the teahouse and waited for the show. The price of tea was reduced from two yuan to a little more than one yuan during the performances, because most attendees were retired workers on fixed incomes. During holidays, the society organized trips for its members, with Sichuan opera the core of its activities.[35]

In the Museum Tea Garden, women were practicing dance steps with red or yellow folded fans in their hands. After that, a chorus in the hall spent more than an hour singing "Socialism Is Good" (Shehui zhuyi hao), "Singing a Folk Song for the CCP" (Changzhi shan'ge gei dangting), and other, primarily "red songs," even though it was before the "Movement of Singing Red Songs" launched by Bo Xilai.[36] After the red songs, they sang the songs from "The Cowherd and the Weaving Girl" (Niu Lang and Zhi Nü), a famous love story from Huangmei opera.[37] This was followed by a radio recording of popular dance tunes. More than a dozen old women then performed the Red Silk Dance, made popular since the war, which immediately attracted a small crowd.[38] These elderly women practiced dancing every Wednesday, and the teahouse charged only three yuan for a bowl of tea.[39] In fact, women played a more active role than men in post-Mao public entertainment, dancing in all kinds of public places such as parks, city squares, and neighborhood exercise areas.[40]

Why was this form of individual entertainment subsumed by revolutionary, politicized songs? The reasons are complex. Most participants were retirees, steeped for decades in revolutionary culture, and such songs might have revived memories of lost youth. In addition, a significant number, particularly those who had been laid off, believed that they did not benefit from the post-Mao reforms, and were nostalgic for the Maoist "iron rice bowl." Singing revolutionary songs might have been a way to express dissatisfaction. Of course, for some, the songs had no political implications, and they sang them only because they were familiar with them. The influence of "revolutionary culture" was evident even after three decades of post-Mao reforms. The Red Silk Dance, for example, came from the Yangge (dance of planting the rice shoots) and has been a common type of popular entertainment since the Yan'an period (1935–1948).[41] The people performing that dance might have been reliving their youth and not really expressing any particular political inclination. Socialist and revolutionary entertainment had accompanied them from youth to old age; for them, "red culture" and "revolutionary culture" were pervasive and accepted. When they participated in social events and public life that had nothing to do with politics, they would unconsciously favor the culture they were most familiar with, or the culture that reminded them of their earlier days. For them and others, teahouses remained venues for social interaction and inexpensive amusement, even as society increasingly became polarized. The fact that teahouses alone could provide such numerous and inexpensive diversions was no doubt one reason why they not only survived, but flourished.

Whereas the teahouse was a man's world in pre-1949 China, gender differentiation in public places decreased under communism, which always claimed equality of women and men. In such public places as parks, city squares, and sometimes teahouses, often more women conducted activities than men. Several factors help account for this. First, women in China retired earlier than men. While male workers and government employees retired at sixty, blue-collar women did so at fifty and white-collar, fifty-five respectively. Second, among the many laid-off factory workers, women had more difficulties becoming re-employed, and many of them thus started their retired life in their forties. Third, women had a longer life expectancy; many widows relied on friends or social circles after their husbands were gone, and they often gathered in public places. Whereas women gained some freedom of employment under Mao, they won more tangible freedom in regard to public life in the post-Mao era. Women frequented teahouses not only as patrons but also made livings there, entering the conventional men's professions such as fortune-telling and earwax picking, as well as peddling and shoe polishing, as seen later in this chapter.

The World of Retired People

One often sees the elderly dancing and practicing tai chi in parks, public squares, and neighborhood exercise areas.[42] But for inexpensive socializing, eating, drinking tea, and playing mahjong, the teahouse was the retiree's preferred destination. It has been remarked that the "old teahouses in Chengdu are mostly the world of the elderly." With abundant free time, retirees could spend as many hours in the teahouse as they liked, interacting with both friends and strangers (see figure 5.2).[43]

We have the example of the Association of Former Postal Workers in Chengdu (Chengdu lao yougong xiehui), which met in teahouses monthly. At first, they went to the Joy Tea Garden, but when renovations there resulted in higher prices, they moved to the Museum Tea Garden (discussed above and in chapter 4). Generally, twenty to forty members would show up; people came and went and bought their own tea unless it was someone's birthday, when they shared the cost. An anthropologist

Figure 5.2 Group of retired people enjoying their pastime in a teahouse in a Chengdu suburb, September 2015. Author photo.

described one of their gatherings: Around 9 a.m., those who first drifted in moved eight tables together. Each paid for his or her own tea, generally buying the least expensive, at two yuan for boiling water for those who brought their own cups and tea leaves. After greeting each other, they chatted on topics ranging from the past, national affairs, social issues and problems, to families and children. If someone missed because of illness, the group would pay that person a visit. By noon, about ten people were left, and the hostess took their orders for lunch: dumplings, noodles, and other standard fare. About twenty minutes later, each received and paid for lunch. After eating, some said their goodbyes and left, and some chatted a bit more before heading home. No one played mahjong.[44]

In the summer of 2000, senior groups at the Great Benevolence Tea Garden were observed and noted in the author's fieldwork. At lunchtime, patrons left their tea bowls behind when they went to the inner hall to eat. Most were retired older women, eating at tables of ten. After lunch, they went back to their tea. Two women were walking out after finishing; one offered the other ten yuan, and the latter insisted, "It was my treat!" The ten yuan bill apparently had been transferred from one to the other many times. Finally, the first woman took back the bill and said with smile, "I do not want to argue with you anymore." Among several others going out, one said, "We should come earlier next Tuesday to get a better spot." Another replied, "So, we will meet here next Tuesday." It seemed they were former coworkers who met there each week. Someone said, "It is too hot inside. Outside is cooler." Some of them sat around the tables and played mahjong while chatting. The people in the pavilion seemed excited: they talked about someone's daughter, who was applying to graduate school in the United States.[45] The weekly get-together kept contacts alive.

For some seniors, the teahouse was the sole outlet. One elderly patron had begun to frequent the teahouse in 1977, going between 7 and 8 a.m. after his night shift and returning home a couple of hours later. After retiring, he often spent the entire day there, either bringing a lunch from home or buying a bowl of noodles for three to four yuan.[46] Mr. Lin, over eighty, grew bored after retiring from an eyeglasses shop, so family members took him to the Museum Tea Garden in the Great Benevolence Temple. He became a regular, coming alone during the week and with his family on weekends, and with his grandson during summer breaks. He preferred to sit under the eaves of the hall and drink quietly in a sort of meditation,

without his wife or grandchildren to distract. Waiters knew his quiet attitude, so they left a thermos with him to keep his tea warm. Mr. Lin did
sometimes chat with others, mostly about glasses. Mr. Yang, a former
middle-school math teacher in his sixties, was fond of the "cultural atmosphere." Later, he moved near the North City Gate, very far from the
temple, but continued to travel to the teahouse weekly by bus to catch up
with his friends. An amateur calligrapher liked to sit in the front yard near
the corridor in order to look at the calligraphy and paintings on the wall.
For him, the teahouse was like a visit to an art exhibition.[47]

Thus, some teahouses—unlike the busier and more expensive cafés,
clubs, hotels, and other places—became domains of the elderly. In
Chengdu, the relationship between the popular teahouses and their elderly
customers was direct and causal. The population of China has been aging,
and age was an important factor—along with educational background,
economic status, and ethnic identity—regarding entertainment genres and
venues. Whereas the young spent long hours confined to their workplaces,
the elderly became the major occupiers of urban, public spaces. Teahouses
met the needs of China's aging, urban residents, and in Chengdu these residents contributed, in turn, to the sustainability of teahouses and teahouse
culture.

Waiters and Waitresses

Many people made their living in teahouses: owners, employees, and associated workers. The most prominent were the waiters and waitresses. In
some small teahouses, the owners or managers took on these roles, as well
as those of stove keeper and accountant, while some larger teahouses had
as many as one hundred employees.[48] During the late Qing and Republican periods—when there were very few waitresses—waiters were called
"masters of tea" (*cha boshi*) or "room officers" (*tangguan*) and were very
skillful and knowledgeable. Today, only a few "masters of tea" survive,
as cultural treasures. One local newspaper depicted a photo of a certain
Master Fang with the following caption: "He is sixty-six years old in a
blue Chinese-style unlined jacket, black trousers, white socks, and a red
cloth on his waist; a long white towel is tied on his head. He carries sixteen sets of bowls and lids stacked over two feet high. He will not lose his

balance even if someone bumps into him. He can pour boiling water into two bowls simultaneously using two kettles, one in each hand, in an act called "two dragons having fun with pearls" (*erlong xizhu*).[49]

While the work was the same, the names of certain occupations had changed. People no longer called waiters *tangguan*, instead calling them *shifu* (master), which became most common for skilled men. In the past, only men were allowed to pour boiling water, but now, with the new openness, women have taken up the task.[50] In some higher-class teahouses, waiters were well educated and had the more elegant moniker of "tea artists" (*chayi shi*). Prosperity Ancient Teahouse had two tea artists who used long-spout, bright copper kettles to pour boiling water, as well as young waitresses, recent graduates of middle school or high school, who wore blue, floral, country-style outfits. The tea artists earned more than 1,000 yuan per month and the girls about 700 yuan. Tea artist Mr. Qiu was thirty-one years old and a graduate of Sichuan Agriculture University, with a major in tea production. He now was in charge of tea leaves, demonstrating expertise in the process of compounding, a secret that was an important part of the teahouse's appeal. He was quite confident in his skills.[51]

In lower-level teahouses, waiters were called "tea workers" (*chagong*) and were responsible for selling tea, pouring water, arranging tables and chairs, and washing and sterilizing bowls. The manager of the Museum Tea Garden said that tea workers had to be young because of the need to move quickly. After arriving at 8 a.m., the workers cleaned up, arranged tables and chairs, and began heating water. When customers arrived, they greeted them, served tea, and poured boiling water. Although their shifts ended at 5:30 p.m., they had to stay until all patrons had left, although theoretically tea workers worked eight hours per day. Most of the workers came from the counties near Chengdu, and some got their jobs through acquaintances in the business (see figure 5.3).[52]

At Museum Tea Garden, one tea worker from a rural village had been working six years, but his wife and children remained behind. He visited them every ten days or two weeks. He previously was a carpenter but started in the teahouse when his business dried up. He liked the teahouse environment and stable salary. As the oldest worker there, he was called "oldest brother." The youngest, also an outsider, got the job before graduating from high school. He said that the work was more strenuous than

Figure 5.3 Teahouse worker in a Chengdu suburb, September 2015. Author photo.

it appeared, and his arms were sore after a day's work. During breaks, he and the others often played mahjong. Their monthly wages were only 400 to 500 yuan, but lunch was provided by the teahouse, and free lodging was available on the grounds of the Great Benevolence Temple.[53]

Some well-educated girls and women became waitresses, including one recent college graduate who wanted to live in Chengdu but could not find another job. She eventually was promoted to head waitress. Her boyfriend asked her to quit her job; but when she discovered that he was too embarrassed to tell his coworkers where she worked, she ended their relationship. She did not necessarily like her job—in fact, she was studying English and computers for a better career—but she would not quit it to save his face.[54] Another example is Nostalgia Teahouse, which employed two teenage girls as waitresses. They were recent graduates of a middle school and were studying computers in a small city in Sichuan, but were too young and inexperienced to get a job in their field in Chengdu. Their salary for fourteen hours per day (8 a.m. to 10 p.m.) was 300 yuan per month, from which they paid 75 yuan each for rent (the owner paying the remainder, as well as providing two meals per workday).[55] One waitress left her home in a small city to work at the Tea Garden Balcony when it first opened, but her parents were not happy. She graduated from a professional school of chemistry but could not find a related job. She claimed that factories did not want female employees. She said her teahouse boss was good, paying for her accommodations and meals, but she did not reveal how much she earned. Each day she worked from 10 a.m. to midnight or even later if patrons were still playing mahjong.[56] The job market was tough for young people, especially those who did not have "social connections" (*guanxi*). Because of the difficulties finding stable, relatively high-paying jobs, many recent college graduates entered the service professions. From the 1980s to the 1990s, the government enacted market reforms that relaxed control of employment in the cities, and by the late 1990s, as one study points out, "the form and context of job-related competition had shifted considerably."[57]

A conversation between waitresses in the Pure Fountain Teahouse on South Stone Man Street tells us how they thought about the operation and management of the teahouse. One said, "Customers won't be happy with a dish of vegetables costing ten yuan." Another replied, "Eighty yuan per hour for a private room will scare customers away." However, one waitress said, "I don't care, and we are not the manager. I've gotten used to the complaints." The conversation then focused on clothing and shoes: where to buy, for how much, whether or not something was a good bargain.[58] Pure Fountain Teahouse and its building were owned by a government office, so the workers were relatively idle, and in the free time they talked. Although business was not good, the workers did not appear to worry much, because they did not have to pay rent. Sometimes it was special arrangements like this that allowed a teahouse to survive the stiff competition.

On the one hand, the post-Mao reforms after 1977 and the resultant commercialization provided more job opportunities for women, and women took advantage of the increasing jobs in the service sector. On the other hand, because businesses now had the freedom to decide about employees, women of middle age and older and those who were unattractive were put at a disadvantage. Many had had "iron rice bowls," but now they suffered weak job security, as younger and better-educated, and better-looking, women entered the job pool. This included even those from rural areas who were willing to do hard work for lower pay. As a middle-aged woman who worked at a state-owned teahouse jokingly said, "If it were not a state-owned teahouse, it would not hire 'old' women like us as waitresses, but young girls."[59] Indeed, employment ads often stated requirements of sex, age, and appearance. In China, there was no law that forbade such discrimination. Therefore, the new and intense economic development did not ensure gender equality. Attitudes of discrimination have been analyzed in a sociological study that found that "society's perception of women as workers" was a hurdle for women.[60]

In my book on the teahouse of the late-Qing and Republican periods, I pointed out that teahouses in Chengdu were a gendered domain. Although women eventually were allowed to enter to watch performances there, elites accused those who did of indecency. The situation changed after 1937 and the War of Resistance against Japan. When the coastal population flowed into the city, the first generation of waitresses emerged, but lasted only two or three years under a constant barrage of attacks by the government, elites, and society at large. After the Mao era, as one observer noted, "it appears that on balance women's positions in society have suffered under the [post-Mao] reforms" and "their position relative to men has in some important ways deteriorated," although "women enjoy an improved overall standard of living as the economy grows."[61] In Chengdu, women's equality was also complex. In the post-Mao reforms of Late Socialism, women in the teahouse as customers, performers, and workers became commonplace; they had many more opportunities for both public life and work in public places, and gender divisions became less prominent. However, in the process of teahouse employment, like employment all across China, women often were still discriminated against, even for their age and appearance. The service industry required large numbers of women, but employers often hired only younger and better-looking ones. What the waitress mentioned above reflected this reality.

"Floating People"

After 1977, with the reforms, a large number of peasants left their rural homes for the cities to make a living.[62] Many worked at factories, workshops, construction sites, restaurants, or became self-employed service providers. Many found careers in teahouses as fortune-tellers, earwax pickers, shoe polishers, and petty peddlers. Their services made teahouse life livelier. Some of these occupations were customarily regarded as debasing, and they were often perceived as appropriate to be undertaken by the "floating population" (*liudong renkou*). The jobs just mentioned had always managed to survive tough political and economic situations, and in Chengdu they flourished in the new world of the marketplace.

Fortune-Tellers

Like the majority of jobs in the teahouse, fortune-telling was an ancient one, and it was among the most colorful. Its relationship with the teahouse had not changed over hundreds of years.[63] The Prosperity Ancient Teahouse hired a fortune-teller in an effort to revive old practices and gain business. The particular fortune-teller was well known, and charged sixty yuan.[64] A female fortune-teller at the Cry of the Crane Teahouse claimed to be a "spirit fortune-teller" and said that she had worked in the area for more than a decade. She was not a Chengdu native but had lived in the city for more than twenty years. She said she told the fortunes only of those who had good futures and refused to tell fortunes for certain types, such as evil minds (*xinshu buzheng*). As for price, she said, "whatever you'd like," adding that someone once paid her one hundred yuan (see figure 5.4).[65]

According to an article in *Shangwu zaobao* (Commerce morning news), some "master fortune-tellers" were active in the high-level teahouses in the area of North and South Zong Streets. Unlike their old-style counterparts, they had "professional certificates," and like everyone around them they communicated via pagers and cell phones. It was said that they had genuine powers and were accurate: some of their businessmen clients achieved great success by following their advice. These fortune-tellers charged a very high fee, as high as 1,000 yuan; some earned about half a million a year. Of course, they competed against each other. The article's author did some investigating and discovered that almost all the area's teahouse employees knew a "White Bearded Great Divinity" (Baihuzi daxian), the most expensive and popular fortune-teller for certain rich businessmen, someone who never needed to seek out new business. One night, the reporter finally caught up with the man, who was sitting alone at a table,

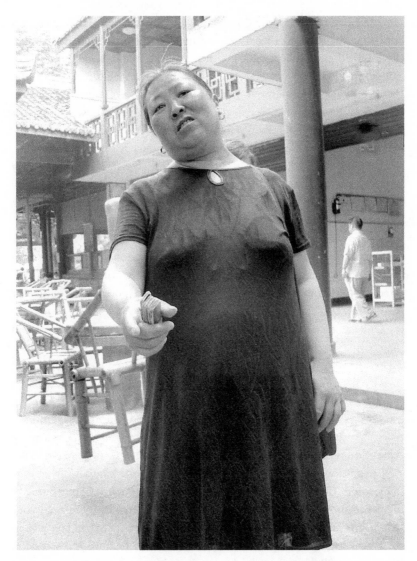

Figure 5.4 Fortune-teller at the Cry of the Crane Teahouse,
June 2003. Author photo.

drinking tea. His white beard was six inches long, drawing great attention
along with his long, white gown, which made him appear to be "utterly
magical" (*xianqi shizu*), but no one approached. A teahouse worker told
the reporter that he often came, and that they served him for free.[66]

The relationship of the "masters" with certain teahouses came out clearly in the reporter's work. He learned that fortune-tellers in the area usually had good relationships with teahouses, and habituated them for long hours. Those who were not well known charged a few dozen to a hundred yuan, but the famous ones could get several hundred or even several thousand. They spent the entire day at teahouses, waiting for customers. They generally did not approach people, but waited for customers to come to them, basing their fees on the customers' appearance. While their skills differed little from those in lower-class teahouses, they were astute observers and arranged their appearance to attract wealthy customers, especially businessmen who were accompanied by young women. Because fortune-tellers attracted business to the teahouses, teahouse employees were friendly, even providing them with free tea when business was good, although they did not allow them to approach the teahouse patrons too forcefully. Moreover, territorial claims created conflict among "masters," which created potential trouble for teahouses.[67]

One summer day in 2000, in a teahouse by the Funan River, an old man could be observed carrying a bunch of bamboo chips.[68] He asked, "Do you want to know your fortune for five yuan?" He said he could make a determination by a random drawing from the chips, or if he based himself on a person's face it was eight yuan. A question was posed to him first: "Tell me anything about myself, so I can tell if your fortune-telling is good." "How old are you?" he asked. I told him my age. He looked at my face and my left palm and said, "You had bad luck in 1995 and 1998." "Wrong," I said. "1995 or 1998," he said, covering himself. But he was then told: "Good things happened to me in both years." "Your lines are light and spread out, and you must have been idle and very relaxed your whole life," he said. I smiled and said, "You are totally wrong! I have been very busy my whole life. Do you assume I am idle because you see me in the teahouse?" This was all a lead-up to an invitation to converse more generally.

He explained that he was seventy-one years old and had made a living telling fortunes for three years. He previously was a farmer in Hebei Province and had received only a few years of education in a private school. He taught himself fortune-telling in the 1980s. He then showed a wrinkled, worn book, *Comprehensive Writings on Spiritual Fortune-Tellers*

(*Shenxiang quanshu*), publisher not stated. At the time, business was not very good, but on his best days he could earn forty yuan, and tips could be as high as twenty yuan. An elderly fortune-teller with long hair and a beard like a Daoist priest happened to walk toward him, but then he turned away and left. One assumes that he avoided areas where he saw competitors.

Later, he said, "I find you have spirit in your eyes, like a knowledgeable person. You must be a scholar, not a military person." I replied, "Everyone can see this," but "Can you tell how I make a living?" He guessed, "A teacher." "This is the first time you got something right," I smiled. He then asked for help in understanding a book, if time allowed for him to go home to retrieve it. Nearly an hour later, he came back with a wrinkled book, *Comprehensive Writings on Lu Ban* (*Lu Ban quanshu*). The print was rough; it was obviously a pirated copy. He turned to a page containing diagrams, pictures, and illustrations regarding the nailing of a wooden "goodness board" (*shanpai*) above a door to improve relations between neighbors. The diagrams explained the size of the board, how to nail it, where the nail should be placed. The captions were traditional Chinese characters without punctuation, which made them difficult to read. In some places, the text read "animal board" (*shoupai*), obviously a misprint of "goodness," since the two characters are quite similar looking. Although some of the jargon was difficult, a decent reading was produced. The fortune-teller inquired if he would see me at this place again, perhaps wondering if he could get more help with the classical Chinese. Unfortunately, though, this did not occur (see figure 5.5).

These stories offer us a great deal of information about the people who made a living in the teahouse. First, many came from outside Chengdu as migrant laborers; they were relatively unskilled and took advantage of the opportunity offered by fortune-telling. As long as they could read, they could find a bit of basic knowledge from fortune-telling books and immediately enter the business. Although they might not earn much, they could at least survive in the strange, new environment of the marketplace. Second, fortune-telling traditionally was a man's profession, but with the post-Mao reforms more women pursued it; this reflected society's growing tolerance for women in historically male domains. Third, fortune-tellers operated at different levels; some became rich, while others hardly made

Figure 5.5 An elderly fortune-teller at a teahouse by the Funan River, July 2004. He is telling the fortune of a foreign visitor. Author photo.

ends meet, depending on experience and reputation. Fourth, fortune-tellers provided entertainment and novelty for teahouse-goers. Not all who paid for the service believed what they were told, but patrons enjoyed the diversion or sought the fortune-teller's blessing. Richard Smith has noted that "divination touched every sector of Chinese society, from emperor to peasant."[69] This was true in the late-imperial period, and to a certain extent it remains true today.

Earwax Pickers

Earwax picking was another old profession in the teahouse, found in almost every one, from late Qing to the Republic. However, like teahouse culture overall, it reached its nadir during the Cultural Revolution. With Late Socialism and the reforms, however, earwax pickers returned. Most were farmers, artisans, and peddlers, with some from rural areas, who turned to earwax picking when they could not find other work. This was

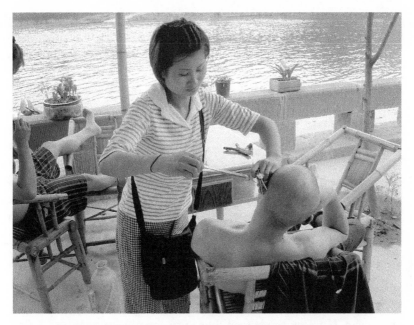

Figure 5.6 Female earwax picker, July 2003. Author photo.

considered a skilled trade, an improvement over manual labor in the fields. This was traditionally a man's job, although women took up the practice toward the end of the twentieth century (see figure 5.6).

The earwax picker at Prosperity Ancient Teahouse was just over thirty years old, from a small town in southern Sichuan, and had been in the business for seven or eight years. He came to Chengdu about six or seven years previously and first plied his trade at a teahouse by the Funan River, which charged him 200 yuan per month out of his earnings, which were about 1,000 yuan. When Prosperity had first opened, the owner, who knew of the picker's skill, invited him to work there. Now the earwax picker paid 6,000 to 7,000 yuan annually to the teahouse but earned about the same as in the teahouse by the Funan River. However, he said that the new location was much more comfortable because it was air-conditioned. He wore white clothing and had a badge on his chest that stated that his basic price was ten yuan, or twenty yuan if the customer wanted him to use disposable tools. He said that most of his patrons were Chengdu natives, because people from other places did not like earwax picking. Also, a majority of his customers were young or middle-aged, because most elderly patrons found his prices too high. The teahouse had a collaborative relationship in which tourist agencies brought foreign tourists to the teahouse, some of whom would request the picker's services. He also provided massages, charging forty to fifty yuan for both earwax picking and a massage (see figure 5.7).[70]

In the Museum Tea Garden, an earwax picker about forty to fifty years old walked between tables soliciting business and announcing his approach with large iron pincers in his hand. He was friendly enough with the waiter to have him get change for a large bill. When he did not have a customer, he joined the waiter at a table to drink tea. After having worked in a barbershop for a few years, he learned the skill from his father at the age of seventeen, and had practiced this craft at the Museum Tea Garden for nine years. He lived in Shuangliu, a suburb of Chengdu. He had even taught an apprentice, his brother-in-law, who now made a living in the teahouses along the Funan River. An apprentice had to learn the skill and practice for a year before working independently.

When he started out, nine years earlier, he charged only one and a half yuan, but now he charged four yuan for new customers and three

Figure 5.7 Earwax picker at Cry of the Crane Teahouse, June 2003. Author photo.

for returning customers. The service lasted from a few minutes to ten minutes. No license was needed, but he had to pay the teahouse 200 yuan by the fifth of each month, and he never had been late with a payment. He claimed that all the teahouses in this temple were his turf, and other earwax pickers would be expelled by the teahouses. He could earn 600 to 700 yuan monthly, for 400 to 500 yuan profit after his fee. His wife polished shoes for patrons in the teahouses, at 1 yuan per pair, and could earn another 500 to 600 yuan each month. He worked from 9 a.m. to late afternoon. When business slowed between 4 p.m. and 5 p.m., he sometimes went to the Funan River teahouses, where he did not have to pay a fee but had to compete with other earwax pickers.

He used five tools. The unique sound of his big iron pincers attracted customers' attention. A long, narrow knife, with a handle, was used to cut the fine hairs just inside the ear that blocked his view into the ear canal. The most important tool, a long and thin brass blade, was used to scratch inside the ear, a pleasant sensation. Smaller pincers were used to extract earwax. Finally, the process concluded with several swipes using a small brush made of goose feathers. The tools, some of which he made and others that were made to his specifications by blacksmiths, cost forty to fifty yuan. His lowest price was three yuan. He said that on a few occasions a customer refused to pay. Once, he worked on three young men, but they said his service was unsatisfactory and refused to pay, which resulted in a verbal dispute that became physical. He was so angry that he overturned their table, which shattered tea bowls. Aided by other workers, he took the young men to a local police station, where they were ordered to pay twelve yuan for the service and eight for the damage.

It was good for him that he was able to keep his whole family together. He and his wife rode a motorbike into the city each day, storing it at his sister's home on Second Ring Road because motorbikes that did not have a Chengdu registration were not allowed into the downtown. He and his wife had a lunch of porridge and steamed bread with free pickles every day for only one and a half yuan at a small restaurant near the temple. They did not need to buy a ticket (one yuan) to enter the temple because the gatekeepers knew them. He had two sons, one in elementary school and the other in middle school. Because it was summer break, both sons stayed at the teahouse every day. He did not, however, want his sons to follow in his footsteps and thought of sending the older one to train as an auto mechanic.

He wanted to open an auto repair shop in the area where he lived, which he said was "a good location for such a business." He also talked about his family in the countryside. He was responsible for a seven-*mu* (about 1.1 acre) rice field, which even during harvest—the busiest season—required only three days of work. His parents helped him take care of the field and his home, where he kept more than twenty each of chickens, ducks, and pigs, plus a water buffalo. The family often sold eggs at the market. The income from the rice paddy, livestock, and other cash crops could reach 10,000 yuan. Adding earwax picking and shoe polishing brought the family's total income to about 16,000 to 17,000 yuan per year. About 10,000 went to living expenses, and the rest was deposited in a bank account.[71]

Many earwax pickers, like this man and other teahouse workers, came from rural areas and managed this sort of juggling of farmwork with a Chengdu job. In the whole nation there were hundreds of millions of migrant workers, whose work situations and new avenues for income profoundly influenced economic development and urban life across China.[72] However, unlike the majority of migrant workers, this earwax picker continued to live in his rural hometown, thus avoiding the pain of long-term separation from family. Furthermore, his wife worked in the same place, so that the family could always be together. Of course, this arrangement was not without costs. Their children spent their days in this bustling place filled with all kinds of people, often subjected to smoking and sometimes crude language. Such conditions might not be healthy and could be seen as holding the children back in terms of education and cultural skills. Although the migrant workers' situation was difficult, nevertheless, compared with those who stayed in their rural areas, incomes tended to be attractive. This earwax picker, for example, knew how to accrue savings and even planned a better future for his sons. The sons' lack of formal education, however, was a certain disadvantage, considering the competition from urbane Chengdu children, and at the end of the day they might end up following their father's footsteps.

Shoe Polishers, Barbers, and Vendors

In addition to waiters, fortune-tellers, and earwax pickers, the teahouse hosted other vocations, such as shoe polishers, barbers, and newspaper vendors. Since roads in the area of the Pure Fragrance Teahouse were under construction and very muddy, shoe polishers were a common sight. They beat a brush against the stool they carried, announcing their arrival with "Shoe polishing! Shoe polishing!" A middle-aged country woman stopped by the teahouse gate and asked if anyone wanted to have shoes cleaned and polished for one yuan. She carried a bag containing brushes, shoe cream, and cloths. She handed the customer a pair of plastic sandals to wear and then carried the muddy shoes out the door. Sitting on a stool she brought, she first scraped off the mud with a toothbrush and water from a plastic bottle. Then she wiped, oiled, and polished the shoes. She said she came from a county in northern Sichuan and worked in the city every winter and summer, when there was not much to do in the fields; she earned 200 to 300 yuan per month. Without this, she could not afford to send her children to school. She said that the job provided more freedom than working for a boss, and she could go home anytime she wished. She estimated that there were more than fifty shoe polishers in the area.[73]

Of course, some teahouses prohibited them in order to prevent the kind of fraud mentioned in a recent newspaper article. It described a street-side teahouse with many customers drinking tea and playing chess as shoe polishers came and went; a female shoe polisher called out, "Shoe polishing! Shoe polishing! Cheap but guaranteed quality!" A young man with a fashionable hairstyle asked, "How much?" The woman looked at his shoes and said, "Fifty cents, just the cost of the shoe oil." The man replied, "This pair of shoes was bought in France and cost more than 1,000 yuan. Can you do a good job?" She replied, "You don't pay if you are not satisfied." The man took off his shoes, and the woman gave him a pair of slippers. The woman took the shoes to a spot under a tree and went to work as the man continued relaxing and reading a newspaper. After he finished reading, he wondered why she had not returned, and realized that she was long gone.[74]

At the end of the twentieth century, some barbers still conducted business at teahouses, especially outside the smaller teahouses; but in general they were not as popular as before. A barber simply placed a chair where he wanted to do business, using hot water provided by the teahouse.[75] If a man needed a haircut, he could enjoy a leisurely wait inside the teahouse. A column in *Shangwu zaobao* named "News on the Sidewalks" ("Jiebian xinwen") told of a barber who put a stall outside the Sandy River Tea Garden

(Shahe chayuan) and enjoyed a very brisk business. Most of his customers were middle-aged or older men. Once, when a man was waiting for his turn, the barber smiled at him and said, "Sir, I have to go back home after I finish with this customer because I have an urgent errand to run." So the man went elsewhere to have his haircut. The following month, the man returned to the teahouse for a haircut; however, the barber did the same thing. Another customer whispered to him, "The barber had nothing to do at home; that was just an excuse because he saw your big forehead and thought it might be difficult to work on. He has no professional ethics." The man then told all the patrons there, "None of us will ask the barber for haircuts ever again. He just wants to earn easy money and does not care about people." The barber's business slumped. When he asked patrons if they needed a haircut, they often replied, "I have to go back home because I have an urgent errand to run," repeating the barber's exact words.[76]

Vendors were active in teahouses, providing a convenience and adding a certain liveliness to the environment. One summer day by the Funan River, food hawkers were plentiful, making it possible for people to remain in their seats for a meal. A middle-aged woman, who looked like she was from the country, carried two baskets containing jars of spices and sauces, and called out, "Cold noodles, bean jelly, tofu pudding," but it was not lunchtime, and nobody bought anything. Later, an old woman came by with a big plate filled with magnolia blossoms with a strong, lovely fragrance, but she also found no buyers.[77] Almost every teahouse had someone selling newspapers, and they had good business. People liked to get caught up on current events with their tea. At the same teahouse and the same time mentioned above, more than a dozen newspaper vendors, men and women, young and old, came and went on bicycles or by foot, crying out *"Zaobao"* (*Shangwu zaobao*, or Morning commerce news), *"Huaxi bao"* (*Huaxi dushi bao*, or West China metropolitan news), and the like.[78] At the Cry of the Crane Teahouse, two or three newspaper vendors conducted business. An old woman with white hair sold *Huaxi bao* (see figure 5.8), while a young man with a Beijing accent sold *Hong Kong Ta Kung Pao* (*Dagong bao*, published in Hong Kong). He looked well-educated and wore a gold watch, unlike the others. At four yuan, his newspaper was more expensive than local ones, so he did not have many customers.[79]

Figure 5.8 Newspaper peddler at the Cry of the Crane Teahouse,
June 2003. Author photo.

All these trades had a long history in the teahouse. Although every
aspect of the city—its politics, economy, culture, and society—had been
fundamentally transformed, the teahouse remained a space where a good
number of people could earn a living, further demonstrating the vitality of a centuries-old service culture. Although vendors reappeared in the
teahouses, they found a different environment, where, unlike before, not
all teahouses welcomed their service, especially the middle-level or high-
level ones, whose customers liked undisturbed privacy. Yet in the open-
air and lower-level teahouses, they enjoyed good business. Workers and
peddlers there became part of teahouse culture and have continued to
play an active role in everyday life, although no one can easily predict
how long their prosperity may last under waves of commercialization and
globalization.

The floating people, especially the peasant workers from rural areas,
became one of the major forces in the enrichment of urban life in Chengdu
and elsewhere, both as workers and consumers: they contributed to

the prosperity of the city. According to anthropologists' investigations, migrant workers made a living in construction, restaurants, factories, domestic service, street cleaning, and other livelihoods that "most urbanities are not willing to take." They had to "break through the constraints of the household registration (*hukou*) system to work and trade in the cities" and overcame many obstacles caused by "social and political tensions exist[ing] between migrant newcomers, the state, and urban society."[80] Dorothy Solinger defines the "floating population" by three criteria: "They have crossed over some territorial, administrative boundary; they have not altered their permanent registration (their *hukou*); and, at least in theory, they 'flow in and out.'" They were not registered as urban citizens, and thus they "were denied free compulsory education, [and] deprived of many of the perquisites that went with permanent employment in state-owned factories." Given the fact that migrant workers did not have rights and faced discrimination, Solinger goes so far as to suggest that "to view Chinese peasants in the metropolises as foreign immigrants there—as noncitizens—is fully in line with the general literature on citizenship."[81]

I should point out that migrant workers, like any large group of people, had many different types of experiences. Some did very well and established businesses and bought homes in the city. We easily find that in Chengdu, like in many other cities, most small businesses are actually owned and run by migrants, who are heavily represented as workers in restaurants, remodeling shops, construction, street-corner teahouses, and other occupations. However, many more continue to struggle for survival in the city, earning low wages, while many of them have become self-employed, making a living in the teahouses or other kinds of places by providing their services as fortune-tellers, earwax pickers, shoe polishers, peddlers, and so on. Although they experienced hardships, their situation might be an improvement for them, with a greater chance for upward mobility than would be the case for those who stayed behind. Certainly their presence greatly enhanced everyday life in the city, contributing significantly to the overall economic development, prosperity, and public life.

6

THE POWER OF MAHJONG

One of the most prominent aspects of the teahouse, especially in Chengdu, was mahjong, which was often played in the street-corner teahouses. Some of these teahouses became pure "houses of mahjong" (*majiang shi*) because the players used every table there. The mahjong phenomenon became such a memorable characterization of Chengdu that a joke took hold throughout China: air travelers could hear the clack of mahjong players when their planes were over Chengdu. Of course, people in planes could not hear this noise; but in fact residents in certain neighborhoods did, and this sometimes caused problems. This chapter takes up a notable, and the first, mahjong lawsuit in China, which was filed in October 2000, in order to examine how an everyday leisure activity inspired a nationwide debate over the issues of "healthy entertainment," a city's image, and modernity itself.

Anthropologist Paul Festa published an excellent study of mahjong in contemporary China; it examines such cultural phenomena as nationalism, "Chineseness," and civility. He discusses these issues with a national perspective by using mahjong "to demonstrate the particular strategies by which the party-state appropriates a private leisure activity in order simultaneously to build the nation and the consumer economy."[1] Festa's viewpoint was national; my approach here, however, is to provide an empirical study based on a single city and to use a microhistorical perspective, before arriving at the involvement and motives at the national level. I discuss mahjong and related issues based on media reports about mahjong from the year 2000 alone; such reports proved to be rich sources of information and reflected popular sentiments.

The focus will be on conflicts not just between individual rights and collective interests, but also conflicts among individuals. I also discuss how the market economy in today's China coexists with older lifestyles, and how such changes have shaped the image of the city. I examine the extent to which daily life has moved away from both the Communists' control and "socialist morality," and how people and the government responded to new standards for "healthy lifestyles" and for improving the city's image. By examining mahjong-related issues, I bring out the way in which teahouses and teahouse culture reflected changes in the larger society, and explore a wave of transformations in Chengdu—involving the economy, society, culture, and politics. These transformations affected China as a whole.

First of all, I look at a personal story, that of Yu Yongjun, to shed light on the conflicts that existed among neighbors. Then, at the level of the community, I examine the role of the residential committee in the neighborhood. Third, I observe the responses to Yu Yongjun's problem by the municipal government and official media that were heavily concerned with the city's image; and finally, from a national perspective, I reveal the socialist state's dilemma of encouraging mahjong (one of the nation's most popular pastimes) as a good use of leisure time, while also handling the problem of gambling that the game often created.

A Lawsuit over Mahjong

Yu Yongjun, a twenty-eight-year-old woman, lived in an apartment in a residential complex in Chengdu. The windows of her apartment on the second floor faced an "activity room" (*huodong shi*) on the lower level that was run by the residential committee (*jumin weiyuanhui*), where residents, mostly retired elders, came to play mahjong from morning to midnight every day. The noise made it difficult for Yu and her child to sleep, and resulted in nervous exhaustion for which she took sleeping pills. She complained to the residential committee repeatedly and even called the police several times, but the problem continued. Yu finally sued the committee, claiming that the noise seriously undermined her health.

The case caused a dramatic reaction from local residents and the media. More than three hundred residents and twenty media outlets were present on the first day of the court hearing on November 16, 2000.[2] The reason the case drew such attention was the enormous impact of mahjong on people's lives. Mahjong is one of the most popular forms of entertainment in China: many wished to know how the case would influence daily life. The issue also affected Chengdu's reputation as a slow-paced, leisurely city: Was the attachment to mahjong something to value and continue, or was there no place for it in the modern world? Furthermore, what constitutes "healthy" entertainment and lifestyles? Finally, and most important, how could society balance the collective interests with individual rights, or, as alluded to above, the rights of contending individuals? China's socialist state has long emphasized the collective, but with intense social and economic development, people have increasingly pursued personal interests. This case directly addressed the matter.

The consideration of mahjong as a social issue is not new; the game cropped up as a topic in late-Qing urban reform, when new elites and local authorities regarded it as a vice that wasted time and encouraged gambling. Opium and gambling became major targets of the police after these activities were criminalized in the first decade of the twentieth century. While the anti-opium campaign was relatively successful, at least before the 1911 Revolution, gambling, mainly at mahjong, still existed, and the police searched homes, teahouses, and street corners and arrested and punished players. This policy was not only a reflection of the reformers' emotional investment against gambling but also their denial of the nation's most popular recreation. No reform could quickly supplant a lifestyle that had emerged over centuries, and mahjong gambling remained very popular in both public and private places in the Republican era because the game had deep and solid cultural roots in both private, family activity and public recreation.[3]

After the Communists' victory in 1949, the new government continued the previous government's policy that outlawed gambling, but had greater success in enforcement. Playing mahjong was identified as a "backward" part of the "feudal" or "bourgeois" lifestyle and came under furious attack from proponents of "revolutionary culture."[4] While mahjong was still played in some family homes, it was no longer seen in public. During the Cultural Revolution, mahjong was regarded as a symbol of the "old culture," and almost all mahjong paraphernalia was destroyed either by the Red Guard or by its owners, in order to avoid any problem or punishment.[5] In the post-Mao era, however, with its economic reform, social openness, and less government control of people's daily lives, the playing of mahjong revived everywhere. Despite the variety of new types of entertainment, mahjong was still the most popular pastime. One heard the saying: "Everywhere the mountains and rivers in this nation are gray" (Quanguo shanhe yipian ma). The word *ma* is used to mean "gray" and as part of the word "mahjong." The saying was borrowed from a popular propaganda slogan during the Cultural Revolution that ran, "Everywhere the mountains and rivers in this nation are red," meaning Maoist thought covered all of China (see figure 6.1).[6]

Chengdu is well-known for its mahjong life, especially as practiced in the teahouses. Traditionally, teahouses in Chengdu were spaces and venues in which all kinds of people could engage in all kinds of activity: talk and gossip, legal and illegal business, job searches, information gathering, political criticisms, meetings, gambling, and playing games such as chess, cards, and mahjong.[7] As previous chapters have examined, after the Communists took over the city, the number of teahouses plummeted, but they made a comeback in Late Socialism. More people than ever before now play mahjong in the teahouses.

Because the population of today's China, like that in most Western countries, is aging, the interests of the elderly become a crucial consideration for local administrators. The living patterns of current residents have contributed to a struggle for public recreational space. In the past, Chengdu residents lived in low-rise (mostly single- or two-story) streetside buildings or in residential compounds, so they had many opportunities to interact and socialize and had easy access to cheap entertainment. Since the intense citywide urban demolitions and construction that began after the post-Mao reforms, people have increasingly moved into high-rise apartment buildings, where families tend not to spend time directly with neighbors. As a result, public activity rooms became important areas for socialization. Some residential committees, following the trend, provided

Figure 6.1 Playing mahjong at Museum Tea Garden at Great Benevolent Temple, May 2003. Author photo.

space for mahjong and tea, ostensibly to provide a variety of activities for elder residents. These facilities become quasi-teahouses, but were tax-exempt. The activity room in Yu Yongjun's case was one such place, the social hub of the neighborhood.

The Personal Story: Conflict among Neighbors

At the first court hearing on November 16, 2000, details of the case were revealed: At 10:20 p.m. on October 7, 2000, residents playing mahjong in the activity room made enough noise that they prevented Yu and her little boy from falling asleep. She asked the players to stop, but nobody paid attention. She grew so angry that she cut the power to the room. The next morning, members of the residential committee detained her and did not allow her to leave until she provided a full explanation of the incident. She called the police, and the police officer who arrived suggested that the committee move the activity to a new location. The committee decided to hold a meeting and let the residents themselves decide. Seventy residents, mostly retirees in their fifties and sixties, attended the meeting. The director of the committee started the meeting with an explanation of the cause of the conflict and a review of relevant items in the "Law of the Urban Residential Committee" (Chengshi jumin weiyuanhui zuzhifa). Then she asked residents to discuss the matter. An overwhelming majority supported the continued playing of mahjong. Many agreed that mahjong was "all right for elders to play . . . , so the activity room for elders should be kept open." They agreed, however, that the hours could be limited. As one of them said, "We cannot sacrifice our interests for her own interest."[8]

Clearly, there was a conflict of rights. In China, people have been told that personal interest should be sacrificed for collective interests, and Yu's action seemed to have violated the principle. The conflict may be seen, in some sense, as an indication of the awakening of individual rights—a challenge to conventional notions. At the same time, collective rights in this case weren't so clear-cut: it could be argued that Yu represented a "collective" comprising all residents who claim the need of harmony and quiet, because those things flow from the human right of housing per se. After all, a residential complex was different from commercial buildings, which are not expected to provide harmony and quiet.

In the meeting, Yu repeated her predicament: "Elders can have many kinds of activities, and why do they only play mahjong? It is okay to play mahjong, but one cannot disturb others' rest." She complained that some people played mahjong from eight o'clock in the morning, continued it after lunch, and went on until near midnight. "How could it be all right that I can get some rest only after midnight?" She requested that the activity room be open from 10 a.m. to noon and from 2 to 6 p.m., with mahjong not permitted at noon when her child napped, nor in the evening, when the child studied. The others scoffed and laughed at her request, asking why she should have the right to restrict when and where they played. They stated, "Over three hundred households in this residential compound do not oppose playing mahjong. . . . You are too bossy!" An old man angrily proclaimed, "If you want quiet, you should not live in this apartment or even in Chengdu." Yu's voice was buried by criticism. At the end of the meeting, the committee director asked for a vote, and sixty-seven voted for and one against the playing of mahjong in the evening. As a compromise, residents agreed to close the room at 10 p.m. in winter and at 11 p.m. in summer, and that anyone being too loud would be asked to leave.[9]

Yu felt that she had no other option but to sue the residential committee. "I cannot call the police every night," Yu said, "so I had no choice except to go to the court."[10] Yu presented the court with three demands: an end to the excessive noise; compensation of 5,000 yuan to cover medical costs and lost wages; and a requirement that the defendants pay the costs of the lawsuit. The representative of the residential committee reiterated that the activity room was legally established according to the requirement of the superior administration, and was not for profit. The room was very small, so the noise of playing mahjong should not be loud enough to damage her health, and there was no direct link between the noise and Yu's symptoms. Yu, however, showed a letter from her doctor confirming that she was suffering from neurasthenia and a written confirmation from the police that acknowledged the noise issue. The court stated that the letters were not adequate support for Yu's claim and pointed out that the key to this case was proving whether the playing of mahjong caused "noise pollution"; but neither party was able to provide authoritative evidence. The court would appoint the Bureau of Environmental Observation and Measurement in Chengdu to measure the noise and resume the case after the data were available.[11]

Initially, Yu was a winner, at least at the surface level. After the lawsuit started, residents no longer played mahjong, and the activity room was closed. But this had problematic implications, because although the committee closed the room while the lawsuit was under way, some residents told Yu that as soon as the case was over, they would go back to playing as before. Yu herself said that, regardless of the outcome of the case, "I have become a sacrifice." Not only did she have a feud with neighbors, but the publicity and pressure surrounding the case caused her to lose her boyfriend. "Of course, I will never compromise and will never leave this place," she promised, because "people across the whole country support me." She said that some people offered emotional and financial support, but that others were hostile. For example, one man called her and asked, "Why do you want to go to the court? You should first find a man for yourself."[12]

After the high-profile hearing on November 16, 2000, which was widely covered by newspapers and television stations, the case dropped from sight, with no follow-up reports about future hearings, trial, or even verdict. For several years, no trace of the lawsuit's result was found. Finally, in March 2007, the *Sichuan Morning Paper* (*Tianfu zaobao*) wrote about what happened to Yu and the case. Before the second hearing, Yu had quietly disappeared from public view. Six years later, when a journalist went looking for her at the apartment complex and asked around about her, residents still remembered her and the famous case. One said, "Everybody in this complex disliked her; how could this woman live here after she made such bad relationships with her neighbors?" The journalist finally found Yu's new place, just ten minutes' walk from her previous home, and interviewed her. "I moved, got a new job, and remarried," Yu said with a smile. While the activity room had been locked after she launched the lawsuit, she had remained unhappy. "It was impossible to continue to live there, with probably a thousand other residents. How can a person fight a thousand? Some people cursed me, and some even spat at me. My son was bullied, and my boyfriend left me. Frankly, I even considered suicide," she added. However, she said that she did not regret her actions. "Why should I? I did nothing wrong. How could a person live such a miserable life with such noise? Nobody could put up with it for very long." She told the reporter that she was now happy, especially with her marriage and new job.[13]

The Neighborhood's Story: The Residential Committee and Its Dilemma

During Early Socialism, under Mao's regime, most urban residents lived inside a local unit called a *danwei*—"the place where Chinese work," but also the "lowest level of the political system." These places included government offices, factories, companies, and cultural organizations—any place where every aspect of employee life, from food in the cafeterias to health care to entertainment, was handled by the *danwei* organization. In Chengdu, as in many cities, the formation of *danwei* life for so many people had a strong impact on the very nature of public life. The *danwei*'s vast takeover of public needs and services also may be considered as part of the story of the decline of teahouse businesses and the teahouse as public space and urban culture during Early Socialism.[14] However, in the city, a large number stayed out of any *danwei* unit. These were people at the lower level of society, who relied solely on their labor for a livelihood. They depended more on public spaces than those who lived in a *danwei*; thus they were a major source of customers for teahouses.

Somewhat different from the *danwei*, in the socialist city, residential committees were the base-level organizations for the purpose of neighborhood control. They were established as soon as the CCP took power; they provided a useful tool of urban control and played a very active role in political movements during Mao's era. Ultimately they helped to form a "planned social life."[15] The committees have actually become a large network in China of about 119,000 neighborhood-based organizations. According to "Law of the Urban Residential Committees," they are "autonomous mass organizations for self-governing, self-educating, and self-serving." Chosen from residents, most of their heads and members are retirees and often have personal relationships with other residents. As a kind of "quasi-official organization," they form a bridge between the state and society, in order, the law says, "to maintain a network of personal relationships between the government bureaucracy and its constituents."[16] Their functions include settlement of disputes among residents, neighborhood security, and the public interest, and they play a role as a representative of the state at the lowest level of urban society.

As Kenneth Lieberthal states, "In one of the major political changes under way since the late 1990s, the urban work unit [the *danwei*] is losing its political role for many city residents, and the CCP and government are moving toward a residential basis of urban political power,"[17] meaning that the turn was toward reliance on residential committees and their total coverage of neighborhoods. The restructuring of work units such as offices and factories, so that the employer was no longer responsible the welfare of workers, caused this transition, while many workers were losing their jobs. Deborah David notices that as the consumer culture rose, employers' impact on people's daily life declined.[18] Furthermore, more retirees reentered the workforce. Over time, the community or neighborhood residential committees developed much closer ties to residents' everyday lives, taking on the role formerly held by employers through the *danwei.*

The mahjong case actually put Yu Yongjun's neighborhood residential committee in a dilemma. The organization of leisure activities—especially for retirees, whose population keeps increasing—often is a task of such committees. It was the residential committee that supported the playing of mahjong, in which gambling often was involved, an activity that the government always disallowed. The question was how to reconcile the committee's providing a facility for mahjong—a game that violated socialist morality—with its official agenda of enriching residents' leisure hours. The report issued by the lawyers of the residential committee stated that the committee had been awarded recognition as an "Excellent Residential Committee" successively for six years, and it was not true there was a "mahjong den." The report said that that charge was based on statements from residents who opposed mahjong and therefore praised Yu as "a hero who is fighting mahjong" (*fanma yongshi*): they had put aside the particulars of the case itself and reduced everything to the issue of the "problem of whether people should play mahjong."[19] Yet, in fact, Yu had fought the other residents alone. According to a reporter who looked into the lawsuit, some anxious residents claimed that they violated no law in playing mahjong, a healthy activity. "Yu becomes famous by damaging the reputation of this residential complex, and we are becoming famous countrywide as being mahjong crazy," a woman complained. To this journalist, the residential committee had been a model and won many awards, but this case "erased all of that."[20]

The same conclusion had been drawn by the above-mentioned report of the lawyers for the committee, namely that people forgot about the nature of the case, which was that "the noise in the room caused noise pollution," and that noise was produced not only by mahjong but also by playing chess and piano music. This was not a question of whether people should play mahjong or not. Would people and the media pay such attention if the noise had been made by piano playing? Their report believed that Yu cleverly used antipathy toward mahjong, so that she could gain support and sympathy. Through their investigation, the report claimed, it was determined that there were no "people playing mahjong until midnight"; in fact, besides mahjong, there were also other games. The committee's goal was not to seek profit, but to better the choices and environment for retirees. The report concluded that the defendants did not violate the plaintiff's right. The accusations of the plaintiff about her neurasthenia and decline in her son's grades had no direct relationship with the playing of mahjong in the activity room. Noise existed everywhere, and the law could be applied only for noise that violated the specific regulations relative to environmental protection. In this case, the noise from playing mahjong was a moral issue, not a violation of laws.[21]

That leaves us still with the popular sentiment about the "demon mahjong," an important motivation for those who supported Yu. A woman criticized the residential committee for acting "under the flag of enriching elders' daily lives" but using the activity room as a way of earning money by encouraging gambling, and adversely affecting residents' quality of life and their health. Therefore, activity rooms for mahjong should be banned. Another woman told a reporter that she got up early and came to court to support Yu, because, as she said, "playing mahjong wastes time and causes trouble." A man expressed a similar point: "Mahjong is a kind of opium, which makes people lose their spirit." However, pro-mahjong voices were also present. An old man said, "Playing mahjong is a good way to spend leisure time. Elders cannot engage in athletic activities; what could they do if they did not play mahjong?" A young man agreed, saying, "Playing mahjong at small stakes has been a lifestyle in Chengdu. Why should we oppose it, now that it has been recognized as a sports game?"[22]

From Yu's case, several dualities emerge: the responses of her neighbors compared to those of the general public; and the distinction between the rights of the individual and the commonsense notion in China that a single entity—a lone individual or family—should not go against what might be called the normative patterns of society. People generally understood the commonsense notion, and there was no question that this was the case with Yu's neighbors. It shows us that the individual finds it very difficult to protect his or her interests in a dispute with "collective interests." Therefore, the residential committee received more support from the neighborhood, where there were many elders who enjoyed mahjong, while the position involving individual rights seems to have earned more support from outside this specific community—from people without a personal investment in the dispute. The case also shows us that it is not easy to conceive of and argue for the residential committee in Later Socialism as simply a neutral upholder of the above-mentioned normative pattern of the collective, let alone make the assumption that a collective has needs as well as rights that protect those needs. The collective at this time in China, it may be argued, was no longer to be found in the mission of the residential committees as "autonomous mass organizations for self-governing, self-educating, and self-serving." That theoretical construct may perhaps already have taken flight, especially since the decline of the *danwei* system, and the committees may otherwise be seen as tools to be used for new, self-aggregated groups of individuals, such as seniors, to protect themselves and their material and legal needs. The following sections go into this in more depth.

The City's Story: How to Present Its Image?

The mahjong controversy inspired many to consider the image and civic spirit of Chengdu. One of the major criticisms of mahjong was that the game could damage the city's reputation. As one scholar noted, "The social mood of playing mahjong should not be encouraged. Mahjong has become the symbol of the city, which we must be concerned about."[23] Some officials believed that during the campaign known as the Great Development of China's West (Xibu dakaifa), the reputation that "all residents play mahjong" (*quanmin jie ma*) in the provincial capital had damaged the image of Chengdu as a "modern economy."[24] This notion about Chengdu reminds one of Mao's era, when modern industry replaced commercial activities (see the discussion in chapter 3). One writer, a Chengdu native, stated that people liked to say Chengdu was a good place to live, but he increasingly felt uncomfortable when he heard this categorization of the city's economy: he had never heard anyone talk about Chengdu as a good place for business. He believed that Chengdu people might become "modern people" (*xiandai ren*) only if they can stop taking pleasure in the "good life."[25] Such a sentiment reflects the idea that developing a solid business base is more important to a city than concentrating on its quality of life. Another journalist, a young woman, worried

Figure 6.2 People of all ages, male and female, playing mahjong at a park, June 2003. Author photo.

about visitors' impressions of Chengdu's leisure lifestyle when they see mahjong players in the parks, on the sidewalks, and in teahouses. She did not like Chengdu's attracting such national attention because of the first mahjong lawsuit in China's history (see figure 6.2).[26]

A reader of *Sichuan Daily*, who was a Chengdu native but lived in Shenzhen, expressed her opinion bluntly: "Chengdu people should reevaluate their lifestyle." When she lived in Chengdu, much of her daily routine was devoted to newspapers, movies, and teahouses, basically a relaxing and satisfying life. Back then, she did not want to think about the future. "Actually this is the lifestyle that most Chengdu people have." She also would worry that she might become a person who had no goals and spirit. Shenzhen, in her view, was different, because people made an effort to build their careers and to sustain high spirits and ambition to improve themselves. Chengdu might have leaped forward if its residents had had half the sense of urgency of those in Shenzhen.[27]

Her comments used career success as a sole criterion, and in her eyes, Chengdu people were losers. In fact, as early as the 1920s, people had argued about the slow-paced lifestyle in Chengdu. Prominent educator Shu Xincheng, for example, writing in the 1930s, understood the Chengdu passion for the teahouse: "When I consider the leisurely lifestyle, I think of the men and women who spend their lives rushing around in the industrialized and commercialized society and of my own rushing about to make a living, but without having a real life. . . . We would be lucky to see the agrarian life described by Zhang Shizhao and should exhort our friends in Sichuan to cherish this life."[28] Shu admired the slow-paced, old-style life found generations earlier and the cheap entertainment that going to the teahouse provided—an attitude directly opposite to that of those who admire the modern life and so-called modern economies.

The introduction of a market economy brought with it more public places for people's leisure, and much less governmental control of people's personal lives. Mahjong quickly occupied their time and space after work, spreading from living rooms, street corners, and sidewalks to teahouses and even workplaces. By 2000, the mahjong craze reached unprecedented heights. In Chengdu, almost all games were forms of gambling, even though most were for very small amounts of money.[29] For many, including government officials and college professors, small-stakes mahjong became the predominant pastime, for the most part because gambling made it exciting.[30] A reporter estimated that there were five million people Chengdu in 2000 (actually six million; see the introduction), 80 percent of whom would play mahjong during the Chinese New Year holiday, totaling one million "battlefields" (mahjong tables).[31] Although such an estimate might be exaggerated, it reflects the game's huge popularity. Commoners' lives in Chengdu at the turn of the century were generalized as "playing small-stakes mahjong, eating spicy hot pots, drinking cheap wine, and watching pornographic videos" (*dadian xiao majiang, chidian malatang, hedian gendoujiu, kandian wailuxiang*). Ordinary residents used this kind of doggerel to ridicule themselves and their lowbrow amusements.[32] When a majority could not afford the high-end entertainments, playing mahjong was the best option. And with the fast pace of modern life, there has developed a fast and simpler form of the game that requires less skill than old-fashioned mahjong, and it has contributed even more to the craze (see figure 6.3).

The teahouse, already the iconic place for sociality, naturally was adopted as the most appropriate setting for mahjong. Eleventh Street, for

Figure 6.3 Playing mahjong in a "farmer's happy house," October 2003.
Author photo.

instance, was regarded as "mahjong street"; only about 150 feet long and 30 feet wide, it had five "old teahouses," whose mahjong tables occupied one-third of the street. Bicycles and "elders' bikes" (*laonian che*, a three-wheel vehicle) blocked traffic outside the teahouses.[33] Every spring, Longquanyi, a suburb of Chengdu, filled with spectacular views of peach blossoms, attracted visitors and became a "mahjong battlefield" (*majiang dazhan*). Local authorities estimated that over ten thousand people played mahjong there. According to a report in March 2001, the "Peach Blossom Village" offered 107 tables for mahjong. Someone described the site as "heaven for playing mahjong, warm temperatures, fresh air, beautiful scenery, plus food, drinks, and good service. I do not feel tired even after playing mahjong for a whole day."[34]

Although most mahjong gatherings were peaceful and good-spirited, some were problematic. Occasionally, people who lost money resorted to harsh words or even violence. Angry disputes are easy to find mentioned in local newspapers. For example, Liu and Cheng were in a group of five men playing mahjong on the sidewalk. Liu stood behind Cheng and constantly gave him advice, but Cheng lost the game by following Liu's suggestions.

When Liu tried once again to give advice, Cheng struck him, breaking his nose.[35] In another case, eight men playing mahjong at a "farmer's happy house" (*nongjia le*, a combination of teahouse, restaurant, and lodge in a rural area) had a fight with another group over a table, using teacups and chairs as weapons and injuring two people.[36] Playing mahjong also caused problems within families. One afternoon, Fan and his wife went to a teahouse to play mahjong, and Fan saw that Zhao, the teahouse owner, placed his hand on the arm of his wife's chair. As soon as the couple returned home, Fan slashed his wife's face. His anger surprised her, and she protested her innocence. At 3 a.m., Fan took his wife to Zhao's home to settle things. As soon as Zhao opened his door, Fan cut Zhao's face with a knife, an injury that required eight stitches. Although Zhao denied any wrongdoing, Fan forced Zhao to pay 2,000 yuan in "compensation." Fan was arrested the next day.[37] Such incidents were fuel for criticisms of the game from elite and official quarters. They also indicate the links that can be argued to exist between mahjong and social discord.

Players could become addicted to mahjong; they would neglect work duties or cause accidents. A resident complained to a local newspaper about his experience in a clinic: He sent his ill wife to the district clinic, but no doctor showed up after his wife had been waiting for an hour. When the on-duty doctor was finally found playing mahjong in the teahouse next door, he said, "Don't be in such a rush; wait for me to finish this round."[38] A four-month-old baby left alone was burned to death after mosquito-repellent incense set the mosquito net on fire while his mother was out playing mahjong.[39] Some mahjong players experienced medical emergencies. There were several reports of pregnant women who played for so long that they suffered medical problems. In some cases, prolonged playing even proved fatal.[40] With the negative coverage constantly being printed in local newspapers, people increasingly raised concerns and criticisms. How to handle the problem became a question for local government officials. When an activity proves so attractive and powerful, it becomes difficult to keep it peaceful. Debates over the playing of mahjong consequently led to the exploration of important social issues.

In February 2000, during the annual meetings of the Municipal People's Congress and Political Consultative Conference in Chengdu, some members suggested that the government ban mahjong on the sidewalks because the activity had become "a devil on the street," not only clogging streets and blocking traffic but also "damaging the image of Chengdu." They complained that the popularity of the game had a negative impact on the business environment and that visitors "dislike very much people playing mahjong everywhere."[41] As a result, in March 2000 the municipal government banned mahjong from the teahouses by the Funan River, a scenic area where throngs played mahjong: the game gave "an impression of Chengdu people's idleness." To get around the regulation, some teahouses simply made sure that "the outside is for drinking tea but the inside is for playing mahjong."[42]

Anti-mahjong activists pointed out that the game encouraged corruption. For instance, some people played so-called "work mahjong" or "business mahjong" (*gongma*) to establish a special relationship with officials; they could gain favors for their businesses if they lost money deliberately.[43] Although this practice was regarded as bribery, it was difficult to prove and rarely prosecuted. The government's response was slow. In late 2000, the government finally set up the rules that prohibited government employees from playing during work hours and punished violators, including lowering rank and reducing year-end bonuses. These rules, however, were not applied to non-work hours.[44] In 2003, the Sichuan Provincial Government carried out a serious measure to ban "business mahjong" by issuing four prohibitions for all levels of cadres: no playing mahjong during work hours at offices, during business meetings in local-level administrations, with people they supervised, and where bribery and gambling were present. The authorities claimed that they did not intend to prohibit mahjong everywhere but simply to end gross violations by those in positions of authority. Soon after the government enacted the "four prohibitions," over thirty cadres were punished. Experts in the Sichuan Academy of Social Sciences held a panel discussion of the "disease of playing mahjong," which centered on the abuse of the game by officials with their subordinates and the detrimental effect this had on the city's economic development.[45]

To promote a better image, the Chengdu Committee for the Millennium Token (Chengdu qiannian xinwu zuweihui) was established in late 2000; the mission was to choose something that represented the best aspect of Chengdu. The item would be buried in an underground time capsule to be opened one thousand years in the future. On November 30, 2000, Sohu, one of the most popular websites in China, conducted a survey about the token. Within a few hours, a large number of people had voted: 55 percent for mahjong, and only 25 percent for the giant panda. The media reported this result as "black humor for Chengdu people." One scholar speculated that the votes might have been a mockery of the city's waste of time and energy.[46]

With the wave of anti-mahjong sentiment, however, there was also the positive view: mahjong as a part of China's cultural heritage could help stabilize society. The idea was that since the game had been recognized by the Bureau of National Sports as a sport, it could be used to promote both Chinese tradition and the elderly in their retirement years. Some argued that too many activities were "high-level entertainment" and not enough served the needs of aged citizens.[47] As a diversion in tough times, the game could also help laid-off workers who had time on their hands. Finally, mahjong could help build family relationships, aid businesses, and enhance communication and friendships (see figure 6.4).[48] This line of thinking naturally wanted no bans on mahjong but did not want the addictive behavior either. To this end, government might delegate "mahjong areas" (*majiang qu*) in places like teahouses. From a moral perspective, all these commentators sympathized with Yu Yongjun, but they also

Figure 6.4 A college class reunion held at a resort teahouse in a Chengdu suburb, June 2003. After lunch, the classmates played mahjong. Author photo.

thought that she overreacted and made a small matter into a big incident that "damaged the image of Chengdu."[49]

Some officials maintained a relatively open-minded view of the issue. In October 2001, in a meeting about tourism development in Chengdu, an official from the Bureau of National Tourism suggested to tag Chengdu as "City of Leisure" (Xiuxian zhi du), especially by promoting the "mahjong culture." He even advocated building a "mahjong street" and publishing a "mahjong newspaper." A number of local intellectuals rejected this. A college professor pointed out that this approach did not fit the "development of modern civilization" because Chengdu residents' affinity for the game eight hours a day and on holidays and vacations shows nothing but "idleness." He suggested holding a conference on leisure and tourism to discuss a diversified approach, promoting, for example, sport, art, food, and gardening.[50]

In the wake of Yu Yongjun's lawsuit, people in other cities began to see Chengdu culture more positively. For instance, the *New Weekly* (*Xinzhoukan*) in 2004 defined Chengdu as the Fourth City in China after Beijing, Shanghai, and Canton because of the "charm of the city." Whereas Shanghai has a culture of "petty bourgeoisie" and Canton a commercial culture, Chengdu's was a "culture of townsfolk" (*shimin wenhua*), and a valuable place for leisurely pursuits. The article said that "whereas Cantonese dearly pursue the good life, Chengdu people already live in the good life." The people of Chengdu emphasize "spiritual and emotional life, alongside economic development."[51]

The National Story: A Local Issue or Chinese Issue?

With the reforms of Late Socialism, state control of everyday life was relaxed, and mahjong revived.[52] Mahjong is not merely a Chengdu phenomenon but a nationwide one. Nevertheless, as mentioned already, from the late Qing, the teahouse and mahjong endured a constant stream of attack as vices, by both social reformers and the government.[53] Voices in their defense were buried under a tidal wave, and many began to think that in any event the teahouse and mahjong were vestiges of the "old society" and would be replaced with new activities as society became increasingly modernized. They never anticipated that more than half a century after dramatic revolution and reforms, not only are teahouses and mahjong not extinguished, but both are flourishing to an unprecedented degree. From the specific issue of mahjong, we can see how the market economy in today's China has coexisted with habitual lifestyles, and how modernization has transformed social life but not to the extent generally thought: there is significant cultural continuity. The environment around mahjong is in flux, but its core—recreation, gambling, and socialization—remain the same.

Since the reforms of Late Socialism, local authorities have not implemented any tough, overall sanction against mahjong, although the media still constantly harp at such games and entertainments. Obviously, the government recognized mahjong's popularity. Even though officials knew that widespread gambling violated socialist morality and government restrictions, they never attempted a real ban, most likely in fear of resentment. Their position has become noncommittal, with moderate policies. This represents a significant step backward from the Mao era's control of so many aspects of daily lives. In theory, any gambling in a teahouse, regardless of the size of the stakes, has been illegal for a long time, but the government has ignored this fact, as long as games do not cause trouble; and it has made accommodating restrictions, such as concerning officials and government employees who played mahjong during working hours. In December 2000, two months after Yu's lawsuit, the first charge of gambling was brought to trial in Chengdu. A certain Mr. Chen did not have a decent job and set up a gambling business in a teahouse as an "easy way to earn money." He was sentenced to five years in jail and fined 3,000 yuan.[54] What the government tried to control in this instance was not gambling per se, but a gambling business.

The significance of Yu's lawsuit extends far beyond the case itself.[55] Again, it inspired people to ask how society balances collective interests and individual rights. In an interview by China Central Television (CCTV), an official of the residential committee described how difficult it was to deal with the situation: "If I satisfied Yu's request, the majority of residents would disagree because we took away the freedom of these people. Every citizen has a right to enjoy life, and neighbors should try to understand and tolerate each other. This is also an issue of attitude, I think." After the initial hearing, CCTV devoted an episode of its well-known *True Words, True Talk* program (*Shihua shishuo*) to a discussion about the issue among invited experts, Yu Yongjun, and audience members. Regarding the protection of the interests of the majority, an expert told CCTV that it is a good principle that the minority obeys the majority, but this should be applied only to public affairs. The conflict over mahjong between Yu and her neighbors was one of private rights, which the committee had no authority to take up.[56]

Most members of the audience hoped that the issue could be solved through better communication, not legal means. Still, Yu maintained that she had no alternative but the lawsuit. "In our compound, you felt weird if you did not play mahjong." Yu believed that many people who were not mahjong players experienced grievances similar to hers, but they were too afraid to speak out. The CCTV host reminded her that the audience's suggestions might be useful and that she might not have handled the relationships with her neighbors in the best possible way. Yu replied that she did not have any other disputes with her neighbors. A lawyer stated that it was her right to pursue her interests through the suit, but only as a last resort. The social pressure she was suffering was obviously much greater than the noise of mahjong.[57]

The preceding look at mahjong highlights significant aspects of urban culture in Late Socialism that seem like new realities. First, the discussion has revealed that given Late Socialism's new direction away from state controls (unlike the opposite direction of Early Socialism toward them), the conflict over mahjong reflected a new sort of grouping of individuals—people now very interested in holding on to their occupation of public space, as well as their personal entertainment, and the rights to both. They simply fended off one other individual, and the residential committee acted as a practical leverage and go-between. Second, we have seen that Chengdu's perceptions of itself as a city, tied for a moment to such a notorious contest over differing rights claims, can, interpretively speaking, still be seen as connected to ideals about modernity. What did Chengdu residents and visitors want Chengdu to be in the bold post-Mao world of competition, freedoms, and the burgeoning business mentality? It seems that part of the answer lies in the worldwide attraction to post–Cold War, Western postmodernity with its goods, money liquidity, competition, narcissism, and urban and commercial development; urban culture in Late Socialism may now have already supplanted any vestiges of the Maoist modernist critique of bourgeois aesthetics that proposed that modernism (industry, obedience) and positivism (science, the future) be used to build the new socialist citizen. The issue for the present study is whether the "new capitalism" riding in with Western postmodernity can be favorable to free-flowing, freely evolving urban culture in Chengdu (or all of China), a culture that relies not on ideology but upon the ebb and flow of individuals in public spaces, leading public lives.

Residents, Neighborhood, and the City in Public Life

This chapter has shown how an individual case of playing mahjong could cause a chain reaction, and how it reflected on the complex relationships among individuals, neighborhoods, the city, and even within the nation. An examination of that case puts it into a larger context and provides better understanding of how and to what extent political transformation and economic development shape people's daily lives and alter these relationships. We also find that the issues and questions raised by the mahjong lawsuit still exist in today's China and have yet to be fully answered.

At the individual level, how should we understand Yu's fate? We should consider the case in terms of political, social, and cultural factors. In China, people have consistently tended to place collective interests before individual rights. When conflict has emerged from the overlap of collective interests and individual interests, the latter always surrendered to the former. Furthermore, Chinese society has traditionally been more tolerant of the behavior of the elderly; in other words, older people have had greater liberty than the younger in the public spaces. When the relatively young Yu presented a conflict with elderly neighbors, she did not get much sympathy, although many elsewhere offered moral support. Finally, another Chinese tendency is to keep civil disputes within the confines of the neighborhood and community and to avoid public exposure through a lawsuit. Yu's neighbors believed that she brought disgrace to the neighborhood by breaking this assumed harmony of daily life. China's socialist state has emphasized that individual rights should be subordinate to collective interests, but some people have begun to challenge this notion. Yu's lawsuit is a key example. Some people gave the issue deeper consideration, and it entered the discourse about the "democratic system of majority rule and protection of individual rights." An article praised Yu for refusing "to be cheated by the flag of 'democracy' but going to the court for justice." The author points out that majority rule in race, religion, and class have suppressed minority opposition even to the point of genocide, in many instances performed under the banner of democracy. Therefore, "a reasonable and limited democratic system of majority rule" (*heli de youxian duoshu minzu zhi*) should be established, which can respect and protect the rights of the minority.[58]

From a neighborhood perspective, it is interesting to note the position of the members of the residential committee in the mahjong lawsuit. As we know, the committee actually represented the demographically lowest rung of state power in its carrying out of the policies promoted by the CCP and the government. The government neither clearly opposed mahjong nor encouraged it.[59] If the committee had pursued a certain sort of "political correctness," it should have opposed mahjong. Ironically, the situation turned out to be just the opposite. From the lawsuit, we can see emerging a certain evidence for the power of "capitalism with Chinese characteristics": although playing mahjong has long been categorized as "backward," "corrupt," and indicative of a "capitalist lifestyle," the residential committee, being the lowest rung of state control, took the *danwei* form of governance to a new interpretive level, namely the issuance of quasi-theoretical determinations about the social good to emerge from individual pleasure. In continuing its role to take care of affairs in its unit, including daily life and entertainment, it considered mahjong as a valid alternative for ordinary retirees with few resources. In this way the game was considered to play an important role in social stability by means of an economic argument. That is why the authorities who looked askance at small-scale gambling were in essence allowing "Chinese characteristics" to paint a new picture of a looser, more populist and tolerant *danwei* governance.

At the city level, we have seen that the residents of Chengdu faced a dilemma. On the one hand, although many enjoyed mahjong, they also resented the use of the game to publicly label their lifestyle; especially, they worried that such a categorization could harm the city's reputation. Therefore, few intellectuals defended the mahjong lifestyle. On the other hand, many people who disliked mahjong did not have the courage to oppose it, because they might face an army of opponents. When Yu Yongjun spoke out, people praised her as a "hero who is fighting mahjong" and condemned "mahjong for disturbing residents" (*raomin majiang*).[60] As soon as these kinds of terms were used to refer to mahjong, proponents of the game were put on the defensive.

All over the city, excessive noise could cause conflicts. In discussing the mahjong case, we must carefully distinguish between "noise as a disturbance" and "noise as a *renao* thing." In China, *renao* has a positive connotation related to prosperity. This term is used to evaluate a city, an event, a market, or a party. Without *renao*, things lack an atmosphere of liveliness (*renqi*). In public life, *renao* brings excitement to all, regardless of age, gender, or economic and educational background. When people are at home, however, they have very different pursuits: quiet (*qingjing*) and privacy. The boundary between public and home and between *renao* and quiet is not absolute, especially regarding noise, which permeates all types of space and causes all types of disputes. Finally, one must not forget that, as discussed above, excessive noise was regarded legally as environmental pollution but had tight parameters. Pollutions of many kinds had increasingly become the focus of people's concerns.

Yu's opposition to the noise of mahjong took place in 2000, but this type of conflict has become even more frequent recently in China. For instance, two similar incidents drew nationwide attention and debate in October 2013 alone, and they bring focus to an increasingly common sight in urban China: groups of people, mostly older women, who gather to dance as exercise on street corners or in parks or public squares in the morning and evening with loudspeakers or cassette players. In Beijing on October 11, 2013, "a man fired a shotgun into the air and set loose three Tibetan mastiffs to scare away a group of women whose public dancing annoyed him." Although the man was arrested, he received "much sympathy online."[61] In Wuhan on October 24, 2013, when a group of old women were dancing in a neighborhood public square, an angry resident flung human excrement at them from an upper floor of an apartment building. It was reported that the conflict between the dancers and residents in the building had gone on for more than a month.[62]

In China, urban dwellers are still grappling with how to understand and balance individual rights with collective interests, even if it is still not clear what kind of legal and moral world the individual actually can occupy and what in fact is the collective. Moreover, the issue discussed here is not merely a simple conflict between individual rights and collective interests but a multilayered and complex set of relations among individuals and between a group and a neighborhood. Consider that the noise caused by either mahjong or dancing actually affects whole groups and even buildings and neighborhoods. Furthermore, a person might suffer from next-door mahjong noise but then also make noise when he or she goes to dance with a loudspeaker in the public square. If the government and residents do not address these issues satisfactorily, then conflicts may continue to tarnish the public image of themselves and their urban culture.

All this underscores the growing role of the state in daily life. Whereas we say that Chinese people enjoyed the most freedom in the 1980s, it is also the case that the state's involvement in cultural and leisure activities grew again, after 1989 and Tiananmen, and increased further throughout the 1990s. As some scholars have noticed, in the mid-1990s "the state's reinvention of the notion of participation was divested of its links to political ideology"—it was not an arm "of either proletarian revolution or democratic polity." Along with its stance in the aftermath of the crackdown on the democracy movement in 1989, the state's participation in cultural affairs cannot simply be categorized as socialism, Late Socialism, or liberalism, "but the making of an egalitarian consumer public theoretically unmarred by vertical hierarchies, in short, participation in the democratic consumption of leisure culture."[63] Therefore, the state has not simply withdrawn from cultural and public life, but rather, its influence has taken different forms and assumed a different scale.

Conclusion

The State, the Teahouse, and the Public Sphere

The teahouse, maintaining its role over hundreds of years of Chinese culture and everyday life, has a long history. During one part of that history, the second half of the twentieth century, it experienced dramatic tumult. The teahouse went from prosperity to decline from 1950 to 1976, then recovered and became prosperous once again after 1977. This reflects the political and economic changes that allow us to periodize Early and Late Socialism in China. Under Mao's radical policies, many people were forced to exercise caution about their public doings and in many cases stayed away, but then, immediately upon the post-Mao reforms, they surged back into public life. To some degree, the reason that their return was quick and vigorous was that long-held, older values about public life stayed at the surface. One can say that Chengdu maintained its historical memory of the usefulness and benefits offered by an urban life rich in urban culture.

In this book, I have examined documents about the municipal government in Chengdu that previously have not been used; the result has been an analysis of the vast extent of control over public life, as reflected in the government's intervention in teahouse operations. In addition, I have observed Chengdu teahouse life in the field. The results have laid bare some of the stark differences between the needs of ordinary people and those of the political and cultural elite, both in Early Socialism, with its unprecedented controls, and in Late Socialism and the opening of a market economy. In the case of the latter, I have noted the rise of the public sphere and the post-1977 renewed vitality of the teahouse, which faced, however, new sorts of blocks and constrictions, due greatly to government-sponsored modernization, changed social patterns, and business competition.

There has been a powerful continuity in the popular culture and the public sphere that pertains to the Chengdu teahouse. The teahouses could not be obliterated by the unprecedented absolutist power of the state that was exerted up until about 1966 and by the Cultural Revolution. In the following discussion, I give a roughly chronological review of particular topics related to my overall study. I hope to provide a picture of how the phenomenon of the Chengdu teahouse fared during just a brief part of its long history, and I take up related points that have emerged throughout the book: the impact of the state's scrutiny of teahouse life, including hundreds of years of entertainment forms; later the lifting of constraints on teahouse-related workers and on women; tension between national and local culture in the context of a threat from "geo-culture"; and the fate of the guild, all in the context of a detailed analysis of the public sphere vis-à-vis civil society.

The Early Years of Socialism: Continuity or Discontinuity?

China's Communist Party leadership, having assumed power after a long military campaign, took up historical models of revolutionary and reformist states that had preceded them and began to implement their notion of "new culture" and "socialist entertainment." This direction reflected in part an attempt to achieve certain modernist ideological goals. The party-state injected communist ideology and propaganda into political and social language: it touted the so-called revolutionary spirit and aimed to strengthen party control over the formation of a new sort of

state-individual relationship and reconstruct the political culture. It promoted heroism, patriotism, and Marxist ideology even in its most mysti-
cal formulations—things of overarching importance to the revolutionary
outlook of the party. Thus, within a short period, the CCP and its new
government were able to control much of society, including speech, kept
opinions, and daily lives. Many in the 1950s were enthusiastic and optimistic, eagerly working to fulfill what they saw as their nation's promise.
The reality, of course, is that the CCP's and the state's forceful imposition
upon the people's extant habits of culture made the survival of that set of
habits extremely difficult.

There is no question that the Communists' revolution brought unprecedented tumult to China, but we cannot assume that socialist China was
built on entirely new bases and practices. Actually, cultural practices and
social customs were not abandoned easily or entirely. Careful observation
reveals that many strands of the older public culture persisted in social
life, underscoring culture's enduring nature. Meanwhile, wave after wave
of ideological attempts to remake China's culture were wearing away at
public lifestyles and public spaces, so as to squeeze and sap them. Therefore, one may say that cultural continuity and discontinuity coexisted during the second half of China's twentieth century.

The state's politically contrived new "culture" made an enormous
impact on public spaces. The party achieved much of this through a certain socialist entertainment, which was designed to transform previous
outlets of entertainment to some degree because they were a "bad influence," but also to keep some aspects that would serve as useful tools for
propaganda that could lead people in the intended direction. Of course,
the CCP was not the first to have this belief. Since the late Qing, folk
performances and arts had been regarded in certain cases as too lowbrow or primitive to be worthy of protecting or patronizing. The elite
of that period frequently used terms such as "scurrilous," "ugly," and
"obscene" to attack popular culture, and this became part of a cultural
hegemony established in the effective orthodox discourse. The Communist revolution inherited this older Chinese cultural hegemony, as well as
the powerful models of cultural manipulation in the spirit of modernity,
as used by the GMD in the 1930s and 1940s, and the revolution pressed
them ever more aggressively. For example, any words pertaining to flirta-
tion, sex or sexuality, and supernatural powers were considered "toxic

entertainment," making the so-called reform of folk lyrics, stories, and dramas the logical outcome. From the late Qing and Nationalist periods, down through the early Communist administration, the nation's political culture changed in fundamental ways, but the hostile attitude toward popular entertainment continued.

Actually, pertaining to the teahouse in particular, careful examination reveals many similarities between the Communist government's policies and the GMD's. Each saw it as a detrimental place that encouraged laziness and other vices, and thus in need of reformation. The GMD government failed to extend its power into the lower levels of society, but after 1949 the Communists' intervention did go quite far, and the teahouse and public life were carefully watched and controlled. A comparison of teahouses after 1950 with those in the Republican period reveals several dramatic changes. First, the transition of ownership from private to collective (and even to state-run) caused sharp changes in the economic structure of the city, namely in the everyday life of many Chengdu urbanites, who by tradition conducted business, pleasure, and sociality and exchanged information in teahouses. Second, government policies exerted an intense impact on the day-to-day management and operation of teahouses, in areas such as registration, employment, taxation, and regulations. Third, a large number of people lived in *danwei*, where all kinds of facilities were provided. For them, there was not much chance of carrying out daily life outside the *danwei*. Such a system prevented people from using teahouses and conducting public life. Fourth, the large political campaigns, such as the Three Antis and Five Antis Campaigns, Socialist Transformation, the Anti-rightist Movement, the Great Leap Forward, and the Cultural Revolution, challenged the survival of the teahouse. Fifth, the structure and forms of teahouse entertainment were transformed and brought under government oversight. Nothing like these policy outcomes had ever occurred in urban life previously.

After 1950, the decrease in small businesses in general resulted in a significant reduction of public spaces and shared public life. This was a logical result of the strengthening of state control. Even though the state was powerful, however, it could not completely conquer small businesses, public places, and daily life in the entire city within a short time. Early Socialism throughout China saw numerous push-backs and popular resistance—flare-ups that occupied much of the top echelon's policy setting and security operations.[1] As we have seen, the old-style economy and lifestyle found in the 1950s continued for quite a long time, then gradually diminished in the face of this new political control. While a shared, public life in the teahouse technically was still possible, it increasingly was interrupted. When so many people were led or were overwhelmed into showing their "progressive" attitudes toward revolutionary, political culture and toward the state by participating in the elimination of "bad habits" such as frequenting the teahouse, the results were to be expected. The number of patrons plummeted, and only the older, diehard teahouse-goers found it difficult to change habits, and thus remained the major cohort of customers, without a younger generation to follow.

The Socialist State and Teahouse Entertainment

After 1949, when socialist ideology and its agenda of political culture dominated society, the teahouse became a hub of political and class struggles into which proprietors and customers alike were actively or passively drawn. Many, perhaps most, proprietors and performers survived the tough environment, but a considerable number were purged in the political campaigns, and teahouses were destroyed. Their very nature as a long-accepted mode of public life could not be tolerated as part of the socialist narrative and revolutionary discourse, which dictated that the teahouse was incompatible with China's economic development and Chengdu's hoped-for transformation into a modern, industrial city. Thus, along with Mao's hasty deployment of urban industries, teahouses were bound to give way.

This book has shown how the CCP and the state infiltrated the lowest levels of enterprise associated with entertainment and changed the management, personnel, and structure of performance troupes, implemented a standardized accounting system, and initiated the transition of performance organizations from loosely structured family-run businesses that catered to popular enjoyment into ventures whose personnel were forced to devote themselves to text-based ideology, as well as to theirs and their peers' morals and political loyalties. Beginning in the early 1950s, socialist propaganda infused all forms of entertainment and tied them to political movements, such as the Land Revolution, the Three Antis and Five Antis, Collectivization, the Great Leap Forward, and the Cultural Revolution. Entertainers and performances in the teahouse became tools of national politics and political culture. The new CCP government in Chengdu used the conventional public arena of the teahouse to disseminate political propaganda and political culture.

In order to effectively control popular entertainment, the government conducted a comprehensive investigation of entertainers in the early 1950s, which laid a foundation for other policies of intrusion. From the late Qing to the Republic, local governments undertook many similar surveys, but none contained this level of detail, reflecting the Communist government's unprecedented hunger and capability for social control. The investigations by party cadres, analyzed in chapter 2, helped the party learn about each troupe's history, present situation, composition of staff, salaries, and political backgrounds, as well as program structures and contents, business operations, management, accounting, training, and performance venues. What is of importance is that all such investigations were conducted by the government, whose motivation was clear: restrict, change, and control. Therefore, the government focused on the problems in the profession rather than on its effectiveness to provide entertainment that could appeal to wide audiences.

We saw that the government sought to eliminate self-entertainment, especially in the form of bench-sitter opera, but found it impossible to completely prohibit it. The authorities focused on those who depended on this quasi-professional entertainment for their small livelihoods. However, the government was unable to control it completely and had to compromise and allow some of these entertainers to perform, although under supervision to ensure "healthy content." Whereas the traditional bench-sitter performance was a form of self-entertainment, arising spontaneously from the audience, when the government forcefully disbanded a large number of performing troupes in the 1950s, the quasi-professionals decreased dramatically. Although the government did not want to acknowledge this, official documents show it to have happened, as analyzed in the present study. When the government addressed the issue, the result was that a number of these quasi-professionals were expelled into the countryside but returned to the city and their previous professions in order to survive, in what might be considered a form of "resistance of the weak."[2]

This is a good example of how those associated with popular entertainment resisted attacks from the socialist state.

The policy requiring folk performers who lacked Chengdu residential registration to return to their rural hometowns reflects the government's negative views of urban life: urban life encouraged vice. In fact, from the 1950s, the Communist government had a policy to send urban residents to rural areas, called "Up to Mountains and Down to the Country" (Shang-shan xiaxiang), which reached the highest point during the Cultural Revolution.[3] In his book *City versus Countryside in Mao's China*, Jeremy Brown uses cases in Tianjin to discuss how the government expelled urban residents to the countryside in order to aid in "purifying the city."[4] The government believed that sending those who did not have a "proper job" back to their hometowns would stabilize urban society as an important part of the Communists' urban reforms.

The government's hostile attitude made it virtually impossible for a person to pursue bench-sitter opera as a livelihood or hobby. Furthermore, the revival of this form of entertainment was complex. As we have seen, the state tightly controlled popular entertainment, and as a result, not only did many residents lose their customary form of amusement, but many also lost their regular jobs and turned to this type of performance in order to survive. The Bureau of Culture in Chengdu refused to recognize it as a legitimate profession and made every effort to eliminate it. However, lower-level government officials had more direct responsibility for the people in their districts: they were relatively more concerned with livelihoods and less concerned with the higher ideals of revolutionary entertainment and socialist propaganda. They did not actively join the campaign against the bench-sitter performers, resulting in trouble for the bureau. Here we can easily see that state power was strong enough to manipulate leisure activities at the lowest levels of society, but it could not do so completely or overnight and became drawn into internecine struggles.

It should be noted, too, that because of the restrictions on this quasi-amateur genre of entertainment, many women had to return home, where they frequently felt "suffocated and unhappy." In the CCP's revolutionary discourse, having an identity beyond the home was an important part of women's liberation. However, when the bench-sitters were restricted, women became "willing to return home to be housewives again," which the government regarded as a positive development. By driving women back home, the government succeeded in persuading them to acknowledge that performing with these groups was a "wrong idea." Apparently, while driving women back home was contrary to the goal of women's liberation, at that moment, in the view of party cadres, the goal of replacing folk entertainment with socialist propaganda was more important.[5] We should recognize that although the government controlled teahouses and other public places during the Mao era, public space, everyday life, and popular culture still maintained certain active aspects, the existence of which challenged the Communist state. Since it was impossible for the state to control everything, then wherever culture and public space gained an opportunity, they would revive. The "bench-sitter opera" is one of the best examples of this.

The Teahouse Revival after the Cultural Revolution: Unleashed Markets

During the Cultural Revolution, the state apparatus on the one hand restricted teahouses and the entertainment they offered, along with other long-established ways of life. On the other hand, it promoted magnificent mass parades and gatherings, which could be seen in every political movement as one of the symbols of socialist political culture.[6] In such a political environment, the individual as a being who moves outside of his house in public spaces with a certain degree of freedom became insignificant, subsumed by wave after wave of revolutionary-type theater. Even under this level of political control, however, the people finally reached the limit of tolerance for the radical leftists and the Cultural Revolution, and began to express their resentment in public places such as the few teahouses that had returned to business, a phenomenon that reached its peak during memorial ceremonies for Premier Zhou Enlai in the spring of 1976. For the first time under the Communists' regime, everyday people started to voice their own independent political thinking, openly expressing anger at the "Gang of Four."[7] Soon afterward, Deng Xiaoping came to power and launched the reformist movement and a vast opening up of many sectors of the economy. With that came the rebirth of the teahouse and public life, after a decade of nonstop calamity across China. Moreover, with the unleashing of the teahouse came a similar lifting of constraints on relatively low-paying professions associated with the teahouse, and new freedoms for women in the same context.

In their study of marketization in post-Mao China, Michel Hockx and Julia Strauss found that the CCP and the state "have shed their old functions of both supporting and suppressing cultural expression, [and] many of these functions are gradually [being] taken over by the market." The most prominent change was that "the emergence of a fast-growing market economy in the PRC had led to a huge increase in consumer-oriented and profit-oriented cultural expression."[8] This phenomenon furthered the increase in and wider use of public spaces and hence urban culture. We can see this trend in Chengdu. After the post-Mao reforms, with opened markets, when the socialist state permitted the establishment of private businesses and political changes rippled through the economy and public life, teahouses recovered very quickly. By the end of the Cultural Revolution, the teahouses that remained in Chengdu had become financially and culturally weak. They possessed only a minimal presence in city life, but this bit of "breathing space," along with the survival of centuries-old traditions, were all they needed to revive, just as seeds planted in dry soil germinate under newly stabilized temperatures and adequate moisture. Teahouses once again became a place where people from all social classes gathered to socialize, partake in hobbies, and otherwise enjoy leisure time. While the elderly were still the primary patrons, younger people began to go as well.

It is obvious that the political burden placed on teahouses was significantly reduced in the post-Mao era primarily as a result of the weakening of the CCP's control, and teahouse-goers had much more freedom to discuss politics there. Individuals were now free to open a teahouse, determine prices, services, and business hours, and hire and fire. The number of teahouses significantly exceeded that of the Republican period. Despite this, we cannot say that the government held a laissez-faire attitude. To run a teahouse required the proprietor to obtain all kinds of permits for safety, sanitation, and taxes, and many of the problems that arose resulted in another type of government scrutiny.

In addition, the new teahouses differed from their earlier counterparts in just about every way, from their appearance to their business operations and ways of providing service, and there were more types of teahouses than ever before. The most prominent change in comparison with the Republican era was the fact that the teahouse guild no longer existed. As a result, of course, teahouses faced fierce competition. As in the past, teahouses continued to provide livelihoods for different types of workers. Some professions that had relied on teahouses in the earlier days, such as fortune-tellers, earwax pickers, shoe polishers, and peddlers, were now able to return and thrive. An obvious difference was the emergence of women employed in trades traditionally filled by men. In the post-Mao era, the constraints and restrictions that applied to women gradually disappeared, reflecting social development, the elevation of women's status, and the continued opening of people's minds, even though habits could poke through negatively, with, as we saw in chapter 5, prejudicial treatment of women teahouse employees according to age and physical appearance.

A Problem of Culture in Late Socialism: National versus Local

State control of society and everyday life was always an issue in twentieth-century China. The intrusion of state power into the very bottom of society existed as early as the late Qing, and it strengthened during the Republic period, although sporadically. With the failure of the GMD and the establishment of the Communists, the nature of the state apparatus per se was conceived of more totalistically than ever.[9] One result was that throughout the second half of the century, local culture was gradually subsumed by national culture.

"Local culture" can mean a regional phenomenon having to do with the ways people in a specific, small area work and live as formed by their geography, products, language, and social patterns. In the past, Chengdu's isolation, combined with a lack of smooth communication with other areas, created a unique culture. A precise definition of "national culture" is difficult for its own reasons, but one should consider at least that the development of modern transportation and communication tools, and the influence of politics, dramatically expanded exchanges between regions and to some degree caused local cultures to change as they became open to outside influence. While the terms "local culture" and "national culture" are flexible and often overlap, I think that a national culture contains at least the following elements: first, it is promoted by state power; second, it serves the goal of centralization; and third, it exists within a nationwide model, with the attendant sense, or ideal, of unity. It is important to state, moreover, that a national (or even the party's) culture is not static but changes and evolves. In fact, compared to local culture, a national culture is more apt on certain occasions of directed leadership and policy to change rapidly.

The investigations undertaken in these chapters have shown that the national increasingly replaced the local. To get to the bottom of this issue, we must assume that public life is a major driver of culture, as discussed in the brief definition given in the introduction. Such life is always conducted under watchful public eyes, and therefore, the government, elites, and media in Chengdu associated street-level, open activity with the city's overall image and with the city's local culture. As discussed in chapter 6, one of the most prominent activities in public places was the game of mahjong. From the study, we learned that mahjong could spark a variety of debates: Is it an innocent entertainment or a misguided way of life? Is it a symbol of a high quality of life or of economic stagnation? Is the highest priority the collective interest or the individual and his or her rights? The debates over mahjong revealed how people were responding to radical social change, how they sought to balance older but still vital customs with modern moral codes, and how they evaluated popular culture.

Mass media, like their predecessors in the late Qing and Republican periods, tried very hard to change popular culture through an infusion of elite values.[10] The media's eagerness to report on problems associated with a popular pastime like mahjong, regardless of how trivial, reflected a skeptical attitude, one might say snobbishness, toward popular culture, and thus the media warned readers of the game's numerous, horrible consequences. We can see that an obvious gap existed between the populace, which largely embraced the game, and the official media, which largely opposed it. The rise of mahjong also tells us something about the way a ubiquitous pursuit of money in the new market economy may follow or mix with people's understandable fascination with gambling.

For its part, the government seemed to focus only on officials and government employees who played mahjong during working hours; it ignored ordinary residents who did the same. The authorities worried more about mahjong as a tool for bribery. Compared with much earlier eras, the government leadership at the time of the mahjong controversy did not conduct an overall anti-mahjong campaign, even though gambling could conceivably have been rooted out. Instead, it implemented restrictions on the times, places, and number of people who could play. Why did the government adopt such a lax policy? In part, perhaps, it was because the game was a diversion, keeping people's attention from clustering around greater, political issues. Finally, although it is difficult to interpret the state's motives for particular decisions without the existence of specific evidence, it is possible to suggest that favoring the individual and his private pursuits was simply a small piece of the larger decision made after Mao's death, namely to take the country in the opposite direction from the chaotic and costly years of social control and the party's problematic policies.

But there is another part to this: the party and its state in the height of Late Socialism and the reforms still found themselves taking a role in the creation of culture, per se—but in quite a new way. When Richard Sennett discusses the "culture of the new capitalism," he asks: "Is the new economy breeding a new politics?" To a great extent, China is a "new capitalist" country, although it is ruled by the CCP. Severe gaps in incomes and opportunities have arisen. "More largely consequent may be the class divide between those who profit from the new economy and those in the middle who do not."[11] With the rise of commercial culture, the state adopted a different strategy to retain its influence on daily life and local culture. As Jing Wang stresses, "That the state has become more entrepreneurial and image-conscious now does not imply that it has given up its means and end of setting the agenda for popular culture."[12] David Goodman expresses a similar point: "In the reform era the party-state, for its part, has by no means surrendered completely its role as a creator of culture of all kinds."[13]

China's new political culture has become tethered through state involvement to local business culture and local consumer patterns. As the government expected, more people, especially the young, have kept a focus on increasing their income and acquisitions, leading, it is thought, toward a better life rather than toward engagement with politics. One aspect of this new political culture is the stark change of ideological platforms: now the state focuses on control of media and publishers, as well as education. This effort has, however, been profoundly hindered by the

Internet. Another aspect is the growing gap between rich and poor. New resentments are seen as possibly sparking a perhaps unwanted interest in politics. In fact, the state's strategy of shifting public attention away from politics might backfire, given current events throughout the country.

Some scholars have introduced the idea of a "geo-culture" (factors of both the natural and human geography of a place) that has arisen out of global capitalism and is now becoming a part of China. Yet they claim that although China is regarded as exerting "highly centralized political control," the central government nevertheless has given cadres "significant leeway to translate . . . central policy guidelines into actions appropriate for the particular locality in which they were appointed to govern."[14] Such an assessment might be true for the late-imperial period of China. However, beginning in the early twentieth century, under the wave of modernization and Westernization, the modernizing state has increasingly seized autonomy from localities. For example, almost all urban reforms follow Western patterns, from urban administration and law enforcement, to landscape aesthetics and forms of entertainment.[15] Even during the Mao era, "mainland Chinese cultural products were, by definition, state products. Mao-era culture is normally associated with monotony and uniformity."[16] Therefore, entertainment was controlled by political ideologies and shaped by socialist political culture—a national culture. It did not offer sufficient space for local cultures to survive and develop within it. This study has found that the perseverance of local culture and the existence of such a "geo-culture" are not a result of "more leeway" given by the government but of the resistance exerted by locals from their local cultures. Although we can find examples of local officials who enthusiastically espoused "local culture," their ideas, formats, and models of development are the same as those in other regions or cities: they are national in essence. Many projects that ostensibly were created for the preservation of local culture have in fact done more harm than good. We can find many cases of commercial development in which actual historic areas were demolished to make way for pseudo-classic streets and faux-historic architecture.

To sum up, the national culture after 1949 was managed and directed by the socialist state under the notion of "unity" (*tongyi*); it was carried out through both the traditional idea of "grand unification" (*da yitong*) in ancient China and Mao's ambitious goal—a strong socialist country under an ideology, a political party, and a leader. The result, from a certain local point of view, was the achievement of mass control over the inherited regional and local cultures of China. The idea of a unified state and culture was instrumental in building state power but was disastrous for local culture. The hegemony of the national has continued its elimination of the local, and local culture has disappeared in the same proportion that national culture has expanded.

Public Life and the Public Sphere

Public space and public life are strong vehicles of local culture; they play a central role in urban life as an arena for social and political activities. The teahouses of Chengdu were a major arena and a reflection of the relationship between the state and society. This has been studied already by Western scholars for whom public associations and civil society have been an important topic, especially as related to European and U.S. history. Then in the late 1980s and early 1990s, Mary Rankin, William Rowe, and David Strand used the term "public sphere" to study China's social transformation since the late-imperial era. The use of the term was contentious; some argued that Jürgen Habermas's concept of a "public sphere" was not appropriate for China.[17] Some years ago, my own work on urban Chengdu's culture focused on the issue of how public space was turned into social and political space and on the role of the "public" in local politics.[18]

Subsequently, I pointed out that, in fact, Habermas's "public sphere" is not just a social and political force that is always, but not binarily or diametrically, in opposition to the state; it also must be considered as a very real physical space, in the way I described it in the introduction, reacting to Whyte's phrase. When people exit their private realms (most likely, their homes), they by definition enter the public sphere. From the perspective of such a "physical" public sphere, the teahouse played a role similar to that of saloons in the United States and cafés in Europe. True, Habermas has a point concerning social and political space in opposition to state power. In Republican-era Chengdu, for example, the teahouse was the place where certain disputes were settled; thus, the state's jurisdiction was enforced at the grassroots level, with the stabilizing effect of a "most democratic court" (although this term is no doubt at least some-what idealized).[19] Now we have clearly shown that the key issue is not the very use of the concept of the "public sphere" in studies of modern China, but rather how to define the concept in a more nuanced way that is meaningful for the unique Chinese context. To this end, it will help to devote a discussion at this point to how the term works inside and outside the concept of civil society.

We can consider the guilds of Chengdu as a form, or element of, the public sphere. Chapter 1 showed that the socialist state's reform of the older guild system resulted in the New Teahouse Guild, which was not effective and simply signaled the destruction of local business groups with any real voice—a reflection of the CCP's policies toward all pre-1949 social and economic organizations. In fact, during the entire Mao era the state controlled nearly all of the nation's resources—political and economic power, and social and cultural artifacts—something unique in Chinese history. The New Teahouse Guild abandoned its previous role and became an indirect arm of the government in the teahouse profession. All guilds existed in name only after the reorganization of the early 1950s, and the New Teahouse Guild disappeared entirely during the "Socialist Transformation" from 1953 to 1956: all social organizations declined with the growing strength of the state. The pattern that had started during the late-imperial period, in which local elites led guilds that were made up of members of local communities, was now dismantled.

How and why did the government do that? Government policy under Early Socialism reduced the influence of guilds in order to prevent chal-lenges to state power. Guilds were considered to be, by their very nature, aligned against the Communist state. The central government pointed out that in the past, guilds were controlled by small groups to suppress small and medium-size businesses (something of an untruth, as discussed in chapter 1). But party leadership understood also that guilds had had a long history and played an important role in sustaining business relations. Therefore, the government chose not to make an all-out ban, but rather to transform the guilds completely. Some scholars do not necessarily believe that the demise of the guild occurred because the CCP and the socialist state wished to thwart the development of the public sphere. For example, Heath Chamberlain can agree that the Communists' regime destroyed the traditional Chinese social structure in the 1950s, but proposes that the result might not have been entirely negative. "Chinese society of the 1950s was a long way from being civil. It was essential that the state intrude rudely and violently to liberate people from the constraints of traditional family and social bonds, precisely in order to prepare the soil for civil society's future growth." Whether "state action has enhanced or blocked the emergence of civil society, however, is exceedingly difficult to judge." He goes on to request that "those who argue that several decades of political dictatorship have served only to retard its progress must provide us with more convincing evidence."[20] His opinion suggests that the public sphere can be uncivil and thus need restraint and reform to prepare it for civility. The present book, while not a comprehensive study of Chinese society, is at least able to respond to Chamberlain's idea. The analysis we have here of Chengdu's teahouses and public life (in the public sphere) from the 1950s up to the late 1970s indicates clearly that the state indeed blocked public life and the public sphere, which I assert are the very wellsprings of civil society, not merely a preparatory period before civil society. The fate of the older teahouse guild after 1949 was the death of a core part of "society." All Chengdu organizations and all levels of units, from streets to *danwei*, became part of the state apparatus. Neither the New Teahouse Guild nor other economic and cultural associations had any autonomy.

Part 2 of the present study focused on the return of voluntary organizations. As these organizations emerged, government controls weakened, and the middle class reinvented itself quickly. The teahouse, as a vibrant public space, helped this along. In the 1980s and 1990s, partially autonomous organizations emerged, such as associations related to commerce, professions, elderly people, clans, and religions. These inevitably weakened the state's control over the populace. Perhaps it can be stated that "society" had gradually returned, if slowly, based on the growth of these associative seeds. In this period, teahouses consequently returned rather vigorously. Whereas in the Republican period a guild controlled the number of teahouses, as the reform era developed, people were given free rein to open teahouses. With competition came the convenience of large numbers and many types of teahouse. Patronage flourished, and it is this in particular that indicates the real return of public life. With the boom in financing and banking, as well as all manner of rental opportunities and contracts, both prosperous and low-end teahouses promoted the development of the public sphere, and the middle class, often more educated and desirous of intellectual arenas, became a major factor. Thus, what we are considering is the overall democratization of business ownership, types of patrons, and intellectual pursuits—what we should acknowledge as a stronger public sphere that was forming in the teahouse. Yet it was not always about criticizing local or national authorities; this new sociality also served people's need to discuss their own lives, as well as social issues and topics, including news from outside just their own city. Although there were no longer the pre-1949 warning signs saying "Do Not Talk about National Affairs," and no longer the real threat that made them guard their words under Mao's regime, people in the 1980s and 1990s reform era actually felt little pressure to say much about anything political. Moreover, I did not find a single case in which anyone was charged with a crime because of words spoken in a teahouse. Such relaxation of talk in public inevitably accelerated the expression of public opinion.

Thus, we might consider that with Late Socialism and all its relaxations and new opportunities, it was the new marketplace itself that helped form a post-Mao civil society. Lowell Dittmer and Lance Gore have stated that the "impact of marketization on politics has been to establish a market culture," thereby forming "the basis for a more autonomous civil society that may ultimately result in a more pluralist and self-critical polity."[21] Frederic Wakeman, earlier, opposed the proposition that "there has been a continuing expansion of the public realm since 1900" that might be thought to constitute "the habituated assertion of civic power against the state."[22] However, Mary Rankin and William Rowe took a more positive view of the rise of the public sphere. As Rankin noted in her study of the public sphere in late-imperial China, "Civil society has been a major theme of Western political theory," but the concept of the public sphere, per se, "is less embedded in either Western political theory or historical literature and is more adaptable to other parts of the world since the early seventeenth century."[23]

This seems to be a claim that "civil society," as a case from Western history, is particularly apt for considering China. Rowe noticed public places such as teahouses and wineshops as places for public opinions, writing that, "although others may not agree, I personally am fully convinced that such phenomena did characterize the late imperial era. I am likewise satisfied that the urban teahouse and wineshop, in all of their varieties, were at least available to serve the same catalytic function in the fostering of popular critical debate of public issues that is routinely attributed to the early modern European cafe and coffee house."[24] My previous study of the teahouse, published in 2008, and the present study of public life, which brings that history forward, would agree; I believe I have provided solid evidence to prove the constant development of the public sphere in twentieth-century China.

Scholars have paid attention to how a changing public space has influenced the concept of the "public sphere" in contemporary China. Of course, "urban public space" includes not only streets, public squares, parks, theaters, coffeehouses, and teahouses, but also relatively grand public spaces such as those associated with monuments, statues, murals, and other art; they "offer a way to discuss the thorny question of China's 'public sphere.'" Some who study post-Mao China, especially sociologists in comparison with historians, favor the term "public sphere." They, and here I quote Richard Kraus, believe that "all societies have a public sphere," while more-cautious scholars believe that while "civil society and public sphere are distinct concepts, the two are still bound together."[25] Even though the notion of "civil society" in China after the Communist revolution and even in the post-Mao reform era is "richly debatable," to them, the concept of the public sphere seems "less controversial." Possibly, those who see something "richly debatable" have not understood the very recent, open criticisms coming from public arenas in China like universities and labor groups, which we usually consider to be strong formulations of civil society.[26]

Let us pause to consider this further. In the early 1990s, sociologist Richard Madsen found that "because of the reforms of the past decade and a half, there have arisen, or have been revived, a large variety of groups within Chinese society that are at least partially autonomous from the state." These include commercial or professional associations, associations to aid the elderly, those for clans, and the like (as I mentioned just above). Actually, in the roughly fifteen years since Madsen's remarks, all such associations have experienced even more development as autonomous factors of civil society. Madsen stated further, in the same work, that the expansion of these associations "weakens the capacity of the state to control its population." This contrasts powerfully with Chamberlain's suggestion, above, that the CCP's authoritarian bans against the development of civil society possibly helped achieve civil society. Madsen boldly argues that it was not the state itself but the voluntary associations that were being oppressed by Mao's state that "eventually contributed to the creation of a democratic public sphere" through a process that did "not necessarily require the establishment of a Western-style liberal democracy." Finally, Madsen invites us to enter society and conduct more concrete studies of the issues, rather than rely on preconceptions. For example, while we know that, as Habermas stated, "coffee houses played a key role in the development of a bourgeois public sphere in eighteenth-century England," we should not assume that "teahouses might play the same role in China." My study of teahouses and public life may be just the sort of empirical groundwork that Madsen calls "find[ing] ways of assessing the qualities that contribute to a civil society capable of leading the way toward a democratic public sphere."[27] Furthermore, the empirical findings here have proven that teahouses indeed shared similar functions with Europe's coffeehouses. This dovetails with the assertion by John Gittings that, "as Party-led political culture loses dominance, there is more space for the emergence of a civil society which is partly autonomous and fast gathering confidence."[28]

Where will the new civil society lead eventually? One answer to that may be the Internet. We have established that the modern teahouse (and other venues) are infused with political activity: people are able to freely meet, read, listen to public lectures, and discuss politics. But as of now, of course, the Internet has become the major outlet for all that. Activity on the Internet, however, unlike that in the teahouse, is conducted in private space. Still, we must understand that the Internet's vitality may be in its teahouse-like ability to be a hub of public opinion. This is emerging, however minimally, via WeChat (something like a Chinese version of Facebook) and other venues. Clearly, the state has found this way of voicing opinion to be difficult to control. Eventually, no force will stop the expansion of the public sphere, when fueled by the increasing vitality of public life overall, and the implications that it has for the permanence and importance of civil society.

CHARACTER LIST

aiguo gongyue　愛國公約
aimei guanxi　曖昧關系
Baihua chashe　百花茶社
Baihua tan　百花潭
Baihuzi daxian　白胡子大仙
ban shoufa ban weifa hu　半守法半違法戶
bandeng xi　板凳戲
bang　幫
Baqi chayuan　八旗茶苑
Bawang bieji　霸王別姬
Beijing sishi tian　北京四十天
bingpi　兵痞
Bishang Liangshan　逼上梁山
bufa huodong　不法活動
buliang zuofeng　不良作風
Caotang si　草堂寺
cha boshi　茶博士

chafang　茶坊
chagong　茶工
chaguan　茶館
chahei jilou　查黑擠漏
chahua　茶花
Chaiquan jie　芭泉街
Changshun jie　長順街
Changzhi shan'ge gei dang ting　唱支山歌給黨聽
Chashe ye tongye gonghui　茶社業同業公會
chayi　茶藝
chayi shi　茶藝師
Chengdu huizhan zhongxin　成都會展中心
Chengdu lao yougong xiehui　成都老郵工協會
Chengdu laonian tixie huodong zhongxin　成都老年體協活動中心
Chengdu qiannian xinwu zuweihui　成都千年信物組委會
Chengdu shi chashe ye tongye gonghui choubei weiyuanhui　成都市茶社業同業公會籌備委員會
Chengdu shi chashe ye tongye gonghui choubei weiyuanhui shuchang chazuo zu jianze caoan　成都市茶社業同業公會籌備委員會書場茶座組簡則草案
Chengdu shi chuanju wanyou xiehui　成都市川劇玩友協會
Chengdu shi chuanju yishu zhongxin,　成都市川劇藝術中心
Chengdu shi gongshangye lianhe choubeihui chashe tongye gonghui choubei weiyuanhui jianzhang　成都市工商業聯合籌備會茶社同業公會籌備委員會簡章
Chengdu shi gongshangye lianhe hui lüzhan chashe ye tongye weiyuanhui　成都市工商業聯合會旅棧茶社業同業委員會
Chengdu shi junshi guanzhi weiyuanhui　成都市軍事管制委員會
Chengdu shi qunzhong yishu guan　成都市群眾藝術館
Chengdu shi quyi chang　成都市曲藝場
Chengdu shi shiyan chuanju yuan　成都市試驗川劇院
Chengdu shi shuiwu xuanchuan gangyao　成都市稅務宣傳綱要
Chengdu shi siying gongshang qiye zhuanxieye yanjiu weiyuanhui　成都市私營工商企業轉歇業研究委員會
Chengdu shi xiqu gaige gongzuo weiyuanhui　成都市戲曲改革工作委員會
Chengdu shougongye zhe de chulu　成都手工業者的出路
Chengdu wenhua jiaoyu ju　成都文化教育局
Chengshi jumin weiyuanhui zuzhifa　城市居民委員會組織法
Chuanju wanyou xiehui　川劇玩友協會

Chuanxi junguan hui　川西軍管會
Chuanxi wenxue yishu jie lianhehui　川西文學藝術界聯合會
Chuli weigu baogao　處理圍鼓報告
Chunhua jie　純化街
Chunxi lu　春熙路
Ci Yun zouguo　慈雲走國
congliang　從良
da daoqin　打道琴
da ge chuanhu　打個傳呼
Da shijie　大世界
da weigu　打圍鼓
da yitong　大一統
Daci si　大慈寺
Dacizhuang chayuan　大慈莊茶園
Dadian xiao majiang, chidian malatang, hedian gendoujiu, kandian
　wailuxiang　打點小麻將，吃點麻辣燙，喝點跟斗酒，看點歪錄像
Daguan chalou　達觀茶樓
danwei　單位
Desheng chaguan　德盛茶館
Desheng xiajie　得勝下街
dianchang lougui　點唱陋規
Dianyuan gonghui　店員公會
Dier shiyan shuchang　第二實驗書場
Dihou wugongdui　敵後武工隊
diji quwei　低級趣味
ditang　底堂
diyi chake　第一茶客
Diyi shiyan shuchang　第一實驗書場
Dongyang dashi　東洋大師
Duanqiao　斷橋
Emei pai chayi　峨眉派茶藝
Erhuan lu　二環路
erlong xizhu　二龍戲珠
Fan gong jiuguo jun　反共救國軍
fangeming　反革命
fangqu zhi　防區制
fanma yongshi　反麻勇士
fanshen jiemei　翻身姐妹
fengjian qixi　封建氣息
Fengshen yanyi　封神演義

Fudaihui　婦代會
Fuzi miao　夫子廟
Gai Lanfang　蓋蘭芳
gairen, gaixi, gaizhidu　改人, 改戲, 改制度
Gaoshan liushui　高山流水
geming de dazhong yule　革命的大眾娛樂
geming qunzhong　革命群眾
geming wenyi　革命文藝
gonggong yinshi ye　公共飲食業
gonghui　公會
gongji jin　公積金
gongma　公麻
Gongnong jutuan　工農劇團
gongren zhen　工人鎮
Gongshang ju　工商局
Gongshanglian chouweihui　工商聯籌委會
Gongshanglian　工商聯
gongsi heying　公私合營
gongyi jin　公益金
gongzhong　公眾
gongzhong yulun　公眾輿論
guanliao ziben　官僚資本
guanmo　觀摩
guapai yanchang　掛牌演唱
gundeng　滾燈
Hangye pingyi weiyuanhui　行業評議委員會
hanyi juankuan　寒衣捐款
he gaiwan cha　喝蓋碗茶
hei wulei　黑五類
heli de youxian duoshu minzhu zhi　合理的有限多數民主制
Heming chashe　鶴鳴茶社
Heshang jie　和尚街
heye　荷葉
hezuo chashe　合作茶社
hezuo shangdian　合作商店
Hongxing lu　紅星路
Hu Zongnan　胡宗南
Huadu chafang　華都茶坊
Huangcheng　皇城
Huangdi yu jinü　皇帝與妓女

Huapaifang jie　花牌坊街
Huaxing jie　華興街
huayuan chazuo　花園茶座
huimen　會門
Huizong　徽宗
huodong shi　活動室
Jia Shusan　賈樹三
jiang shengyu　講聖諭
jiaozi　餃子
jiben shoufa hu　基本守法戶
Jidu xiyang hong　幾度夕陽紅
jiebian xinwen　街邊新聞
jiedao gongchang　街道工廠
jiegu fei　解雇費
jieji yiji fenzi　階級異己分子
Jieyi lou　結義樓
Jigong zhuan　濟公傳
jiji fenzi　積極分子
Jile chaguan　集樂茶館
Jile laoren zhijia　集樂老人之家
Jinchun chashe　錦春茶社
jingtang mu　驚堂木
Jinjiang juchang　錦江劇場
Jinli chashe　金利茶社
Jinniu　金牛
jinqian ban　金錢板
Jinsheng chashe　近聖茶社
jiti suoyou zhi　集體所有制
jumin chuanju tuan　居民川劇團
jumin weiyuanhui　居民委員會
Junguan hui　軍管會
Lao chake xianhua　老茶客閑話
Lao xiangzi　老巷子
Laogong chashe　勞工茶社
laohu zao　老虎灶
laonian che　老年車
Laowu　老屋
laozi liangli　勞資兩利
laozi xieshang hui　勞資協商會
Li Boqing　李伯清

Li Decai　李德才

Li Xiaolong luxiang pai cha　李小龍錄像牌茶

Li Yueqiu　李月秋

Liaozhai　聊齋

Lidong chashe　利東茶社

Lin Zexu jinyan　林則徐禁煙

lishi zhang　理事長

liudong renkou　流動人口

Lu Ban quanshu　魯班全書

luanshuo luanchang　亂說亂唱

Luoguo xiang　鑼鍋巷

luohou qunzhong　落後群眾

majiang dazhan　麻將大戰

majiang feng　麻將瘋

majiang guan　麻將館

majiang qu　麻將區

Majiang xue　麻將學

mangmu xing　盲目性

Meng Wentong　蒙文通

Mingqing chalou　明清茶樓

Mingren ju　茗仁居

minzhu de fangshi　民主的方式

mixin yongpin　迷信用品

mixin zhiye　迷信職業

Nanfeng chalou　南風茶樓

nongjia le　農家樂

Ouluoba　歐羅巴

paichu suo　派出所

paoge　袍哥

pibao gongsi　皮包公司

Pifang jie　皮房街

pingtan　評彈

pingyi xiaozu　評議小組

Qing'an chashe　清安茶社

qingchang　清唱

Qingcheng shijiu xia　青城十九俠

Qingfang chayuan　清芳茶園

qingfei fanba, jianzu tuiya　清匪反霸,減租退押

Qinghe chazuo　清河茶座

qingjing　清靜

qingmian　情面

Qingquan chafang　清泉茶坊

Qingyang gong　青羊宮

qingyin　清音

Qintai lu　琴臺路

quanguo shanhe yipian ma　全國山河一片麻

quanmin jie ma　全民皆麻

quanmin jingshang　全民經商

Qugaihui choubeihui　曲改會籌備會

qunzhong　群眾

qunzhuan zu　群專組

quyi ju　曲藝劇

Quyi yiren bianxie zu　曲藝藝人編寫組

raomin majiang　擾民麻將

renao　熱鬧

renbao zu　人保組

Renmin chashe　人民茶社

Renmin nanlu　人民南路

renqi　人氣

Sanda Zhujiazhuang　三打祝家莊

Sangui chayuan　三桂茶園

Sanguo　三國

Sanguo yanyi　三國演義

sanmian hongqi　三面紅旗

Sanqiao bei jie　三橋北街

Sanqingtuan　三青團

Sansheng jie　三聖街

Sanxian jianshe　三線建設

Sanyigong　三益公

Shahe chayuan　沙河茶園

shangshan xiaxiang　上山下鄉

shanpai　善牌

Shaocheng gongyuan　少城公园

shehui jinbu renshi　社會進步人士

shehui zhazi　社會渣滓

Shehui zhuyi hao　社會主義好

Shehui zhuyi jiaoyu yundong　社會主義教育運動

shengchan chengshi　生產城市

Shengtaosha　聖淘沙

Shenxiang quanshu　神相全書

Shewu weiyuanhui　社務委員會
Shi yuzhuo　拾玉鐲
Shiba mo　十八摸
shifu　師傅
Shihua shishuo　實話實說
Shimei tu　十美圖
shimin wenhua　市民文化
Shiren nanlu　石人南路
Shiyi renmin jiuyi du, haiyou yiyi zuo houbu　十億人民九億賭，
　還有一億做候補
shoufa hu　守法戶
shoupai　獸牌
shourong　收容
shourong suo　收容所
Shouzhang de yiguan　首長的衣冠
Shu　蜀
Shubao　蜀報
shuchang　書場
shuchang chazuo zu　書場茶座組
shuiba　水吧
Shuihu　水滸
Shuiwu tuijin weiyuanhui　稅務推進委員會
shunkouliu　順口溜
Shunxing lao chaguan　順興老茶館
Shuo Yue　說岳
shupeng　書棚
Shusheng qinshe　蜀聲琴社
Shusheng qinshe yanchang hui　蜀聲琴社演唱會
Shuwa jie　暑襪街
Shuyuan nanjie　書院南街
Si xiucai　思秀才
sixiang jiefang　思想解放
sixue　私學
Suiyuan chashe　隨園茶社
Taiping tianguo　太平天國
tangguan　堂倌
Tiao huache　挑滑車
Tidu jie　提督街
tigao zhengzhi renshi　提高政治認識
Tongle　同樂

tongye gonghui　同業公會
tongye gonghui weiyuanhui　同業公會委員會
Tongzhan bu　統戰部
Wang Banxian　王半仙
Wang Gui yu Li Xiangxiang　王桂與李香香
Wangjiang (district)　望江(區)
Wangri qinghuai chafang　往日情懷茶坊
Wanhualou chashe　萬花樓茶社
Wanyou xiehui　玩友協會
Wenbo chayuan　文博茶園
Wenbo yishu lüyou gongsi　文博藝術旅遊公司
wenhua gong　文化宮
Wenhua jiaoyu ju　文化教育局
Wenhua ju xiquke　文化局戲曲科
wenhua leyuan　文化樂園
Wenjiao jieguan weiyuanhui　文教接管委員會
Wenshu yuan　文殊院
Wenyi chu　文藝處
Wuhou ci　武侯祠
Wuyue juyuan　五月劇院
Wuyue wenhua fuwu she　五月文化服務社
Wuyue wenyu chayuan　五月文娛茶園
Wuyue yeyu qiyi zu　五月業余棋藝組
xialiu yongsu　下流庸俗
xiandai ren　現代人
Xiangji chu chalou　香積廚茶樓
Xianglin sao　祥林嫂
xianqi shizu　仙氣十足
Xiao Erhei jiehun　小二黑結婚
Xiaoao jianghu　笑傲江湖
xiaofei chengshi　消費城市
Xibu da kaifa　西部大開發
Xie Guozhen　謝國楨
xieshang hutui　協商互推
xieshang tuixuan　協商推選
xieye jiegu hetong　歇業解雇合同
Xiju bao　戲劇報
Xin minzhu zhuyi geming　新民主主義革命
xinde wenyi yundong　新的文藝運動
Xinrong chashe　新蓉茶社

Xinrong pingju tuan　新蓉平劇團
xinshu buzheng　心術不正
xiqu　戲曲
Xiuxian zhidu　休閑之都
Xiyu jie　西禦街
Xu Zhongshu　徐中書
xujia fanrong　虛假繁榮
yanchang zheng　演唱證
yanchu zheng　演出證
Yang Bajie youchun　楊八姐遊春
yangqin　洋琴
Yewu zhidao weiyuanhui　業務指導委員會
yinci　淫詞
yingjuyuan chazuo　影劇院茶座
Yinxiao chashe　吟嘯茶社
Yixiang chayuan　頤香茶園
Yizhi chalou　益智茶樓
Yuanda chaguan　遠大茶館
Yuekuan chashe　月寬茶社
Yuelai chayuan　悅來茶園
Yufu shan　魚腹山
Yunhai chaguan　雲海茶館
Yushi dai　玉獅帶
Yutang chun　玉堂春
zanzhu zheng　暫住證
zaocha　早茶
Zeng Bingkun　曾炳昆
Zhao Shuli　趙樹理
zhengdun xiaozu　整頓小組
Zhengsheng jingju she　正聲京劇社
Zhenliu chashe　枕流茶社
zhongzuo　中左
Zhouwu chahui　周五茶會
Zhuojiang chashe　濯江茶社
zhuqin　竹琴
zhuren　主任
zhuyeqing　竹葉青
Zhuyeqing chafang　竹葉青茶坊
Zongfu jie　總府街
Zou Zhongxin　鄒忠新
zuotanhui　座談會

NOTES

Frequently cited sources have been identified by the abbreviations below.

Archives

All citations of documents in the Chengdu Municipal Archives follow the archives' cataloging conventions: numbers following the abbreviation (e.g., CGTGD) refer to category (*quanzong*), catalog (*mulu*), and volume (*juan*) (e.g., CGTGD 52-128-12). Two groups of numbers after the abbreviation indicate that this archive has only a category and volume, with no catalog (e.g., CSSD, 104-1388).

CGTGD	Chengdu shi gehang geye tongye gonghui dang'an [Archive of Chengdu guilds in all professions]. Chengdu Municipal Archives, *quanzong* 52.
CSGJD	Chengdu shi gongshang ju dang'an [Archive of the Chengdu bureau of industry and commerce]. Chengdu Municipal Archives, *quanzong* 119.
CSGSLD	Chengdu shi gongshanglian dang'an [Archive of the Chengdu association of industry and commerce]. Chengdu Municipal Archives, *quanzong* 103.
CSGXD	Chengdu shi gongshang xingzheng dengji dang'an [Archive of the registry of Chengdu commercial administrations]. Chengdu Municipal Archives, *quanzong* 40.
CSJJD	Chengdu shenghui jingcha ju dang'an [Archive of the Chengdu provincial capital police force]. Chengdu Municipal Archives, *quanzong* 93.
CSSD	Chengdu shi shanghui dang'an [Archive of the Chengdu Chamber of Commerce]. Chengdu Municipal Archives, *quanzong* 104.

CSSYEJ   Chengdu shi shangye erju dang'an [Archive of the Chengdu Second Bureau of
          Commerce]. Chengdu Municipal Archives, *quanzong* 117.
CSTZD   Chengdu shiwei tongzhanbu dang'an [Archive of the Chengdu municipal
          party committee united front section]. Chengdu Municipal Archives, *quan-
          zong* 76.
CSWHJ   Chengdu shi wenhua ju dang'an [Archive of the Chengdu Bureau of Culture].
          Chengdu Municipal Archives, *quanzong* 124.
CSZGD   Chengdu shi zhengfu gongshang dang'an [Archive of Chengdu industry and
          commerce. Republican period]. Chengdu Municipal Archives, *quanzong* 38.

Chinese Newspapers

Chengdu shangbao [Chengdu commercial news]
Chengdu wanbao [Chengdu evening news]
Huaxi dushi bao [West China metropolitan news]
Renmin ribao [People's daily]
Shandong zhengbao [Shandong government report]
Shangwu zaobao [Commerce morning news]
Shubao [Shu region news]
Sichuan qingnian bao [Sichuan youth news]
Sichuan ribao [Sichuan daily]
Tianfu zaobao [Sichuan morning news]
Xiju bao [Opera news]
Xinwen jie [News world]
Xinxin xinwen [Newest news]
Zhongguo qingnian bao [China youth news]

Introduction

1. *Xinxin xinwen*, December 31, 1949.
2. Li Xianke 1995.
3. Chengdu shi difangzhi bianzuan weiyuanhui 1999, 400.
4. On storytellers' audiences see D. Wang 2003, 77–79.
5. On late-Qing and Republican-era teahouse entertainment see D. Wang 2008b,
chaps. 4 and 5.
6. See D. Wang 2003, 221–25; D. Wang 2008b, 20.
7. For the daily routines see D. Wang 2008b, chap. 3.
8. D. Wang 1993; He Yimin 2002; Chengdu shi tongjiju 2000.
9. D. Wang 2003, chap. 7, and 2008b, chap. 8.
10. Heller 1984, 244.
11. There are many studies of the impact of globalization on local places and culture. See
Harvey 1990; Bird et al. 1993; Massey 1994 and 1995; Hayden 1995; Cox 1997; Mitchell
2000; and Ching 2000. For studies of Chinese regions and regional culture see Skinner 1976
and 1977; Harrell 1995; Oi 1995; Cartier 2002a; and Goodman and Segal 2002.
12. Lao Xiang 1942.
13. By 2000, according to a conservative estimate, Chengdu had at least three thousand
teahouses (*Shangwu zaobao*, May 19, 2000).
14. Regarding this region see Skinner 1964–65; D. Wang 1993, chaps. 1 and 2; D. Wang
2003, 4–6.
15. D. Wang 2003, 119–20; D. Wang 2008b, 125, 155–57, 165, 166, 175, 212.

16. Bao Yaming, Wang Hongtu, and Zhu Shengjian have given a vivid description of bars in Shanghai (2002), while poet Zhai Yongming wrote a book on bars and bar culture in today's Chengdu (2009).

17. W. Whyte 1980.

18. D. Wang 2008b, 1.

19. Post-Mao China has moved away from "socialism" economically, although China is still ruled by the party. Given the market economy, the rise of the private sector, and the increasing gap between rich and poor, to a large extent China might no longer be a real "socialist country" in terms of orthodox Marxism. Or we might say it is a hybrid of capitalism and socialism, or, as some studies have suggested, it could be called "late socialism" (the term that I have adopted in this book) or "post-socialism" (Wittman 1983; Solinger 1989; Gore 2001; An Chen 2002; McNally 2004; Zhang 2001b, 2; Bandelj and Solinger 2012). Some studies call the Mao era "High Socialism" (Brown and Johnson 2015).

20. For example, Aminda Smith has studied people's resistance against the movements of thought reform and reeducation (2013).

21. Brown and Pickowicz 2007b, 2.

22. L. Zhang 2001b, 5, 11.

23. J. Wang 2001b, 71, and 2001c.

24. Rankin 1986, 1990, and 1993; Rowe 1989, 1990, and 1993.

25. Rowe 1990.

26. Richard Sennett, in his influential book *The Fall of Public Man*, pointed out that today "public life has also become a matter of formal obligation" (1977, 3). Here, he regards the modern notion of "public life" as a person's political life, in some sense looking to public service and political office and elections. In early modern European cities, however, public life, Sennett held, was what transpired in public places "apart from the realm of family and close friends" and from the "public realm of acquaintances and strangers," where activities might be somewhat shielded. He also points out that to study "public life," one must find out "who 'the public' were, and where one was when one was out 'in public.'" In early eighteenth-century Paris and London, the bourgeois class became "less concerned to cover up their social origins," and their cities were becoming "a world in which widely diverse groups in society were coming into contact" (Sennett 1977, 17). In *Public Life in Renaissance Florence* (1980), Richard Trexler assumes a different focus; he examines "classic public ritual." His term "public ritual life" happens to include the struggles of "marginal social groups" and their "challenge to traditional social and ritual organization." He ultimately would disagree with Sennett about "public man" in decline (Trexler 1980, xxiii).

27. For example, John Forester, in his *Critical Theory and Public Life* (1988), places the term "public life" under Jürgen Habermas's critical communications theory of society and defines it as "everyday life and social action in workplaces, in schools, in planning processes, and in broader social, political, and cultural settings" (1988, ix). Yet it is Yael Navaro-Yashin who has given the broadest description of public life. In her *Faces of the State: Secularism and Public Life in Turkey* (2002), "public life" is analyzed as "the public sphere," "public culture," "civil society," and "the state" and then examined as domains of "power" and "resistance." By using the notion of public life, she analyzes "people and the state, not as an opposition, but as the same domain" (2002, 2).

28. Sennett 1977, 17.

29. Y. Yan 2000, 224.

30. A good example is the Mao cult and related spectacles of worship and rituals (Leese 2011).

31. Y. Yan 2000, 224.

32. Gabriel Almond and G. Bingham Powell defined "political culture" as "the set of attitudes, beliefs, and feelings about politics current in a nation at a given time. This political culture has been shaped by the nation's history and by the processes of social, economic, and political activities" (Almond 1956; Almond and Powell 1978, 25). In 1971, the political scientist Richard H. Solomon published *Mao's Revolution and the Chinese Political Culture*; in it he used the term "political culture" to explore "Chinese social attitudes, emotional concerns, and moral norms which influence political behavior" and to analyze "social and cultural systems" (1971, 2). In Solomon's notion, "political culture" exists almost everywhere; for instance, it is shown in a "society's socialization practices," "the manner in which parents educate their children," and teachers' instruction for their students "to deal with the world they will know as adults," and so forth (xiii). Similarly, Lucian W. Pye's article "Culture and Political Science: Problems in the Evaluation of the Concept of Political Culture" (1972) considered "political culture" as attitudes, beliefs, sentiments, political processes, governing behavior, political ideals, public opinion, political ideology, basic consensus, values, and political sentiments. These studies are broad: they cast a very wide net in order to delineate what political culture is, ranging from "feelings" to "moral norms" to "ideology."

33. Unlike the political scientists, Lynn Hunt and others use the concept of political culture in a relatively narrower way, as contrasted with the broad approach. In an early work, *Politics, Culture, and Class in the French Revolution* (1984), Hunt examined "the political culture of the Revolution" and uncovered "the rules of political behavior," including the values, expectation, and implicit rules that "expressed and shaped collective intentions and actions." For Hunt, political culture takes in both "the logic of revolutionary political action" and "symbolic practices" such as language, imagery, and gestures (1984, 10–13). Peter Burke also sees different spheres in which political culture operates. He points out that the concept links two "domains, focusing on the political attitudes or assumptions of different groups of people, and the ways in which these attitudes are instilled" (Burke 2008, 105–6). On the political culture of the French Revolution see Baker 1987. On political culture generally see Pye and Verba 1965; Brown and Gray 1979; Weisband and Thomas 2015. For studies of political culture in China see Metzger 1979; Adelman 1983; Zarrow 1990; Jin 1993; Wasserstrom and Perry 1994; Moody 1994; H. Goodman 1998; Hua 2001; A. Wang 2006; Yang Zhong 2012. On the political culture of the French Revolution see Baker 1987. On political culture generally see Pye and Verba 1965; Brown and Gray 1979; Weisband and Thomas 2015.

34. One exception is John Wilson Lewis's edited collection of essays in 1971 that deal with control and transformation of Chinese cities during Early Socialism; it covered public security bureaus, urban cadres, unions, businesses, education, and human resource management. The essays show how the Communist regime gained control at the urban, grassroots level, where every resident was surveilled by a totalistic administration (Lewis 1971). Also, Janet Weitzner Salaff's "Urban Residential Communities in the Wake of the Cultural Revolution" and Jerome Alan Cohen's "Drafting People's Mediation Rules" are likely the earliest studies of urban grassroots organizations in Communist China (Salaff 1971; Cohen 1971). See also Sit (1979), the first to examine small shops at the local level.

35. Most data came from interviews of 133 individuals from fifty cities in mainland China, mostly from the Lingnan region to Hong Kong, during 1977 and 1978. (The authors had no access to materials from mainland China when they conducted their research.) Whyte and Parish 1984, 5.

36. M. K. Whyte 1991, 740. On the urban economy during this period see Solinger 1984 and Meliksetov 1996. Certain general histories of the PRC by Chinese historians may also be considered in this approach. So far, the most systematic and comprehensive study on 1950s

China is Yang Kuisong's *History of the Founding of the People's Republic of China* (Zhonghua renmin gongheguo jianguo shi yanjiu), dealing with the major political and management issues facing "New China," such as the Land Revolution, the Suppression of Counterrevolutionaries, the Three Antis and Five Antis Campaigns, cadre appointments, the wage system, and the bourgeoisie. The work mainly takes a national perspective, with two chapters devoted to Shanghai (Yang Kuisong 2009b). Jin Guantao edited the ten-volume *History of the People's Republic of China, 1949–1981* (Zhonghua renmin gongheguo shi, 1949–1981), chronologically constructing the histories of major political movements, the economy, and diplomacy (Jin Guantao 2009). However, neither of the above two deals with urban life, leisure, and entertainment. There is a general history of Chengdu edited by He Yimin (2002) titled *Reforms and Development: A Study of Modernization of China's Inland-City Chengdu* (Biange yu fazhan: Zhongguo neilu chengshi Chengdu xiandaihua yanjiu), a large contribution to modern Chengdu history, but the period from 1949 to 1976 is overlooked.

37. The book is divided into four parts. All three articles in the section "Urban Takeover" are about Shanghai: Frederic Wakeman on Shanghai's new order, Elizabeth Perry on the working class, and Nara Dillon on private charity (Wakeman 2007; Perry 2007; Dillon 2007). In the section "Occupying the Periphery," two articles deal with entertainment of Early Socialism. Perry Link points out that the comic performances of *xiangsheng* (cross-talkers) were satirical, making the actors relatively more vulnerable to persecution by the state. Cross-talkers enthusiastically participated in the establishment of revolutionary culture but were eventually betrayed by the new regime. In his examination of Shi Hui's post-1949 fate, Paul Pickowicz shows that a famous movie actor tried to contribute to revolutionary movies but committed suicide during the Anti-rightist Movement. Works by Joseph Esherick and Sherman Cochran reveal the experience of intellectuals and capitalists (and their families) after 1949. Esherick describes the Ye brothers in Beijing: "For the brothers of the Ye family, the early years of the People's Republic were most remarkable as a long-delayed period of normalcy, after years of war and revolution." But, "Only gradually did politics enter the picture, as a slowly encroaching shadow that would darken the years to come" (Esherick 2007, 336). In Cochran's study, we see capitalist Liu Hongsheng cooperating with the CCP, after which he "not only survived but greatly benefited from the outcome." Cochran concludes that "it now seems possible that the Lius' belief in the compatibility of capitalism and communism in China might be vindicated after all" (Cochran 2007, 380, 385).

38. Brown and Pickowicz 2007b, 5–6. James Gao's monograph on the Communists' takeover of Hangzhou, for instance, is based on items in the municipal archives and explores the transition from Nationalist to CCP government through issues such as the development of urban policy, cadres, the Korean War and the city, and the Three Antis and Five Antis Campaigns (J. Gao 2004). In 2012, the journal *Frontiers of History in China* published a special issue on "Remolding Chinese Society: People, Cadres, and Mass Campaigns in the 1950s and 1960s"; most of this research stemmed from archival material. With the exception of my article on Chengdu, the focus was on Shanghai and its slums, religious organizations, and antiques collectors. In 2011, the same journal also published Antonia Finnane's article on tailors in early 1950s Beijing (Henriot 2012; D. Wang 2012; Jessup 2012; Joseph Lee 2012; Denise Ho 2012; Finnane 2011).

39. Three volumes of the series Contemporary Chinese History (Dangdai Zhongguo shi yanjiu) have been published so far; they include several articles on urban society and culture and represent the latest achievements in the study of Chinese urban history. This includes Zhang Jishun on the institutional changes of private newspapers in Shanghai, especially the transition from private to the CCP control; Ruan Qinghua on the cleanup and reconstruction of the urban grassroots community in early 1950s Shanghai; Wang Haiguang on the

establishment of China's urban and rural household registration system and the CCP's political manipulation; Feng Xiaocai on the procedures of public-private partnerships for businessmen in Shanghai and on the socialist transformation of hawkers after 1956; and Lin Chaochao on the CCP takeover and transformation of cities (Yang Kuisong 2009a, 2011; Zhang Jishun 2009; Wang D. 2009; Ruan Qinghua 2009; Wang Haiguang 2011; Feng Xiaocai 2011a, 2011b; and Lin Chaochao 2011). Another of Zhang Jishun's works, on Shanghai residents' committees in the early 1950s, is excellent; it allows us to see the extent of state control over urban, grassroots activities (Zhang Jishun 2004). Gao Zhongwei (2011) has produced a work on the establishment of urban, low-level administrations in Chengdu during Early Socialism, addressing issues such as the Communists' takeover, renovation, formation of the *danwei* system, and residents' committees.

40. Brown and Johnson 2015, 1–2.

41. Tang and Parish 2000.

42. Li Zhang observes the massive population movement after the reforms and the formation of immigrant communities, such as "Zhejiang Village" in Beijing. State control was undermined by the more than one hundred million "floating people" each year, plus the increasing growth of commercial culture and social networks, and the "privatization" of space and power (L. Zhang 2001b). Regarding the floating population, also see Dutton 1998 and Friedmann 2005. Qin Shao's *Shanghai Gone* is the most recent study of the reconstruction of Shanghai, which explores the personal hardship in the demolishing movement (Shao 2013).

43. Yeh 1995, 121.

44. Regarding this workshop see Perry, Li Lifeng, et al. 2015.

45. Oksenberg 1969, 580.

46. Oksenberg 1969, 581.

1. The Demise of the Chengdu Teahouse Guild and the Fall of Small Business

1. Imahori 1953; Morse (1909) 1967; P. Ho 1966; Golas 1977; Rowe 1984; B. Goodman 1995; Qiu Pengsheng 1990; Zhu Ying 2004. The latter provides an extensive discussion of guilds in the Republic and their revival under Late Socialism, but up until now there has not been a study of the transformation of guilds in the early 1950s. However, there have been studies of early 1950s guilds in Chinese: Cui Yuefeng 2005 and Wei Wenxiang 2008. Regarding recent studies of the socialist transformation see Liu and Wang 2006; Lin Yunhui 2009.

2. See Chand 1958; Gluckstein 1957; Brugger 1976; Meliksetov 1996; Meliksetov and Pantsov 2001; H. Li 2006. Several exceptions for local studies are Vogel 1969; Gardner 1969; Lieberthal 1980. For studies of the economy during this period see Liu and Wang 2006; Kubo 2010; Matsumoto 2010; Finnane 2011.

3. Chai 2000. For urban control and reform during Early Socialism see Lewis 1971, which collected articles on the mediation system, public security, fostering of cadres, unions, etc., but not on guilds.

4. For a case of state infiltration of the lowest levels of society during the Republican period see D. Wang 2008b, chap. 2.

5. D. Wang 2008b, chap. 2.

6. CSSD 104-1401.

7. D. Wang 2008b, chap. 2.

8. Regarding studies of New Democracy see Chin and Lin 1982; Meliksetov 1996; Dillon 2007.

9. Chengdu shi difang zhi bianzuan weiyuanhui 2000, 96–97.

10. Wei Wenxiang 2008, 89; Cui Yuefeng 2005, 107.

11. Chengdu shi difang zhi bianzuan weiyuanhui 2000, 98.

12. Wei Wenxiang 2008, 90.

13. Chengdu shi difang zhi bianzhuan weiyuan hui 2000, 106–7. Reform of street vendors was a national policy at the time. In March 1950, the Ministry of Finance of the central government issued "Regulations for Licensing and Taxation of Street Vendors," which required that "any person who engages in street vending must apply for a license and pay taxes" (*Shandong zhengbao* no. 3, 1950). After that, every major city followed suit. See Zhonggong Beiping shiwei 2004; Zhang Chen 2003. For street vendors in late-Qing and early Republican Chengdu see D. Wang 2003, 32–38, 132–34. For a general study of peddlers in modern Chinese cities see Hu Junxiu and Suo Yu 2012.

14. CSGXD 40-65-13. The money mentioned here was the old currency. The exchange rate in 1955 when the new currency came in was 1 to 10,000 (*Renmin ribao*, February 21, 1955).

15. CSZGD 38-11-97, 38-11-544; CSSYEJ 117-2-1252; CSSD 104-2-1388; CSJJD 93-2-1447.

16. CSGSLD 103-1-167. As an example, the application of the Golden Profit Teahouse (Jinli chashe) promised: "(1) I want to firmly take the socialist road, (2) my shop has a balanced budget and makes some profit every month, and (3) my shop's debts have been settled." The application of the Purity and Peace Teahouse (Qing'an chashe) claimed, "Since our shop became a public-private copartnership in January, we have gained a better understanding of the system and our management style and have decided to make some major changes to improve our business operation and accumulate capital. Our shop has a balanced budget, and any debt is solely the responsibility of the manager."

17. CGTGD 52-128-1.

18. CGTGD 52-128-1.

19. See D. Wang 2008b, chap. 2.

20. CGTGD 52-128-1.

21. CGTGD 52-128-1.

22. CGTGD 52-128-1. In chapter 3 I will discuss how the city was transformed from a "city of consumption" to a "city of production."

23. CGTGD 52-128-1.

24. CGTGD 52-128-1.

25. CGTGD 52-128-1.

26. CGTGD 52-128-1.

27. CGTGD 52-128-1.

28. CGTGD 52-128-1. According to the "List of the Names and Résumés of the Teahouse Guild Board Members" dated November 1950, there was no entry for Liao Wenchang, president of the old Teahouse Guild; but Wang Xiushan, his predecessor, remained a member (CGTGD 52-128-1, 52-128-2).

29. Of them, those twenty to twenty-nine years olds numbered four; thirty to thirty-nine numbered ten; forty to forty-nine numbered four; fifty to fifty-nine had five; and sixty and over only two.

30. CGTGD 52-128-2.

31. CGTGD 52-128-1. Until 1953, when the New Teahouse Guild registered with the government, five cinemas were still attached to teahouses, and these were called "cinema teahouses" (*yingjuyuan chazuo*). See CGTGD 52-128-11.

32. CGTGD 52-128-1.

33. CGTGD 52-128-1.

34. On February 1, 1950, the new government took over fourteen district offices of the previous government and divided the city into eight new district offices (four urban and four suburban) named in numerical order from one to eight. The *baojia* system was entirely abandoned (Guo Wenzhi 1995, 14). For teahouse categorization the result was eight large groupings (based on the eight districts), and hierarchically underneath each of these large groups every fifteen to twenty teahouses became a small group.

35. CGTGD 52-128-1.

36. CGTGD 52-128-2.

37. CGTGD 52-128-2.

38. CGTGD 52-128-2.

39. These documents provide important information on teahouses and employment. The list of employees, for example, reveals that Broad View had one manager, six general workers, five waiters, two shop assistants, two water carriers, one stove keeper, and one back-of-the-house man. The "daily salary" column indicates that, in addition to the manager (i.e., the owner), six people (a man and five women) worked without pay, likely as members of the manager's family. The shop assistants earned 2,000 yuan per day; the stove keeper, 6,400 yuan; waiters, from 2,000 to 2,800 yuan; water carriers, 3,600 yuan each; and the back-of-the-house man, 2,800 yuan. Interestingly, the stove keeper earned the highest wages, triple a waiter's salary. From the "asset survey inventory" we know that the teahouse had five rooms, 368 sets of tea bowls, 280 copper saucers, and one hot water vat, plus electric lightbulbs, raw materials, and so on, all of which are listed in great detail (CSGXD 40-65-13).

40. CSGXD 40-65-13.

41. CSGXD 40-65-4. For example, Gong, an employee since June 1947, had a daily wage of twenty-one bowls of tea, or about 250,000 yuan per month, plus 50,000 yuan for meals. His severance pay was three months' worth of wages and meals, or a total of 900,000 yuan. Lan came to the teahouse in December 1949 and received a monthly wage of 0.75 *dan* of rice, plus 50,000 yuan for meals, so he was paid a total of 2.25 *dan* rice and 150,000 yuan cash, plus an unpaid regular wage of 1.8 *dan* rice. To convert *dan* into pounds is difficult because there was no standard rate; not only did different regions in China have different weight systems, but even in Chengdu there was no single standard. Generally, one *dan* of rice in East China was about 160 to 180 pounds, a poundage that was much less than in Sichuan. In late Qing-era Chengdu, one *dan* was between 280 and 300 *jin*, and in the 1940s it was also 280 *jin*, or about 307 to 330 pounds (D. Wang 2008b, 266).

42. CGTGD 52-128-11.

43. CGTGD 52-128-11.

44. For studies of these campaigns see Brugger 1976; M. Sheng 2006. Scholars in China have looked at the campaigns from a positive side, especially as regards certain benefits from fighting corruption. See Zhang Junguo 2008; Zhang Yue 2004. However, some recent studies have started to revisit this movement, such as Yang Kuisong 2006; Liu Dejun 2009; Shang Hongjuan 2008. Some have pointed out that the negative impact hit industry and commerce. See Zhang Yuyu 2011.

45. D. Wang 2008b, 66–71.

46. Wu Yongxiao 1989, 11–13.

47. Wu Yongxiao 1989, 11–13.

48. Wu Yongxiao 1989, 13.

49. Of 31,609 private business proprietors, 6,322 were "law-abiders" (*shoufa hu*); 19,540 were "fundamental law-abiders" (*jiben shoufa hu*); and 5,044 were "half law-abiders" (*ban shoufa ban weifa hu*). Those who broke the law on a serious scale numbered 666; those who totally violated the law, 37. The total amounts of tax evasion was 17.54 million yuan (Chengdu shi difang zhi bianzuan weiyuanhui 2000, 101–2).

50. CGTGD 52-128-12.

51. CGTGD 52-128-1, 52-128-12.

52. CGTGD 52-128-12. The money mentioned here was the old currency. Eight million was about 800 yuan, not a small amount at that time.

53. CGTGD 52-128-12; 52-128-2. The archives contain hundreds of pages regarding teahouse tax violations and evasions in 1950 and 1951, including confessions, investigations, and secret reports. These materials help us understand how the campaigns were undertaken at the lowest level of the city. However, there are some problems in using such materials. For example, the reports do not have a unified form, the makeup of some parallel items in fact varies, and some data were obviously changed repeatedly. Furthermore, certain of the data resulted from political pressure, others were used as a way of attacking business rivals, and still others were based on hearsay (CGTGD 52-128-12).

54. Chengdu shi difang zhi bianzuan weiyuanhui 2000, 98–100.

55. Wu Yongxiao 1989, 11. In fact, there were still 448 teahouses in 1957; see CSSYEJ 117-2-244.

56. Wu Yongxiao 1989, 18.

57. Ma Shihong 1994, 13. The money mentioned was the old currency.

58. CSGXD 40-65-29, 40-65-15, 40-65-154.

59. Shaocheng was a Manchu walled area within Chengdu. The wall was dismantled after the 1911 Revolution.

60. CSGXD 40-65-111, 40-65-119, 40-65-58.

61. CSGXD 40-65-95, 40-65-51.

62. CSGXD 40-65-33.

63. Zhang Xiande 1999, 54.

64. Strauss 2006, 896.

65. Dillon 2007, 93.

66. Perry 2007, 79. Also see J. Chen 1994, 2001.

67. Gardner 1969, 539.

68. Dillon 2007, 102.

69. Brown and Pickowicz 2007a, 8.

70. Solinger 1984, 20.

71. Lieberthal 2004, 99.

2. State Control and the Rise of Socialist Entertainment

1. Qiao Zengxi, Li Canhua, and Bai Zhaoyu 1983, 9–11.

2. There are few studies of cultural and art policies under Early Socialism, but Chang-tai Hung has studied revolutionary dance of *yangge* (2005), and Eddy U (2007) and Zhang Jishun (2010) have studied thought reform. In addition, Jin Jiang's book on Yue opera actresses has a chapter about this period (Jiang 2009, 181–90). For this topic, Chinese scholars largely concentrate on Shanghai (see Jiang Jin 2007; Zhang Jishun 2012; Sun Xiaozhong 2012; Xiao Wenming 2013), although Yan Feng examines the cultural transformation from nationalism to communism from a national perspective (Yan Feng 2007).

3. McDougall 1984a, viii.

4. Link 1984, 83.

5. McDougall 1984a, xii.

6. Jin Jiang 2009, 257.

7. Q. He 2012, 14–15.

8. On culture and the arts having become tools for revolution and education see Ka-ming Wu's study of revolutionary storytelling in Yan'an (Wu 2011).

9. Most studies of the Communist takeover of Chinese cities focus on Shanghai, such as Pang Song 1997; Wu Jingping and Zhang Xule 2003; Zhang Yi 2006; Yang Liping 2010. For the Communists' control of Hangzhou in the early 1950s see J. Gao 2004. There are studies of the takeover seen at the national level, such as Li Wenfang 2000; Li Liangyu 2002; He Libo 2009; Wang Fei 2012. For the early socialist government in Chengdu see Wu Ke 2010; Gao Zhongwei 2011.

10. Chengdu shi difang zhi bianzuan weiyuanhui 1999, 400. The five offices under the Department of Literature and Art were propaganda, drama, film, print, and general affairs, as well as an office for clerical support, a cultural work team, and a movie-screening team. The office of drama had a traditional drama group, a modern drama group, and a folk performance group.

11. In January 1953, however, this was divided into two departments: the Bureau of Culture and the Bureau of Education.

12. Kang Mingyu and Li Qing 2002, 146. The most popular types of folk performance used different styles and instruments. For example, bamboo clapper singers carried three bamboo slats, two in the left hand and one in the right, with which they beat a rhythm (D. Wang 2003, 79–80).

13. Those dramas included *Three Attacks on the Zhu Family Village* (*Sanda Zhujiazhuang*), *Forty Days in Beijing* (*Beijing sishi tian*), *Fish Stomach Mountain* (*Yufu shan*), *Driven to Revolt* (*Bishang Liangshan*), and *Wang Gui and Li Xiangxiang* (*Wang Gui yu Li Xiangxiang*). So-called superstitious dramas, such as *Nineteen Swordsmen of Qingcheng* (*Qingcheng shijiu xia*) and *Jade Lion Belt* (*Yushi dai*), which had long dominated in popular culture, were prohibited. See Kang Mingyu and Li Qing 2002, 147–50; Chengdu shi difang zhi bianzuan weiyuanhui 1999, 400–401.

14. This drama (based on a short story by Zhao Shuli) concerned a young farmer, Xiao Erhei, and his girlfriend, Xiao Qin, who sought freedom through marriage. The story was set in the area controlled by the CCP in North China during the Civil War. For more on its influence and position in revolutionary literature see Fu Xiuhai. 2012. In recent years, however, some scholars have revisited the "masterpieces of revolutionary literature" and found a dark side to this story in the tide of revolution (Xie Yong 2008; Zhai Yejun 2013).

15. Kang Mingyu and Li Qing 2002, 147–50; Chengdu shi difang zhi bianzuan weiyuanhui 1999, 400–401. *The Emperor and the Prostitute*, which well-known playwright Song Zhidi wrote in 1950, tells the story of Northern Song Emperor Huizong (1082–1135) and Li Shishi, a famous prostitute. For other studies of popular entertainment in the 1950s see the analysis by Jin Jiang (2009) of Yue opera, and Perry Link's research on cross-talk and its use as a propaganda tool during the War to Resist the United States and Aid Korea (2007). In his new book on *pingtan*, Qiliang He describes the "Cutting the Tail" movement, that is, "cutting feudalism's tail," or taking out feudalist-sounding ideas from folk performances in Shanghai from 1951 to 1953 (2012, chap. 2).

16. For the Three Reforms Policy and its influence see Liu Naichong 1990; Liu Yilun 2007; Jiang Jin 2007; Liu Dejun 2009; Zhang Lianhong 2010.

17. Liu Dejun 2009, 389.

18. D. Wang 2008b, chap. 5.

19. Kang and Li 2002, 151.

20. Liu Dejun 2009, 405.

21. Chengdu shi difang zhi bianzuan weiyuanhui 1999, 400–01; CSWHJ 124-1-39, 124-1-83.

22. D. Wang 2008b, chap. 2.

23. However, the actual number is larger because many teahouse theaters did not register with the police. According to an investigation dated August 4, 1950, there were twenty

registered teahouse theaters. Of these, ten were established before 1949, eight in 1950, and the dates of two unknown. Among these, four offered Ping opera, three shadow plays, and one music and dance. The largest could hold 240 people and the smallest 70, for a total of 2,470 seats (CGTGD 52-128-1).

24. Interview with eighty-eight-year-old Xiong Zhuoyun at Xiong's home, August 9, 2001; Zou Qutao 1998, 201. The society's name revealed its political orientation. From the memoir of an early organizer, we learn that people often called the month of May "red May" because it had quite a few special days of political commemoration, such as International Labor Day on May 1, Youth Day on May 4, Karl Marx's birthday on May 5, and National Humiliation Day on the May Thirtieth Movement (1925) (Zou Qutao 1998, 202).

25. Zou Qutao 1998, 203–4.

26. Famous folk performers performed there: e.g., Jia Shusan on bamboo dulcimer, Li Decai on dulcimer, Zeng Binkun in comic dialogue, Li Yueqiu in pure singing, Zou Zongxin on bamboo clappers, and Gai Lanfang in drum singing (Zou Qutao 1998, 203–7).

27. Peking opera programs included new and revolutionary works such as *Forty Days in Beijing* and *Bethune*, as well as popular, traditional dramas such as *The Story of Su San* (*Yutang chun*), *Pushing on the Pulleys* (*Tiao huache*), and *Picking Up a Jade Bracelet* (*Shi yuzhuo*). Bethune is Henry Norman Bethune (1890–1939), a Canadian surgeon, who joined the War of Resistance in helping China and died there.

28. Zou Qutao 1998, 203–7. In 1955, the First Experimental Teahouse Theater was renamed the Chengdu Theater of Folk Performance (Chengdu shi quyi chang). See Chengdu shi difang zhi bianzuan weiyuanhui 1999, 325; CSWHJ 124-1-83.

29. The Great World in Shanghai, built in 1917, previously was the most attractive place for recreation, offering various theaters for opera, folk performance, dance, song, and side-shows, as well as a movie theater, shops, and restaurants. The Confucius Temple in Nan-jing was important because of its temple fair, which became prosperous from the Ming and Qing to Republican periods, along with the popularity of lantern boats on the Qinhuai River.

30. Zou Qutao 1998, 202–3, 207–8.

31. Almost every city has a Center of Culture and Art for the Populace to promote cultural and artistic activities. See Pan Hongtao 2011.

32. Zou Qutao 1998, 208.

33. Chengdu shi difang zhi bianzuan weiyuanhui 1999, 325; CSWHJ 124-1-83.

34. CSWHJ 124-1-83.

35. CSWHJ 124-1-83.

36. Including fifty-five "major operas" and twenty-one highlights from operas.

37. CSWHJ 124-1-83. *Eighth Sister Yang Sightseeing in Spring* is about generals of the Yang family during the Song dynasty (960–1279). Eighth Sister Yang had a spring outing in the suburbs and inadvertently met the emperor, who fell in love with her and asked her to marry him. *Mistress Xiang Lin* is Lu Xun's tragic masterpiece about a maid from the country-side. An investigation in 1956 found that the theater offered eight kinds of folk performances each week (one show per day with two on Sunday) of "good traditional programs" and "new programs that reflect current lives and promote new people and things." Furthermore, the troupe "made significant progress," with more than three hundred "new pieces" performed over a few years (CSWHJ 124-1-83).

38. On the national level, many troupes changed ownership as socialist control deep-ened. For example, sixty-nine troupes in Shanghai became state owned in early 1956 (*Xiju bao*, no. 2, 1956).

39. CSWHJ 124-1-83. Regarding women's liberation in the 1950s see Hershatter 2002; T. Chen 2003a; Z. Wang 2006.

40. The rent of 10 yuan per day (300 per month) was later reduced to 200 yuan per month. The theater had 577 seats but no toilet facilities or lobby / waiting room (CSWHJ 124-1-83).

41. CSWHJ 124-1-83.

42. Wen Wenzi 1985, 455; Jing Huan and Zeng Ronghua 1982, 133.

43. CSWHJ 124-1-39. For studies of the Gowned Brotherhood see Stapleton 1996, McIsaac 2000, and D. Wang 2008a.

44. CSWHJ 124-1-39.

45. CSWHJ 124-1-39. These amateurs actually made significant contributions to the development of Sichuan opera. See Zeng Xiangyu and Zhong Zhiru 1990 and Yu Yingshi 1990.

46. "Vulgar taste" was a term often used by the state and elite from the late Qing and Republic to the Communist regime. For a study of popular tastes see Bourdieu 1984.

47. CSWHJ 124-1-39.

48. CSWHJ 124-1-39. These people were attacked nationwide as soon as the PRC was established. For prostitution reform see Hershatter 1997, chap. 10; Huang Jinping 2005; Ma Huifang and Gao Yanchun 2008; Dong Limin 2010. Regarding politics and measures for other political, religious, and social issues see Li Lu 1989; Jia Wei 1995; Shang Jinming and Bei Guangsheng 1996; Lü Chenxi 2004; Sun Huiqiang 2009.

49. CSWHJ 124-1-39.

50. CSWHJ 124-1-39.

51. CSWHJ 124-1-39.

52. CSWHJ 124-1-83. Regarding this lifestyle in Sichuan see D. Wang 1993, chap. 4.

53. CSWHJ 124-1-83.

54. CSWHJ 124-1-39.

55. CSWHJ 124-1-39.

56. CSWHJ 124-1-83.

57. CSWHJ 124-1-83.

58. For a study of housewives in China see S. Song 2007.

59. CSWHJ 124-1-83.

60. CSWHJ 124-1-83.

61. CSWHJ 124-1-83.

62. "Neighborhood offices" were the lowest level of urban administration. For studies of neighborhood offices in Chinese cities see Bai Yihua 1991; Zhou Ping 2001; Rao Changlin and Chang Jian 2011; Zhang and Yang 2012.

63. CSWHJ 124-1-83.

64. Under the "taking in" policy, adopted after 1949, the government took in homeless or vagrant people or sent them back to their hometown by force. It is a recent topic of discussion. Many appealed to end the practice after the Sun Zhigang case in 2003. Sun was from Hubei Province, working for a company in Guangzhou. He was taken in because he did not have a temporary residence permit (*zanzhu zheng*) and was beaten to death in a take-in house (*shou-rong suo*). Regarding the Sun Zhigang case see Tang Xingxiang, Li Zhigang, and Kuang Ying-tong 2003. For the taking-in practice see Zhu Wenyi 2003 and Wang Xingjian 2004.

65. CSWHJ 124-1-83.

66. Huang Zhenyuan 1956.

67. Huang Zhenyuan 1956.

68. *Renmin ribao*, May 28, 1957.

69. Regarding the Anti-rightist Movement see C. Wong 1978; C. Chang 1987; Chung 2011; Shen 2011.

70. CSWHJ 124-1-83.

71. CSWHJ 124-1-83.

72. The first aspect included a speech by a high-level official with the Bureau of Culture, absorbing the Ministry of Culture's instructions, and holding informal meetings and individual interviews. These measures were intended to assuage performers' concerns and motivate them to participate in this effort. Meanwhile, the team diligently gathered information regarding each troupe's history, business patterns, structure, and major problems and categorized each actor as "positive," "middle," or "backward." The survey was the second aspect. Under the work team's leadership, each troupe established a professional affairs office and finance office, and the team organized people to identify each troupe's major problems in each area. The third was to help each troupe craft a working plan. All kinds of materials from the investigation were to be compiled and copies filed with the Bureaus of Culture at the district, city, and provincial levels. When these were completed, troupes received a "certificate of performance" (*yanchu zheng*) from the provincial Bureau of Culture, and each folk performer was issued a "certificate of singing" (*yanchang zheng*) from the municipal Bureau of Culture. Once the working plans were in place, the district-level offices of culture became the direct authorities overseeing all troupes and performers (CSWHJ 124-1-83).

73. Questions on the historical background included when and where the troupe was established; which level of the government approved its creation; whether or not it had been reformed; and what changes and progress had been made. For organizational structure, the government wanted to know what offices the troupe contained; their responsibilities; regulations; and whether any branches of the CCP or Communist Youth League had been established, and if so, how many members each had. The information on personnel included members' family histories and political backgrounds; how many joined the profession before 1949 and how many after; the number and total percentages of people working as actors, musicians, stagehands, staff, and apprentices; and their literacy levels and specialties. The government also sought details regarding programs, including how many scripts and musical scores had been written or revised; how many scripts and scores were in the overall repertoire; how many of the troupe's plays were traditional and how many were contemporary; how a troupe adhered to the "censorship system"; how many plays the troupe performed and which were most popular; and so forth. The government also wanted to know which plays the troupe performed in the countryside in 1955, and how often, how many were in each audience, and the dates for each performance. Furthermore, the government asked for details pertaining to the troupe's training, management, and venues: how often "political studies" were carried out; what documents had been and were currently studied; how they were working to eliminate illiteracy; how many people associated with the troupe were illiterate; how professional training had been undertaken; the contents and methodologies of this training; and what percentage of people in the troupe came from working-class or peasant backgrounds. Economic information concerned the troupe's management, accounting system, income and expenditures (itemized as a percentage of the total assets), budgets, income distributions, and salary ranges. Regarding venues, the investigation asked if a troupe had a regular theater, and if so, when it was built; if any repairs or remodeling work had been done; who owned the theater; and how much it paid in monthly rent. Finally, questions about the local environment centered on the neighborhood where each venue was located: its economic status, traffic flow, and the presence of other entertainment establishments (CSWHJ 124-1-83).

74. Notably, this report did not mention "sacred-edict preaching" (*jiang shengyu*) because this had disappeared, dwindling from twenty-plus in 1950 to none in 1952 (Shi Youshan and Fang Chongshi 1986, 183). One account said that the preachers recognized the "harmful elements of superstition" and voluntarily ceased their activities without the government's involvement. For studies of local entertainment see Ward 1985. For performers, especially actresses, see Cheng 1996; Luo 2005; and Yeh 2005. For storytelling see D. Wang 2003, 77–79; Fei 2004;

and Børdahl 2009. For cross-talk see Kaikkonen 1990 and Link 2007. For shadow plays see Tsang 1999.

75. Here are the numbers broken down: 1950, 42; 1951, 20; 1952, 49; 1953, 23; 1954, 32.

76. CSWHJ 124-1-83.

77. Based on the report, of 405 people, 17 were special agents, 13 drug dealers, 9 core members of the GMD and Youth Corps, 9 members of superstitious sects and secret societies, 6 military officers, 3 bandits, and 1 head of a *bao*. In addition, 89 members of superstitious sects and secret societies and 24 common members of the GMD and Youth Corps had multiple identities.

78. CSWHJ 124-1-83.

79. The report mentioned above is the final general report, which synthesized the individual surveys for each genre that are no longer available. However, I did find a report by the Association for Folk Performance Reform, written a few months after the completion of the general report. It states that there were 104 ballad singers (compared to 113 stated in the general report), divided into two groups: group 1 for ballad singers and group 2 for singers of Peking operas. Of the seventy-two performers in group 1, nineteen worked at different teahouses in the city, while the rest were concentrated on three teahouse theaters in the market outside the north city gate. Of the thirty-two performers in group 2, twenty-seven performed in various locations, and five were associated with the Great Wisdom Tea Balcony (Yizhi chalou) and the Labor Teahouse (Laogong chashe). This report states that of all folk performers, ballad singers were the most numerous, the most "complicated," and the most mobile, making them the target of investigation by the Bureau of Culture. Based on secret reports from "activists" (*jiji fenzi*) who were close to the CCP, as well as other evidence, the bureau targeted forty-three singers who could not clearly tell their "true history" and had many other issues. This group comprised eighteen prostitutes, twelve professional performers, five housewives, two military officers, and one small businessman, one craftsman, one clerk, one "army riffraff" (*bingpi*), one hooligan, and one whose provenance was unclear. Regarding their daily income, eight earned 6,000 to 8,000 yuan; twenty 4,000 to 6,000; and fifteen below 4,000. The investigation also evaluated their "professional skills" and claimed that no one in group 1 was "highly skilled" or could adequately perform ballad singing and other forms of folk performance (CSWHJ 124-1-83). From this we can see that 18 of the 104 were former prostitutes, "liberated" as victims during the government's anti-prostitution campaign in the early 1950s. In the government's subsequent "reformation" of folk performance, however, these were regarded as "bad elements." We may question to what extent accusations of "evil lifestyles," "prostitution," and "defrauding" were true and how many were based on discrimination, bias, or rumor.

80. CSWHJ 124-1-83.

81. This investigation shows that teahouses were the most common venue, with fifty-nine locations in the East City District, where 131 performers made a living by means of seventy-four shows per day. The West City District had forty-seven locations and sixty-one shows per day, supporting 105 people. The River View District had thirty-five such businesses, with thirty shows daily (CSWHJ 124-1-83).

82. CSWHJ 124-1-83.

83. "Eighteen Touches" is a popular, sexually provocative duet, with performers touching a girl's body from head to toe.

84. "The Broken Bridge" is based on the famous *Madam White Snake* (*Baishe zhuan*), a love story set by the West Lake.

85. CSWHJ 124-1-83.

86. In another example, an actress seduced a shoemaker and swindled him out of more than one hundred pairs of shoes, forcing the shoemaker out of business (CSWHJ 124-1-83).

87. CSWHJ 124-1-83.

88. *Stories of Jigong* is about monk Jigong's efforts to help poor people fight rich bullies; *The Picture of Ten Beauties* is about how two of Zeng's sons sought revenge after Chief Minister Yan Hao executed their father, Governor Zeng Xuan; and *Missing the Scholar* is a love story between a young woman and a scholar.

89. CSWHJ 124-1-83. The "model show" was a very interesting cultural phenomenon of socialist China, a free performance offered exclusively to people working in "units" (*danwei*), such as government offices, schools, and factories. During the Cultural Revolution, there were no commercial performances, as all forms of entertainment were subsumed into political propaganda. As a result, "model shows" became a major form of entertainment, and while tickets were never sold but entirely free of charge, party officials and government dignitaries received all they needed, and commoners had no such privilege.

90. CSWHJ 124-1-83.

91. Holm 1984, 32.

92. Gardner 1969, 479.

93. DeMare 2015.

94. Loh 1984, 179. Also see Y. Chen 2016.

95. Yung, Rawski, and Watson 1996.

96. For example, during the Great Leap Forward, folk songs became a powerful tool for mobilizing masses (Chang Shuai 2008).

97. I. Wong 1984, 112–14.

98. Hoffmann 2003.

99. McDougall 1984b, 291.

100. McDougall 1984b, 269.

3. The Decline of Public Life under Mao's Rule

1. Regarding post-1949 social control see Salaff 1971; Chiang 1986; Troyer, Clark, and Rojek 1989; Lau 2001; Y. Zhong 2003; Hung 2007; S. Guo 2012.

2. For post-1949 public spaces see Mazur 1999; Watson 2011.

3. Between 1949 and 1977 class struggle was a relentlessly pursued political agenda; see Farina 1980; Loh 1984; Liu Peiping 1994; Li Pingnan 2006; Cai 2001; Sun Kang 2010.

4. Ma Shitu 2004, 474.

5. Abrami 2002, 96.

6. Lu Sigui 1956.

7. Wo Ruo 1987.

8. Liu Zhengyao 1999, 150–51. *Ci Yun's Revenge* is about Crown Prince Ci Yun of the Song dynasty (960–1279), who was betrayed and thus lived as a commoner until, with help from loyal supporters, he regained authority and punished his enemies.

9. A Nian 1997, 7, 19.

10. Huang Shang 1999, 322–23. The correlation of the Chinese foot to the Western standards varied from late Qing times to the 1950s. Huang may be referring to a Chinese foot that was about thirteen inches.

11. Zhang Xiande 1999, 54, 57.

12. For the government's attacks on bench-sitter opera see chapter 2.

13. The *Legend of Yue Fei* is about General Yue Fei of the early Southern Song dynasty (1127–1279), a hero who fought the Jin dynasty (military opponents of China in the north) but was falsely accused and executed by Chief Minister Qin Gui. *Water Margin* is one of the so-called Four Classic novels; it describes Song Jiang's leading 108 loyal fighters against the government in Liangshanpo, Shandong Province, during the Northern Song (960–1127). *Romance of the Three Kingdoms* is another of the Four Classics, describing the military

collapse of the Han dynasty into three rival states between 220 and 280. *Ghost Stories*, by Pu Songling (1640–1715), depicts human struggles and interactions with ghosts.

14. Zhang Xiande 1999, 56. Lin Zexu was a commissioner sent by the emperor to end the opium trade in Canton. His destruction of enormous amounts of opium in 1839 triggered a British military response and the first Opium War. *Fighting Workers*, a novel by Feng Zhi, is set during the War of Resistance against Japan and is regarded as one of the "Red Classics."

15. Interview with Mr. Huang, forty-four years old, an editor of Sichuan Minorities Publisher, July 22, 2000.

16. Interview with Ms. Wu, seventy years old, at the Teahouse of the Institute of Paintings in Chengdu, May 2, 2003.

17. CSWHJ 124-1-83.

18. CSWHJ 124-1-83.

19. D. Wang 2008b, 188–96.

20. Zhang Xiande 1999, 54.

21. Zhang Xiande 1999, 57–58.

22. *Zhongguo qingnian bao*, September 1, 2004. Meng Wentong (1894–1968) was a famous historian who taught at Sichuan University for many years.

23. Liu Heng 1954. For business practices in China during the Republican and early PRC see Zheng 1997.

24. Liu Heng 1954.

25. Zhang Yan 1956.

26. Zhang Yan 1956.

27. Regarding the floods in Republican-era Chengdu see D. Wang 2003, 66.

28. Zhang Yan 1956.

29. Kau 1969, 219.

30. Studies of socialist transformation are mostly in Chinese; see Huang Rutong 1994; Lou Shenghua 2000; Sha Jiansun 2005.

31. Chengdu shi difang zhi bianzuan weiyuanhui 2000, 57.

32. Chengdu shi difang zhi bianzuan weiyuanhui 2000, 105. There are few studies of the collective ownership of urban enterprises in English, but many in Chinese. See Hong Yuanpeng and Weng Qiqian 1980; Xu Yulong and Ni Zhanyuan 1980; Zhu Chuan 1980; Li Qingrui and Xi Guizhen 1980; Wang Shuchun 2001.

33. CSSYEJ 117-2-244.

34. For studies of the Great Leap Forward see MacFarquhar 1983; Joseph 1986; Bachman 1991; Li and Yang 2005; Manning and Wemheuer 2011; Liu Jianguo 2000; Gao Qirong 2004; Zeng Honglu 1998; Liu Yuan 2010.

35. See Li Meng and Hou Bo 2013, 324; Yang Jisheng 2008, 162.

36. Yu Jingqi and Liu Zongtang 1958.

37. Regarding the Chengdu Conference see Pei Di 1988.

38. For politics in the teahouse during the Republican period see D. Wang 2008b, chap. 8.

39. Zhang Xiande 1999, 55. For the relationship between teahouses and the Gowned Brothers see D. Wang 2000; CSWHJ 124-2-133.

40. There have been many Western studies of the Hundred Flowers Bloom and Anti-rightist Campaigns, mostly concerning intellectuals. See Das 1979; S. Chan 1980; Nieh 1981; Goldman 1987; Kraus 2011; Shen 2011. In China there have been very few, most of which hold that the campaigns were necessary, and that broadening the scope was the real problem—the tune sounded by the CCP. See Wang Huaichen 1994.

41. CSTZD 76-2-76.

42. CSWHJ 124-1-106.

43. CSWHJ 124-1-106.

44. Link 1984.

45. For Liu Shaoqi's economic policies after the "Three Bad Years" see Lardy 1987, 391–97.

46. Link 2007. Regarding cross-talking see Link 1984.

47. Dittmer and Gore 2001, 20. The "Three Selves" were having 5 percent arable land for private use, small private handicraft shops, and sales of products at rural free markets. The "One Guarantee": fulfillment of agricultural production quotas set by the government.

48. For the number in 1955 see CSWHJ 124-1-83. Also see chap. 2.

49. CSWHJ 124-1-236.

50. CSWHJ 124-1-236.

51. CSWHJ 124-1-236.

52. Chengdu shi difang zhi bianzuan weiyuanhui 1999, 342.

53. I have discussed the continuity and endurance of popular culture. See D. Wang 2003, chaps. 1 and 8.

54. Abrami 2002, 316–18.

55. Chengdu shi difang zhi bianzhuan weiyuanhui 2000, 58–62.

56. CSGJD 119-2-752, 119-2-754, 119-2-755. At the time, Chengdu had three districts: East, West, and the suburb called Golden Cow (Jinniu).

57. CSGJD 119-2-752. Interestingly, all "starting of business" registrations were dated July 20, 1958, except for five on October 1, 1962. I am dubious that actual startups in 1958 (during the Great Leap Forward campaign) reflect the right year, probably just the registration dates. It seems that not very many shops were opened during the Great Leap Forward campaign.

58. For the number of teahouses in 1949 see D. Wang 2008b, 30; for the number of employees in 1951 see CSGJD 119-2-167.

59. Ma Shitu 2004, 474.

60. Xie Guozhen 1999, 352–32.

61. D. Wang 2008b, chap. 8.

62. Interview of Mr. Jiang, at Joy Tea Garden, July 21, 2000. The "Three Red Flags" were the General Line for Socialist Construction, Great Leap Forward, and People's Communes.

63. The Cultural Revolution has drawn a great deal of attention from scholars in the West. For a general history see Hiniker 1983; Pye 1986; Esherick, Pickowicz, and Walder 2006; MacFarquhar and Schoenhals 2009. For neighborhood organizations see Salaff 1971. For Mao's strategies see H. Lee 1979. For the relationship between the Cultural Revolution and post-Mao Reform see Tsou 1986. For personal experiences see Y. Gao 1987. For the attacks on intellectuals see Thurston 1988. For violence see L. White 1989. For the cultural aspects of the Cultural Revolution see Roberts 2006; J. Jiang 2009; King, Sheng, and Watson 2010. For women see Sausmikat 1999.

64. Zhang Xiande 1999, 58.

65. Jung Chang 2003, 290–91.

66. Regarding the Red Guard Movement see Walder 2009.

67. Whyte 1991, 727.

68. Whyte 1991, 717.

69. Jiang and Ashley 2013.

70. Whyte 1991, 725–26.

71. Tang Minghui 1994.

72. During the Cultural Revolution, radicals used "revolutionary masses" (*geming qunzhong*) as a "people's security group" and "mass dictatorship group" to control "people's enemies."

73. Zhang Xiande 1999, 59. In his recent study of the Cultural Revolution, Yiching Wu (2014) has pointed out how various personal spaces were left unmolested at the margins, beyond the reach of the radical mainstream.

4. The Resurgence of Teahouses in the Reform Era

1. There is rich scholarship on China's reform and opening up. For general studies see Chiu 1981; Perry 1985; Tsou 1986; Harding 1986; Schwarcz 1986–1987; P. Cohen 1988; Halpern 1991; Goldman and MacFarquhar 1999. For economic reforms see Solinger 1991, 1993; Oi 1995. For educational reforms see Silver 2008. For urban changes see Cartier 2002b; Gaubatz 1995. For family life in the reform era see Davis and Harrell 1993. For studies of post-Mao Chengdu see Dwyer 1986.

2. Lieberthal 2004, 190.

3. Dittmer and Gore 2001, 39–40. For studies of small businesses in post-Mao China see Gold 1985; Lockett 1986; Chaichian 1994; J. Wu 1999; Siu and Liu 2005; Head 2005; Atherton and Fairbanks 2006; Cunningham and Rowley 2010.

4. Solinger 1984, 108.

5. Studies of teahouses in post-Mao China are mostly in Chinese and deploy sociology and anthropology; see, e.g., Lü Zhuohong 2003 and Dai Lichao 2005.

6. Regarding control of the number of teahouses in Republican Chengdu see D. Wang 2008b, chap. 2.

7. The number of teahouses in the Republican period peaked in 1934, at 748 (D. Wang 2008b, 30).

8. For post-Mao government and social control see Mohanty 1981; Lieberthal and Lampton 1992; G. White 1996; Oi 2004; M. Pei 2000; Shambaugh 2000.

9. For studies of management in privately owned businesses in the post-Mao era see Gates 1996, 1999; Siu 2000, 2001; Yen and Ho 2005; Cooke 2011.

10. For example, at the Pure and Fragrant Tea Garden (Qingfang chayuan) on South Stone Man Road (Shiren nanlu), all kinds of permits were on the wall, e.g., "Certificate of Fire Control," "Registration of Taxes," "Business License for Private Industrial and Commercial Households," "Responsibility for Shop Fronts," and "Standards and Responsibilities of Patriotic Sanitation"; see author's fieldwork, under entry for Pure and Fragrant Tea Garden, South Stone Man Road, July 13, 2000.

11. Chengdu shi difang zhi bianzuan weiyuanhui 2000, 83–87, 131–34.

12. This "Southern Tour" occurred in early 1992 when the top leaders had almost stopped reforms. Along the way, Deng gave talks about the reforms and forced Jiang Zemin and Li Peng to continue carrying out his policies.

13. Zhang Xiande 1999, 59.

14. Gu Zhizhong 1984.

15. Gu Zhizhong 1984.

16. Zhang Xiande 1999, 59–60.

17. Naitō 1991, 203–4.

18. Takeuchi 2006.

19. Takeuchi 2006. In the 1970s, Takeuchi edited *Chakan* (Teahouse); it dealt generally with Chinese culture, and the first chapter was about the teahouse. He believes that the teahouse, to a large extent, represented Chinese culture (Takeuchi 1974).

20. From 2003 to 2008, this area underwent large-scale renovations, after which teahouses sought to attract tourists and raised their prices, thus pricing themselves beyond the means of many local residents. For the history and current state of this area see the special issue of *Wide and Narrow Alleys* in *Ducheng* [Reading the city], no. 6, 2008.

21. For the Manchu City see D. Wang 2003, chap. 2.

22. Just a few steps down was another tiny teahouse, the Fragrant Tea Garden (Yuxiang chayuan). Its front room was actually a store, likely converted from a living area, and rural-seeming patrons played mahjong. Next, under a cloth banner, was the Teastand by Pure River (Qinghe chazuo)—quiet, with one customer. Author's fieldwork, under entry for Wide and Narrow Alleys, June 7, 2003.

23. Author's fieldwork, under Gathered Happiness Teahouse, Buddhist Monk Street, June 27, 2000.

24. Author's fieldwork, under Gathered Happiness Teahouse, Buddhist Monk Street, June 27, 2000.

25. Author's fieldwork, under Gathered Happiness Teahouse, Buddhist Monk Street, June 27, 2000.

26. Passersby continually came in to use the phone (thirty cents for the first three minutes, sixty cents for three to five minutes, and ninety cents for more than six minutes). This telephone served as a type of neighborhood public phone: someone answering might shout for someone working at the hair salon across the street.

27. Author's fieldwork, under Cloudy Sea Teahouse, Three Sages Street, July 3, 2000.

28. Author's fieldwork, under Nostalgic Teahouse, Flower Arch Street, July 7, 2000.

29. Veeck 2000, 108.

30. Y. Yan 2000; Farrer 2000; D. Wang 2000; Kraus 2000.

31. Balcony teahouses had unique décor, and all were comfortable. For example, the Flowering Capital Teahouse (Huadu chafang) was located in a commercial area but was quiet, combining traditional Chinese and Western styles in bright open spaces that offered painting, chess, and occasional musical performances. The Benevolence Tea Chamber (Mingren ju) offered a "pastoral flavor" that attracted businessmen and white-collar employees from nearby offices. As one customer noted, "This teahouse gives me a comfortable feeling" (Deng Gaoru 1995; Qin Hongyan 2000).

32. Yu Yao 2007, 43.

33. *Shangwu zaobao*, July 13, 2000.

34. *Shangwu zaobao*, July 13, 2000. Although most teahouses were privately owned, some—mainly mid-level—were state owned, such as the Pure Fountain Teahouse (Qingquan chafang) occupying the third floor (above another teahouse) of a building at an intersection on South Stone Man Street. Despite being stated owned, it was actually run by a contractor. It was a big teahouse and had an open-air rooftop garden with fifteen concrete tables and more than one hundred bamboo or plastic chairs, and bamboo trees and other plants and flowers, including an ivy-covered shed. Inside were several private rooms furnished in Japanese style, and a large conference room. The main hall contained several dozen tables with a pendant lamp above each. The young son of a waitress watched a show on the large-screen color television set. Two pool tables, which cost six yuan per hour to use, stood unused in the middle of the hall. This space, which until two years earlier was a furniture store, was owned by the transportation company of the Chengdu government and thus did not pay rent. It could accommodate five hundred guests, but was never full. Customers could spend an entire day there for fifteen yuan, including lunch. Business was good, and a competing teahouse had opened on the second floor. When I asked if the place was the Pure Fountain "*chaguan*," a waitress corrected me by saying it was "*chafang*." The difference was that a *chafang* was of a higher level than a *chaguan* (author's fieldwork, under Pure Fountain Teahouse, South Stone Man Street, July 19, 2000).

35. Author's fieldwork, under Sentosa, West Extension Route, July 24, 2000.

36. Author's fieldwork, under Shunxing Ancient Teahouse, Convention and Exhibition Center, May 24, 2003.

37. Author's fieldwork, under Wuhou Temple, June 12, 2003. During my 2003 fieldwork in Chengdu, I went to one of the two teahouses at the Humble Cottage Temple (Caotang si), one of the city's major attractions, popular with tourists and the elderly (who were admitted for free) but less so with ordinary residents because of the high admission, thirty yuan. The one I visited was a nice tea garden, with tea ranging in price from eight yuan to over fifty yuan. Tea was served with a traditional three-piece set, and the walls were decorated with many handicrafts, mainly woodcarvings and poems on wooden boards, all relating to tea and tea culture. I found that there were not many customers, only three tables occupied by people playing mahjong (author's fieldwork, under Humble Cottage Temple, May 27, 2003). This was during the peak of the SARS scare, and most people chose to stay home. (For the SARS situation see Rosenthal 2003a, 2003b.)

38. Author's fieldwork, under Cry of the Crane Teahouse, June 28, 2003. For its history see D. Wang 2008b, 43–45, 61, 88, 175, and 208.

39. Other questions included "What type of car would you like to buy?" "Are you going to buy a car soon?" "What is your price range?" and so on.

40. Author's fieldwork, under Teahouse by the Funan River, July 10, 2000.

41. Lü Zhuohong 2003, 62.

42. Lü Zhuohong 2003, 63.

43. One *jin* of tea leaves was usually used to make as many as 100 to 120 bowls in the Republican period, so 140 bowls means less tea leaves for each bowl, which was probably a result of increasing costs.

44. At the same time, monthly expenses for the teahouse rose to at least 20,000 yuan, including about 4,000 in wages and more than 1,300 for utilities and other expenses, plus 800 per year to renew the sanitation license. All total, the teahouse apparently could not make ends meet (Lü Zhuohong 2003, 65–66).

45. Author's fieldwork, under Museum Tea Garden, Great Benevolence Temple, July 5, 2000.

46. Author's fieldwork, under Great Benevolence Tea Garden, Great Benevolence Temple, July 5, 2000. A teahouse in the Manjusri Monastery (Wenshu yuan) mainly served as a resting place for pilgrims and was open from 8 a.m. to 5:30 p.m. Its cheapest tea was jasmine, at five yuan. Although against Buddhist doctrine, the teahouse sold alcohol. Senior citizens were admitted free, and most of the visitors were elderly women. Mahjong was not allowed because it was too noisy, but visitors could play poker. At one time, the teahouse had sales of as much as 10,000 yuan daily, but after the monastery was designated a key cultural heritage preservation site, ticket prices were raised, resulting in a dramatic drop in the number of visitors so that daily sales averaged only 1,000 to 2,000 yuan (Yu Yao 2007, 19).

47. Regarding migrant laborers see Solinger 1999.

48. Dai Shankui 1998; He Xiaozhu 2006, 31.

49. Author's fieldwork, under Bruce Lee Video/Poker Teahouse, August 8, 2000.

50. Author's fieldwork, under Woying Tea Garden, July 12, 2000.

51. Author's fieldwork, under Wide and Narrow Alleys, June 7, 2003.

52. Author's fieldwork, under Easy Tea Garden, Sansheng Village, Outer East Chengdu, October 25, 2003.

53. Author's fieldwork, under Hotel/Teahouse of the Commercial Company of the Golden Cow District, Flower Arch Street, July 17, 2000.

54. Dittmer and Gore 2001, 29.

55. Dai Shankui 1984.

56. Yu Yao 2007, 33.

57. Han Nanzheng 1990, 13–15.

58. *Chengdu wanbao*, June 4, 1987.

59. He Xiaozhu 2006, 28, 31.

60. Abrami 2002, 16.

61. W. Whyte 1980, 63.

62. *Huaxi dushi bao*, August 21, 2000.

63. *Tianfu zaobao*, October 26, 2003.

64. *Farewell, My Concubine* is a popular historical story based on the war between Xiang Yu (232–202 BCE) and Liu Bang (256–195 BCE, founder of the Han dynasty).

65. *Tianfu zaobao*, October 27, 2003. An American, named Jami, also showed off his skill in pouring water (*Huaxi dushi bao*, October 26, 2003).

66. *Tianfu zaobao*, October 24, 2003. The high-end tea balconies advertised in newspapers. For example, there were eighty-two teahouse ads in *Chengshi gouwu daobao* (Guide to urban shipping) on July 17, 2002 (Lü Zhuohong 2003, 19).

67. *Huaxi dushi bao*, November 30, 2003.

68. Zhong Minghua 2000.

69. Zhong Minghua 2000.

70. Lieberthal 2004, 296.

71. Bruun 1993, 202.

72. Dittmer and Gore 2001, 23.

5. Urban Residents and Migrant Workers in Public Life

1. Davis 2000, 5.

2. According to Ann Veeck's study of food markets in 1990s Nanjing, the markets were crucial for urban residents, and the expanded food choices allowed food shoppers to enrich their daily lives (Veeck 2000, 123).

3. L. Zhang 2002, 275.

4. L. Zhang 2001b, 3–4.

5. For studies of public entertainment spaces in Chinese cities see Atkinson 1994 and 1997; Palmer 2006; X. Zhang 2007.

6. There have been some studies of the influence of the reforms on urban everyday life and cultural life. See Farrer 2000. For a number of systematic studies of post-Mao culture in one volume see Link, Madsen, and Pickowicz 2002, containing the following: Andrew Morris, "'I Believe You Can Fly': Basketball Culture in Postsocialist China"; Perry Link and Kate Zhou, "*Shunkouliu*: Popular Satirical Sayings and Popular Thought"; Julia Andrews and Kuiyi Shen, "The New Chinese Woman and Lifestyle Magazines in the Late 1990s"; Anita Chan, "The Culture of Survival: Lives of Migrant Workers through the Prism of Private Letters"; Amy Hanser, "The Chinese Enterprising Self: Young, Educated Urbanites and the Search for Work"; Deborah Davis, "When a House Becomes His Home"; Robert Geyer, "In Love and Gay"; L. Zhang, "Urban Experiences and Social Belonging among Chinese Rural Migrants."

7. Zhang Xiande 1999, 54.

8. *Shangwu zaobao*, May 19, 2000.

9. D. Wang 2008b, 34.

10. For studies of hobbies and self-organized activities see K. Wong 1984; Witzleben 1987; Nakajima 2006; Crespi 2010.

11. Hao Keqiang 1981.

12. Bing Feng and Qiang Jinwu 2003, 220.

13. M. Whyte 1990.

14. Her future husband, a stranger, first noticed her when she was at a teahouse with friends. When she spoke on her cell phone, he heard that she had to go to another teahouse for a business meeting. He offered to drive her, and they quickly fell in love (Zhang Yixian 2000).

15. Author's fieldwork; item under Museum Tea Garden, at the Great Benevolence Temple, July 8, 2007.

16. Yu Yao 2007, 41.

17. He Xiaozhu 2005.

18. He Xiaozhu 2006, 31. For discussion of a novel on lives in Chengdu see Gentil 2004.

19. Zhai Yongming 2009, 12.

20. Wang Yue 1999, 2.

21. Lü Zhuohong 2003, 66–67.

22. Writer Xi Menmei described the emergence of Bacon Road in the 1990s, when bars, bookstores, snack shops, but mostly teahouses, opened up. There were both street-corner and courtyard teahouses; in particular, open-air courtyard teahouses run as family businesses enjoyed great success and were crowded all the time (Xi Menmei 2006, 171–72).

23. You 2001, 3–6.

24. He Xiaozhu 2006, 31.

25. Lü Zhuohong 2003, 66–67.

26. There have been many studies of popular entertainment and leisure in post-Mao China. For tourism see Chen and Gassner 2012. For bars see Farrer 2009–2010. For karaoke see Fung 2009–2010. For golf see Giroir 2007. For games and plays see Hansson, McDougall, and Weightman 2002. For the politics of leisure see S. Wang 1995.

27. Xu Juan, unpublished manuscript. Prosperity Ancient Teahouse hosted Sichuan opera for an hour every night and a half hour on weekend afternoons, performances by a troupe it organized. The programs were mostly the famous parts of Sichuan operas, such as changing faces, blowing fire, and rolling lamps (*gundeng*). In a rolling lamp show, the performer places a lamp on his head while performing all kinds of movements; author's fieldwork, under Prosperity Ancient Teahouse, Convention Center in Chengdu, July 22, 2000.

28. Zeng Zhizhong and You Deyan 1999, 391–93.

29. Zeng Zhizhong and You Deyan 1999, 391–93.

30. Qiong Yao 1990, 165–67. "Lotus singing" and "beating the Daoist instrument" were traditional folk performances. See D. Wang 2003, 53, 80, 202.

31. Author's fieldwork, under Museum Tea Garden, Great Benevolence Temple, July 5, 2000.

32. Lü Zhuohong 2003, 63, 73; Qin Geng 1988, 45–46. In the post-Mao reform era there is a rise of such associations. For such studies see Liu Housheng 1997; Su Minhua 1998.

33. Author's fieldwork, under Museum Tea Garden, Great Benevolence Temple, May 17, 2003.

34. Zhang Xiande 1999, 193–94.

35. Zhang Xiande 1999, 195–96.

36. The singing of "red songs" was a campaign launched by Bo Xilai, former member of the Politburo, in 2007 and 2012 as a part of the "Chongqing experiment" (Z. Cui 2011). For other studies of this movement see Zhang Shengliang 2008; He Shihong 2010; Tao Wenzhao 2011; Zhou Yong 2011; Barmé 2012; Du Jianhua 2012. The relevant articles in China described this activity as positive, but Bo's downfall came after police chief Wang Lijun fled to the U.S. Consulate in Chengdu, and the praise disappeared. It is impossible for state-run media to air critical views in China's current political environment. Ironically, Bo, who flew the banner of Mao, was revealed to be shockingly corrupt and abusive of his power.

37. The legend of the Cowherd and the Weaving Girl is about a once-happy man and woman who were turned into stars that became separated by the Milky Way. They could see each other only once a year, when magpies flew in unison to form a bridge for them.

38. Regarding revolutionary dance see Hung 2005.

39. Author's fieldwork, under Museum Tea Garden, Great Benevolence Temple, July 5, 2000.

40. Chinese women in the post-reform era have been much studied in the West. For women in literature see C. He 2008; S. Wei 2011. For gender roles in economic activities see Ding 2006. For women's political participation see Q. Wang 2004. For women's lives see Liu 2006. For women's image see Yanru Chen 2008; Y. Sun 2011. For women's equality with men see Min 2011.

41. Regarding studies of *yangge* see Holm 1984; Hung 2005.

42. There have been several studies of Chinese elderly and the aging society, mostly from sociological or anthropological perspectives. For community and the elderly see C. Chan 1993. For social roles of the elderly see Olson 1994. For issues of the elderly see Fleischer 2006. For lives of the elderly see Ying Liu 2004. For living conditions of the elderly see Meng and Luo 2008. For incomes of the elderly see Raymo and Xie 2000. For the welfare of the elderly and their social services see Tsai 1987; Berger 2002. For the health issues of the elderly see Yu and Wang 1993.

43. Dai Shankui 1998.

44. Lü Zhuohong 2003, 69.

45. Author's fieldwork, under Great Benevolence Tea Garden, Great Benevolence Temple, July 5, 2000.

46. Yu Yao 2007, 27.

47. Lü Zhuohong 2003, 71.

48. There has been little study of Chinese waiters and waitresses, only D. Wang 2004. For studies of their Western counterparts see Paules 1991.

49. *Rongcheng zhoubao*, February 11, 1992, cited in Yang Zhongyi 1992, 116. But some masters were not as skilled as their predecessors. In the late 1980s, the famous writer Qiong Yao returned to Chengdu in search of her "roots." One night, her host arranged for her to see a show at a teahouse and praised the skill of a stunt artist. It became obvious, however, that the performer had not practiced in a long time, and Qiong was not at all impressed with his show (Qiong Yao 1990, 166).

50. For women's economic activities in the reform era see Rai 1988; Hooper 1994, 1998; Loscocco and Bose 1998.

51. Author's fieldwork, under Prosperity Ancient Teahouse, Convention Center in Chengdu, July 22, 2000.

52. Lü Zhuohong 2003, 65–66.

53. Lü Zhuohong 2003, 65–66. Many floating people worked in the teahouse or became loyal teahouse customers. For floating populations and the city see Leong and Wright 1997; Dutton 1998; Ma and Xiang 1998; Bakken 2000; Chen, Clark, et al. 2001; Friedmann 2005.

54. A. Qiu 2000. Regarding job searching among educated young people see Hanser 2002.

55. Author's fieldwork, under Nostalgia Teahouse, Flower Arch Street, July 7, 2000.

56. Author's fieldwork, under Tea Garden Balcony, South Stone Man Street, July 8, 2000.

57. Hanser 2002, 192.

58. Author's fieldwork, under Pure Fountain Teahouse, South Stone Man Street, July 19, 2000.

59. Author's fieldwork, under Pure Fountain Teahouse, South Stone Man Street, July 19, 2000.

60. Hanser 2002, 200–201. Also see X. Liu 1992; X. Wu 2000; Gong 2002; Fernandez-Stembridge 2005; Dong et al. 2007; Ding, Dong, and Li 2009.

61. Lieberthal 2004, 310. For studies of women under socialism see Andors 1983; Kruks, Rapp, and Young 1989.

62. Regarding peasants and rural China in the post-Mao era see Day 2013.

63. For studies of fortune-tellers see R. Smith 1991; Yenna Wu 1998; Endicott-West 1999; D. Wang 2003, 85–86; D. Wang 2008b, 172; Poon 2008.

64. The author's fieldwork, under Prosperous Old Teahouse, Convention Center in Chengdu, July 22, 2000.

65. Author's fieldwork, under Cry of the Crane Teahouse, People's Park, June 28, 2003.

66. The next night, the journalist returned, but the fortune-teller did not show up. As the journalist was about to leave, he met another fortune-teller, called the Japanese Master (Dongyang dashi), who was wearing a golden-yellow T-shirt, blue glasses, pink jeans, and brown leather shoes. He had wavy hair, a mustache, and heavy dark brows that were obviously accentuated by cosmetic surgery. The Japanese Master gave the reporter a business card that had the Japanese national emblem and the words "Telling fortunes in the Japanese style from Hokkaido, Japan," with a Chengdu address below. On the back was printed, "I am a Half Deity Wang (Wang Banxian), who learned fortune-telling from a Japanese master. By following my instructions, you will turn bad luck into good." He took out his cell phone and said he usually did not answer it because so many people—especially young women—tried to find him. He emphasized that his phone was a Motorola model, a gift from a business owner. He tried to persuade the reporter to have his fortune told for 200 yuan, a discount from the usual 600 yuan. When the reporter said he did not want to pay so much, he reduced the price to 100 yuan because he "regarded the reporter as a friend." The reporter claimed that he actually tried to find a fortune-teller for his boss, who did not care to pay so much. The fortune-teller promised to find another master the next day. The following night, the Japanese Master introduced another fortune-teller, Master Wang, to the reporter. Wang, clad in designer clothing, handed the reporter his business card, on which was written "The unique and most scientific predictions of the new century; master of fortune-telling at the Cultural Research Center of Henan Province; Fengshui master at the Institute of *Book of Changes* in Henan; and Adviser to the Japanese Palm Reading Enterprise." Wang told the reporter that the Japanese Master did not have any skill at all and that he could take care of this business alone, without any involvement by the Japanese Master. When the reporter explained that he wanted to find the white-bearded man, Wang became unhappy and left in a huff, after telling the reporter to contact him if his boss wanted his services. The next day, the reporter ran into the Japanese Master, who told him not to trust Wang, who was boastful and tricky, unwilling to share his profits, and lacking "professional ethics." He suggested that he could introduce the white-bearded man to him if he got a commission. He also told the reporter that he should be present when the white-bearded man provided his services. Before leaving, the Japanese Master sighed and said, clearly jealous, that the white-bearded man earned good money only because of his unique and magnificent beard that helped him put on a quite good show (*Shangwu zaobao*, June 12, 2000).

67. *Shangwu zaobao*, June 12, 2000.

68. The following study of this particular fortune-teller is based on the author's fieldwork, under the item Teahouse by the Funan River, July 10, 2000.

69. R. Smith 1991, 9.

70. Author's fieldwork, under Prosperity Ancient Teahouse, Convention Center in Chengdu, July 22, 2000. Mr. Li had made a living as an earwax picker in a teahouse for three years, after the remodeling company he owned failed owing to his lack of education and poor management. Although business was bad when he first started out, after he became skillful he had many regular clients. Since the job was not seasonal, a picker who was diligent enough to go to a teahouse every day could easily earn 100 to 200 yuan per day. Generally, an earwax picker worked in a single teahouse, which received a fee (in this case, 720 yuan per year, or 60 yuan per month). In order to avoid conflict and to protect their own interests, pickers would

not encroach on one another's territories. Although he paid the fee, he did not work every day; he had good business on weekends and holidays. Within a month of the Chinese New Year, he already had earned 3,900 yuan, generally charging 10 yuan for each service (Yu Yao 2007, 23). The Cry of the Crane Teahouse in the People's Park had at least four earwax pickers.

71. Author's fieldwork, under Museum Tea Garden, Great Benevolence Temple, July 5, 2000.

72. Western studies of migrant workers are extensive. On family life see M. Whyte 1993; on urban experiences see A. Chan 2002; Florence 2007; Zhou and Sun 2010; on hardships and discrimination see Wenran Jiang 2009; Li and Li 2013; D. Wang 2009; J. Wu 2010. For state policies regarding migrant workers see Chan, Pun, and Chan 2010.

73. Author's fieldwork, under Pure Fragrance Tea Garden, South Stone Man Road, July 13, 2000. At Cry of the Crane Teahouse there was only a single shoe polisher, who walked around carrying a pair of plastic sandals, looking for customers. He would give a customer the sandals while he took the shoes back to his stall to clean (author's fieldwork, under Cry of the Crane Teahouse, People's Park, June 28, 2003). Some high-end teahouses, such as Prosperity Ancient Teahouse, did not allow shoe polishers in because they were afraid of lowering their reputation (author's fieldwork, under Prosperity Ancient Teahouse, Convention Center in Chengdu, July 22, 2000).

74. *Shangwu zaobao*, July 1, 2000.

75. For barbers in late-Qing and Republican teahouses see D. Wang 2003, 45, 95.

76. *Shangwu zaobao*, May 27, 2000.

77. Author's fieldwork, under Teahouse by the Funan River, July 10, 2000.

78. Author's fieldwork, under Teahouse by the Funan River, July 10, 2000.

79. Author's fieldwork, under Cry of the Crane Teahouse, People's Park, June 28, 2003. Panhandlers also were common in open-air teahouses. At Cry of the Crane, an old man, carrying a yellow bag and wearing a Mao suit despite the heat, begged for money. His suit was worn but clean, and he even wore a pair of glasses. According to my observation, at least half of the patrons there gave him money. I estimated that he probably received more money from begging than the earwax pickers earned (author's fieldwork, under Cry of the Crane Teahouse, People's Park, June 28, 2003).

80. L. Zhang 2001b, 1–2.

81. Solinger 1999, 4, 15.

6. The Power of Mahjong

1. Festa 2006, 26. He has also published an article on mahjong in Taiwan, "analyzing the culturally intimate codes and ritual practices by which men conjure fate and battle luck" (Festa 2007, 101).

2. Xiao Longlian 2000; CCTV 2000a.

3. D. Wang 1993, 641–43, and Stapleton 2000, 133–34. Gambling, unlike opium smoking, most often occurred in public places and was virtually indistinguishable from many other leisure activities, particularly mahjong. The police took this issue seriously; they searched houses and streets to arrest gamblers and collected information on gaming establishments, their purveyors and participants, and made quick arrests of violators, who received fines and in some cases corporal punishment (D. Wang 2003, chap. 5).

4. Festa 2006, 13.

5. Regarding the history of mahjong see Chen Hsi-yüan. 2009. On the campaign to "Destroy the Four Olds" (ideologies, culture, customs, and habits) see D. D. Ho 2006, 64–95.

6. Steinmüller 2011, 265. Regarding popular culture and subculture of the new middle class in 1990s China see J. Wang 2005b.

7. D. Wang 2008b, chap. 4. For studies of teahouses in other areas see Suzuki 1982; Shao 1998; Goldstein 2003.

8. CCTV 2000a.

9. CCTV 2000a.

10. Xiao Longlian 2000; CCTV 2000a.

11. *Tianfu zaobao*, November 17, 2000.

12. *Tianfu zaobao*, November 18, 2000.

13. Tan Xiaojuan 2007.

14. Lü and Perry 1997.

15. See Zhang Jishun 2004.

16. Read 2000, 816. For other studies of urban neighborhood organizations in China under socialism see Whyte and Parish 1984; Lü and Perry 1997.

17. Lieberthal 2004, 172, 184.

18. Davis 2005, 705.

19. Sichuan sifangda lüshi shiwusuo 2000.

20. *Tianfu zaobao*, November 18, 2000.

21. Sichuan sifangda lüshi shiwusuo 2000.

22. *Tianhu zaobao*, November 17, 2000. Mahjong was recognized by the National Bureau of Sports as a sports activity in 1998.

23. Zha Yi 2003.

24. Xiao Longlian 2000. The "Great Opening of the Western Zone" was a major plan made by the central government in 1999 to decrease the economic imbalance between the coastal and inland regions. See D. Goodman 2004.

25. *Sichuan ribao*, November 24, 2000.

26. *Zhongguo qingnian bao*, November 24, 2000.

27. *Sichuan ribao*, November 22, 2000.

28. Shu Xincheng 1934, 144–45. Shu mentioned Zhang Shizhao (1881–1973), a well-known scholar and educator who was the minister of education during the warlord period. In the 1920s, he published articles and gave lectures praising the traditional agrarian life-style and opposing industrialization. These articles and lectures have been collected in Zhang Shizhao 2000.

29. There are numerous studies of gambling: Downes et al. 1976; Eadington 1976; Basu 1991; Steinmüller 2011.

30. Of course, the "craze of playing mahjong" (*majiang feng*) was not an issue only in Chengdu, but was a nationwide phenomenon. For example, a 1991 article in *Shehui* (Society) discusses the "craze of playing mahjong" and found that one-fourth of Shanghai residents, from small children to senior citizens more than eighty years old, played. Furthermore, almost all were involved in small-stakes gambling (Huang Yuemin 1991, 22–23).

31. *Tianfu zaobao*, March 12, 2000.

32. Perry Link and Kate Zhou have studied *shunkouliu* and their political implications (Link and Zhou 2002).

33. *Huaxi dushi bao*, April 9, 2001.

34. Zha Yi 2003.

35. *Chengdu shangbao*, April 7, 2000.

36. *Chengdu wanbao*, December 9, 2000. Additional articles on violence in teahouses caused by playing mahjong are in *Tianfu zaobao*, January 3, 2000, and *Huaxi dushi bao*, July 17, 2000, and October 4, 2000.

37. *Shangwu zaobao*, March 22, 2000. For a similar case see *Shangwu zaobao*, August 6, 2000.

38. *Shangwu zaobao*, February 28, 2000.

39. *Sichuan qingnian bao*, October 27, 2000.

40. *Tianfu zaobao*, March 12, 2000. A similar example can be found in *Chengdu shangbao*, February 25, 2000. Two mahjong-related incidents of illness occurred in a single day. See *Chengdu shangbao*, February 23, 2000; *Tianfu zaobao*, March 12, 2000.

41. *Tianfu zaobao*, February 24, 2000.

42. Zhongguo xinwen she 2000.

43. Xiao Longlian 2000. Interview by author, July 16, 2000, at the Europa (Ouluoba) resort in Chengdu. For more examples of business mahjong see Li Xianfu 1994, 80–90.

44. *Chengdu wanbao*, December 15, 2000. Since the government is unable to control mahjong, it tries to lead the game in the "right" direction, such as promoting "healthy mahjong" or transforming it into a kind of sport or "competition mahjong" (Festa 2006, 15–16). In 1990s Beijing, the government promoted "the consumption of leisure culture," which became a part of the CCP's ideological agenda (J. Wang 2001b, 77–78).

45. Zha Yi 2003.

46. *Huaxi dushi bao*, December 29, 2000.

47. Research comparing mahjong and reading found that while reading contributes significantly to the mental stimulation of the elderly, which can help prevent Alzheimer's disease, mahjong playing does not, contrary to common belief (Y.-C. Ho and A. S. Chan 2005).

48. Playing mahjong is regarded as a "Chineseness" factor (see Lo 2001; Festa 2006). Even during the anti-mahjong period, several books on how to play it were published. One, for example, titled *The Study of Mahjong* (*Majiang xue*), tries to promote the game as a legitimate tradition and sport (Sheng Q. 1999).

49. Xiao Longlian 2000.

50. *Tianfu zaobao*, October 31, 2001.

51. *Xinwenjie*, no. 4, 2004, 102.

52. As Michel Hockx and Julia Strauss point out, "As Party and state have shed their old functions of both supporting and suppressing cultural expression, many of these functions are gradually being taken over by the market" (Hockx and Strauss 2005, 526). Regarding the relationship between state and popular culture see J. Wang 2001a and 2001b.

53. D. Wang 2003, chap. 5; 2008b, introduction and chap. 8.

54. *Shangwu zaobao*, December 7, 2000.

55. Regarding conflicts in everyday life see Heller 1984, chap. 12.

56. CCTV 2000b.

57. CCTV 2000b; *Zhongguo qingnian bao*, November 24, 2000.

58. Song Zheng 2002.

59. See Dutton 1998; Chen et al. 2001; Link, Madsen, and Pickowicz 2002.

60. *Sichuan qingnian bao*, November 10, 2000; *Tianfu zaobao*, November 17, 2000.

61. *Economist* 2013, 54.

62. Yang Jing 2013.

63. J. Wang 2001b, 73, who also discusses *yangge* dance in 1990s Beijing.

Conclusion

1. Frank Dikötter's new book follows a chronology, covering both the run-up to and the entire Cultural Revolution, that abounds in personal, local, and regional resistances to state harassment and cruelty (Dikötter 2016).

2. Scott 1985.

3. Yu Yunhan 2000.

4. Brown 2012, chap. 6.

5. Regarding women's liberation after 1949 see Andors 1983; Chien 1994; Yee 2001; Evans 2003; Zang 2011; X. Zhong 2011.

6. Hung 2007.

7. Zhang Xiande 1999, 113.

8. Hockx and Strauss 2005, 526.

9. For control of leisure in Republican Shanghai see Wakeman 1995.

10. D. Wang 2003, chaps. 1 and 4; Duara 1988, 1991.

11. Sennett 2006, 131.

12. J. Wang 2001c, 41.

13. Goodman 2001, 248. Litzinger 2001 also speaks of the close connection of the state with the consumer culture.

14. J. Wang 2005, 10, in her introduction to the edited volume on geo-culture.

15. Esherick 2000; Stapleton 2000; D. Wang 2003, chaps. 4, 5.

16. Hockx and Strauss 2005, 525.

17. Rankin 1986, 1990; Rowe 1989, 1990; Strand 1989; Habermas 1989; P. Huang 1993; Wakeman 1993; Chamberlain 1993; Brook and Frolic 1997.

18. D. Wang 2003, chaps. 6 and 7.

19. D. Wang 2008b, 254–55.

20. Chamberlain 1993, 210.

21. Dittmer and Gore 2001, 41.

22. Wakeman 1993, 133.

23. Rankin 1993, 159.

24. Rowe points out that because there is an "absence of a detailed study of these institutions in the Ming and Qing," he could only "point to the suggestiveness of early twentieth-century literary depictions of these institutions, as for example in Lao She's *Teahouse* and Lu Xun's 'In the Wineshop'" (Rowe 1993, 146).

25. Kraus 2000, 288–89.

26. Solinger 1999, 284–86.

27. Madsen 1993, 190.

28. Gittings 2005, 4.

WORKS CITED

A Nian. 1997. *Huainian jiuju* [Recalling my old home]. Beijing: Zhongyang minzu daxue chubanshe.

A Qiu. 2000. "Zhuimeng nühai: Chengdu bu xiangxin yanlei" [The girl who chased dreams: Chengdu does not believe in tears]. *Shangwu zaobao* [Commerce morning news], April 16.

Abrami, Regina Marie. 2002. "Self-Making, Class Struggle and Labor Autarky: The Political Origins of Private Entrepreneurship in Vietnam and China." PhD diss., University of California, Berkeley.

Adelman, Jonathan R. 1983. "The Impact of Civil Wars on Communist Political Culture: The Chinese and Russian Cases." *Studies in Comparative Communism* 16.1–2 (Spring–Summer): 25–48.

Akita, Shigeru, and Nicholas J. White, eds. 2010. *The International Order of Asia in the 1930s and 1950s*. Farnham: Ashgate.

Almond, Gabriel. 1956. "Comparative Political Systems." *Journal of Politics* 18.3 (August): 391–409.

Almond, Gabriel, and G. Bingham Powell. 1978. *Comparative Politics: System, Process, Policy*. Boston: Little, Brown.

Andors, Phyllis. 1983. *The Unfinished Liberation of Chinese Women, 1949–1980*. Bloomington: Indiana University Press.

Andrews, Julia F., and Kuiyi Shen. 2002. "The New Chinese Woman and Lifestyle Magazines in the Late 1990s," 137–62. In Link, Madsen, and Pickowicz 2002.

Atherton, Andrew, and Alaric Fairbanks. 2006. "Stimulating Private Sector Development in China: The Emergence of Enterprise Development Centres in Liaoning and Sichuan Provinces." *Asia Pacific Business Review* 12.3 (July): 333–54.

Atkinson, Lisa. 1994. "Fun for the '90s: Entertainment Just May Be China's Newest Growth Industry." *China Business Review* 21.5 (September): 16–22.

——. 1997. "What's Entertainment? New Censorship and Consolidation Concerns Plague China's Entertainment Market." *China Business Review* 24.2 (March–April): 38–40.

Bachman, David M. 1991. *Bureaucracy, Economy, and Leadership in China: The Institutional Origins of the Great Leap Forward*. New York: Cambridge University Press.

Bai Yihua. 1991. "Woguo chengshi jiedao banshichu de lishi, xianzhuang he gaige" [History, status, and reforms of China's urban neighborhood committee offices]. *Chengshi wenti* [Urban issues] 6:62–66.

Baker, Keith Michael, ed. 1987. *The French Revolution and the Creation of Modern Political Culture*. Vol. 1, *The Political Culture of the Old Regime*. Oxford: Pergamon.

Bakken, B. 2000. *The Exemplary Society: Human Improvement, Social Control, and the Dangers of Modernity in China*. New York: Oxford University Press.

Bandelj, Nina, and Dorothy J. Solinger, eds. 2012. *Socialism Vanquished, Socialism Challenged: Eastern Europe and China, 1989–2009*. New York: Oxford University Press.

Bao Yaming, Wang Hongtu, and Zhu Shengjian. 2002. *Shanghai jiuba* [Shanghai bars]. Kaohsiung: Hongwen tushu.

Barmé, Geremie. 2012. "Red Allure and the Crimson Blindfold." *China Perspectives* 90:29–40.

Barnett, A. Doak, ed. 1969. *Chinese Communist Politics in Action*. Seattle: University of Washington Press.

Basu, Ellen Oxfeld. 1991. "Profit, Loss, and Fate: The Entrepreneurial Ethic and the Practice of Gambling in an Overseas Chinese Community." *Modern China* 17.2 (April): 227–59.

Berger, Yakov. 2002. "Social Support of the Elderly in Contemporary China." *Far Eastern Affairs* 30.1: 79–112.

Bing Feng and Qiang Jinwu. 2003. *Chengdu shiba guai* [Eighteen strange things about Chengdu]. Chengdu: Shidai chubanshe.

Bird, John, Barry Curtis, Tim Putnam, and Lisa Tickner, eds. 1993. *Mapping the Futures: Local Cultures, Global Change*. London: Routledge.

Børdahl, Vibeke. 2009. "Written Scripts in the Oral Tradition of Yangzhou Storytelling." In *Lifestyle and Entertainment in Yangzhou*, edited by Lucie B. Olivová and Vibeke Børdahl, 245–70. Copenhagen: NIAS.

Bourdieu, Pierre. 1984. *Distinction: A Social Critique of the Judgment of Taste*. Translated by Richard Nice. Cambridge, MA: Harvard University Press.

Brook, Timothy, and B. Michael Frolic, eds. 1997. *Civil Society in China*. Armonk, NY: M. E. Sharpe.

Brown, Archie, and Jack Gray, eds. 1979. *Political Culture and Political Change in Communist States*. London: Macmillan.

Brown, Jeremy. 2012. *City versus Countryside in Mao's China: Negotiating the Divide.* Cambridge: Cambridge University Press.

Brown, Jeremy, and Mathew Johnson, eds. 2015. *Maoism at the Grassroots: Everyday Life in China's Era of High Socialism.* Cambridge, MA: Harvard University Press.

Brown, Jeremy, and Paul G. Pickowicz, eds. 2007a. *Dilemmas of Victory: The Early Years of the People's Republic of China.* Cambridge, MA: Harvard University Press.

———. 2007b. "The Early Years of the People's Republic of China: An Introduction." In Brown and Pickowicz 2007a, 1–18.

Brugger, William. 1976. *Democracy and Organization in the Chinese Industrial Enterprise, 1948–1953.* New York: Cambridge University Press.

Bruun, Ole. 1993. *Business and Bureaucracy in a Chinese City: An Ethnography of Private Business Households in Contemporary China.* Berkeley: Institute of East Asian Studies, University of California.

Burke, Peter. 2008. *What Is Cultural History?* 2nd ed. Cambridge: Polity.

Cai, Wenhui. 2001. *Class Struggle and Deviant Labeling in Mao's China: Becoming Enemies of the People.* Lewiston, NY: Edwin Mellen.

Cartier, Carolyn. 2002a. "Origins and Evolution of a Geographical Idea: The Macroregion in China." *Modern China* 28.1 (January): 79–143.

———. 2002b. "Transnational Urbanism in the Reform Era Chinese City: Landscapes from Shenzhen." *Urban Studies* 39.9 (2002): 1513–32.

CCTV 2000a. "Yiren fandui da majiang nengfou tuifan jumin jiti jueyi" [Can a person who opposes playing mahjong overturn a resolution made by the collective of residents?]. http://www.people.com.cn/GB/channel7/498/20001111/324250.html. Posted December 29.

CCTV 2000b. "Majiang shengsheng" [The sounds of mahjong]. http://www.people.com.cn/GB/channel7/498/20001108/305318.html. Posted December 29.

Chai, Joseph C. H. 2000. *The Economic Development of Modern China.* Northampton, MA: Edward Elgar Publishing Limited.

Chaichian, Mohammad A. 1994. "The Development of Small Business and Petty Commodity Production in the People's Republic of China." *Asian Profile* 22.4 (August): 167–76.

Chamberlain, Heath B. 1993. "On the Search for Civil Society in China." *Modern China* 19.2 (April): 199–215.

Chan, Anita. 2002. "The Culture of Survival: Lives of Migrant Workers through the Prism of Private Letters." In Link, Madsen, and Pickowicz 2002, 163–88.

Chan, Cecilia. 1993. "Urban Neighborhood Mobilization and Community Care for the Elderly in the People's Republic of China." *Journal of Cross-Cultural Gerontology* 8.3 (July): 253–70.

Chan, Chris King-Chi, Ngai Pun, and Jenny Chan. 2010. "The Role of the State, Labour Policy and Migrant Workers' Struggles in Globalized China." In *Globalization and Labour in China and India: Impacts and Responses,* edited by Paul Bowles and John Harriss, 45–63. London: Palgrave Macmillan.

Chan, Sylvia. 1980. "The Blooming of a 'Hundred Flowers' and the Literature of the 'Wounded Generation.'" In *China since the Gang of Four,* edited by Bill Brugger, 174–201. New York: St. Martin's.

Chand, Gyan. 1958. *The New Economy of China: Factual Account, Analysis and Interpretation*. Bombay: Vora.

Chang, Chen-pang. 1987. "Anti-rightist in Politics, Anti-leftist in Economics." *Issues and Studies* 23.8: 5–8.

Chang, Jung. 2003. *Wild Swans: Three Daughters of China*. New York: Touchstone.

Chang Shuai. 2008. "Quanmin wutuobang de gechang: Yi 'Hongqi geyao' weili chanshi 1958 nian xinminge yundong" [Singing the utopian songs of all the people: 'Red Flag Songs' as an example to explain the New Folk Song Movement]. *Anhui wenxue yuekan* [Anhui literature monthly], no. 8: 88–89.

Cheek, Timothy. 1981. "Deng Tuo: Culture, Leninism and Alternative Marxism in the Chinese Communist Party." *China Quarterly* 87 (September): 470–91.

Chen, An. 2002. "Capitalist Development, Entrepreneurial Class, and Democratization in China." *Political Science Quarterly* 117.3 (Fall): 401–22.

Chen Hsi-yüan. 2009. "Cong madiao dao majiang: Xiaowanyi yu dachuantong jiaozhi de yiduan lishi yinyuan" [From madiao to mahjong: The historical reason behind the mingling of petty things with great traditions]. *Zhongyang yanjiuyuan lishi yuyan yanjiusuo jikan* [Collected papers of the Institute of History and Philology of Academia Sinica] 80:137–96.

Chen, Jian. 1994. *China's Road to the Korean War: The Making of the Sino-American Confrontation*. New York: Columbia University Press.

——. 2001. *Mao's China and the Cold War*. Chapel Hill: University of North Carolina Press.

Chen, Nancy N., Constance D. Clark, Suzanne Z. Gottschang, and Lyn Jeffery. 2001. *China Urban: Ethnographies of Contemporary Culture*. Durham, NC: Duke University Press.

Chen, Sandy C., and Michael Gassner. 2012. "An Investigation of the Demographic, Psychological, Psychographic, and Behavioral Characteristics of Chinese Senior Leisure Travelers." *Journal of China Tourism Research* 8.2: 123–45.

Chen, Tina Mai. 2003a. "Female Icons, Feminist Iconography? Socialist Rhetoric and Women's Agency in 1950s China." *Gender and History* 15.2: 268–95.

——. 2003b. "Propagating the Propaganda Film: The Meaning of Film in Chinese Communist Party Writings, 1949–1965." *Modern Chinese Literature and Culture* 15.2: 154–93.

Chen, Yanru. 2008. "From Ideal Women to Women's Ideal: Evolution of the Female Image in Chinese Feature Films, 1949–2000." *Asian Journal of Women's Studies* 14.3: 97–129.

Chen, Yunqian. 2016. "Bursting with Mountain Songs: Gender Resistance and Class Struggle in Liu Sanjie." *Frontiers of History in China* 11.1: 133–58.

Cheng, Weikun. 1996. "The Challenge of the Actresses: Female Performers and Cultural Alternatives in Early Twentieth Century Beijing and Tianjin." *Modern China* 22.2: 197–233.

Chengdu shi difang zhi bianzuan weiyuanhui, ed. 1999. *Chengdu shizhi: Wenhua yishu zhi* [Gazetteer of Chengdu: Culture and arts]. Chengdu: Sichuan cishu chubanshe.

——, ed. 2000. *Chengdu shizhi: Gongshang xingzheng guanli zhi* [Gazetteer of Chengdu: Administration of industry and commerce]. Chengdu: Sichuan cishu chubanshe.

Chengdu shi tongjiju. 2000. "Chengdu shi tongjiju guanyu 2000 nian diwuci quanguo renkou pucha zhuyao shuju gongbao" [Report of the Chengdu City Statistics Bureau on an investigation of important data from the fifth national census of 2000]. http://www.xjtjj.gov.cn/upimg/sys061025161337.doc. Posted date unknown.

Chiang, Chen-ch'ang. 1986. "Social Control under the Chinese Communist Regime." *Issues and Studies* 22.5 (May): 87–111.

Chien, Ying-Ying. 1994. "Revisioning 'New Women': Feminist Readings of Representative Modern Chinese Fiction." *Women's Studies International Forum* 17.1 (January–February): 33–45.

Chin, S. S. K., and A. H. Y. Lin. 1982. "Persevering in Socialism or Returning to New Democracy? A Case of the Verification of Mao Tse-tung Thought by Practice." *Journal of Oriental Studies* 20.2: 173–88.

Ching, Leo. 2000. "Globalizing the Regional, Regionalizing the Global: Mass Culture and Asianism in the Age of Late Capitalism." *Public Culture* 12.1 (Winter): 233–57.

Chiu, Hungdah. 1981. "Socialist Legalism: Reform and Continuity in Post Mao Communist China." *Issues and Studies* 17.11: 45–69.

Chung, Yen-lin. 2011. "The Witch-Hunting Vanguard: The Central Secretariat's Roles and Activities in the Anti-rightist Campaign." *China Quarterly* 206 (June): 391–411.

Clausen, Søren. 1998. "Party Policy and 'National Culture': Towards a State-Directed Cultural Nationalism in China?" In *Reconstructing Twentieth-Century China: State Control, Civil Society, and a National Identity*, edited by Kjeld Erik Brødsgaard and David Strand, 253–79. Oxford: Clarendon Press.

Cochran, Sherman. 2007. "Capitalists Choosing Communist China: The Liu Family of Shanghai, 1948–56." In Brown and Pickowicz 2007a, 359–85.

Cohen, Jerome Alan. 1971. "Drafting People's Mediation Rules." In Lewis 1971, 29–50.

Cohen, Paul A. 1988. "The Post-Mao Reforms in Historical Perspective." *Journal of Asian Studies* 47.3 (August): 518–40.

——. 2003. "Reflections on a Watershed Date: The 1949 Divide in Chinese History." In *Twentieth-Century China: New Approaches*, edited by Jeffrey N. Wasserstrom, 27–36. New York: Taylor & Francis.

Cooke, Fang Lee. 2011. "Entrepreneurship, Humanistic Management and Business Turnaround: The Case of a Small Chinese Private Firm." In *Humanistic Management in Practice*, edited by Ernst Von Kimakowitz, Michael Pirson, Heiko Spitzeck, and Claus Dierksmeier, 119–30. New York: Palgrave Macmillan.

Cox, Kevin R., ed. 1997. *Spaces of Globalization: Reassuring the Power of the Local.* New York: Guilford.

Crespi, John A. 2010. "Treasure-Seekers: The Poetry of Social Function in a Beijing Recitation Club." *Modern Chinese Literature and Culture* 22.2 (Fall): 1–38.

Cui Yuefeng. 2005. "1949–1958 nian Beijing shi tongye gonghui zuzhi de yanbian" [Transformation of guild organizations in Beijing, 1949–1958]. *Beijing shehui kexue* [Social sciences in Beijing] 1:106–13.

Cui, Zhiyuan. 2011. "Partial Intimations of the Coming Whole: The Chongqing Experiment in Light of the Theories of Henry George, James Meade, and Antonio Gramsci." *Modern China* 37.6 (December): 646–60.

Cunningham, Li Xue, and Chris Rowley. 2010. "Small and Medium-Sized Enterprises in China: A Literature Review, Human Resource Management and Suggestions for Further Research." *Asia Pacific Business Review* 16.3: 319–37.

Dai Lichao. 2005. "Chaguan guancha: Nongcun gonggong kongjian de fuxing yu jiceng shehui zhenghe" [Observation of the teahouse: Revival of rural public spaces and social integration at the base]. *Shehui* [Society] 5:96–117.

Dai Shankui. 1984. "Chaguan" [The teahouse]. *Renmin ribao* [People's daily], August 19.

——. 1998. "Chengdu pao chaguan" [Frequenting Chengdu teahouses]. *Renmin ribao* [People's daily], July 10.

Das, Naranarayan. 1979. *China's Hundred Weeds: A Study of the Anti-Rightist Campaign in China*. Calcutta: K. P. Bagchi.

Davis, Deborah, ed. 2000. *The Consumer Revolution in Urban China*. Berkeley: University of California Press.

——. 2002. "When a House Becomes His Home." In Link, Madsen, and Pickowicz 2002, 231–50.

——. 2005. "Urban Consumer Culture." *China Quarterly* 183 (September): 692–709.

Davis, Deborah, and Stevan Harrell, eds. 1993. *Chinese Families in the Post-Mao Era*. Berkeley: University of California Press.

Davis, Deborah, Richard Kraus, Barry Naughton, and Elizabeth J. Perry, eds. 1995. *Urban Spaces in Contemporary China: The Potential for Autonomy and Community in Post-Mao China*. New York: Cambridge University Press.

Day, Alexander. 2013. *The Peasant in Postsocialist China: History, Politics, and Capitalism*. Cambridge: Cambridge University Press.

DeMare, Brian. 2015. *Mao's Cultural Army: Drama Troupes in China's Rural Revolution*. Cambridge: Cambridge University Press.

Deng Gaoru. 1995. "Yincha" [Drinking tea]. *Renmin ribao* [People's daily], November 3.

Dikötter, Frank. 2016. *The Cultural Revolution: A People's History, 1962–1976*. New York: Bloomsbury.

Dillon, Nara. 2007. "New Democracy and the Demise of Private Charity in Shanghai." In Brown and Pickowicz 2007a, 80–102.

Ding, Sai, Xiao-yuan Dong, and Shi Li. 2009. "Women's Employment and Family Income Inequality during China's Economic Transition." *Feminist Economics* 15.3 (July): 163–90.

Ding, Yuling. 2006. "Economic Activities and the Construction of Gender Status among the Xunpu Women in Fujian." In *Southern Fujian: Reproduction of Traditions in Post-Mao China*, edited by Chee-Beng Tan, 163–83. Hong Kong: Chinese University Press.

Dittmer, Lowell, and Lance Gore. 2001. "China Builds a Market Culture." *East Asia* 19.3 (September): 9–50.

Dong Limin. 2010. "Shenti, lishi yu xiangxiang de zhengzhi: Zuowei wenxue shijian de 50 niandai jinü gaizao" [The body, history, and imagination of politics: Prostitution reforms in the 1950s as a literary matter]. *Wenxue pinglun* [Literature review] 1:113–21.

Dong, Xiao-Yuan, et al. 2007. "Women's Employment and Public Sector Restructuring: The Case of Urban China." In *Unemployment in China: Economy, Human Resources and Labour Markets*, edited by Grace O. M. Lee and Malcolm Warner, 87–107. London: Routledge.

Downes, David, B. P. Davies, M. E. David, and P. Stone. 1976. *Gambling, Work and Leisure: A Study across Three Areas.* London: Routledge & Kegan Paul.

Du Jianhua. 2012. "'Hongse jiyi' de shanbian: Dui 'hongge' meiti chengxian de kaocha, 1979–2011" [Transformation of "red memory": A study of the media phenomenon of "red songs" (1979–2011)]. Unpublished diss., Fudan University.

Duara, Prasenjit. 1988. "Superscribing Symbols: The Myth of Guandi, Chinese God of War." *Journal of Asian Studies* 47.4 (November): 778–95.

——. 1991. "Knowledge and Power in the Discourse of Modernity: The Campaigns against Popular Religion in Early Twentieth-Century China." *Journal of Asian Studies* 50.1 (February): 67–83.

Ducheng [Reading the city]. 2008. Special issue of *Wide and Narrow Alleys.*

Dutton, Michael Robert. 1998. *Streetlife China.* New York: Cambridge University Press.

Dwyer, D. J. 1986. "Chengdu, Sichuan: The Modernisation of a Chinese City." *Geography* 71.3: 215–27.

Eadington, William R. 1976. *Gambling and Society: Interdisciplinary Studies on the Subject of Gambling.* Springfield, IL: Charles C. Thomas.

Economist. 2013. "Dancing Queens: Grooving Grannies Encounter Opposition." October 26, 54.

Endicott-West, Elizabeth. 1999. "Notes on Shamans, Fortune-Tellers and Yin-Yang Practitioners and Civil Administration in Yüan China." In *The Mongol Empire and Its Legacy*, edited by Reuven Amitai-Preiss and David O. Morgan, 224–39. Leiden: Brill.

Esherick, Joseph W., ed. 2000. *Remaking the Chinese City: Modernity and National Identity, 1900–1950.* Honolulu: University of Hawai'i Press.

——. 2007. "The Ye Family in New China." In Brown and Pickowicz 2007a, 311–36.

Esherick, Joseph, Paul G. Pickowicz, and Andrew G. Walder, eds. 2006. *The Chinese Cultural Revolution as History.* Stanford, CA: Stanford University Press.

Evans, Harriet. 2003. "The Language of Liberation: Gender and *Jiefang* in Early Chinese Communist Party Discourse." In *Twentieth-Century China: New Approaches*, edited by Jeffrey N. Wasserstrom, 193–220. New York: Routledge.

Farina, Marina Basso. 1980. "Urbanization, Deurbanization and Class Struggle in China, 1949–79." *International Journal of Urban and Regional Research* 4.4 (December): 485–502.

Farrer, James. 2000. "Dancing through the Market Transition: Disco and Dance Hall Sociability in Shanghai." In Davis 2000, 226–49.

——. 2009–2010. "Shanghai Bars: Patchwork Globalization and Flexible Cosmopolitanism in Reform-Era Urban-Leisure Spaces." *Chinese Sociology and Anthropology* 42.2 (Winter): 22–38.

Fei, Li. 2004. "Performance Technique and Schools of Yangzhou Storytelling." In *Four Masters of Chinese Storytelling: Full-Length Repertoires of Yangzhou Storytelling on Video*, edited by Vibeke Børdahl, Li Fei, and Ying Huang, 17–27. Copenhagen: NIAS.

Feng Xiaocai. 2011a. "Shehui zhuyi de bianyuan ren: 1956 nian qianhou de xiaoshang xiaofan gaizao wenti" [Marginalized people of socialism: Problems in reforming petty traders and peddlers before and after 1956]. In Huadong shifan daxue Zhongguo dangdai shi yanjiu zhongxin 2011b, 3–45.

——. 2011b. "Zhengzhi shengcun yu jingji shengcun: Shanghai shangren ruhe zoushang gongsi heying zhilu?" [Political survivors and economic survivors: How did merchants in Shanghai take up public-private ownership?]. In Huadong shifan daxue Zhongguo dangdai shi yanjiu zhongxin 2011a, 91–138.

Feng Zhicheng, ed. 1999. *Shimin jiyi zhong de lao Chengdu* [Old Chengdu in the memories of its residents]. Chengdu: Sichuan wenyi chubanshe.

Fernandez-Stembridge, Leila. 2005. "Shaping Rural Migrant Women's Employment: The Role of Housemaid Agencies." *European Journal of East Asian Studies* 4.1: 31–53.

Festa, Paul E. 2006. "Mahjong Politics in Contemporary China: Civility, Chineseness, and Mass Culture." *Position* 14.1: 7–35.

——. 2007. "Mahjong Agonistics and the Political Public in Taiwan: Fate, Mimesis, and the Martial Imaginary." *Anthropological Quarterly* 80.1 (Winter 2007): 93–125.

Finnane, Antonia. 2011. "Tailors in 1950s Beijing: Private Enterprise, Career Trajectories, and Historical Turning Points in the Early PRC." *Frontiers of History in China* 6.1 (March): 117–37.

Fleischer, Friederike. 2006. "Speaking Bitter-Sweetness: China's Urban Elderly in the Reform Period." *Asian Anthropology* 5.1: 31–55.

Florence, Eric. 2007. "Migrant Workers in the Pearl River Delta: Discourse and Narratives about Work as Sites of Struggle." *Critical Asian Studies* 39.1 (March): 121–50.

Forester, John. 1988. "Introduction: The Applied Turn in Contemporary Critical Theory." In *Critical Theory and Public Life*, edited by John Forester, ix–xvii. Cambridge, MA: MIT Press.

Friedmann, John. 2005. *China's Urban Transition*. Minneapolis: University of Minnesota Press.

Fu Chongju. 1910. *Chengdu tonglan* [Investigation of Chengdu]. Vol. 3. Chengdu: Tongsu baoshe.

Fu Xiuhai. 2012. "Zhao Shuli de geming xushi yu xiangtu jingyan: Yi 'Xiao Erhei jiehun' de zai jiedu wei zhongxin" [Zhao Shuli's revolutionary narrative and hometown experience: Reinterpretation of *A Peasant Takes a Wife*]. *Wenxue pinglun* [Literature review] 2:72–80.

Fung, Anthony. 2009–2010. "Consuming Karaoke in China: Modernities and Cultural Contradiction." *Chinese Sociology and Anthropology* 42.2 (Winter): 39–55.

Gao, James Z. 2004. *The Communist Takeover of Hangzhou: The Transformation of City and Cadre, 1949–1954*. Honolulu: University of Hawai'i Press.

Gao Qirong. 2004. "Jin shinian lai guanyu Dayuejin yundong chengyin yanjiu zongshu" [Overview of research concerning the causes of the Great Leap Forward]. *Dangshi yanjiu yu jiaoxue* [Research and teaching of CCP history] 5:93–96.

Gao, Yuan. 1987. *Born Red: A Chronicle of the Cultural Revolution*. Stanford, CA: Stanford University Press.

Gao Zhongwei. 2011. *Xin Zhongguo chengli chuqi chengshi jiceng shehui zuzhi de chonggou yanjiu: Yi Chengdu wei zhongxin de kaocha, 1949–1957* [A study of the reconstruction of urban grassroots social organizations in the period soon after establishment of the PRC: Chengdu as a major investigation]. Chengdu: Sichuan daxue chubanshe.

Gardner, John. 1969. "The Wu-fan Campaign in Shanghai." In Barnett 1969, 477–539.

Gates, Hill. 1996. "Owner, Worker, Mother, Wife: Taibei and Chengdu Family Businesswomen." In *Putting Class in Its Place: Worker Identities in East Asia*, edited by Elizabeth J. Perry, 127–65. Berkeley: Institute of East Asian Studies, University of California.

———. 1999. *Looking for Chengdu: A Woman's Adventures in China*. Ithaca, NY: Cornell University Press.

Gaubatz, Piper Rae. 1995. "Urban Transformation in Post-Mao China: Impacts of the Reform Era on China's Urban Form." In Davis et al. 1995, 28–60.

Gentil, Sylvie. 2004. "Chengdu, Leave Me Alone Tonight, or Life as a Drowning Experience." *Chinese Cross Currents* 1.2 (April): 58–69.

Geyer, Robert. 2002. "In Love and Gay." In Link, Madsen, and Pickowicz 2002, 251–74.

Giroir, Guillaume. 2007. "Spaces of Leisure: Gated Golf Communities in China." In *China's Emerging Cities: The Making of New Urbanism*, edited by Fulong Wu, 235–55. London: Routledge.

Gittings, John. 2005. *The Changing Face of China: From Mao to Market*. New York: Oxford University Press.

Gluckstein, Ygael. 1957. *Mao's China: Economic and Political Survey*. London: George Allen & Unwin.

Golas, Peter J. 1977. "Early Ch'ing Guilds." In *The City in Late Imperial China*, edited by G. William Skinner, 555–80. Stanford, CA: Stanford University Press.

Gold, Thomas B. 1985. "China's Private Entrepreneurs: Small-Scale Private Business Prospers under Socialism." *China Business Review* 12.6 (November–December): 46–50.

Goldman, Merle. 1987. "The Party and the Intellectuals." In MacFarquhar and Fairbank 1987, 218–58.

Goldman, Merle, and Roderick MacFarquhar, eds. 1999. *The Paradox of China's Post-Mao Reforms*. Cambridge, MA: Harvard University Press.

Goldstein, Joshua. 2003. "From Teahouses to Playhouse: Theaters as Social Texts in Early-Twentieth-Century China." *Journal of Asian Studies* 62.3 (August): 753–79.

Gong, Ting. 2002. "Women's Unemployment, Re-employment and Self-employment in China's Economic Restructuring." In *Transforming Gender and Development in East Asia*, edited by Esther Ngan-ling Chow, 125–39. New York: London: Routledge.

Goodman, Bryna. 1995. *Native Place, City, and Nation: Regional Networks and Identities in Shanghai, 1853–1937*. Berkeley: University of California Press.

Goodman, David S. G. 2001. "Contending the Popular: The Party State and Culture." *Positions* 9.1: 245–52.

———, ed. 2004. *China's Campaign to "Open Up the West": National, Provincial, and Local Perspectives*. New York: Cambridge University Press.

Goodman, David S. G., and Gerald Segal. 2002. *China Deconstructs: Politics, Trade and Regionalism*. London: Routledge.

Goodman, Howard L. 1998. *Ts'ao P'i Transcendent: The Political Culture of Dynasty-Founding in China at the End of the Han*. London: Routledge.

Gore, Lance L. P. 2001. "Dream On: Communists of the Dengist Brand in Capitalistic China." In *The Nanxun Legacy and China's Development in the Post-Deng Era*, edited by John Wang and Yongnian Zheng, 197–219. Singapore: Singapore University Press and World Scientific.

Gu Zhizhong. 1984. "Xianhua chaguan" [Teahouse gossip]. *Renmin ribao* [People's daily], May 26.

Guo, Sujian. 2012. *Chinese Politics and Government: Power, Ideology and Organization.* London: Routledge.

Guo Wenzhi. 1995. "Dongchengqu jiedao banshichu de yanbian he fazhan" [Evolution and development of neighborhood committees in the East City District]. *Jinjiang wenshi ziliao* [Jinjiang literary and historical materials] 3:14–30.

Habermas, Jürgen. 1989. *The Structural Transformation of the Public Sphere: An Inquiry into a Category of Bourgeois Society.* Translated by Thomas Burger. Cambridge: Polity.

Halpern, Nina P. 1991. "Economic Reform, Social Mobilization, and Democratization in Post-Mao China." In *Reform and Reaction in Post-Mao China: The Road to Tiananmen*, edited by Richard Baum, 38–59. London: Routledge.

Han Nanzheng. 1990. "Chaguan yu chahui" [Teahouses and tea parties]. In *Ba Shu chaoyong kuimen kai: Sichuan gaige jianwen yu sikao* [Ba and Shu surging through the Kuimen gateway: Firsthand knowledge and reflections on Sichuan reforms], edited by Wang Mulin and Han Nanzheng, 13–15. N.p.

Hanser, Amy. 2002. "The Chinese Enterprising Self: Young, Educated Urbanites and the Search for Work." In Link, Madsen, and Pickowicz 2002, 189–206.

Hansson, Anders, Bonnie S. McDougall, and Frances Weightman, eds. 2002. *The Chinese at Play: Festivals, Games, and Leisure.* New York: Kegan Paul.

Hao Keqiang. 1981. "Xingwang de Chengdu qiyuan" [Flourishing chess gardens in Chengdu]. *Renmin ribao* [People's daily], January 1.

Harding, Harry. 1986. "Political Development in Post-Mao China." In *Modernizing China: Post-Mao Reform and Development*, edited by A. Doak Barnett and Ralph N. Clough, 13–37. Boulder, CO: Westview.

Harrell, Stevan, ed. 1995. *Cultural Encounters on China's Ethnic Frontiers.* Seattle: University of Washington Press.

Harvey, David. 1990. *The Condition of Post-Modernity: An Enquiry into the Conditions of Cultural Change.* Oxford: Blackwell.

Hayden, Delores. 1995. *The Power of Place: Urban Landscapes as Public History.* Cambridge, MA: MIT Press.

He, Chengzhou. 2008. "Women and the Search for Modernity: Rethinking Modern Chinese Drama." *Modern Language Quarterly* 69.1 (March): 45–60.

He Libo. 2009. "Xin Zhongguo chengli qianhou de junguan zhidu" [Military control systems before and after the establishment of the PRC]. *Dangshi zonglan* [The broad view of CCP history] 5:11–17.

He, Qiliang. 2011. "High-Ranking Party Bureaucrats and Oral Performing Literature: The Case of Chen Yun and Pingtan in the People's Republic of China." *CHINOPERL Papers* 30:77–101.

———. 2012. *Gilded Voices: Economics, Politics, and Storytelling in the Yangzi Delta since 1949.* Leiden: Brill.

He Shizhong. 2010. "Hongmei huaxiang bian shancheng: Chongqing shi kaizhan 'chang du jiang chuan' huodong de shijian yu sikao" [Red plum fragrance imbues the mountain city: Practicing and reflecting on Chongqing's development of the "songs, reading, lectures, and tradition" movement]. *Qiushi* [Seeking truth] 9:53–55.

He Xiaozhu. 2005. "Chengdu chaguan jiyi" [Memories of teahouses in Chengdu]. *Huaxi dushi bao* [West China metropolitan news], December 11.

———. 2006. *Chengdu chaguan: Yishi jumin ban chake* [Chengdu teahouses: Half the residents are teahouse-goers]. Chengdu: Chengdu shidai chubanshe.

He Yimin, ed. 2002. *Biange yu fazhan: Zhongguo neilu chengshi Chengdu xiandaihua yanjiu* [Reform and development: A study of the modernization of China's inland-city Chengdu]. Chengdu: Sichuan daxue chubanshe.

Head, Thomas C. 2005. "Structural Changes in Turbulent Environments: A Study of Small and Mid-Size Chinese Organizations." *Journal of Leadership & Organizational Studies* 12.2: 82–93.

Heller, Ágnes. 1984. *Everyday Life*. Translated by G.L. Campbell. London: Routledge & Kegan Paul.

Hendrischke, Hans. 2005. "Popularization and Localization: A Local Tabloid Newspaper Market in Transition." In *Locating China: Space, Place, and Popular Culture*, edited by Jing Wang, 115–32. London: Routledge.

Henriot, Christian. 2012. "Slums, Squats, or Hutments? Constructing and Deconstructing an In-Between Space in Modern Shanghai (1926–65)." *Frontiers of History in China* 7.4 (December): 499–528.

Hershatter, Gail. 1997. *Dangerous Pleasures: Prostitution and Modernity in Twentieth-Century Shanghai*. Berkeley: University of California Press.

———. 2002. "The Gender of Memory: Rural Chinese Women and the 1950s." *Journal of Women in Culture and Society* 28.1 (August): 43–70.

Hiniker, Paul J. 1983. "The Cultural Revolution Revisited: Dissonance Reduction or Power Maximization." *China Quarterly* 94 (June): 282–303.

Ho, Dahpon David. 2006. "To Protect and Preserve: Resisting the Destroy the Four Olds Campaign, 1966–1967." In Esherick, Pickowicz, and Walder 2006, 64–95.

Ho, Denise Y. 2012. "Reforming Connoisseurship: State and Collectors in Shanghai in the 1950s and 1960s." *Frontiers of History in China* 7.4 (December): 608–37.

Ho, Ping-ti. 1966. "The Geographic Distribution of Hui-kuan (Landsmannschaften) in Central and Upper Yangtze Provinces." *Tsinghua Journal of Chinese Studies*, n.s., 5.2 (December): 120–52.

Ho, Yim-Chi, and A. S. Chan. 2005. "Comparing the Effects of Mahjong Playing and Reading on Cognitive Reserve of the Elderly." *Journal of Psychology in Chinese Societies* 6.1: 5–26.

Hockx, Michel, and Julia Strauss. 2005. Introduction to *China Quarterly* 183 (September): 523–31.

Hoffmann, David L. 2003. *Stalinist Values: The Cultural Norms of Soviet Modernity, 1917–1941*. Ithaca, NY: Cornell University Press.

Holm, David. 1984. "Folk Art as Propaganda: The Yangge Movement in Yan'an." In McDougall 1984a, 3–35.

Hong Yuanpeng and Weng Qiquan. 1980. "Shilun chengshi jiti suoyouzhi gongye" [Essay on urban collectively owned industry]. *Jingji yanjiu* [Studies in economics] 1:62–67.

Hooper, Beverley. 1994. "Women, Consumerism and the State in Post-Mao China." *Asian Studies Review* 17.3 (April): 73–83.

——. 1998. "'Flower Vase and Housewife': Women and Consumerism in Post-Mao China." In *Gender and Power in Affluent Asia*, edited by Krishna Sen and Maila Stivens, 167–93. London: Routledge.

Hu Junxiu and Suo Yu. 2012. "Liudong tanfan yu Zhongguo jindai chengshi dazhong wenhua" [Itinerant vendors and popular culture in modern Chinese cities]. *Gansu shehui kexue* [Gansu social sciences] 6:164–67.

Hua, Shiping, ed. 2001. *Chinese Political Culture, 1989–2000*. Armonk, NY: M. E. Sharpe.

Huadong shifan daxue Zhongguo dangdai shi yanjiu zhongxin, ed. 2009. *Zhongguo dangdai shi yanjiu* [Studies of contemporary China]. Vol. 1. Beijing: Jiuzhou chubanshe.

——, ed. 2011a. *Zhongguo dangdai shi yanjiu* [Studies of contemporary China]. Vol. 2. Beijing: Jiuzhou chubanshe.

——, ed. 2011b. *Zhongguo dangdai shi yanjiu* [Studies of contemporary China]. Vol. 3. Beijing: Jiuzhou chubanshe.

Huang Jinping. 2005. "Jinghua shehui huanjing, cujin shehui hexie: Shanghai jiefang chuqi de jinü gaizao" [Purifying the social environment and promoting social harmony: Prostitution reforms in early liberated Shanghai]. *Shanghai dangshi yu dangjian* [History and the establishment of the CCP in Shanghai] 3:40–41.

Huang, Philip C. C. 1993. "'Public Sphere' / 'Civil Society' in China? The Third Realm between State and Society." *Modern China* 19.2 (April): 216–40.

Huang Rutong. 1994. "Ziben zhuyi gongshang ye shehui zhuyi gaizao de lishi huigu" [Historical retrospect on socialist reforms of capitalist industry and commerce]. *Dangdai Zhongguo shi yanjiu* [Studies of contemporary Chinese history] 2:83–94.

Huang Shang. 1999. "Xian" [Leisure]. In Zeng Zhizhong and You Deyan 1999, 321–26.

Huang Yuemin. 1991. "Dui zhili 'majiang feng' de ruogan sikao" [Some thoughts on correcting and controlling the mahjong craze]. *Shehui* [Society] 12:22–24.

Huang Zhenyuan. 1956. "Qingting women de huyu" [Please hear our appeal]. *Xiju bao* [Drama news] 9:4–5.

Hung, Chang-tai. 2005. "The Dance of Revolution: Yangge in Beijing in the Early 1950s." *China Quarterly* 181 (March): 82–99.

——. 2007. "Mao's Parades: State Spectacles in China in the 1950s." *China Quarterly* 190 (January): 411–31.

Hunt, Lynn A. 1984. *Politics, Culture, and Class in the French Revolution*. Berkeley: University of California Press.

Imahori Seiji. 1953. *Chūgoku no shakai kōzō: Anshan rejiimu ni okeru "kyōdōtai"* [Chinese social structure: "Community" in the ancient regime]. Tokyo: Yūhikaku.

Jessup, J. Brooks. 2012. "Beyond Ideological Conflict: Political Incorporation of Buddhist Youth in the Early PRC." *Frontiers of History in China* 7.4 (December): 551–81.

Jia Wei. 1995. "Sanqingtuan de chengli yu Zhonggong de duice" [Establishment of the Youth League of the Three People's Principles and the proposal by the CCP]. *Jindaishi yanjiu* [Studies of modern Chinese history] 2:222–42.

Jiang, Jiehong, ed. 2007. *Burden or Legacy: From the Chinese Cultural Revolution to Contemporary Art*. Hong Kong: Hong Kong University Press.

Jiang Jin. 2007. "Duanlie yu yanxu: 1950 niandai Shanghai de wenhua gaizao" [Discontinuity and continuity: Cultural reforms in 1950s Shanghai]. In *Dushi wenhua zhong de xiandai Zhongguo* [Modern China from within metropolitan culture], edited by Jiang Jin, 481–97. Shanghai: Huadong shifang daxue chubanshe.

——. 2009. *Women Playing Men: Yue Opera and Social Change in Twentieth-Century Shanghai.* Seattle: University of Washington Press.

Jiang, Wenran. 2009. "Prosperity at the Expense of Equality: Migrant Workers Are Falling Behind in Urban China's Rise." In *Confronting Discrimination and Inequality in China: Chinese and Canadian Perspectives,* edited by Errol P. Mendes and Sakunthala Srighanthan, 16–29. Ottawa: University of Ottawa Press.

Jiang, Yarong, and David Ashley. 2013. *Mao's Children in the New China: Voices from the Red Guard Generation.* London: Routledge.

Jin, Guantao. 1993. "Socialism and Tradition: The Formation and Development of Modern Chinese Political Culture." *Journal of Contemporary China* 3 (Summer): 3–17.

——, ed. 2009. *Zhonghua renmin gongheguo shi, 1949–1981* [History of the People's Republic of China, 1949–1981]. Hong Kong: Xianggang zhongwen daxue chubanshe.

Jing Huan and Zeng Ronghua. 1982. "Jincheng yiyuan hua Tian Lai" [Stories of Tian Lai in Chengdu's artistic world]. *Chengdu wenshi ziliao xuanji* [Selection of Chengdu literary and historical materials] 3:133–41.

Joseph, William A. 1986. "A Tragedy of Good Intentions: Post-Mao Views of the Great Leap Forward." *Modern China* 12.4 (October): 419–57.

Kaikkonen, Marja. 1990. *Laughable Propaganda: Modern Xiangsheng as Didactic Entertainment.* Stockholm: Institute of Oriental Languages, Stockholm University.

Kang Mingyu and Li Qing. 2002. "Jianguo chuqi Chengdu shi wenhua tuanti bei jieguan yu gaizao de jingguo" [Process by which Chengdu cultural groups were taken over and reformed in the early years of the People's Republic]. In *Chengdu wenshi ziliao* [Chengdu literary and historical materials] 32, 146–54. Chengdu: Sichuan daxue chubanshe.

Kau, Ying-mao. 1969. "The Urban Bureaucratic Elite in Communist China: A Case Study of Wuhan, 1949–65." In Barnett 1969, 216–67.

King, Richard, Sheng Tian Zheng, and Scott Watson, eds. 2010. *Art in Turmoil: The Chinese Cultural Revolution, 1966–76.* Vancouver: UBC Press.

Kraus, Richard. 2000. "Public Monuments and Private Pleasures in the Parks of Nanjing: A Tango in the Ruins of the Ming Emperor's Palace." In Davis 2000, 287–311.

——. 2011. "Let a Hundred Flowers Blossom, Let a Hundred Schools of Thought Contend." In *Words and Their Stories: Essays on the Language of the Chinese Revolution,* edited by Ban Wang, 249–62. Leiden: Brill.

Kruks, Sonia, Rayna Rapp, and Marilyn B. Young, eds. 1989. *Promissory Notes: Women in the Transition to Socialism.* New York: Monthly Review.

Kubo, Toru. 2010. "China's Economic Development and the International Order of Asia, 1930s–1950s." In Akita and White 2010, 233–54.

Lao Xiang. 1942. "Tan Chengduren chicha" [Talking about tea drinking by Chengdu people], pts. 1–3. *Huaxi wanbao* [West China evening news], December 26–28.

Lardy, Nicholas R. 1987. "The Chinese Economy under Stress, 1958–1965." In MacFarquhar and Fairbank 1987, 360–97.

Lau, Raymond W. K. 2001. "Socio-political Control in Urban China: Changes and Crisis." *British Journal of Sociology* 52.4 (December): 605–20.

Lee, Hong Yung. 1979. "Mao's Strategy for Revolutionary Change: A Case Study of the Cultural Revolution." *China Quarterly* 77 (March): 50–73.

Lee, Joseph Tse-Hei. 2012. "Co-optation and Its Discontents: Seventh-Day Adventism in 1950s China." *Frontiers of History in China* 7.4 (December): 582–607.

Leese, Daniel. 2011. *Mao Cult: Rhetoric and Ritual in China's Cultural Revolution.* Cambridge: Cambridge University Press.

Leong, Sow-Theng, and Tim Wright, eds. 1997. *Migration and Ethnicity in Chinese History: Hakkas, Pengmin, and Their Neighbors.* Stanford, CA: Stanford University Press.

Lewis, John Wilson, ed. 1971. *The City in Communist China.* Stanford, CA: Stanford University Press.

Li, Hua-yu. 2006. *Mao and the Economic Stalinization of China, 1948–1953.* Boulder, CO: Rowman & Littlefield.

Li Liangyu. 2002. "Jianguo qianhou jieguan chengshi de zhengce" [Policies for taking over cities before and after the establishment of the PRC]. *Jiangsu daxue xuebao* [Journal of Jiangsu University] 3:1–10.

Li Lu. 1989. "Sanmin zhuyi qingnian tuan de chuangli yu xiaowang" [Establishment and demise of the Youth League of Three People's Principles]. *Dangshi yanjiu yu jiaoxue* [Research and teaching of CCP history] 2:48–54.

Li Meng and Hou Bo. 2013. *Mao Zedong chongzheng jiu heshan: 1949–1960* [Mao Zedong rebuilds the old lands]. Hong Kong: Hong Kong Open Publishing.

Li, Peilin, and Wei Li. 2013. "The Work Situation and Social Attitudes of Migrant Workers in China under the Crisis." In *China's Internal and International Migration,* edited by Peilin Li and Laurence Roulleau-Berger, 3–25. London: Routledge.

Li Pingnan. 2006. "Lun woguo qian 20 nian shehui zhuyi jianshe de jiaoxun" [On the lessons of the first 20 years of socialist construction]. *Dangdai shijie yu shehui zhuyi* [Today's world and socialism] 5:83–87.

Li Qingrui and Xi Guizhen. 1980. "Shilun chengshi da jiti qiye de suoyouzhi xingzhi" [Essay on the nature of large collectively owned urban enterprises]. *Beijing daxue xuebao* [Journal of Beijing University] 2:45–48.

Li, Wei, and Dennis Tao Yang. 2005. "The Great Leap Forward: Anatomy of a Central Planning Disaster." *Journal of Political Economy* 113.4 (August): 840–77.

Li Wenfang. 2000. "Zhonggong jieguan chengshi de chenggong shijian" [Successful practice of the CCP's takeover of cities]. *Beijing dangshi* [History of the CCP in Beijing] 6:15–18.

Li Xianfu. 1994. "Majiang shengsheng: Guanyu majiang feng de baogao" [Sounds of mahjong: Concerning the report on the mahjong craze]. In *Majiang shengsheng: Shehui wenti baogao wenxue ji* [Sounds of mahjong: A collection of reportage on social issues], edited by Li Xianfu, 54–106. Beijing: Guangming ribao chubanshe.

Li Xianke. 1995. "Jiefang Chengdu" [Liberation of Chengdu]. *Sichuan dangshi* [History of the CCP in Sichuan] 5:55–58.

Lieberthal, Kenneth. 1980. *Revolution and Tradition in Tientsin, 1949–1952.* Stanford, CA: Stanford University Press.

———. 2004. *Governing China: From Revolution through Reform.* New York: W. W. Norton.

Lieberthal, Kenneth, and David M. Lampton, eds. 1992. *Bureaucracy, Politics, and Decision Making in Post-Mao China.* Berkeley: University of California Press.

Lin Chaochao. 2011. "Zhonggong dui chengshi de jieguan he gaizao: Yige chubu de yanjiu huigu yu sikao" [CCP's takeover and reforms of cities: Initial research retrospectives and thoughts]. In Huadong shifan daxue Zhongguo dangdai shi yanjiu zhongxin 2011a, 139–63.

Lin Yunhui. 2009. *Xiang shehui zhuyi guodu: Zhongguo jingji yu shehui de zhuanxing, 1953–1955* [Toward a socialist transition: Transformations of the Chinese economy and society, 1953–55]. In vol. 2, *Zhonghua renmin gongheguo shi, 1949–1981* [History of the People's Republic of China, 1949–1981], edited by Jin Guantao. Hong Kong: Xianggang zhongwen daxue chubanshe.

Link, Perry. 1984. "The Genie and the Lamp: Revolutionary Xiangsheng." In McDougall 1984a, 83–111.

———. 2007. "The Crocodile Bird: Xiangsheng in the Early 1950s." In Brown and Pickowicz 2007a, 207–31.

Link, Perry, Richard P. Madsen, and Paul G. Pickowicz, eds. 2002. *Popular China: Unofficial Culture in a Globalizing Society.* Lanham, MD: Rowman & Littlefield.

Link, Perry, and Kate Zhou. 2002. "*Shunkouliu*: Popular Satirical Sayings and Popular Thought." In Link, Madsen, and Pickowicz 2002, 89–110.

Litzinger, Ralph A. 2001. "Government from Below: The State, the Popular, and the Illusion of Autonomy." *Positions* 9.1: 253–66.

Liu Dejun. 2009. "'Sanfan wufan' yundong zai kaocha" [Further thoughts on the Three Antis and Five Antis Campaigns]. *Tianfu xinlun* [New approaches from Sichuan] 3:128–31.

Liu Heng. 1954. "Chengdu shougongye zhe de chulu" [Employment of handicraft workers in Chengdu]. *Renmin ribao* [People's daily], May 15.

Liu Housheng. 1997. "Guanyu minjian zhiye jutuan de jidian sikao" [Several points concerning professional folk performance troupes]. *Guangdong yishu* [Performing arts in Guangdong] 1:21–24.

Liu Jianguo. 2000. "Shehui zhuyi zhenying de ganchao langchao yu Zhongguo dayuejin yundong de fasheng" [Surpassing waves in the socialist camp and the appearance of the Great Leap Forward in China]. *Jianghan luntan* [Jianghan forum] 4:75–78.

Liu, Jianhui, and Hongxu Wang. 2006. "The Origins of the General Line for the Transition Period and of the Acceleration of the Chinese Socialist Transformation in Summer 1955." *China Quarterly* 187 (September): 724–31.

Liu, Jieyui. 2006. "Researching Chinese Women's Lives: 'Insider' Research and Life History Interviewing." *Oral History* 34.1 (Spring): 43–52.

Liu Naichong. 1990. "'Gaixi, gairen, gaizhi' gei women de qishi" [Our inspiration from the "reforms of operas, performers, and institutions"]. *Zhongguo xiju* [Chinese opera] 1:38–41.

Liu Peiping. 1994. "Lun jieji douzheng kuoda hua cuowu chansheng de lilun yuanyin" [On the theoretical reasons for the mistaken outcomes of the spread of class struggle]. *Wen shi zhe* [Literature, history, and philosophy] 4:46–52.

Liu, Siyuan. 2009. "Theatre Reform as Censorship: Censoring Traditional Theatre in China in the Early 1950s." *Theatre Journal* 61 (2009): 387–406.

Liu, Xiaocong. 1992. "A Comparative Study on Women's Employment in Beijing, Guangzhou and Hong Kong." *Chinese Journal of Population Science* 4.1: 85–93.

Liu Yilun. 2007. "Jianguo chuqi xiqujie 'sangai' de shehui yingxiang" [The social influence of the theater world's "three reforms" in the early PRC]. *Xin dongfang* [New orient] 10:42–46.

Liu, Ying. 2004. "The Lives and Needs of Elderly Women in Urban China." In *Holding Up Half the Sky: Chinese Women Past, Present, and Future*, edited by Jie Tao, Bijun Zheng, and Shirley L. Mow, 193–203. New York: Feminist Press at the City University of New York.

Liu Zhenyao. 1999. "Desheng chaguan yi quyi" [Recalling folk performances in the Prosperity Teahouse]. In Feng Zhicheng. 1999, 150–51.

Lo, Amy. 2001. *The Book of Mahjong: An Illustrated Guide*. Boston: Tuttle.

Lockett, Martin. 1986. "Small Business and Socialism in Urban China." *Development and Change* 17.1 (January): 35–68.

Loh, Wai-fong. 1984. "From Romantic Love to Class Struggle: Reflections on the Film Liu Sanjie." In McDougall 1984a, 165–76.

Loscocco, Karyn A., and Christine E. Bose. 1998. "Gender and Job Satisfaction in Urban China: The Early Post-Mao Period." *Social Science Quarterly* 79.1 (March): 91–109.

Lou Shenghua. 2000. "Shehui zhuyi gaizao he jizhong dongyuan xing tizhi de xingcheng" [Socialist reform and the formation of a system of centralized mobilization]. *Nanjing shehui kexue* [Social sciences in Nanjing] 11:33–38.

Lü Chenxi. 2004. "Luelun jianguo chuqi de chengshi shehui wenti" [General discussion of issues concerning urban society in the early PRC]. *Sichuan daxue xuebao* [Journal of Sichuan University] S1: 113–16.

Lu Sigui. 1956. "Bupa kunnan de chashe gongren" [A teahouse worker who does not fear difficulties]. *Chengdu ribao* [Chengdu daily], July 6.

Lü, Xiaobo, and Elizabeth J. Perry, eds. 1997. *Danwei: The Changing Chinese Workplace in Historical and Comparative Perspective*. Armonk, NY: M. E. Sharpe.

Lü Zhuohong. 2003. "Chuanxi chaguan: Zuowei gonggong kongjian de shengcheng he bianqian" [Teahouses in West Sichuan: Formation and changes in public spaces]. Unpublished diss., Central Minority College.

Luo, Suwen. 2005. "Gender on Stage: Actresses in an Actors' World (1895–1930)." In *Gender in Motion: Divisions of Labor and Cultural Change in Late Imperial and Modern China*, edited by Bryna Goodman and Wendy Larson, 75–95. Lanham, MD: Rowman & Littlefield.

Ma, Laurence, and Biao Xiang. 1998. "Native Place, Migration and the Emergence of Peasant Enclaves in Beijing." *China Quarterly* 155 (September): 546–81.

Ma Shihong. 1994. "Huiyi jiefang chuqi Chengdu shi de gongshang shuishou gongzuo" [Memories of the work of collecting industrial and commercial tax revenues in Chengdu soon after liberation]. *Wuhou wenshi ziliao xuanji* [Selection of Wuhou district literary and historical materials] 3:3–14.

Ma Shitu. 2004. "Sichuan de chaguan" [Sichuan's teahouses]. In *Zhongguo wenhua mingren tan guxiang* [China's cultural celebrities talk about hometowns], pt. 2, edited by Deng Jiuping, 472–75. Beijing: Dazhong wenyi chubanshe.

MacFarquhar, Roderick. 1983. *The Origins of the Cultural Revolution*. Vol. 2, *The Great Leap Forward, 1958–1960*. New York: Columbia University Press.

MacFarquhar, Roderick, and John King Fairbank, eds. 1987. *The Cambridge History of China*. Vol. 14, *The People's Republic, Part 1: The Emergence of Revolutionary China, 1949–1965*. Cambridge: Cambridge University Press.

MacFarquhar, Roderick, and Michael Schoenhals. 2009. *Mao's Last Revolution*. Cambridge, MA: Harvard University Press.

Madsen, Richard. 1993. "The Public Sphere, Civil Society and Moral Community: A Research Agenda for Contemporary China Studies." *Modern China* 19.2 (April): 183–98.

Manning, Kimberley Ens, and Felix Wemheuer, eds. 2011. *Eating Bitterness: New Perspectives on China's Great Leap Forward and Famine*. Vancouver: UBC Press.

Massey, Doreen. 1994. *Space, Place, and Gender*. Minneapolis: University of Minnesota Press.

——. 1995. "The Conceptualization of Place." In *A Place in the World? Places, Cultures and Globalization*, edited by Doreen Massey and Pat Jess, 45–86. Milton Keynes, UK: Open University Press.

Matsumoto, Toshiro. 2010. "Continuity and Discontinuity from the 1930s to the 1950s in Northeast China: The 'Miraculous' Rehabilitation of the Anshan Iron and Steel Company Immediately after the Chinese Civil War." In Akita and White 2010, 255–73.

Mazur, Mary G. 1999. "Public Space for Memory in Contemporary Civil Society: Freedom to Learn from the Mirror of the Past?" *China Quarterly* 160 (December): 1019–35.

McDougall, Bonnie S., ed. 1984a. *Popular Chinese Literature and Performing Arts in the People's Republic of China, 1949–79*. Berkeley: University of California Press.

——. 1984b. "Writers and Performers, Their Works, and Their Audiences in the First Three Decade." In McDougall 1984a, 269–304.

McIsaac, Lee. 2000. "'Righteous Fraternities' and Honorable Men: Sworn Brotherhoods in Wartime Chongqing." *American Historical Review* 105.5 (August): 1641–55.

McNally, Christopher A. 2004. "Sichuan: Driving Capitalist Development Westward." *China Quarterly* 178 (June 2004): 426–47.

Meliksetov, Arlen V. 1996. "'New Democracy' and China's Search for Socio-economic Development Routes, 1949–1953." *Far Eastern Affairs* 1:75–92.

Meliksetov, Arlen V., and Alexander V. Pantsov. 2001. "Stalin, Mao, and the New Democracy in China." *Herald of Moscow State University* 2:24–39.

Meng, Xin, and Chuliang Luo. 2008. "What Determines Living Arrangements of the Elderly in Urban China?" In *Inequality and Public Policy in China*, edited by Björn A. Gustafsson, Li Shi, and Terry Sicular, 267–86. New York: Cambridge University Press.

Metzger, Thomas A. 1979. "Chinese Communism and the Evolution of China's Political Culture: A Preliminary Analysis." *Issues and Studies* 15.8 (August): 51–63.

Min, Dongchao. 2011. "From Men-Women Equality to Gender Equality: The Zigzag Road of Women's Political Participation in China." *Asian Journal of Women's Studies* 17.3: 7–24.

Mitchell, Donald. 2000. *Cultural Geography: A Critical Introduction*. Oxford: Blackwell.

Mohanty, Manoranjan. 1981. "Party, State, and Modernization in Post-Mao China." In *China, the Post-Mao View*, edited by Vidya Prakash Dutt, 45–66. New Delhi: Allied.

Moody, Peter R., Jr. 1994. "Trends in the Study of Chinese Political Culture." *China Quarterly* 139 (September): 731–40.

Morris, Andrew. 2002. "'I Believe You Can Fly': Basketball Culture in Postsocialist China." In Link, Madsen, and Pickowicz 2002, 9–38.

Morse, Hosea Ballou. (1909) 1967. *The Gilds of China, with an Account of the Gild Merchant or Co-hong of Canton*. 2nd ed., 1932; reprint 1967. New York: Russell & Russell.

Naitō Rishin. 1991. *Sun de mita Seito: Shoku no kuni ni miru Chūgoku no nichijo seikatsu* [Chengdu as I lived it: China's everyday life as seen in the land of Shu]. Tokyo: Saimaru Shuppankai.

Nakajima, Seio. 2006. "Film Clubs in Beijing: The Cultural Consumption of Chinese Independent Films." In *From Underground to Independent: Alternative Film Culture in Contemporary China*, edited by Paul G. Pickowicz and Yingjin Zhang, 161–208. Lanham, MD: Rowman & Littlefield.

Navaro-Yashin, Yael. 2002. *Faces of the State: Secularism and Public Life in Turkey*. Princeton, NJ: Princeton University Press.

Nieh, Hualing, ed. 1981. *Literature of the Hundred Flowers: Criticism and Polemics*. New York: Columbia University Press.

Oi, Jean C. 1995. "The Role of the Local State in China's Transitional Economy." *China Quarterly* 144 (December): 1132–49.

——. 2004. "Realms of Freedom in Post-Mao China." In *Realms of Freedom in Modern China*, edited by William C. Kirby, 264–84. Stanford, CA: Stanford University Press.

Oksenberg, Michel. 1969. "Sources and Methodological Problems in the Study of Contemporary China." In Barnett 1969, 577–606.

Olson, Philip G. 1994. "The Changing Role of the Elderly in the People's Republic of China." In *The Graying of the World: Who Will Care for the Frail Elderly?*, edited by Laura Katz Olson, 261–87. New York: Haworth.

Palmer, Augusta Lee. 2006. "Mainland China: Public Square to Shopping Mall and the New Entertainment Film." In *Contemporary Asian Cinema: Popular Culture in a Global Frame*, edited by Anne Tereska Ciecko, 144–55. New York: Berg.

Pan Hongtao. 2011. "Qunzhong yishu guan zai shequ wenhua jianshe zhong de zuoyong" [The role of people's arts halls in the construction of community culture]. *Kexue zhi you* [Friends of science] 18:155.

Pang Song. 1997. "Luelun jiefang zhanzheng shiqi zhonggong dui Shanghai de jieguan" [Brief study of the CCP takeover of Shanghai in the time of the War of Liberation]. *Jindai shi yanjiu* [Studies of modern Chinese history] 2:284–312.

Paules, Greta Foff. 1991. *Dishing It Out: Power and Resistance among Waitresses in a New Jersey Restaurant.* Philadelphia: Temple University Press.

Pei Di. 1988. "1958 nian Chengdu huiyi shuping" [Review of the Chengdu conference in 1958]. *Zhonggong dangshi yanjiu* [Studies of CCP history] 5:37–43.

Pei, Minxin. 2000. "Political Change in Post-Mao China: Progress and Challenges." In *China's Future: Constructive Partner or Emerging Threat?*, edited by Ted Galen Carpenter and James A. Dorn, 291–315. Washington, DC: Cato Institute.

Perry, Elizabeth J. 1985. *The Political Economy of Reform in Post-Mao China.* Cambridge, MA: Council on East Asian Studies, Harvard University.

——. 2007. "Masters of the Country? Shanghai Workers in Early People's Republic." In Brown and Pickowicz 2007a, 59–79.

Perry, Elizabeth J. (Pei Yili), Li Lifeng, et al. 2015. "Zaisi 1949 nian fenshuiling: Zhengzhixue yu lishixue de duihua" [Rethinking the 1949 divide: Dialogue between political science and history]. *Xuehai* [Sea of knowledge], no. 1: 5–49.

Poon, Shuk-wah. 2008. "Religion, Modernity, and Urban Space: The City God Temple in Republican Guangzhou." *Modern China* 34.2 (April): 247–75.

Pye, Lucian W. 1972. "Culture and Political Science: Problems in the Evaluation of the Concept of Political Culture." *Social Science Quarterly* 53.4 (September): 285–96.

——. 1986. "Reassessing the Cultural Revolution." *China Quarterly* 108 (December): 597–612.

Pye, Lucian W., and Sidney Verba. 1965. *Political Culture and Political Development.* Princeton, NJ: Princeton University Press.

Qiao Zengxi, Li Canhua, and Bai Zhaoyu. 1983. "Chengdu shizheng yange gaishu" [Summary of the developments in Chengdu municipal administration]. *Chengdu wenshi ziliao xuanji* [Selection of Chengdu literary and historical materials] 5:1–22.

Qin Geng. 1988. "'Wanyou' yu wanyou" ["Amateur" and amateur]. *Sichuan xiju* [Sichuan opera] 3:45–46.

Qin Hongyan. 2000. "Chengdu: Reliao chashui lengliao kafei" [Chengdu: Warm tea and cold coffee]. *Renmin ribao* [People's daily], September 8.

Qiong Yao. 1990. "Jianbuduan de xiangchou" [Never-ending homesickness]. Beijing: Zuojia chubanshe.

Qiu Pengsheng. 1990. *Shiba shijiu shiji Suzhou cheng de xinxing gongshang ye tuanti* [New organizations of industry and commerce in eighteenth- and nineteenth-century Suzhou]. Taipei: Guoli Taiwan daxue chuban weiyuanhui (*Taida wenshi congkan*, no. 86).

Rai, Shirin. 1988. "Market Economy and Gender Perception in Post-Mao China." *China Report* 24.4 (October–December): 463–67.

Rankin, Mary B. 1986. *Elite Activism and Political Transformation in China: Zhejiang Province, 1865–1911.* Stanford, CA: Stanford University Press.

——. 1990. "The Origins of a Chinese Public Sphere: Local Elites and Community Affairs in the Late Imperial Period." *Études chinoises* 9.2: 14–60.

——. 1993. "Some Observations on a Chinese Public Sphere." *Modern China* 19.2: 158–82.

Rao Changlin and Chang Jian. 2011. "Woguo chengshi jiedao banshichu guanli tizhi bianqian yu zhidu wanshan" [Transformation and institutional improvement of the management of China's urban neighborhood committee offices]. *Zhongguo xing-zheng guanli* [Public administration in China] 2:85–88.

Raymo, James M., and Yu Xie. 2000. "Income of the Urban Elderly in Postreform China: Political Capital, Human Capital, and the State." *Social Science Research* 29.1 (March): 1–24.

Read, Benjamin L. 2000. "Revitalizing the State's Urban 'Nerve Tips.'" *China Quarterly* 163 (September): 806–20.

Roberts, Rosemary. 2006. "Gendering the Revolutionary Body: Theatrical Costume in Cultural Revolution China." *Asian Studies Review* 30.2 (June): 141–59.

Rosenthal, Elisabeth. 2003a. "The SARS Epidemic: The Path from the Provinces, a Crafty Germ Spreads." *New York Times*, April 27.

——. 2003b. "SARS Makes Beijing Combat an Old but Unsanitary Habit." *New York Times*, May 28.

Rowe, William T. 1984. *Hankow: Commerce and Society in a Chinese City, 1796–1889.* Stanford, CA: Stanford University Press.

——. 1989. *Hankow: Conflict and Community in a Chinese City, 1796–1895.* Stanford, CA: Stanford University Press.

——. 1990. "The Public Sphere in Modern China." *Modern China* 16.3 (July): 309–29.

——. 1993. "The Problem of 'Civil Society' in Late Imperial China." *Modern China* 19.2: 139–57.

Ruan Qinghua. 2009. "'Geliu': 1950 niandai chuqi Shanghai dushi jiceng shehui de qingli yu gaizao" [Cutting tumors: Cleanup and reform of grassroots society in early 1950s metropolitan Shanghai]. In Huadong shifan daxue Zhongguo dangdai shi yanjiu zhongxin 2009, 143–55.

Salaff, Janet Weitzner. 1971. "Urban Residential Communities in the Wake of the Cultural Revolution." In *The City in Communist China*, edited by John Wilson Lewis, 289–323. Stanford, CA: Stanford University Press.

Sausmikat, Nora. 1999. "Female Autobiographies from the Cultural Revolution: Returned Xiaxiang Educated Women in the 1990s." In *Internal and International Migration: Chinese Perspectives*, edited by Frank N. Pieke and Hein Mallee, 297–314. London: Routledge.

Schwarcz, Vera. 1986–1987. "Behind a Partially-Open Door: Chinese Intellectuals and the Post-Mao Reform Process." *Pacific Affairs* 59.4 (Winter): 577–604.

Scott, James C. 1985. *Weapons of the Weak: Everyday Forms of Peasant Resistance.* New Haven, CT: Yale University Press.

Sennett, Richard. 1977. *The Fall of Public Man: On the Social Psychology of Capitalism.* New York: Vintage Books.

——. 2006. *The Culture of the New Capitalism.* New Haven, CT: Yale University Press.

Sha Jiansun. 2005. "Guanyu shehui zhuyi gaizao wenti de zai pingjia" [Reevaluation of questions about the remolding of socialism]. *Dangdai Zhongguo shi yanjiu* [Studies of current Chinese history] 1:115–28.

Shambaugh, David. 2000. "The Chinese State in the Post-Mao Era." In *The Modern Chinese State*, edited by David Shambaugh, 161–87. Cambridge: Cambridge University Press.

Shang Hongjuan. 2008. "Shilun jianguo chuqi zhonggong de 'yundong zhiguo' moshi: Yi 'sanfan yundong' weili" [Essay on the early CCP's pattern of using movements to govern the state: A case study of the Three Antis Campaign]. *Jianghuai luntan* [Jiang Huai forum] 2:99–105.

Shang Jinming and Bei Guangsheng. 1996. "Qudi Yiguandao, gonggu xinsheng de renmin zhengquan" [Ban on the Yiguandao and the stabilization of the newborn people's state]. *Beijing dangshi yanjiu* [Studies of Beijing CCP history] 3:41–43.

Shao, Qin. 1998. "Tempest over Teapots: The Vilification of Teahouse Culture in Early Republican China." *Journal of Asian Studies* 57.4 (November): 1009–41.

——. 2013. *Shanghai Gone: Domicide and Defiance in a Chinese Megacity.* Lanham, MD: Rowman & Littlefield.

Shen, Zhihua. 2011. "Mao Zedong and the Origins of the Anti-rightist Rectification Campaign." In *The People's Republic of China at 60: An International Assessment*, edited by William C. Kirby, 25–40. Cambridge, MA: Harvard University Asia Center.

Sheng, Michael M. 2006. "Mao Zedong and the Three-Anti Campaign (November 1951 to April 1952): A Revisionist Interpretation." *Twentieth-Century China* 32.1 (November): 56–80.

Sheng Qi. 1999. *Majiang xue* [A study of mahjong]. Beijing: Tongxin chubanshe.

Shi Youshan and Fang Chongshi. 1986. "Shengyu jianshi" [Brief history of the Sacred Edict]. *Jinniu wenshi ziliao xuanji* [Selection of Jinniu literary and historical materials] 3:176–99.

Shu Xincheng. 1934. *Shuyou xinying* [Reflections on Sichuan travels]. Shanghai: Zhonghua shuju.

Sichuan sifangda lüshi shiwusuo. 2000. "Majiang raomin an yinlai zhongduo guanzhu" [The case of mahjong's harassing people has attracted great attention]. http://www.sifangda.com/html/detail.asp?classid=0216&id=8908. Posted February 10, 2003.

Silver, Mariko. 2008. "Higher Education and Science Policy in China's Post-Mao Reform Era." *Harvard Asia Quarterly* 11.1 (Winter): 42–53.

Sit, Victor Fung-shuen. 1979. "Neighbourhood Workshops in the Socialist Transformation of Chinese Cities." *Modernization in China* 3:91–101.

Siu, Wai-Sum. 2000. "Chinese Small Business Management: A Tentative Theory." In *The Dragon Millennium: Chinese Business in the Coming World Economy*, edited by Frank-Jürgen Richter, 149–61. Westport, CT: Quorum.

——. 2001. "Small Firm Marketing in China: A Comparative Study." *Small Business Economics* 16.4 (June): 279–92.

Siu, Wai-sum, and Zhi-chao Liu. 2005. "Marketing in Chinese Small and Medium Enterprises (SMEs): The State of the Art in a Chinese Socialist Economy." *Small Business Economics* 25.4 (November): 333–46.

Skinner, G. William. 1964–65. "Marketing and Social Structure in Rural China." *The Journal of Asian Studies.* 24.1: 3–43; 24.2: 195–228; 24.3: 363–99.

——. 1976. "Mobility Strategies in Late-Imperial China: A Regional Systems Analysis." In *Regional Analysis*, vol. 1, *Economic Systems*, edited by Carol A. Smith, 327–64. New York: Academic.

——. 1977. "Cities and the Hierarchy of Local Systems." In *The City in Late Imperial China*, edited by G. W. Skinner, 275–351. Stanford, CA: Stanford University Press.

Smith, Aminda. 2012. *Thought Reform and China's Dangerous Class: Reeducation, Resistance, and the People*. Lanham, MD: Rowman & Littlefield.

Smith, Richard Joseph. 1991. *Fortune-Tellers and Philosophers: Divination in Traditional Chinese Society*. Boulder, CO: Westview.

Solinger, Dorothy J. 1984. *Chinese Business under Socialism: The Politics of Domestic Commerce in Contemporary China*. Berkeley: University of California Press.

——. 1989. "Capitalist Measures with Chinese Characteristics." *Problems of Communism* 38.1 (January–February 1989): 19–33.

——. 1991. *From Lathes to Looms: China's Industrial Policy in Comparative Perspective, 1979–1984*. Stanford, CA: Stanford University Press.

——. 1993. *China's Transition from Socialism: Statist Legacies and Market Reforms, 1980–1990*. Armonk, NY: M. E. Sharpe.

——. 1999. *Contesting Citizenship in Urban China: Peasant Migrants, the State, and the Logic of the Market*. Berkeley: University of California Press.

Solomon, Richard H. 1971. *Mao's Revolution and the Chinese Political Culture*. Berkeley: University of California Press.

Song, Shaopeng. 2007. "The State Discourse on Housewives and Housework in the 1950s in China." In *Rethinking China in the 1950s*, edited by Mechthild Leutner, 49–63. Berlin: Lit Verlag.

Song Zheng. 2002. "Duoshu minzhuzhi yu shaoshuren quanli zhi baohu: You yiqi 'majiang guansi' suo xiangdao de" [Majoritarian democracy and the protection of minority rights: Thoughts arising from the mahjong lawsuit]. http://www.china lawedu.com/news/16900/174/2003/12/zh621314563418213002243810_76995. htm. Posted December 8, 2003.

Stapleton, Kristin. 1996. "Urban Politics in an Age of 'Secret Societies': The Cases of Shanghai and Chengdu." *Republican China* 22.1 (November): 23–64.

——. 2000. *Civilizing Chengdu: Chinese Urban Reform, 1875–1937*. Cambridge, MA: Harvard University Asia Center.

Steinmüller, Hans 2011. "The Moving Boundaries of Social Heat: Gambling in Rural China." *Journal of the Royal Anthropological Institute*, n.s., 17:263–80.

Strand, David. 1989. *Rickshaw Beijing: City People and Politics in the 1920s*. Berkeley: University of California Press.

Strauss, Julia. 2006. "Morality, Coercion and State Building by Campaign in the Early PRC: Regime Cosolidation and After, 1949–1956." *China Quarterly* 188 (December): 891–912.

Su Minhua. 1998. "Minjian zhiye jutuan zai yanchu shichang zhong de diwei he zuoyong" [Position and role of professional folk troupes in the entertainment market]. *Fujian yishu* [Performing arts in Fujian] 2:9–10.

Sun Huiqiang. 2009. "1950 Beijing chanchu yiguandao xiejiao" [Uprooting the Yiguandao cult in 1950 Beijing]. *Dang'an chunqiu* [Archival history] 9:12–16.

Sun Kang. 2010. "Jihua jingji shi jieji douzheng kuoda hua de zhidu genyuan" [The planned economy was the institutional source of the spread of class struggle]. *Yanhuang chunqiu* [History of the Chinese] 4:34–37.

Sun Xiaozhong. 2012. "1950 niandai de Shanghai gaizao yu wenhua zhili" [1950s Shanghai reforms and the administration of culture]. *Zhongguo xiandai wenxue yanjiu congkan* [Modern Chinese literature research series] 1:95–105.

Sun, Yi. 2011. "Reading History in Visual Rhetoric: The Chinese Images of Chinese Women, 1949–2009." *Chinese Historical Review* 18.2 (Fall): 125–50.

Suzuki Tōmō. 1982. "Shinmatsu Kō-Seku no chakan ni tsuite" [Jiangsu and Zhejiang teahouses in late Qing times]. In *Rekishi ni okeru minshū to bunka: Sakai Tadao sensei koki shukuga kinen ronshū* [People and culture in history: Essay collection in honor of the seventieth birthday of Master Sakai Tadao], 529–40. Tokyo: Kokusho kankkai.

Takeuchi Minoru. 1974. *Chakan: Chūgoku no fudo to sekaizo* [The teahouse: China's localities and world image]. Tokyo: Taishukan shoten.

—— (Zhunei Shi). 2006. "Shuguo Chengdu de chaguan" [Chengdu teahouses in the land of Shu]. In *Zhunei Shi wenji* [Collected works of Takeuchi Minoru], vol. 9, translated by Cheng Ma, 230–37. Beijing: Zhongguo wenlian chubanshe.

Tan Xiaojuan. 2007. "Mancheng yiran xuezhan daodi, 'fanma doushi' yinshen jianghu" [Mahjong wars everywhere in the city while the 'Anti-mahjong warrior' lives a hidden life]. *Tianfu zaobao* [Sichuan morning news], March 8.

Tang Minghui. 1994. "Heming shengyi jing" [Business practices at Cry of the Crane Teahouse]. *Longmenzhen* [Longmen chats] 3:82–84.

Tang, Wenfang, and William Parish. 2000. *Chinese Urban Life under Reform: The Changing Social Contract*. Cambridge: Cambridge University Press.

Tang Xingxiang, Li Zhigang, and Kuang Yingtong. 2003. "Cong qiansong dao jiuzhu: Cong Sun Zhigang an kan shourong zhidu de bianqian" [From turning back to giving aid: Seeing the transformation of the intake system from the case of Sun Zhigang]. *Zhengfu fazhi* [Government legal institutions] 17:14–15.

Tao Wenzhao. 2011. "'Chang hong' bei zhiyi de fuza shehui yinsu" [Complex social factors behind the questioning of "singing red songs"]. *Renmin luntan* [People's forum] 33:37.

Thøgersen, Stig. 2000. "Cultural Life and Cultural Control in Rural China: Where Is the Party?" *China Journal* 44 (July): 129–41.

Thurston, Anne F. 1988. *Enemies of the People: The Ordeal of the Intellectuals in China's Great Cultural Revolution*. Cambridge, MA: Harvard University Press.

Trexler, Richard C. 1980. *Public Life in Renaissance Florence*. Ithaca, NY: Cornell University Press.

Troyer, Ronald J., John P. Clark, and Dean G. Rojek, eds. 1989. *Social Control in the People's Republic of China*. New York: Praeger.

Tsai, Wen-hui. 1987. "Life after Retirement: Elderly Welfare in China." *Asian Survey* 27.5 (May): 566–76.

Tsang, Ka Bo. 1999. "Tiger Story: A Set of Chinese Shadow Puppets from Chengdu, Sichuan Province." *Oriental Art* 45.2 (Summer): 38–49.

Tsou, Tang. 1986. *The Cultural Revolution and Post-Mao Reforms: A Historical Perspective*. Chicago: University of Chicago Press.

U, Eddy. 2007. "The Making of Chinese Intellectuals: Representations and Organization in the Thought Reform Campaign." *China Quarterly* 192 (December): 971–89.

Veeck, Ann. 2000. "The Revitalization of the Marketplace: Food Markets of Nanjing." In Davis 2000, 107–23.

Vogel, Ezra F. 1969. *Canton under Communism: Programs and Politics in a Provincial Capital, 1949–1968*. Cambridge, MA: Harvard University Press.

Wakeman, Frederic, Jr. 1993. "The Civil Society and Public Sphere Debate: Western Reflections on Chinese Political Culture." *Modern China* 19.2 (April): 108–38.

——. 1995. "Licensing Leisure: The Chinese Nationalists' Attempt to Regulate Shanghai, 1927–49." *Journal of Asian Studies* 54.1 (February): 19–42.

——. 2007. "'Cleanup': The New Order in Shanghai." In Brown and Pickowicz 2007a, 21–58.

Walder, Andrew G. 2009. *Fractured Rebellion: The Beijing Red Guard Movement*. Cambridge, MA: Harvard University Press.

Wang, Aihe. 2006. *Cosmology and Political Culture in Early China*. Cambridge: Cambridge University Press.

Wang, Di. 1993. *Kuachu fengbi de shijie: Changjiang shangyou quyu shehui yanjiu, 1644–1911* [Breaking out of a closed world: A study of society in the upper Yangzi region, 1644–1911]. Beijing: Zhonghua shuju.

——. 2000. "The Idle and the Busy: Teahouses and Public Life in Early Twentieth-Century Chengdu." *Journal of Urban History* 26.4 (May): 411–37.

——. 2003. *Street Culture in Chengdu: Public Space, Urban Commoners, and Local Politics, 1870–1930*. Stanford, CA: Stanford University Press.

——. 2004. "'Masters of Tea': Teahouse Workers, Workplace Culture, and Gender Conflict in Wartime Chengdu." *Twentieth-Century China* 29.2 (April): 89–136.

——. 2008a. "Mysterious Communication: The Secret Language of the Gowned Brotherhood in Nineteenth-Century Sichuan." *Late Imperial China* 29.1: 77–103.

——. 2008b. *The Teahouse: Small Business, Everyday Culture, and Public Politics in Chengdu, 1900–1950*. Stanford, CA: Stanford University Press.

——. 2009. "Guojia kongzhi yu shehui zhuyi yule de xingcheng: 1950 niandai qianqi dui Chengdu chaguan zhong de quyi he quyi yiren de gaizao he chuli" [State control and the formation of socialist entertainment: Reforms and disposition of Chengdu teahouse folk performances and performers in the early 1950s]. In Huadong shifan daxue Zhongguo dangdai shi yanjiu zhongxin 2009, 76–105.

——. 2012. "Reorganization of Guilds and State Control of Small Business: A Case Study of the Teahouse Guild in Early 1950s Chengdu." *Frontiers of History in China* 7.4 (December): 529–50.

Wang Fei. 2012. "Xin Zhongguo chengli qianhou de chengshi junshi guanzhi zhidu" [Urban military control systems before and after the establishment of the PRC]. *Dang'an tiandi* [Archival scope] 2:42–48.

Wang, Gan. 2000. "Cultivating Friendship through Bowling in Shenzhen." In Davis 2000, 250–67.

Wang Haiguang. 2011. "Cong zhengzhi kongzhi dao shehui kongzhi: Zhongguo chengxiang eryuan huji zhidu de jianli" [From political control to social control: Establishment of the urban-rural dual household registration system]. In Huadong shifan daxue Zhongguo dangdai shi yanjiu zhongxin 2011a, 3–48.

Wang Huaichen. 1994. "Luelun fan youpai douzheng de lishi jingyan he jiaoxun" [Synopsis of the historical experiences and lessons of the anti-rightist struggle]. *Jinyang xuekan* [Jinyang journal] 2:28–32.

Wang, Jing, ed. 2001a. *Chinese Popular Culture and the State.* Special issue of *Positions. East Asia Cultures Critique* 9.1.

——. 2001b. "Culture as Leisure and Culture as Capital." In J. Wang 2001a, 69–104.

——. 2001c. "The State Question in Chinese Popular Cultural Studies." *Inter-Asia Cultural Studies* 2.1: 35–52.

——. 2005a. "Introduction: The Politics and Production of Scales in China: How Does Geography Matter to Studies of Local, Popular Culture?" In *Locating China: Space, Place, and Popular Culture,* edited by Jing Wang, 1–30. London: Routlege.

——. 2005b. "Bourgeois Bohemians in China? Neo-Tribes and the Urban Imaginary." *China Quarterly,* no. 183: 532–48.

Wang, Meiyan. 2009. "Wage Arrears and Discrimination against Migrant Workers in China's Urban Labor Market." In *The China Population and Labor Yearbook,* vol. 1, *The Approaching Lewis Turning Point and Its Policy Implications,* edited by Fang Cai and Yang Du, 153–75. Leiden: Brill.

Wang, Qingshu. 2004. "The History and Current Status of Chinese Women's Participation in Politics." In *Holding up Half the Sky: Chinese Women Past, Present, and Future,* edited by Jie Tao, Bijun Zheng, and Shirley L. Mow, 92–106. New York: Feminist Press at the City University of New York.

Wang, Shaoguang. 1995. "The Politics of Private Time: Changing Leisure Patterns in Urban China." In Davis et al. 1995, 149–72.

Wang Shuchun. 2001. "Chengshi jiti jingji de zhidu bianqian jiqi qushi" [Changes in the urban collective-enterprise system and its trends]. *Zhongguo jiti jingji* [China's collective businesses] 3:4–8.

Wang Xingjian. 2004. "Shehui jiuzhu zhidu de yihua he biange: Cong shourong qiansong dao jiuzhu guanli" [Alienation and change in the social assistance system: From in/out accommodation to assistance management]. *Tianfu xinlun* [New approaches from Sichuan] 6:87–90.

Wang Yue. 1999. *Lao chake xianhua* [Old teahouse-goer's gossip]. Chengdu: Sichun wenyi chubanshe.

Wang, Yuefeng. 1993. "Urban Crimes in Mainland China: A Social Ecological Approach." *Issues and Studies* 29.8: 101–17.

Wang, Zheng. 2006. "Dilemmas of Inside Agitators: Chinese State Feminists in 1957." *China Quarterly* 188 (December): 913–32.

Ward, Barbara E. 1985. "Regional Operas and Their Audiences: Evidence from Hong Kong." In *Popular Culture in Late Imperial China,* edited by David Johnson, Andrew J. Nathan, and Evelyn S. Rawski, 161–87. Berkeley: University of California Press.

Wasserstrom, Jeffrey N., and Elizabeth J. Perry, eds. 1994. *Popular Protest and Political Culture in Modern China.* Boulder, CO: Westview.

Watson, James L. 2011. "Feeding the Revolution: Public Mess Halls and Coercive Commensality in Maoist China." In Zhang, Kleinman, and Tu 2011, 33–46.

Wei, S. Louisa. 2011. "The Encoding of Female Subjectivity: Four Films by China's Fifth-Generation Women Directors." In *Chinese Women's Cinema: Transnational Contexts,* edited by Lingzhen Wang, 173–90. New York: Columbia University Press.

Wei Wenxiang. 2008. "Zhuanye yu tongzhan: Jianguo chuqi Zhonggong dui gongshang tongye gonghui de gaizao celüe" [Professions and the united front: CCP tactics for reforming guilds in the early People's Republic]. *Anhui shixue* [Studies of Anhui history] 2:88–93.

Weisband, Edward, and Courtney I. P. Thomas. 2014. *Political Culture and the Making of Modern Nation-States*. London: Routledge.

Wen Wenzi, ed. 1985. *Sichuan fengwu zhi* [Essay on Sichuan folklore]. Chengdu: Sichuan renmin chubanshe.

White, Gordon. 1996. "The Dynamics of Civil Society in Post-Mao China." In *The Individual and the State in China*, edited by Brian Hook, 196–221. New York: Oxford University Press.

White, Lynn T. 1989. *Policies of Chaos: The Organizational Causes of Violence in China's Cultural Revolution*. Princeton, NJ: Princeton University Press.

Whyte, Martin King. 1990. "Changes in Mate Choice in Chengdu." In *Chinese Society on the Eve of Tiananmen: The Impact of Reform*, edited by Deborah Davis and Ezra Vogel, 181–213. Cambridge, MA: Council on East Asian Studies, Harvard University.

——. 1991. "Urban Life in the People's Republic." In *Cambridge History of China*, vol. 15, *The People's Republic, Part 2: Revolutions within the Chinese Revolution, 1966–1982*, edited by Roderick Macfarquhar and John K. Fairbank, 682–742. Cambridge: Cambridge University Press.

——. 1993. "Adaptation of Rural Family Patterns to Urban Life in Chengdu." In *Urban Anthropology in China*, edited by Greg Guldin and Aidan Southall, 358–80. Leiden: Brill.

Whyte, Martin King, and William L. Parish. 1984. *Urban Life in Contemporary China*. Chicago: University of Chicago Press.

Whyte, William H. 1980. *The Social Life of Small Urban Spaces*. New York: Project for Public Spaces.

Wittman, Marlene R. 1983. "Shanghai in Transition? Implications of the Capitalist Intrusion." *Issues and Studies* 19.6 (June): 66–79.

Witzleben, J. Lawrence. 1987. "Jiangnan Sizhu Music Clubs in Shanghai: Context, Concept and Identity." *Ethnomusicology* 31.2: 240–60.

Wo Ruo. 1987. "Nanwang de chaguan" [An unforgettable teahouse]. *Chengdu wanbao* [Chengdu nightly], May 10.

Wong, Chun. 1978. "From 'Anti-rightist Struggle' to Taking Off Rightist's Hat." *Asian Outlook* 13.7 (July): 28–32.

Wong, Isabel K. F. 1984. "*Geming Gequ*: Songs for the Education of the Masses." In McDougall 1984a, 112–43.

Wong, Kathy. 1984. "Chinese Chess Differs Only in Detail from Its Western Counterpart: In Anticipation of War, a Peaceful Pastime." *Free China Review* 34.3: 56–58.

Wu, Jieh-min. 2010. "Rural Migrant Workers and China's Differential Citizenship: A Comparative Institutional Analysis." In *One Country, Two Societies: Rural-Urban Inequality in Contemporary China*, edited by Martin King Whyte, 55–81. Cambridge, MA: Harvard University Press.

Wu, Jinglian. 1999. "The Key to China's Transition: Small and Midsize Enterprises." *Harvard China Review* 1.2: 7–12.

Wu Jingping and Zhang Xule. 2003. "Jieguan Shanghai guanliao ziben jinrong jigou shulun" [Description of the takeover of the Shanghai bureaucracy's financial system]. *Jindaishi yanjiu* [Journal of modern Chinese history] 4:113–39.

Wu, Ka-ming. 2011. "Tradition Revival with Socialist Characteristics: Propaganda Storytelling Turned Spiritual Service in Rural Yan'an." *China Journal* 66:101–17.

Wu Ke. 2010. "Zhonggong dui Chengdu jieguan zhong de zhengzhi dongyuan jiqi xiaoli" [Political mobilization and its effect in the CCP takeover of Chengdu]. *Dangdai Zhongguo shi yanjiu* [Studies of current Chinese history] 5:125–26.

Wu, Xiaoping. 2000. "The Market Economy, Gender Equality, and Women's Development from the Viewpoint of Women's Employment." *Chinese Education and Society* 33.6 (November–December 2000): 44–54.

Wu, Yenna. 1998. "Satiric Realism from *Jin Ping Mei* to *Xingshi Yinyuan Zhuan*: The Fortunetelling Motif." *Chinese Culture Quarterly* 39.1: 147–71.

Wu, Yiching. 2014. *The Cultural Revolution at the Margins: Chinese Socialism in Crisis*. Cambridge, MA: Harvard University Press.

Wu Yongxiao. 1989. "Chengdu shi zai dui ziben zhuyi gongshangye de shehui zhuyi gaizao zhong de shuiwu gongzuo" [The work of the tax administration in Chengdu's socialist transformation of capitalist industry and commerce]. *Chengdu dangshi tongxun* [Bulletin of Chengdu CCP history] 3:10–19.

Xi Menmei. 2006. "Peigen lu zuihou de qiutian" [The last autumn on Bacon Road]. In *Jielu ji* [Record of my cottage], 169–72. Shijiazhuang: Hebei renmin chubanshe.

Xiao Longlian. 2000. "Chengdu: Majiang guansi nanjie nanfen" [Chengdu: The inextricably locked up mahjong lawsuit]. *Fazhi ribao* [Law daily], December 6.

Xiao Wenming. 2013. "Guojia chujiao de xiandu zhi zai kaocha: Yi xin Zhongguo chengli chuqi Shanghai de wenhua gaizao wei gean" [Reinvestigation of the limits of the state's antennae: The case of cultural reforms in early PRC Shanghai]. *Kaifang shidai* [Opened era] 3:130–52.

Xie Guozhen. 1999. *Jincheng youji* [Chengdu travel notes]. In Zeng and You 1999, 349–76.

Xie Yong. 2008. "Bainian Zhongguo wenxue zhong de 'Zhao Shuli beiju': Cong 'Xiao Erhei jiehun' de yige xijie shuoqi" [The "Tragedy of Zhao Shuli" in a century of Chinese literature: Discussion based on a detail of *A Peasant Takes a Wife*]. *Kaifang shidai* [Opened era] 6:158–62.

Xu Juan. n.d. "Jin wushi nian Chengdu laoshi chaguan de bianqian" [Changes in Chengdu's old-style teahouses in the last fifty years]. Unpublished manuscript.

Xu Yulong and Ni Zhanyuan. 1980. "Luetan chengshi jiti jingji de xingzhi jiqi zai guomin jingji zhong de diwei" [Brief discussion of the nature of urban collectives and their position in the people's economy]. *Caijing wenti yanjiu* [Studies of finance and economy] 1:61–65.

Yan Feng. 2007. "Shilun woguo jianguo chuqi de wenhua guodu" [Essay on cultural excesses in the early PRC]. *Guangxi shehui kexue* [Guangxi social sciences] 2:185–89.

Yan, Yunxiang. 2000. "Of Hamburger and Social Space: Consuming McDonald's in Beijing." In Davis 2000, 201–25.

Yang Jing. 2013. "Wuhan dama guangchang tiaowu zao pofen" [Dancing grannies in the square in Wuhan were showered by human excrement]. *Wuhan wanbao* [Wuhan nightly news]. October 25.

Yang Jisheng. 2008. *Mubei: Zhongguo liushi niandai dajihuang jishi* [Epitaphs: A true record of China's 1960s Great Famine]. Hong Kong: Tiandi tushu youxian gongsi.

Yang Kuisong. 2006. "Mao Zedong yu 'sanfan' yundong" [Mao Zedong and the Three Antis Campaign]. *Shilin* [Forest of history] 4:51–69.

——. 2009a. "Jianguo chuqi zhonggong ganbu renyong zhengce kaocha" [Investigation of the policy of cadre appointments in the early years of the nation]. In Huadong shifan daxue Zhongguo dangdai shi yanjiu zhongxin 2009, 3–39.

——. 2009b. *Zhonghua renmin gongheguo jianguo shi yanjiu* [Studies in the history of the establishment of the PRC]. Nanchang: Jiangxi renmin chubanshe.

——. 2011. "Xin Zhongguo xinwen baokan tongzhi jizhi de xingcheng jingguo: Yi jianguo qianhou Wang Yunsheng de 'touxiang' yu *Dagongbao* gaizao weili" [Forms and procedures in news control mechanisms in the PRC: A case study of Wang Yunsheng's "surrender" and the reform of the *Dagong bao* before and after the establishment of the PRC]. In Huadong shifan daxue Zhongguo dangdai shi yanjiu zhongxin 2011a, 49–90.

Yang Liping. 2010. "Xin Zhongguo chengli chuqi de Shanghai linong zhengdun" [Neighborhood reorganizations and control in early PRC Shanghai]. *Dangdai Zhongguo shi yanjiu* [Studies of current Chinese history] 5:50–57.

Yang Zhongyi. 1992. "Chengdu chaguan" [Chengdu teahouses]. *Nongye kaogu* [Agricultural archeology] 4 (special edition on Chinese tea): 114–17.

Yee, Janice. 2001. "Women's Changing Roles in the Chinese Economy." *Journal of Economics* 27.2: 55–67.

Yeh, Catherine Vance. 2005. "Playing with the Public: Late Qing Courtesans and Their Opera Singer Lovers." In *Gender in Motion: Divisions of Labor and Cultural Change in Late Imperial and Modern China*, edited by Bryna Goodman and Wendy Larson, 145–68. Lanham, MD: Rowman & Littlefield.

——. 2007. "Shanghai Leisure, Print Entertainment, and the Tabloids, Xiaobao." In *Joining the Global Public: Word, Image, and City in Early Chinese Newspapers, 1870–1910*, edited by Rudolf G. Wagner, 201–33. Albany: SUNY Press.

Yeh, Wen-Hsin. 1995. "Corporate Space, Communal Time: Everyday Life in Shanghai's Bank of China." *American Historical Review* 100.1 (February): 97–122.

Yen, Benjamin, and Phoebe Ho. 2005. "PGL: The Entrepreneur in China's Logistics Industry." In *Small Business Management and Entrepreneurship in Hong Kong: A Casebook*, edited by Ali Farhoomand, 230–43. Hong Kong: Hong Kong University Press.

You Ye. 2001. *Lailu buming de yewan* [Dim night]. Chengdu: Sichuan wenyi chubanshe.

Yu Jingqi and Liu Zongtang. 1958. "Rang sheyuan shenghuo fengfu duocai" [Let commune members have rich and varied lives]. *Renmin ribao* [People's daily], December 1.

Yu, Lucy C., and Minqi Wang. 1993. "Social Status, Physical, Mental Health, Well-Being, and Self Evaluation of Elderly in China." *Journal of Cross-Cultural Gerontology* 8.2: 147–59.

Yu Yao. 2007. "Chaguan minsu yu charen shenghuo: Sumin shiye zhong de Chengdu chaguan" [Teahouse folkways and teahouse lives: Chengdu teahouses seen through the eyes of regular folk]. Unpublished MA thesis, Shanghai University.

Yu Yingshi. 1990. "Chuanju wanyou: Zhenxing chuanju bu ke hushi de liliang" [Sichuan opera amateurs: A force not to be overlooked in promoting Sichuan opera]. *Sichuan xiju* [Sichuan opera] 2:7–8.

Yu Yunhan. 2000. "Shangshan xiaxiang yundong yu Zhongguo chengshihua" [The movement of going to rural areas and China's urbanization]. *Xueshu yanjiu* [Academic studies], no. 9: 78–83.

Yung, Bell, Evelyn S. Rawski, and Rubie S. Watson, eds. 1996. *Harmony and Counterpoint: Ritual Music in Chinese Context.* Stanford, CA: Stanford University Press.

Zang, Jian. 2011. "The Soviet Impact on 'Gender Equality' in China in the 1950s." In *China Learns from the Soviet Union, 1949–Present,* edited by Thomas P. Bernstein and Hua-Yu Li, 259–74. Lanham, MD: Lexington Books.

Zarrow, Peter. 1990. *Anarchism and Chinese Political Culture.* New York: Columbia University Press.

Zeng Honglu. 1998. "Zailun 'dayue jin' de lishi chengyin" [Another essay on the historical contributing factors of the Great Leap Forward]. *Nanjing daxue xuebao* [Journal of Nanjing University] 4:74–79.

Zeng Xiangyu and Zhong Zhiru. 1990. "Wanyou dui Chuanju changqiang gaige de gongxian" [Amateurs' contributions to reforms in Sichuan opera vocal music]. *Sichuan xiju* [Sichuan opera] 4:39–40.

Zeng Zhizhong and You Deyan, eds. 1999. *Wenhuaren shiyezhong de lao Chengdu* [Old Chengdu in the view of intellectuals]. Chengdu: Sichuan wenyi chubanshe.

Zha Yi. 2003. "Sichuan: Ganbu weigui damajiang 'sha'" [Sichuan: Cadres playing mahjong violate rules and must be stopped]. *Xibu kaifa bao* [Development of West China news], May 15.

Zhai Yejun. 2013. "Cong 'Xiao Erhei jiehun' kan AQ geming" [Seeing Ah Q's revolution from *A Peasant Takes a Wife*]. *Shanghai wenhua* [Shanghai culture] 1:36–43.

Zhai Yongming. 2009. *Baiye tan* [Tales of white nights]. Guangzhou: Huacheng chubanshe.

Zhang Chen. 2003. "Jiefang chuqi Shanghai tanfan de guanli" [Management of Shanghai street peddlers soon after liberation]. *Dang'an yu shixue* [Archives and historical studies] 1:68–70.

Zhang, Everett, Arthur Kleinman, and Weiming Tu, eds. 2011. *Governance of Life in Chinese Moral Experience: The Quest for an Adequate Life.* London: Routledge.

Zhang Jishun. 2004. "Shanghai linong: Jiceng zhengzhi dongyuan yu guojia shehui yitihua zouxiang, 1950–1955" [Shanghai's alley neighborhoods: Grassroots political mobilization and the trend toward integration of state and society]. *Zhongguo shehui kexue* [Social sciences in China] 2:178–88.

———. 2009. "Cong minban dao dangguan: Shanghai siying baoye tizhi biange zhong de sixiang gaizao yundong" [From local management to party control: Brainwashing movement in the reform of Shanghai's privately owned newspaper business]. In Huadong shifan daxue Zhongguo dangdai shi yanjiu zhongxin 2009, 40–75.

———. 2010. "Thought Reform and Press Nationalization in Shanghai: The Wenhui Newspaper in the Early 1950s." *Twentieth-Century China* 35.2: 52–80.

———. 2012. "Shehui wenhua shi de jianshi: 1950 niandai Shanghai yanjiu de zai sikao" [Examination of sociocultural history: Revisiting of studies of 1950s Shanghai]. *Huadong shifan daxue xuebao* [Journal of East China Normal University] 2:1–7.

Zhang Junguo. 2008. "'Sanfan wufan' yundong yanjiu shuping" [Critique of scholarship on the Three Antis and Five Antis Campaigns]. *Hubei sheng shehui zhuyi xueyuan xuebao* [Journal of the Hubei College of Socialism] 2:75–80.

Zhang, Li. 2001a. "Contesting Crime, Order, and Migrant Spaces in Beijing." In Chen et al. 2001, 201–24.

———. 2001b. *Strangers in the City: Reconfigurations of Space, Power, and Social Networks within China's Floating Population.* Stanford, CA: Stanford University Press.

———. 2002. "Urban Experiences and Social Belonging among Chinese Rural Migrants." In Link, Madsen, and Pickowicz 2002, 275–300.

Zhang Lianhong. 2010. "Zailun xin Zhongguo xiqu gaige yundong de lishi zuobiao" [Further essay on the historical coordinates of the opera reform movement in the new China]. *Shanghai xiju* [Shanghai opera] 12:20–22.

Zhang Shengliang. 2008. "Lun 'Zhongguo hongge hui' de xingqi" [On the rise of the Chinese Red Songs Association]. *Zuojia* [Writers] 2:256–57.

Zhang Shizhao. 2000. "Wenhua yundong yu nongcun gailiang" [Cultural movements and rural improvements]; "Nongguobian" [A debate on the agricultural state]; and "Zhang Xingyan zai nongda zhi yanshuoci" [Notes on Zhang Shizhao's lecture at the Agricultural College]. In *Zhang Shizhao quanji* [Complete works of Zhang Shizhao], vol. 4, 144–46; 266–72; 403–5. Shanghai: Shanghai wenhui chubanshe.

Zhang Xiande. 1999. *Chengdu: Jin wushi nian de siren jiyi* [Chengdu: Personal memories of the last fifty years]. Chengdu: Sichuan wenyi chubanshe.

Zhang, Xiaoling. 2007. "Seeking Effective Public Space: Chinese Media at the Local Level." *China: An International Journal* 5.1: 55–77.

Zhang Xiyong and Yang Jiwu. 2012. "Lishi zhidu zhuyi shiyu xia woguo chengshi jiedao banshichu de zhidu bianqian" [Institutional transformation of the neighborhood offices in Chinese cities from the view of historical institutionalism]. *Zhongguo xingzheng guanli* [Chinese public administration] 12:69–73.

Zhang Yan. 1956. "Hui Chengdu" [Return to Chengdu]. *Renmin ribao* [People's daily], September 13.

Zhang Yi. 2006. "Jiefang zhanzheng shiqi zhonggong dui Shanghai jieguan de lishi jingyan" [Historical experience of the CCP takeover of Shanghai during the civil war]. *Zhongnan minzu daxue xuebao* [Journal of South Central Minorities University] S1: 108–12.

Zhang Yixian. 2000. "Guji zhong dansheng de 'aiqing'" [Love emerging from loneliness]. *Shangwu zaobao* [Commerce morning news], April 26.

Zhang Yue. 2004. "'Sanfan' yundong de yiyi jiqi dui woguo xian jieduan fan fubai gongzuo de qishi" [Significance of the Three Antis Campaign and its inspiration for anticorruption work at China's present stage]. *Qiushi* [Seeking truth] S4: 126–27.

Zhang Yuyu. 2011. "Shilun 'wufan' yundong hou woguo siying gongshangye de shengcun zhuangkuang" [Essay on the existing condition of China's private businesses after the Five Antis Campaign]. *Shanghai jiaotong daxue xuebao* [Journal of Shanghai Jiaotong University] 2:82–88.

Zheng, X. 1997. "Chinese Business Culture from the 1920s to the 1950s." In *Economic Development in Twentieth-Century East Asia: The International Context*, edited by Aiko Ikeo, 55–65. London: Routledge.

Zhong Minghua. 2000. "Chengdu chalou kao 'tian' chifan" [Chengdu teahouses depend on weather to stay in business]. *Shangwu zaobao* [Commerce morning news], May 26.

Zhong, Xueping. 2011. "Women Can Hold Up Half the Sky." In *Words and Their Stories: Essays on the Language of the Chinese Revolution*, edited by Ban Wang, 227–47. Leiden: Brill.

Zhong, Yang. 2003. *Local Government and Politics in China: Challenges from Below*. Armonk, NY: M. E. Sharpe.

———. 2012. *Political Culture and Participation in Rural China*. New York: Routledge, 2012.

Zhonggong Beiping shiwei. 2004. "Guanyu zhengli tanfan gongzuo de zongjie" [Summary of the work to rectify street vendors]. *Beijing dangshi* [History of the CCP in Beijing] 2:44–45.

Zhongguo xinwen she [China news agency]. March 31, 2000. "Chengdu Funan hepan jinda majiang" [Ban playing mahjong by the Funan river in Chengdu]. http://news.sina.com.cn/society/2000-3-31/77315.html.

"Zhonghua renmin gongheguo chengshi jumin weiyuanhui zuzhifa" [Bylaws of the urban residential committees in the People's Republic of China]. 1989. http://www.mca.gov.cn/artical/content/PJCN/2003122290821.htm.

Zhou, Daming, and Xiaoyun Sun. 2010. "Research on 'Job Hopping' by Migrant Workers from the Countryside: A Second Study on Turnover among Migrant Workers Employed by Businesses." *Chinese Sociology and Anthropology* 43.2: 51–69.

Zhou Ping. 2001. "Jiedao banshichu de dingwei: Chengshi shequ zhengzhi de yige genben wenti" [Orienting neighborhood offices: A basic issue of urban community politics]. *Zhengzhi xue yanjiu* [Journal of political science] 2:76–82.

Zhou Yong. 2011. "Chongqing de 'chang du jiang chuan' yu guojia wenhua ruan shili" [The "songs, reading, lectures, and tradition" movement in Chongqing and the soft power of national culture]. *Chongqing shehui kexue* [Social sciences in Chongqing] 5:93–94.

Zhu Chuan. 1980. "Lun chengzhen jiti suoyouzhi jingji de fazhan" [Discussion of developments in locality-owned businesses]. *Shehui kexue jikan* [Journal of social sciences] 2:3–10.

Zhu Wenyi. 2003. "Woguo shourong zhidu shimo" [Full story of China's intake systems]. *Zhengfu fazhi* [Government legal institutions] 17:15.

Zhu Ying, ed. 2004. *Zhongguo jindai tongye gonghui yu dangdai hangye xiehui* [Modern China's guilds and current professional associations]. Beijing: Zhongguo renmin daxue chubanshe.

Zou Qutao. 1998. "Chengdu Wuyue wenhua fuwu she" [Chengdu May Cultural Services]. In *Chengdu zhanggu* [Anecdotes of Chengdu], vol. 2, edited by Chengdu shi qunzhong yishu guan, 201–8. Chengdu: Sichuan daxue chabanshe.

INDEX